Oxford
Solver

Oxford
Puzzle Solver

Compiled by
Market House Books Ltd

OXFORD
UNIVERSITY PRESS

OXFORD

UNIVERSITY PRESS

Great Clarendon Street, Oxford OX2 6DP

Oxford University Press is a department of the University of Oxford.
It furthers the University's objective of excellence in research, scholarship,
and education by publishing worldwide in

Oxford New York

Athens Auckland Bangkok Bogotá Buenos Aires Calcutta
Cape Town Chennai Dar es Salaam Delhi Florence Hong Kong Istanbul
Karachi Kuala Lumpur Madrid Melbourne Mexico City Mumbai
Nairobi Paris São Paulo Singapore Taipei Tokyo Toronto Warsaw

and associated companies in Berlin Ibadan

Oxford is a registered trade mark of Oxford University Press
in the UK and in certain other countries

Published in the United States
by Oxford University Press Inc., New York

© Oxford University Press 1999

Database right Oxford University Press (maker)

First published 1999

All rights reserved. No part of this publication may be reproduced,
stored in a retrieval system, or transmitted, in any form or by any means,
without the prior permission in writing of Oxford University Press,
or as expressly permitted by law, or under terms agreed with the appropriate
reprographics rights organization. Enquiries concerning reproduction
outside the scope of the above should be sent to the Rights Department,
Oxford University Press, at the address above

You must not circulate this book in any other binding or cover
and you must impose this same condition on any acquirer

British Library Cataloguing in Publication Data
Data available

Library of Congress Cataloging in Publication Data
Data available

ISBN 0–19– 860222–7

10 9 8 7 6 5 4 3 2 1

Typeset by Market House Books Ltd
Printed in Great Britain
on acid-free paper by
Mackays of Chatham
Chatham, Kent

PREFACE

The *Oxford Puzzle Solver* is ideal for anyone who enjoys solving crosswords or playing word games. It was compiled to provide answers to general knowledge crossword clues and quiz questions and to be useful in a wide variety of games. It includes lists in tabular form, such as Religious Festivals; Capital Cities; and Planets and their Satellites; and thematic lists, such as Fish; Musical Instruments; and Sportspeople.

To help the reader locate a particular subject, the book has been divided into twelve broad sections:
Famous People;
History, Politics, and War;
Religion and Mythology;
Geography;
Transport;
Science and Technology;
Medicine and the Human Body;
Animals, Plants, and Agriculture;
The Arts;
Literature and Language;
Sport; and
Miscellaneous.

The *Oxford Puzzle Solver* contains a wealth of information and the editors believe that it will prove useful as a reference resource in its own right.

ACKNOWLEDGEMENTS

Editor
Fran Alexander

Contributing Editors
Peter Blair
Jonathan Law
Mark Salad

Computerization
Dr John Daintith

Compiled and Typeset by
Market House Books Ltd., Aylesbury

CONTENTS

FAMOUS PEOPLE

RULERS OF ENGLAND
(with dates of reign)

Edwy *or* Eadwig	955–7
Edgar	959–75
Edward the Martyr, St	975–8
Ethelred the Unready	978–1013
Sweyn Forkbeard	1013–4
Ethelred the Unready	1014–6
Edmund Ironside	1016
Canute	1016–35
Harold I (Harefoot)	1035–40
Hartacnut	1040–2
Edward the Confessor, St	1042–66
Harold II	1066
William I (the Conqueror)	1066–87
William II (Rufus)	1087–1100
Henry I	1100–35
Stephen	1135–54
Henry II	1154–89
Richard I	1189–99
John	1199–1216
Henry III	1216–72
Edward I	1272–1307
Edward II	1307–27
Edward III	1327–77
Richard II	1377–99
Henry IV	1399–1413
Henry V	1413–22
Henry VI	1422–61; 1470–1
Edward IV	1461–83
Edward V	1483
Richard III	1483–5
Henry VII	1485–1509
Henry VIII	1509–47
Edward VI	1547–53
Jane (Lady Jane Grey)	1553
Mary I*	1553–8
Philip*	1554–8
Elizabeth I	1558–1603
James I	1603–25
Charles I	1625–49
The Commonwealth	*1649–60*
Oliver Cromwell (Lord Protector)	1653–8
Richard Cromwell (Lord Protector)	1658–9
Charles II	1660–85
James II	1685–8
*William and Mary, King and Queen of England	1689–94
William III	1694–1702
Anne	1702–14
George I	1714–27
George II	1727–60
George III	1760–1820
George IV	1820–30
William IV	1830–7
Victoria	1837–1901
Edward VII	1901–10
George V	1910–36
Edward VIII (Duke of Windsor)	1936
George VI	1936–52
Elizabeth II	from 1952

* Indicates joint reign.

RULERS OF SCOTLAND
(with dates of reign)

Kenneth I (MacAlpine)	c. 844–58	William the Lion	1165–1214
Donald I	858–62	Alexander II	1214–49
Constantine I	862–77	Alexander III	1249–86
Aedh	877–8	Margaret, Maid of	
Girac*	878–89	Norway	1286–90
Eocha*	878–89	John Balliol	1292–6
Donald II	889–900	(Edward I of England 1296–1306)	
Constantine II	900–43	Robert I (Bruce)	1306–29
Malcolm I	943–54	David II	1329–32
Indolf or Indolphus	954–62	Edward Balliol	1332–56
Duff	962–6	David II (restored)	1356–71
Colin	966–71	Robert II	1371–90
Kenneth II	971–95	Robert III	1390–1406
Constantine III	995–7	James I	1406–37
Kenneth III	997–1005	James II	1437–60
Malcolm II	1005–34	James III	1460–88
Duncan I	1034–40	James IV	1488–1513
Macbeth	1040–57	James V	1513–42
Malcolm III	1057–93	Mary Stuart, Queen	
Donald III (Bane)	1093–4, 1094–7	of Scots	1542–67
Duncan II	1094	James VI of Scotland and I of England	1567–1625 1603–25
Edgar	1097–1107		
Alexander I	1107–24		
David I	1124–53		
Malcolm IV	1153–65	*Indicates joint reign.	

PRIME MINISTERS OF THE UK
(with dates in office)

Sir Robert Walpole	1721–42
Earl of Wilmington	1742–3
Henry Pelham	1743–54
Duke of Newcastle	1754–6
Duke of Devonshire	1756–7
Duke of Newcastle	1757–62
Earl of Bute	1762–3
George Grenville	1763–5
Marquess of Rockingham	1765–6
Earl of Chatham	1766–8
Duke of Grafton	1768–70
Lord North	1770–82
Marquess of Rockingham	1782
Earl of Shelburne	1782–3
Duke of Portland	1783
William Pitt	1783–1801
Henry Addington	1801–4
William Pitt	1804–7
Lord William Grenville	1806–7
Duke of Portland	1807–9
Spencer Perceval	1809–12
Earl of Liverpool	1812–27
George Canning	1827
Viscount Goderich	1827–8
Duke of Wellington	1828–30
Earl Grey	1830–4
Viscount Melbourne	1834
Duke of Wellington	1834
Sir Robert Peel	1834–5
Viscount Melbourne	1835–41
Sir Robert Peel	1841–6
Earl Russell	1846–52
Earl of Derby	1852
Earl of Aberdeen	1852–5
Viscount Palmerston	1855–8
Earl of Derby	1858–9
Viscount Palmerston	1859–65
Earl Russell	1865–6
Earl of Derby	1866–8
Benjamin Disraeli	1868
William Ewart Gladstone	1868–74
Benjamin Disraeli	1874–80
William Ewart Gladstone	1880–5
Marquess of Salisbury	1885–6
William Ewart Gladstone	1886
Marquess of Salisbury	1886–92
William Ewart Gladstone	1892–4
Earl of Rosebery	1894–5
Marquess of Salisbury	1895–1902
Arthur James Balfour	1902–5
Sir Henry Campbell-Bannerman	1905–8
Herbert Henry Asquith	1908–16
David Lloyd George	1916–22
Andrew Bonar Law	1922–3
Stanley Baldwin	1923–4
Ramsay MacDonald	1924
Stanley Baldwin	1924–9
Ramsay MacDonald	1929–35
Stanley Baldwin	1935–7
Neville Chamberlain	1937–40
Winston Spencer Churchill	1940–5
Clement Attlee	1945–51
Sir Winston Spencer Churchill	1951–5
Sir Anthony Eden	1955–7
Harold Macmillan	1957–63
Sir Alec Douglas-Home	1963–4
Harold Wilson	1964–70
Edward Heath	1970–4
Harold Wilson	1974–6
James Callaghan	1976–9
Margaret Thatcher	1979–90
John Major	1990–7
Tony Blair	from 1997

PRESIDENTS OF THE USA
(with dates in office)

George Washington	1789–97	William McKinley	1897–1901
John Adams	1797–1801	Theodore Roosevelt	1901–9
Thomas Jefferson	1801–9	William Howard Taft	1909–13
James Madison	1809–17	Thomas Woodrow	
James Monroe	1817–25	Wilson	1913–21
John Quincy Adams	1825–9	Warren Gamaliel	
Andrew Jackson	1829–37	Harding	1921–3
Martin Van Buren	1837–41	Calvin Coolidge	1923–9
William Henry Harrison	1841	Herbert Clark Hoover	1929–33
John Tyler	1841–5	Franklin Delano	
James Knox Polk	1845–9	Roosevelt	1933–45
Zachary Taylor	1849–50	Harry S. Truman	1945–53
Millard Fillmore	1850–3	Dwight David	
Franklin Pierce	1853–7	Eisenhower	1953–61
James Buchanan	1857–61	John Fitzgerald	
Abraham Lincoln	1861–5	Kennedy	1961–3
Andrew Johnson	1865–9	Lyndon Baines Johnson	1963–9
Ulysses Simpson Grant	1869–77	Richard Milhous Nixon	1969–74
Rutherford Birchard		Gerald Rudolph Ford	1974–7
Hayes	1877–81	James Earl Carter, Jr.	1977–81
James Abram Garfield	1881	Ronald Wilson Reagan	1981–9
Chester Alan Arthur	1881–5	George Herbert Walter	
Stephen Grover		Bush	1989–93
Cleveland	1885–9	William Jefferson	
Benjamin Harrison	1889–93	Clinton	from 1993
Stephen Grover			
Cleveland	1893–7		

ROMAN EMPERORS
(with dates of reign)

Augustus	27 BC–AD 14	Domitian	81–96
Tiberius	14–37	Nerva	96–8
Caligula	37–41	Trajan	98–117
Claudius	41–54	Hadrian	117–38
Nero	54–68	Antoninus Pius	138–61
Galba	68–9	Marcus Aurelius	161–80
Otho	69	Lucius Verus	161–9
Vitellius	69	Commodus	180–92
Vespasian	69–79	Pertinax	193
Titus	79–81	Didius Julianus	193

ROMAN EMPERORS (cont.)
(with dates of reign)

Septimius Severus**	193–211	Maximin	310–3
Caracalla**	198–217	Constantine I	
Geta**	209–12	(the Great)	312–37
Macrinus	217–8	Constantine II	337–40
Heliogabalus	218–22	Constans I**	337–50
Alexander Severus	222–35	Constantius II**	337–61
Maximinus I	235–8	Magnentius	350–1
Gordian I**	238	Julian	360–3
Gordian II**	238	Jovian	363–4
Balbinus**	238	*Valentinian I	364–75
Maximus**	238	†Valens	364–78
Gordian III	238–44	†Procopius	365–6
Philip	244–9	*Gratian	375–83
Decius	249–51	*Valentinian II	375–92
Hostilian**	251	Theodosius I	379–95
Gallus**	251–3	†Arcadius	395–408
Aemilian	253	*Honorius**	395–423
Valerian**	253–60	Flavius Claudius	
Gallienus**	253–68	Constantinus**	407–11
Claudius II	268–9	†Theodosius II	408–50
Quintillus	269–70	*Constantius III	421–3
Aurelian	270–5	Valentinian III	423–55
Tacitus	275–6	†Marcian	450–7
Florian	276	*Petronius Maximus	455
Probus	276–82	*Avitus	455–6
Carus	282–3	†Leo I	457–74
Carinus**	283–5	*Majorian	457–61
Numerian**	283–4	*Libius Severus	461–7
*Diocletian	284–305; abdicated	*Anthemius	467–72
		*Olybrius	472–73
*Maximian	286–305; 306–8	*Julius Nepos	474–5
		†Leo II	474
*Constantius I	305–6	†Zeno	474–91
†Galerius	305–11	*Romulus Augustulus	475–6
*Severus	306–7		
*Maxentius	306–12		
†Licinius	308–24		

*During the reign of Diocletian, the Roman Empire was divided and from then on sometimes had both a Western and an Eastern emperor.
*Indicates Emperors of the Western Roman Empire only.
†Indicates Emperors of the Eastern Roman Empire.
** Indicates emperors that shared power.

POPES FROM 1492
(with dates in office)

Alexander VI	1492–1503	Innocent XI	1676–89
Pius III	1503	Alexander VIII	1689–91
Julius II	1503–13	Innocent XII	1691–1700
Leo X	1513–21	Clement XI	1700–21
Adrian VI	1522–3	Innocent XIII	1721–4
Clement VII	1523–34	Benedict XIII	1724–30
Paul III	1534–49	Clement XII	1730–40
Julius III	1550–5	Benedict XIV	1740–58
Marcellus II	1555	Clement XIII	1758–69
Paul IV	1555–9	Clement XIV	1769–74
Pius IV	1559–65	Pius VI	1775–99
Pius V	1566–72	Pius VII	1800–23
Gregory XIII	1572–85	Leo XII	1823–9
Sixtus V	1585–90	Pius VIII	1829–30
Urban VII	1590	Gregory XVI	1831–46
Gregory XIV	1590–1	Pius IX	1846–78
Innocent IX	1591	Leo XIII	1878–1903
Clement VIII	1592–1605	Pius X	1903–14
Leo XI	1605	Benedict XV	1914–22
Paul V	1605–21	Pius XI	1922–39
Gregory XV	1621–3	Pius XII	1939–58
Urban VIII	1623–44	John XXIII	1958–63
Innocent X	1644–55	Paul VI	1963–78
Alexander VII	1655–67	John Paul I	1978
Clement IX	1667–9	John Paul II	from 1978
Clement X	1670–6		

ARCHBISHOPS OF CANTERBURY
(with dates in office)

Augustine	597–604	Jaenbeorht	765–92
Laurentius	604–19	Æthelheard	793–805
Mellitus	619–24	Wulfred	805–32
Justus	624–7	Feologild	832
Honorius	627–53	Ceolnoth	833–70
Deusdedit	655–64	Æthelred	870–89
Theodorus	668–90	Plegmund	890–914
Beorhtweald	693–731	Æthelhelm	914–23
Tatwine	731–4	Wulfhelm	923–42
Nothelm	735–9	Oda	942–58
Cuthbeorht	740–60	Ælfsige	959
Breguwine	761–4	Beorhthelm	959

ARCHBISHOPS OF CANTERBURY (cont.)
(with dates in office)

Dunstan	960–88	John Stafford	1443–52
Æthelgar	988–90	John Kempe	1452–4
Sigeric Serio	990–4	Thomas Bourgchier	1454–86
Ælfric	995–1005	John Morton	1486–1500
Ælfheah	1005–12	Henry Deane	1501–3
Lyfing	1013–20	William Warham	1504–32
Æthelnoth	1020–38	Thomas Cranmer	1532–55
Eadsige	1038–50	Reginald Pole	1555–8
Robert of Jumièges	1051–2	Matthew Parker	1559–75
Stigand	1052–70	Edmund Grindal	1575–83
Lanfranc	1070–89	John Whitgift	1583–1604
Anselm	1093–1109	Richard Bancroft	1604–10
Ralph d'Escures	1114–22	George Abbot	1611–33
William of Corbeil	1123–36	William Laud	1633–45
Theobald of Bec	1138–61	William Juxon	1660–3
Thomas à Becket	1162–70	Gilbert Sheldon	1663–77
Richard of Dover	1174–84	William Sancroft	1677–90
Baldwin	1184–90	John Tillotson	1691–4
Hubert Walter	1193–1205	Thomas Tenison	1694–1715
Stephen Langton	1206–28	William Wake	1715–37
Richard Grant		John Potter	1737–47
(Wethershed)	1229–31	Thomas Herring	1747–57
Edmund Rich	1233–40	Matthew Hutton	1757–8
Boniface of Savoy	1241–70	Thomas Secker	1758–68
Robert Kilwardby	1272–8	Frederick Cornwallis	1768–83
John Pecham	1279–92	John Moore	1783–1805
Robert Winchelsey	1293–1313	Charles Sutton	1805–28
Walter Reynolds	1313–27	William Howley	1828–48
Simon Mepham	1327–33	John Sumner	1848–62
John Stratford	1333–48	Charles Longley	1862–8
John Offord	1348–9	Archibald Tait	1868–82
Simon Islip	1349–66	Edward Benson	1883–96
Simon Langham	1366–8	Frederick Temple	1896–1902
William Whittlesey	1368–74	Randall Davidson	1903–28
Simon Sudbury	1375–81	Cosmo Lang	1928–42
William Courtenay	1381–96	William Temple	1942–4
Thomas Arundel	1396–7	Geoffrey Fisher	1945–61
Roger Walden	1397–9	Arthur Ramsey	1961–74
Thomas Arundel		Frederick Coggan	1974–80
(restored)	1399–1414	Robert Runcie	1980–91
Henry Chichele	1414–43	George Carey	from 1991

HISTORICAL, POLITICAL, AND MILITARY FIGURES

Abbas, Ferhat (1899–1989) Algerian nationalist leader, President of Algeria 1958–61

Abdul Hamid II (known as 'the Great Assassin' and 'the Red Sultan') (1842–1918) Sultan of the Ottoman Empire (1876–1909)

Abdullah, Sheikh Muhammad (known as 'the Lion of Kashmir') (1905–82) Nationalist leader in Kashmir

Abdullah ibn Hussein (1882–1951) king of Jordan 1946–51

Abdul Rahman, Tunku (1903–90) Malaysian statesman, Prime Minister of Malaya 1957–63 and of Malaysia 1963–70

Aberdeen, 4th Earl of (title of George Hamilton Gordon) (1784–1860) British Conservative statesman, Prime Minister 1852–5

Abiola, Moshood (Kashimawo Olawale) (1937–98) Nigerian politician

Acheson, Dean Gooderham (1893–1971) American statesman

Adams, John (1735–1826) American Federalist statesman, 2nd President of the US 1797–1801

Adams, John Quincy (1767–1848) American statesman, 6th President of the US 1825–9

Addams, Jane (1860–1935) American social reformer and feminist

Addington, Henry, 1st Viscount Sidmouth (1757–1844) British Tory statesman, Prime Minister 1801–4

Adenauer, Konrad (1876–1967) German statesman, first Chancellor of the Federal Republic of Germany 1949–63

Aeschines (c. 390–c. 314 BC) Athenian statesman and orator

Aga Khan, title of the imam or leader of the Nizari sect of Ismaili Muslims

Agricola, Gnaeus Julius (AD 40–93) Roman general and governor of Britain 78–84

Agrippa, Marcus Vipsanius (63–12 BC) Roman general

Aitken, William Maxwell See BEAVERBROOK

Akbar, Jalaludin Muhammad (known as Akbar the Great) (1542–1605) Mogul emperor of India 1556–1605

Akhenaten (also Akhenaton, Ikhnaton) (14th century BC) Egyptian pharaoh of the 18th dynasty, reigned 1379–1362 BC

Alaric (c. 370–410) king of the Visigoths

Albert, Prince (1819–61) consort to Queen Victoria

Albuquerque, Alfonso de (known as Albuquerque the Great) (1453–1515) Portuguese colonial statesman

Alcibiades (c. 450–404 BC) Athenian statesman and general

Alexander, Harold (Rupert Leofric George), 1st Earl Alexander of Tunis (1891–1969) British Field Marshal and Conservative statesman

Alexander (known as Alexander the Great) (356–323 BC) king of Macedon 336–323

Alexander I (c. 1077–1124) king of Scotland

Alexander I (1777–1825) tsar of Russia

Alexander II (1198–1249) king of Scotland

Alexander III (1241–86) king of Scotland

Alexander III (1845–94) tsar of Russia

Alexander Nevsky (also Nevski) (canonized as St Alexander Nevsky) (c. 1220–63) Prince of Novgorod (1236–63) and Grand Prince of Vladimir (1252–63)

Alexander the Liberator (1818–81) tsar of Russia

Alfonso XIII (1886–1941) king of Spain 1886–1931

Alfred (known as Alfred the Great) (849–99) king of Wessex 871–99

Ali, Muhammad See MUHAMMAD ALI

Allenby, Edmund Henry Hynman, 1st Viscount (1861–1936) British soldier

HISTORICAL, POLITICAL, AND MILITARY FIGURES (cont.)

Allende, Salvador (1908–73) Chilean statesman, President 1970–3

Allen, Ethan (1738–89) American soldier

Amenhotep I (16th century BC) Egyptian pharaoh, reigned 1546–1526

Amin, Idi (full name Idi Amin Dada) (born 1925) Ugandan soldier and head of state 1971–9

Amundsen, Roald (1872–1928) Norwegian explorer

Andrew, Prince, Andrew Albert Christian Edward, Duke of York (born 1960) second son of Elizabeth II

Andropov, Yuri (Vladimirovich) (1914–84) Soviet statesman, General Secretary of the Communist Party of the USSR 1982–4 and President 1983–4

Anne Boleyn See BOLEYN

Anne (1665–1714) queen of England and Scotland (known as Great Britain from 1707) and Ireland 1702–14

Anne of Cleves (1515–57) fourth wife of Henry VIII

Anne, Princess, Anne Elizabeth Alice Louise, the Princess Royal (born 1950) daughter of Elizabeth II

Antall, Jozsef (1933–93) Hungarian statesman, Prime Minister 1990–3

Antiochus III (known as Antiochus the Great) (c. 242–187 BC) Seleucid king

Antoninus Pius (86–161) Roman emperor 138–61

Antony, Mark (Latin name Marcus Antonius) (c. 83–30 BC) Roman statesman and general

Anyaoku, Eleazar Chukwuemeka (born 1933) Nigerian diplomat

Aquitaine, Eleanor of See ELEANOR OF AQUITAINE

Arafat, Yasser (born 1929) Palestinian leader

Aragon, Catherine of See CATHERINE OF ARAGON

Aristides (known as Aristides the Just) (5th century BC) Athenian statesman and general

Arrow, Kenneth Joseph (born 1921) American economist

Artaxerxes I (died 425 BC) king of ancient Persia, reigned 464–425 BC

Arthur, traditionally king of Britain, historically perhaps a 5th or 6th-century Romano-British chieftain or general

Arthur, Chester Alan (1830–86) American Republican statesman, 21st President of the US 1881–5

Ashdown, Jeremy John Durham ('Paddy') (born 1941) British Liberal Democrat politician

Ashmole, Elias (1617–92) English antiquary

Ashurbanipal, king of Assyria c. 668–627 BC

Asoka (died c. 232 BC) Indian emperor

Asquith, Herbert Henry, 1st Earl of Oxford and Asquith (1852–1928) British Liberal statesman, Prime Minister 1908–16

Assad, Hafiz al- (born 1928) Syrian Baath statesman, President since 1971

Astor, Nancy Witcher Langhorne, Viscountess (1879–1964) American-born British Conservative politician

Atatürk, Kemal (born Mustafa Kemal; also called Kemal Pasha) (1881–1938) Turkish statesman and general, President of Turkey (1923–38)

Athelstan (895–939) king of England 925–39

Atkinson, Sir Harry (Albert) (1831–92) New Zealand statesman, Prime Minister 1876–7, 1883–4, and 1887–91

Attila (406–53) king of the Huns 434–53

Attlee, Clement Richard, 1st Earl Attlee (1883–1967) British Labour statesman, Prime Minister 1945–51

Augustus (born Gaius Octavianus; also called (until 27 BC) Octavian) (63 BC–AD 14) the first

HISTORICAL, POLITICAL, AND MILITARY FIGURES (cont.)

Roman emperor

Aung San (1914–47) Burmese nationalist leader

Aung San Suu Kyi (born 1945) Burmese political leader

Aurangzeb (1618–1707) Mogul emperor of Hindustan 1658–1707

Aurelian (Latin name Lucius Domitius Aurelianus) (c. 215–75) Roman emperor

Aurelius, Marcus (full name Caesar Marcus Aurelius Antoninus Augustus) (121–80) Roman emperor 161–80

Ayatollah Khomeini See KHOMEINI

Ayub Khan, Muhammad (1907–74) Pakistani soldier and statesman, President 1958–69

Azikiwe, (Benjamin) Nnamdi (1904–96) Nigerian statesman, President 1963–6

Babur (born Zahir al-Din Muhammad) (1483–1530) Mogul emperor of India c. 1525–30

Bacon, Francis, Baron Verulam and Viscount St Albans (1561–1626) English statesman and philosopher

Baden-Powell, Robert (Stephenson Smyth), 1st Baron Baden-Powell of Gilwell (1857–1941) English soldier and founder of the Boy Scout movement

Bader, Sir Douglas (Robert Steuart) (1910–82) British airman

Baffin, William (c. 1584–1622) English navigator and explorer

Bakunin, Mikhail (Aleksandrovich) (1814–76) Russian anarchist

Balboa, Vasco Núñez de (1475–1519) Spanish explorer

Baldwin, Stanley, 1st Earl Baldwin of Bewdley (1867–1947) British Conservative statesman, Prime Minister 1923–4, 1924–9, and 1935–7

Balfour, Arthur James, 1st Earl of Balfour (1848–1930) British Conservative statesman, Prime Minister 1902–5

Ball, John (died 1381) English rebel

Banda, Hastings Kamuzu (1906–97) Malawian statesman, Prime Minister 1964–94 and President 1966–94

Bandaranaike, Sirimavo Ratwatte Dias (born 1916) Sinhalese stateswoman, Prime Minister of Sri Lanka 1960–5, 1970–7, and since 1994

Barbarossa (born Khair ad-Din) (c. 1483–1546) Barbary pirate

Barbarossa See FREDERICK I

Bar-Cochba, Jewish leader of a rebellion in AD 132

Barents, Willem (died 1597) Dutch explorer

Barton, Sir Edmund (1849–1920) Australian statesman and jurist, first Prime Minister of Australia 1901–3

Batista, Fulgencio (full name Fulgencio Batista y Zaldívar) (1901–73) Cuban soldier and statesman, President 1940–4 and 1952–9

Bayard, Pierre du Terrail, Chevalier de (1473–1524) French soldier

Beale, Dorothea (1831–1906) English educationist

Beatty, David, 1st Earl Beatty of the North Sea and of Brooksby (1871–1936) British admiral

Beaverbrook, (William) Max(-well) Aitken, 1st Baron (1879–1964) Canadian-born British Conservative politician and newspaper proprietor

Becket, St Thomas à (c. 1118–70) English prelate and statesman

Begin, Menachem (1913–92) Israeli statesman, Prime Minister 1977–84

Belshazzar (6th century BC) last king of Babylon

Ben Bella, (Muhammad) Ahmed (born 1916) Algerian statesman, Prime Minister 1962–3 and President 1963–5

Beneš, Edvard (1884–1948) Czechoslovak statesman, Prime Minister 1921–2, President 1935–8 and 1945–8

Famous People

HISTORICAL, POLITICAL, AND MILITARY FIGURES (cont.)

Ben-Gurion, David (1886–1973) Israeli statesman, Prime Minister 1948–53 and 1955–63

Benn, Anthony (Neil Wedgwood) ('Tony') (born 1925) British Labour politician

Berenice (3rd century BC) Egyptian queen, wife of Ptolemy III

Beria, Lavrenti (Pavlovich) (1899–1953) Soviet politician and head of the secret police (NKVD and MVD) 1938–53

Bering, Vitus (Jonassen) (1681–1741) Danish navigator and explorer

Bernadotte, Folke, Count (1895–1948) Swedish statesman

Bernadotte, Jean Baptiste Jules (1763–1844) French soldier, king of Sweden (as Charles XIV) 1818–44

Bevan, Aneurin ('Nye') (1897–1960) British Labour politician

Beveridge, William Henry, 1st Baron (1879–1963) British economist and social reformer, born in India

Bevin, Ernest (1881–1951) British Labour statesman and trade unionist

Bhutto, Benazir (born 1953) Pakistani stateswoman, Prime Minister 1988–90 and 1993–6

Bhutto, Zulfikar Ali (1928–79) Pakistani statesman, President 1971–3 and Prime Minister 1973–7

Biko, Stephen ('Steve') (1946–77) South African radical leader

Billy the Kid See BONNEY

Bismarck, Otto (Eduard Leopold) von, Prince of Bismarck, Duke of Lauenburg (known as 'the Iron Chancellor') (1815–98) German statesman

Black Prince (name given to Edward, Prince of Wales and Duke of Cornwall) (1330–76) eldest son of Edward III of England

Blair, Anthony Charles Lynton ('Tony') (born 1953) British Labour Prime Minister since 1997

Bligh, William (1754–1817) British naval officer

Bloody Mary, nickname of Mary I of England

Blum, Léon (1872–1950) French statesman, Prime Minister 1936–7, 1938, 1946–7

Blunt, Anthony (Frederick) (1907–83) British art historian, Foreign Office official, and Soviet spy

Boadicea See BOUDICCA

Bodley, Sir Thomas (1545–1613) English scholar and diplomat

Boethius, Anicius Manlius Severinus (c. 480–524) Roman statesman and philosopher

Bokassa, Jean Bédel (1921–96) Central African Republic statesman and military leader, President 1972–6, emperor 1976–9

Boleyn, Anne (1507–36) second wife of Henry VIII and mother of Elizabeth I

Bolger, James B(rendan) (born 1935) New Zealand statesman, Prime Minister 1990–7

Bolingbroke, surname of Henry IV of England

Bolívar, Simón (known as 'the Liberator') (1783–1830) Venezuelan patriot and statesman

Bonaparte (Italian, Buonaparte) See NAPOLEON

Bonney, William H. (Billy the Kid) (1859–81) American outlaw

Bonnie Prince Charlie See STUART

Boone, Daniel (c. 1734–1820) American pioneer

Borgia, Cesare (c. 1476–1507) Italian statesman

Borgia, Lucrezia (1480–1519) Italian noblewoman

Boris Godunov See GODUNOV

Bormann, Martin (1900–c. 1945) German Nazi politician

Botha, Louis (1862–1919) South African soldier and statesman, first Prime Minister of the Union of South Africa 1910–19

Botha, P(ieter) W(illem) (born 1916) South African statesman, Prime Minister 1978–84, State

HISTORICAL, POLITICAL, AND MILITARY FIGURES (cont.)

President 1984–9

Bothwell, 4th Earl of (title of James Hepburn) (*c.* 1536–78) Scottish nobleman and third husband of Mary, Queen of Scots

Boudicca (also Boadicea) (died AD 62) queen of the Britons, ruler of the Iceni tribe in eastern England

Bougainville, Louis Antoine de (1729–1811) French explorer

Bourguiba, Habib ibn Ali (born 1903) Tunisian nationalist and statesman, President 1957–87

Boutros-Ghali, Boutros (born 1922) Egyptian diplomat and politician, Secretary-General of the United Nations 1992–6

Bowie, James ('Jim') (1799–1836) American frontiersman

Brandt, Willy (born Karl Herbert Frahm) (1913–92) German statesman, Chancellor of West Germany 1969–74

Braun, Eva (1910–45) German mistress of Adolf Hitler

Brezhnev, Leonid (Ilich) (1906–82) Soviet statesman, General Secretary of the Communist Party of the USSR 1966–82 and President 1977–82

Bright, John (1811–89) English Liberal politician and reformer

Brown, John (1800–59) American abolitionist

Bruce, James ('the Abyssinian') (1730–94); Scottish explorer

Bruce, Robert the See ROBERT THE BRUCE

Brundtland, Gro Harlem (born 1939) Norwegian Labour stateswoman, Prime Minister 1981, 1986–9, 1990–6

Bruton, John (Gerard) (born 1947) Irish Fine Gael statesman, Taoiseach (Prime Minister) 1994–7

Brutus, Marcus Junius (85–42 BC) Roman senator

Buchanan, James (1791–1868) American Democratic statesman, 15th President of the US 1857–61

Bukharin, Nikolai (Ivanovich) (1888–1938) Russian revolutionary activist and theorist

Bulganin, Nikolai (Aleksandrovich) (1895–1975) Soviet statesman, Chairman of the Council of Ministers (Premier) 1955–8

Buonaparte See NAPOLEON

Burgess, Guy (Francis de Moncy) (1911–63) British Foreign Office official and spy

Burghley, William Cecil, 1st Baron (1520–98) English statesman

Burgoyne, John ('Gentleman Johnny') (1722–92) English general and dramatist

Burke, Edmund (1729–97) British man of letters and Whig politician

Burke, Robert O'Hara (1820–61) Irish explorer

Burke, William (1792–1829) Irish murderer

Burr, Aaron (1756–1836) American Democratic Republican statesman

Burton, Sir Richard (Francis) (1821–90) English explorer, anthropologist, and translator

Bush, George (Herbert Walter) (born 1924) American Republican statesman, 41st President of the US 1989–93

Buss, Frances Mary (1827–94) English educationist

Bute, 3rd Earl of (title of John Stuart) (1713–92) Scottish courtier and Tory statesman, Prime Minister 1762–3

Buthelezi, Chief Mangosuthu (Gatsha) (born 1928) South African politician

Cabot, John (Italian name Giovanni Caboto) (*c.* 1450–*c.* 1498) Italian explorer and navigator

Cadbury, George (1839–1922) English cocoa and chocolate manufacturer and social reformer

Cade, John ('Jack') (died 1450) Irish rebel

Caesar See JULIUS CAESAR

Calamity Jane (born Martha Jane

HISTORICAL, POLITICAL, AND MILITARY FIGURES (cont.)

Cannary) (*c.* 1852–1903) American frontierswoman

Caligula (born Gaius Julius Caesar Germanicus) (AD 12–41) Roman emperor 37–41

Callaghan, (Leonard) James, Baron Callaghan of Cardiff (born 1912) British Labour statesman, Prime Minister 1976–9

Cambyses (died 522 BC) son of Cyrus, king of Persia 529–522 BC

Campbell-Bannerman, Sir Henry (1836–1908) British Liberal statesman, Prime Minister 1905–8

Canmore, nickname of Malcolm III of Scotland

Canning, George (1770–1827) British Tory statesman, Prime Minister 1827

Canute (also Cnut) (died 1035) Danish king of England 1017–35, Denmark 1018–35, and Norway 1028–35

Capet, Hugh (or Hugo) (938–96) king of France 987–96

Capone, Alphonse ('Al') (1899–1947) American gangster, of Italian descent

Caracalla (born Septimius Bassanius; later called Marcus Aurelius Severus Antoninus Augustus) (188–217) Roman emperor 211–17

Caratacus (also Caractacus) (1st century AD) British chieftain, son of Cunobelinus

Carnegie, Andrew (1835–1919) Scottish-born American industrialist and philanthropist

Carter, James Earl ('Jimmy') (born 1924) American Democratic statesman, 39th President of the US 1977–81

Cartier, Jacques (1491–1557) French explorer

Casanova, Giovanni Jacopo (full surname Casanova de Seingalt) (1725–98) Italian adventurer

Casement, Sir Roger (David) (1864–1916) Irish nationalist

Cassius, Gaius (full name Gaius Cassius Longinus) (died 42 BC)

Roman general

Castle, Barbara (Anne), Baroness Castle of Blackburn (born 1911) British Labour politician

Castlereagh, Robert Stewart, Viscount (1769–1822) British Tory statesman

Castro, Fidel (born 1927) Cuban statesman, Prime Minister 1959–76 and President since 1976

Catherine II (known as Catherine the Great) (1729–96) empress of Russia, reigned 1762–96

Catherine de' Medici (1519–89) queen of France

Catherine of Aragon (1485–1536) first wife of Henry VIII

Catiline (Latin name Lucius Sergius Catilina) (*c.* 108–62 BC) Roman nobleman and conspirator

Cato, Marcus Porcius (known as Cato the Elder or Cato the Censor) (234–149 BC) Roman statesman, orator, and writer

Cavell, Edith (Louisa) (1865–1915) English nurse

Cavour, Camillo Benso, Conte di (1810–61) Italian statesman, Prime Minister 1852–9, 1860–1

Ceauşescu, Nicolae (1918–89) Romanian Communist statesman, first President of the Socialist Republic of Romania 1974–89

Cecil, William See BURGHLEY

Cetshwayo (also Cetewayo) (*c.* 1826–84) Zulu king

Chaka See SHAKA

Chamberlain, (Arthur) Neville (1869–1940) British Conservative statesman, Prime Minister 1937–40

Chamberlain, Joseph (1836–1914) British Liberal statesman

Champlain, Samuel de (1567–1635) French explorer and colonial statesman

Chandragupta Maurya (*c.* 325–297 BC) Indian emperor

Charlemagne (Latin Carolus Magnus Charles the Great) (742–814) king of the Franks 768–814 and Holy

HISTORICAL, POLITICAL, AND MILITARY FIGURES (cont.)

Roman emperor

Charles I (1500–58) king of Spain, reigned 1516–56 and Holy Roman emperor

Charles I (1600–49) king of England, Scotland, and Ireland, reigned 1625–49

Charles II (1630–85) king of England, Scotland, and Ireland, reigned 1660–85

Charles Martel (c. 688–741) Frankish ruler of the eastern part of the Frankish kingdom from 715 and the whole kingdom from 719

Charles, Prince, Charles Philip Arthur George, Prince of Wales (born 1948) heir apparent to Elizabeth II

Charles VII (1403–61) king of France 1422–61

Charles XII (also Karl XII) (1682–1718) king of Sweden 1697–1718

Chatham, 1st Earl of See PITT

Cheops (Egyptian name Khufu) (fl. early 26th century BC) Egyptian pharaoh of the 4th dynasty

Chiang Kai-shek (also Jiang Jie Shi) (1887–1975) Chinese statesman and general, President of China 1928–31 and 1943–9 and of Taiwan 1950–75

Chifley, Joseph Benedict (1885–1951) Australian Labor statesman, Prime Minister 1945–9

Childers, (Robert) Erskine (1870–1922) Irish writer and political activist, born in England

Chirac, Jacques (René) (born 1932) French statesman, Prime Minister 1974–6 and 1986–8 and President since 1995

Chou En-lai See ZHOU ENLAI

Chrétien, (Joseph-Jacques) Jean (born 1934) Canadian Liberal statesman, Prime Minister since 1993

Christian, Fletcher (c. 1764–c. 1793) English seaman and mutineer

Churchill, Sir Winston (Leonard Spencer) (1874–1965) British Conservative statesman, Prime Minister 1940–5 and 1951–5

Cid, El (also the Cid) (born Rodrigo Díaz de Vivar), Count of Bivar (c. 1043–99) Spanish soldier

Clarendon, Earl of (title of Edward Hyde) (1609–74) English statesman and historian

Clark, William (1770–1838) American explorer

Claudius (full name Tiberius Claudius Drusus Nero Germanicus) (10 BC–AD 54) Roman emperor 41–54

Clausewitz, Karl von (1780–1831) Prussian general and military theorist

Cleisthenes (c. 570 BC–c. 508 BC) Athenian statesman

Clemenceau, Georges (Eugène Benjamin) (1841–1929) French statesman, Prime Minister 1906–9 and 1917–20

Cleopatra (also Cleopatra VII) (69–30 BC) queen of Egypt 47–30

Cleveland, (Stephen) Grover (1837–1908) American Democratic statesman, 22nd and 24th President of the US 1885–9 and 1893–7

Clinton, William Jefferson ('Bill') (born 1946) American Democratic statesman, 42nd President of the US (since 1993)

Clive, Robert, 1st Baron Clive of Plassey (known as Clive of India) (1725–74) British general and colonial administrator

Clovis (465–511) king of the Franks 481–511

Cnut See CANUTE

Cobden, Richard (1804–65) English political reformer

Colbert, Jean Baptiste (1619–83) French statesman, chief minister to Louis XIV

Collins, Michael (1890–1922) Irish nationalist leader and politician

Columbus, Christopher (Spanish name Cristóbal Colón) (1451–1506) Italian-born Spanish explorer

Constantine (known as Constantine the Great) (c. 274–337) Roman emperor 312–37

HISTORICAL, POLITICAL, AND MILITARY FIGURES (cont.)

Cook, Captain James (1728–79)
English explorer

Cook, Thomas (1808–92) English
founder of the travel firm Thomas
Cook

Coolidge, (John) Calvin (1872–1933)
American Republican statesman,
30th President of the US 1923–9

Corday, Charlotte (full name Marie
Anne Charlotte Corday d'Armont)
(1768–93) French political assassin

Coriolanus, Gaius (*or* **Gnaeus**)
Marcius (5th century BC) Roman
general

Cortés, Hernando (also Cortez)
(1485–1547) first of the Spanish
conquistadores

Cosimo de' Medici (known as Cosimo
the Elder) (1389–1464) Italian
statesman and banker

Crassus, Marcus Licinius ('Dives') (*c.*
115–53 BC) Roman politician

Crazy Horse (Sioux name Ta-Sunko-
Witko) (*c.* 1849–77) Sioux chief

Crichton, James (known as 'the
Admirable Crichton') (1560–*c.* 1585)
Scottish adventurer

Crippen, Hawley Harvey (known as
Doctor Crippen) (1862–1910)
American-born British murderer

Crockett, David ('Davy') (1786–1836)
American frontiersman, soldier,
and politician

Croesus (6th century BC) last king of
Lydia *c.* 560–546 BC

Cromwell, Oliver (1599–1658) English
general and statesman

Cromwell, Thomas (*c.* 1485–1540)
English statesman, chief minister to
Henry VIII

**Cumberland, William Augustus, Duke
of** (1721–65) English military
commander

Cunard, Sir Samuel (1787–1865)
Canadian-born British shipowner

Cunobelinus See CYMBELINE

Curtin, John (Joseph Ambrose)
(1885–1945) Australian Labor
statesman, Prime Minister 1941–5

Custer, George (Armstrong)

(1839–76) American cavalry general

Cymbeline (also Cunobelinus) (died
c. 42 AD) British chieftain

Cyrus (known as Cyrus the Great)
(died *c.* 530 BC) king of Persia
559–530 BC

Cyrus (known as Cyrus the Younger)
(died 401 BC) Persian prince

Da Gama, Vasco (*c.* 1469–1524)
Portuguese explorer

Dalhousie, 1st Marquess of (title of
James Andrew Broun Ramsay)
(1812–60) British colonial
administrator

Dampier, William (1652–1715)
English explorer and adventurer

Danton, Georges (Jacques) (1759–94)
French revolutionary

Darius I (known as Darius the Great)
(*c.* 550–486 BC) king of Persia
521–486 BC

Darling, Grace (1815–42) English
heroine

Darnley, Lord (title of Henry Stewart
or Stuart) (1545–67) Scottish
nobleman, second husband of
Mary, Queen of Scots

David (died *c.* 962 BC) King of Judah
and Israel *c.* 1000–*c.* 962 BC

David I (*c.* 1084–1153) king of
Scotland, reigned 1124–53

Dayan, Moshe (1915–81) Israeli
statesman and general

Deakin, Alfred (1856–1919) Australian
Liberal statesman, Prime Minister
1903–4, 1905–8, and 1909–10

**Decius, Gaius Messius Quintus
Trajanus** (*c.* 201–51) Roman
emperor 249–51

**de Gaulle, Charles (André Joseph
Marie)** (1890–1970) French general
and statesman, President 1959–69

de Klerk, F(rederik) W(illem) (born
1936) South African statesman,
President 1989–94

Delors, Jacques (Lucien Jean) (born
1925) French socialist politician,
president of the European
Commission 1985–94

de' Medici, Catherine See CATHERINE

HISTORICAL, POLITICAL, AND MILITARY FIGURES (cont.)

DE' MEDICI
de Montfort, Simon See MONTFORT
Demosthenes (384–322 BC) Athenian orator and statesman
Deng Xiaoping (also Teng Hsiao-p'ing) (1904–97) Chinese Communist statesman
Derby, 14th Earl of (title of Edward George Geoffrey Smith Stanley) (1799–1869) British Conservative statesman, Prime Minister 1852, 1858–9, and 1866–8
de Valera, Eamon (1882–1975) American-born Irish statesman, Prime Minister (1932–48)
Diana, Princess (formally called Diana, Princess of Wales; born Lady Diana Frances Spencer) (1961–97) Former wife of Prince Charles
Dias, Bartolomeu (also Diaz) (c. 1450–1500) Portuguese navigator and explorer
Díaz, Porfirio (1830–1915) Mexican general and statesman, President 1877–80 and 1884–1911
Diocletian (full name Gaius Aurelius Valerius Diocletianus) (245–313) Roman emperor 284–305
Dionysius I (known as Dionysius the Elder) (c. 430–367 BC) ruler of Syracuse
Disraeli, Benjamin, 1st Earl of Beaconsfield (1804–81) British Tory statesman, of Italian Jewish descent; Prime Minister 1868 and 1874–80
Dole, Robert Joseph ('Bob') (born 1923) American Republican politician
Dollfuss, Engelbert (1892–1934) Austrian statesman, Chancellor of Austria 1932–4
Domitian (full name Titus Flavius Domitianus) (AD 51–96) Roman emperor 81–96
Douglas-Home, Sir Alec, Baron Home of the Hirsel of Coldstream (1903–95) British Conservative statesman, Prime Minister 1963–4
Dowding, Hugh (Caswall

Tremenheere), Baron (1882–1970) British Marshal of the RAF
Drake, Sir Francis (c. 1540–96) English sailor and explorer
Dreyfus, Alfred (1859–1935) French army officer, of Jewish descent
Dubček, Alexander (1921–92) Czechoslovak statesman
Dudley, Robert, Earl of Leicester (c. 1532–88) English nobleman
Dulles, John Foster (1888–1959) American Republican statesman
Durham, John George Lambton, Earl of (1792–1840) British Whig statesman
Duvalier, François (known as 'Papa Doc') (1907–71) Haitian statesman, President 1957–71
Dzerzhinsky, Feliks (Edmundovich) (1877–1926) Russian Bolshevik leader, of Polish descent
Eadwig See EDWY
Earp, Wyatt (Berry Stapp) (1848–1929) American gambler and marshal
Eden, (Robert) Anthony, 1st Earl of Avon (1897–1977) British Conservative statesman, Prime Minister 1955–7
Edgar (944–75) king of England 959–75
Edinburgh, Duke of See PHILIP, PRINCE
Edmund Ironside, nickname of Edmund II of England
Edmund, St (born Edmund Rich) (c. 1175–1240) English churchman and teacher
Edmund the Martyr, St (c. 841–70) king of East Anglia 855–70
Edward I to VIII, kings of England
Edward, Prince, Edward Antony Richard Louis (born 1964) third son of Elizabeth II
Edward, Prince of Wales See BLACK PRINCE
Edward the Confessor, St (c. 1003–66) son of Ethelred the Unready, king of England 1042–66
Edward the Elder (c. 870–924) son of Alfred the Great, king of

HISTORICAL, POLITICAL, AND MILITARY FIGURES (cont.)

Wessex 899–924

Edward the Martyr, St (*c.* 963–78) son of Edgar, king of England 975–8

Edwy (also Eadwig) (died 959) king of England 955–7

Egbert (died 839) king of Wessex 802–39

Eichmann, (Karl) Adolf (1906–62) German Nazi administrator

Eisenhower, Dwight David ('Ike') (1890–1969) American general and Republican statesman, 34th President of the US 1953–61

Elagabalus See HELIOGABALUS

El Cid See CID, EL

Eleanor of Aquitaine (*c.* 1122–1204) queen of France 1137–52 and of England 1154–89

Elgin, 8th Earl of (title of James Bruce) (1811–63) British colonial statesman

Elizabeth I (1533–1603) daughter of Henry VIII, queen of England and Ireland 1558–1603

Elizabeth II (born Princess Elizabeth Alexandra Mary) (born 1926) daughter of George VI, queen of the United Kingdom since 1952

Elizabeth, the Queen Mother (born Lady Elizabeth Angela Marguerite Bowes-Lyon) (born 1900) wife of George VI

Ellsworth, Lincoln (1880–1951) American explorer

Enver Pasha (1881–1922) Turkish political and military leader

Ericsson, Leif (also Ericson) (*fl. c.* 1000) Norse explorer, son of Eric the Red

Eric the Red (*c.* 940–*c.* 1010) Norse explorer

Eugénie (born Eugénia María de Montijo de Guzmán) (1826–1920) Spanish empress of France 1853–71 and wife of Napoleon III

Eyre, Edward John (1815–1901) British-born Australian explorer and colonial statesman

Fabius (full name Quintus Fabius Maximus Verrucosus, known as 'Fabius Cunctator') (died 203 BC) Roman general and statesman

Fairfax, Thomas, 3rd Baron Fairfax of Cameron (1612–71) English Parliamentary general

Faisal I (1885–1933) king of Iraq, reigned 1921–33

Faisal II (1935–1958) king of Iraq, reigned 1939–58

Farnese, Alessandro, Duke of Parma (1545–92) Italian general and statesman

Farouk (1920–65) king of Egypt, reigned 1936–52

Fawkes, Guy (1570–1606) English conspirator

FDR, nickname of Franklin Delano Roosevelt

Ferdinand (known as Ferdinand of Aragon or Ferdinand the Catholic) (1452–1516) king of Castile 1474–1516 and of Aragon 1479–1516

Fillmore, Millard (1800–74) American Whig statesman, 13th President of the US 1850–3

Flinders, Matthew (1774–1814) English explorer

Foch, Ferdinand (1851–1929) French general

Ford, Gerald R(udolph) (born 1913) American Republican statesman, 38th President of the US 1974–7

Ford, Henry (1863–1947) American motor manufacturer

Forkbeard, Sweyn See SWEYN I

Forrest, John, 1st Baron (1847–1918) Australian explorer and statesman, Premier of Western Australia 1890–1901

Fox, Charles James (1749–1806) British Whig statesman

Francis I (1494–1547) king of France 1515–47

Franco, Francisco (1892–1975) Spanish general and statesman, head of state 1939–75

Frank, Anne (1929–45) German Jewish diarist

Franz Josef (1830–1916) emperor of

HISTORICAL, POLITICAL, AND MILITARY FIGURES (cont.)

Austria 1848–1916 and king of
Hungary 1867–1916

Fraser, (John) Malcolm (born 1930)
Australian Liberal statesman, Prime
Minister 1975–83

Frederick I (known as Frederick
Barbarossa, 'Redbeard') (c.
1123–90) king of Germany and Holy
Roman emperor 1152–90

Frederick II (known as Frederick the
Great) (1712–86) king of Prussia
1740–86

Frederick William (known as 'the
Great Elector') (1620–88) Elector of
Brandenburg 1640–88

Frémont, John Charles (known as
'the Pathfinder') (1813–90)
American explorer and politician

**Freyberg, Bernard Cyril, 1st Baron
Freyberg of Wellington and of
Munstead** (1889–1963) British-born
New Zealand general

Friedman, Milton (born 1912)
American economist

Frisch, Ragnar (Anton Kittil)
(1895–1973) Norwegian economist

Frobisher, Sir Martin (c. 1535–94)
English explorer

Froebel, Friedrich (Wilhelm August)
(1782–1852) German educationist
and founder of the kindergarten
system

Fuad I (1868–1936) king of Egypt,
reigned 1922–36

Fuchs, Sir Vivian (Ernest) (born 1908)
English geologist and explorer

Fulbright, (James) William (1905–95)
American senator

Gaddafi, Mu'ammer Muhammad al
(also Qaddafi) (born 1942) Libyan
colonel, head of state since 1970

Gaitskell, Hugh (Todd Naylor)
(1906–63) British Labour politician

Galba (full name Servius Sulpicius
Galba) (c. 3 BC–AD 69) Roman
emperor AD 68–9

Galbraith, John Kenneth (born 1908)
Canadian-born American
economist

Galtieri, Leopoldo Fortunato (born

1926) Argentinian general and
statesman, President 1981–2

Gama, Vasco da See DA GAMA

Gandhi, Mahatma (born Mohandas
Karamchand Gandhi) (1869–1948)
Indian nationalist and spiritual
leader

Gandhi, Mrs Indira (1917–84) Indian
stateswoman, Prime Minister
1966–77 and 1980–4

Gandhi, Rajiv (1944–91) Indian
statesman, Prime Minister 1984–9

Garfield, James A(bram) (1831–81)
American Republican statesman,
20th President of the US
March–September 1881

Garibaldi, Giuseppe (1807–82) Italian
patriot and military leader

Garvey, Marcus (Mosiah) (1887–1940)
Jamaican political activist and black
nationalist leader

Gaulle, Charles de See DE GAULLE

Gaunt John of See JOHN OF GAUNT

Gemayel, Amin (born 1942) Lebanese
President 1982–8

Gemayel, Pierre (1905–84) Lebanese
political leader

Genghis Khan (1162–1227) the
founder of the Mongol empire

George I to **IV,** kings of Great Britain
and Ireland

George V, king of Great Britain and
Ireland (from 1920 of the United
Kingdom)

George VI, king of the UK

Geronimo (c. 1829–1909) Apache
chief

Getty, Jean Paul (1892–1976)
American industrialist

Giap, Vo Nguyen (born 1912)
Vietnamese military and political
leader

Gilbert, Sir Humphrey (c. 1539–83)
English explorer

Giolitti, Giovanni (1842–1928) Italian
statesman, Prime Minister five
times between 1892 and 1921

Giscard d'Estaing, Valéry (born 1926)
French statesman, President
1974–81

HISTORICAL, POLITICAL, AND MILITARY FIGURES (cont.)

Gladstone, William Ewart (1809–98) British Liberal statesman, Prime Minister 1868–74, 1880–5, 1886, and 1892–4

Glendower, Owen (also Glyndwr) (c. 1354–c. 1417) Welsh chief

Gloriana, nickname of Elizabeth I of England and Ireland

Glyndwr See GLENDOWER

Göbbels See GOEBBELS

Godiva, Lady (died 1080) English noblewoman, wife of Leofric, Earl of Mercia

Godunov, Boris (1550–1605) tsar of Russia 1598–1605

Goebbels, (Paul) Joseph (also Göbbels) (1897–1945) German Nazi leader and politician

Goering, Hermann Wilhelm (1893–1946) German Nazi leader and politician

Gokhale, Gopal Krishna (1866–1915) Indian political leader and social reformer

Goldman, Emma (known as 'Red Emma') (1869–1940) Lithuanian-born American political activist

Gorbachev, Mikhail (Sergeevich) (born 1931) Soviet statesman, General Secretary of the Communist Party of the USSR 1985–91 and President 1988–91

Gordon, Charles George (1833–85) British general and colonial administrator

Gowon, Yakubu (born 1934) Nigerian general and statesman, head of state 1966–75

Gracchus, Tiberius Sempronius (c. 163–133 BC) Roman tribune

Grafton, Augustus Henry Fitzroy, 3rd Duke of (1735–1811) British Whig statesman, Prime Minister 1768–70

Grant, Ulysses S(impson) (born Hiram Ulysses Grant) (1822–85) American general and 18th President of the US 1869–77

Grenville, George (1712–70) British Whig statesman, Prime Minister 1763–5

Gresham, Sir Thomas (c. 1519–79) English financier

Grey, Charles, 2nd Earl (1764–1845) British statesman, Prime Minister 1830–4

Grey, Lady Jane (1537–54) queen of England 9–19 July 1553

Grey, Sir George (1812–98) British statesman and colonial administrator, Prime Minister of New Zealand 1877–9

Griffith, Arthur (1872–1922) Irish nationalist leader and statesman, President of the Irish Free State 1922

Grimond, Joseph ('Jo'), Baron (1913–93) British Liberal politician

Grivas, George (Theodorou) (1898–1974) Greek-Cypriot patriot and soldier

Gromyko, Andrei (Andreevich) (1909–89) Soviet statesman, President of the USSR 1985–8

Guevara, Che (full name Ernesto Guevara de la Serna) (1928–67) Argentinian revolutionary and guerrilla leader

Guggenheim, Meyer (1828–1905) Swiss-born American industrialist

Gulbenkian, Calouste Sarkis (1869–1955) Turkish-born British oil magnate and philanthropist, of Armenian descent

Gustavus Adolphus (1594–1632) king of Sweden 1611–32

Hadrian (full name Publius Aelius Hadrianus) (AD 76–138) Roman emperor 117–38

Haig, Douglas, 1st Earl Haig of Bemersyde (1861–1928) British Field Marshal

Haile Selassie (born Tafari Makonnen) (1892–1975) emperor of Ethiopia 1930–74

Halifax, George Montagu Dunk, 2nd Earl of (1716–71) British Tory statesman

Hallowes, Odette (born Marie Céline) (1912–95) French heroine of the Second World War

HISTORICAL, POLITICAL, AND MILITARY FIGURES (cont.)

Hamilcar (*c.* 270–229 BC) Carthaginian general and father of Hannibal

Hamilton, Alexander (*c.* 1757–1804) American Federalist politician

Hamilton, Lady Emma (born Amy Lyon) (*c.* 1765–1815) English beauty and mistress of Lord Nelson

Hammarskjöld, Dag (Hjalmar Agne Carl) (1905–61) Swedish diplomat and politician

Hammurabi (died 1750 BC) the sixth king of the first dynasty of Babylonia, reigned 1792–1750 BC

Hannibal (247–182 BC) Carthaginian general

Hardie, (James) Keir (1856–1915) Scottish Labour politician

Harding, Warren (Gamaliel) (1865–1923) American Republican statesman, 29th President of the US 1921–3

Hare, William (*fl.* 1820s) Irish murderer

Harefoot, Harold See HAROLD

Harmsworth, Alfred Charles William See NORTHCLIFFE

Harold I (known as Harold Harefoot) (died 1040) reigned 1035–40

Harold II (*c.* 1022–66) king of England 1066

Haroun-al-Raschid See HARUN AR-RASHID

Harris, Sir Arthur (Travers), 1st Baronet (known as 'Bomber Harris') (1892–1984) British Marshal of the RAF

Harrison, Benjamin (1833–1901) American Republican statesman, 23rd President of the US 1889–93

Harrison, William Henry (1773–1841) American Whig statesman, 9th President of the US, 1841

Harrod, Charles Henry (1800–85) English grocer and tea merchant

Harun ar-Rashid (also Haroun-al-Raschid) (763–809) fifth Abbasid caliph of Baghdad 786–809

Hasdrubal (died 207 BC) Carthaginian general, son of Hamilcar

Hasdrubal (died 221 BC) Carthaginian general, son-in-law of Hamilcar

Hastings, Warren (1732–1818) British colonial administrator

Hathaway, Anne (*c.* 1557–1623) the wife of Shakespeare, whom she married in 1582

Hatshepsut (died 1482 BC) Egyptian queen of the 18th dynasty, reigned *c.* 1503–1482 BC

Havel, Václav (born 1936) Czech dramatist and statesman, President of Czechoslovakia 1989–92 and of the Czech Republic from 1993

Hawke, Robert James Lee ('Bob') (born 1929) Australian Labor statesman, Prime Minister 1983–91

Hawkins, Sir John (also Hawkyns) (1532–95) English sailor

Hayes, Rutherford B(irchard) (1822–93) American Republican statesman, 19th President of the US 1877–81

Heath, Sir Edward (Richard George) (born 1916) British Conservative statesman, Prime Minister 1970–4

Helena, St (AD *c.* 255–*c.* 330) Roman empress and mother of Constantine the Great

Heliogabalus (also Elagabalus) (born Varius Avitus Bassianus) (AD 204–22) Roman emperor 218–22

Hengist (died 488) semi-mythological Jutish leader

Henrietta Maria (1609–69) daughter of Henry IV of France, queen consort of Charles I of England

Henry (known as Henry the Navigator) (1394–1460) Portuguese prince

Henry I (1068–1135) king of England, youngest son of William I, reigned 1100–35

Henry I (Henry the Fowler) (*c.* 876–936) king of the Germans, reigned 919–36

Henry II (1133–89) king of England, reigned 1154–89

Henry II (Saint Henry) (973–1024) king of the Germans, reigned 1002–24

Henry III (1207–72) king of England,

HISTORICAL, POLITICAL, AND MILITARY FIGURES (cont.)

reigned 1216–72

Henry III to **VII,** kings of the Germans

Henry IV (Henry Bolingbroke) (1367–1413) king of England, reigned 1399–1413

Henry V (1387–1422) king of England, reigned 1413–22

Henry VI (1421–71) king of England, reigned 1422–61 and 1470–1

Henry VII (Henry Tudor) (1457–1509) king of England, reigned 1485–1509

Henry VIII (1491–1547) king of England, reigned 1509–47

Henry Bolingbroke See HENRY IV of England

Henry IV (known as Henry of Navarre) (1553–1610) king of France 1589–1610

Henry Tudor See HENRY VII of England

Hereward the Wake (11th century) semi-legendary Anglo-Saxon rebel leader

Herod the Great (c. 74–4 BC) ruler of Palestine, ruled 37–4 BC

Herod Antipas (22 BC–AD 40) tetrarch of Galilee and Peraea 4 BC–AD 40

Herod Agrippa I (10 BC–AD 44) king of Judaea AD 41–4

Herod Agrippa II (AD 27–c. 93) king of (parts of) Palestine 50–c. 93

Hess, (Walther Richard) Rudolf (1894–1987) German Nazi politician

Hickok, James Butler (known as 'Wild Bill Hickok') (1837–76) American frontiersman and marshal

Hicks, Sir John Richard (1904–89) English economist

Hill, Octavia (1838–1912) English housing reformer

Hillary, Sir Edmund (Percival) (born 1919) New Zealand mountaineer and explorer

Himmler, Heinrich (1900–45) German Nazi leader, chief of the SS (1929–45) and of the Gestapo (1936–45)

Hindenburg, Paul Ludwig von Beneckendorff und von (1847–1934) German Field Marshal and statesman, President of the Weimar Republic 1925–34

Hirohito (born Michinomiya Hirohito) (1901–89) emperor of Japan 1926–89

Hiss, Alger (1904–96) American public servant

Hitler, Adolf (1889–1945) Austrian-born Nazi leader, Chancellor of Germany 1933–45

Ho Chi Minh (born Nguyen That Thanh) (1890–1969) Vietnamese Communist statesman, President of North Vietnam 1954–69

Hoffa, James Riddle ('Jimmy') (1913–c. 1975) American trade union leader

Holyoake, Sir Keith (Jacka) (1904–83) New Zealand National Party statesman, Prime Minister 1957 and 1960–72

Home of the Hirsel of Coldstream, Baron See DOUGLAS-HOME

Honecker, Erich (1912–94) East German Communist statesman, head of state 1976–89

Hoover, Herbert C(lark) (1874–1964) American Republican statesman, 31st President of the US 1929–33

Hoover, J(ohn) Edgar (1895–1972) American lawyer and director of the FBI 1924–72

Hoover, William (Henry) (1849–1932) American industrialist

Horsa (died 455) semi-mythological Jutish leader

Hotspur, nickname of Sir Henry Percy

Howard, Catherine (c. 1521–42) fifth wife of Henry VIII

Howard, John (1726–90) English philanthropist and prison reformer

Howard, John (Winston) (born 1939) Australian Liberal statesman, Prime Minister from 1996

Hoxha, Enver (1908–85) Albanian statesman, Prime Minister 1944–54 and First Secretary of the Albanian Communist Party 1954–85

Hudson, Henry (c. 1565–1611) English explorer

HISTORICAL, POLITICAL, AND MILITARY FIGURES (cont.)

Humboldt, Friedrich Heinrich Alexander, Baron von (1769–1859) German explorer and scientist

Husák, Gustáv (1913–91) Czechoslovak statesman, leader of the Communist Party of Czechoslovakia 1969–87 and President 1975–89

Hussein, Abdullah ibn See ABDULLAH IBN HUSSEIN

Hussein, ibn Talal (also Husain) (born 1935) king of Jordan since 1953

Hussein, Saddam (also Husain) (full name Saddam bin Hussein at-Takriti) (born 1937) Iraqi President from 1979

Hyde, Edward See CLARENDON

Ibarruri Gomez, Dolores (known as 'La Pasionaria') (1895–1989) Spanish Communist politician

Ibn Batuta (c. 1304–68) Arab explorer

ibn Hussein, Abdullah See ABDULLAH IBN HUSSEIN

Ikhnaton See AKHENATEN

Ine, king of Wessex 688–726

Iron Chancellor, nickname of Bismarck

Iron Duke, nickname of Wellington

Iron Lady, nickname of Margaret Thatcher

Isabella I (known as Isabella of Castile or Isabella the Catholic) (1451–1504) queen of Castile 1474–1504 and of Aragon 1479–1504

Isabella of France (1292–1358) daughter of Philip IV of France

Isocrates (436–338 BC) Athenian orator

Ito, Prince Hirobumi (1841–1909) Japanese statesman, Premier four times between 1884 and 1901

Ivan I (c. 1304–41) ruler of Russia, grand duke of Muscovy 1328–40

Jackson, Andrew (1767–1845) American general and Democratic statesman, 7th President of the US 1829–37

Jackson, Jesse (Louis) (born 1941) American politician and clergyman

Jackson, Thomas Jonathan (known as 'Stonewall Jackson') (1824–63) American general

Jack the Ripper (19th-century) unidentified English murderer

James, Jesse (Woodson) (1847–82) American outlaw

James I to **VII,** Stuart kings of Scotland

James I (1566–1625) son of Mary, Queen of Scots, king of Scotland (as James VI) 1567–1625, and of England and Ireland 1603–25

James II (1633–1701) king of England, Ireland, and (as James VII) of Scotland (1685–8)

Jaruzelski, Wojciech (born 1923) Polish general and Communist statesman, Prime Minister 1981–5, head of state 1985–9, and President 1989–90

Jefferson, Thomas (1743–1826) American Democratic Republican statesman, 3rd President of the US 1801–9

Jeffreys, George, 1st Baron (c. 1645–89) Welsh judge

Jehu (842–815 BC) king of Israel

Jellicoe, John Rushworth, 1st Earl (1859–1935) British admiral

Jenkins, Roy (Harris), Baron Jenkins of Hillhead (born 1920) English Labour and Social Democrat MP and scholar

Jervis, John, Earl St Vincent (1735–1823) British admiral

Jiang Jie Shi See CHIANG KAI-SHEK

Jiménez de Cisneros, Francisco (also Ximenes de Cisneros) (1436–1517) Spanish statesman, regent of Spain 1516–17

Jinnah, Muhammad Ali (1876–1948) Indian statesman and founder of Pakistan

Joan of Arc, St (known as 'the Maid of Orleans') (c. 1412–31) French national heroine

Joffre, Joseph Jacques Césaire (1852–1931) French Marshal

John (known as John Lackland) (1165–1216) son of Henry II, king of

HISTORICAL, POLITICAL, AND MILITARY FIGURES (cont.)

England 1199–1216
John I (known as John the Great) (1357–1433) king of Portugal, reigned 1385–1433
John III (known as John Sobieski) (1624–96) king of Poland 1674–96
John of Gaunt (1340–99) Duke of Lancaster
John Sobieski See JOHN III
Johnson, Andrew (1808–75) American Democratic statesman, 17th President of the US 1865–9
Johnson, Lyndon Baines (known as 'LBJ') (1908–73) American Democratic statesman, 36th President of the US 1963–9
Jones, John Paul (born John Paul) (1747–92) Scottish-born American naval officer
Josephine (born Marie Joséphine Rose Tascher de la Pagerie) (1763–1814) Empress of France 1796–1809
Juan Carlos (full name Juan Carlos Victor María de Borbón y Borbón) (born 1938) grandson of Alfonso XIII, king of Spain since 1975
Juárez, Benito Pablo (1806–72) Mexican statesman, President 1861–4 and 1867–72
Judas Maccabaeus (died c. 161 BC) Jewish leader
Jugurtha (died 104 BC) joint king of Numidia c. 118–104
Julian (known as the Apostate) (full name Flavius Claudius Julianus) (AD c. 331–63) Roman emperor 360–3, nephew of Constantine
Julius Caesar, Gaius (100–44 BC) Roman general and statesman
Justinian (Latin name Flavius Petrus Sabbatius Justinianus) (483–565) Byzantine emperor 527–65
Kádár, János (1912–89) Hungarian statesman, First Secretary of the Hungarian Socialist Workers' Party 1956–88 and Prime Minister 1956–8 and 1961–5
Kaiser Wilhelm See WILHELM II
Kalinin, Mikhail Ivanovich (1875–

1946) Soviet statesman, head of state of the USSR 1919–46
Karl XII See CHARLES XII
Kaunda, Kenneth (David) (born 1924) Zambian statesman, President 1964–91
Keating, Paul (John) (born 1944) Australian Labor statesman, Prime Minister 1991–6
Kellogg, Will Keith (1860–1951) American food manufacturer
Kelly, Edward ('Ned') (1855–80) Australian outlaw
Kelly, Petra (Karin) (1947–92) German political leader
Kemal Pasha See ATATÜRK
Kennedy, Edward Moore ('Teddy') (born 1932) American Democratic politician
Kennedy, John F(itzgerald) (known as 'JFK') (1917–63) American Democratic statesman, 35th President of the US 1961–3
Kennedy, Robert F(rancis) (1925–68) American Democratic statesman
Kenneth I (known as Kenneth MacAlpine) (died 858) king of Scotland c. 844–58
Kenyatta, Jomo (c. 1891–1978) Kenyan statesman, Prime Minister of Kenya 1963 and President 1964–78
Keynes, John Maynard, 1st Baron (1883–1946) English economist
Khama, Sir Seretse (1921–80) Botswanan statesman, Prime Minister of Bechuanaland 1965 and President of Botswana 1966–80
Khan, Ayub See AYUB KHAN
Khomeini, Ruhollah (known as Ayatollah Khomeini) (1900–89) Iranian Shiite Muslim leader
Khrushchev, Nikita (Sergeevich) (1894–1971) Soviet statesman, Premier of the USSR 1958–64
Khufu See CHEOPS
Kidd, William (known as Captain Kidd) (1645–1701) Scottish pirate
Kim Il Sung (born Kim Song Ju) (1912–94) Korean Communist

HISTORICAL, POLITICAL, AND MILITARY FIGURES (cont.)

statesman, first Premier of North Korea 1948–72 and President 1972–94

King, Martin Luther (1929–68) American Baptist minister and civil-rights leader

King, William Lyon Mackenzie (1874–1950) Canadian Liberal statesman, Prime Minister 1921–6, 1926–30, and 1935–48

Kissinger, Henry (Alfred) (born 1923) German-born American statesman and diplomat, Secretary of State 1973–7

Kitchener, (Horatio) Herbert, 1st Earl Kitchener of Khartoum (1850–1916) British soldier and statesman

Klerk, F. W. de See DE KLERK

Knut See CANUTE

Kohl, Helmut (born 1930) German statesman, Chancellor of the Federal Republic of Germany 1982–90, and of Germany 1990–8

Kosciusko, Thaddeus (or Tadeusz) (1746–1817) Polish soldier and patriot

Kossuth, Lajos (1802–94) Hungarian statesman and patriot

Kosygin, Aleksei Nikolaevich (1904–80) Soviet statesman, Premier of the USSR 1964–80

Krishnamurti, Jiddu (1895–1986) Indian spiritual leader

Kropotkin, Prince Peter (1842–1921) Russian anarchist

Kruger, Stephanus Johannes Paulus (known as 'Oom (= uncle) Paul') (1825–1904) South African soldier and statesman

Krupp, Alfred (1812–87) German arms manufacturer

Kublai Khan (1216–94) Mongol emperor of China, grandson of Genghis Khan

Ladislaus I (canonized as St Ladislaus) (c. 1040–95) king of Hungary 1077–95

Ladislaus II (Polish name Władysław) (c. 1351–1434) king of Poland

1386–1434

Lafayette, Marie Joseph Paul Yves Roch Gilbert du Motier, Marquis de (also La Fayette) (1757–1834) French soldier and statesman

La Salle, René-Robert Cavelier, Sieur de (1643–87) French explorer

Laurier, Sir Wilfrid (1841–1919) Canadian Liberal statesman, Prime Minister 1896–1911

Law, (Andrew) Bonar (1858–1923) Canadian-born British Conservative statesman, Prime Minister 1922–3

Lee, Robert E(dward) (1807–70) American general

Leghari, Farooq Ahmed (born 1940) Pakistani statesman, President since 1993

Leicester, Earl of See DUDLEY

Leichhardt, (Friedrich Wilhelm) Ludwig (1813–48) Australian explorer, born in Prussia

Leif Ericsson See ERICSSON

Lenin, Vladimir Ilich (born Vladimir Ilich Ulyanov) (1870–1924) the principal figure in the Russian Revolution and first Premier (Chairman of the Council of People's Commissars) of the Soviet Union 1918–24

Leo III (c. 680–741) Byzantine emperor 717–41

Leopold I (1790–1865) first king of Belgium 1831–65

Lepidus, Marcus Aemilius (died c. 13 BC) Roman statesman and triumvir

Lesseps, Ferdinand Marie, Vicomte de (1805–94) French diplomat

Leverhulme, 1st Viscount (born William Hesketh Lever) (1851–1925) English industrialist and philanthropist

Lewis, Meriwether (1774–1809) American explorer

Lie, Trygve Halvdan (1896–1968) Norwegian Labour politician, first Secretary-General of the United Nations 1946–53

Lin Biao (1908–71) Chinese Communist statesman and general

HISTORICAL, POLITICAL, AND MILITARY FIGURES (cont.)

Lincoln, Abraham (1809–65)
American Republican statesman,
16th President of the US 1861–5
Lin Piao See LIN BIAO
Liverpool, 2nd Earl of (title of Robert
Banks Jenkinson) (1770–1828)
British Tory statesman, Prime
Minister 1812–27
Llewelyn (also Llywelyn ap Gruffydd)
(died 1282) prince of Gwynedd in
North Wales
**Lloyd George, David, 1st Earl Lloyd
George of Dwyfor** (1863–1945)
British Liberal statesman, Prime
Minister 1916–22
Llywelyn ap Gruffydd See LLEWELYN
Lorenzo de' Medici (known as
Lorenzo the Magnificent) (1449–92)
Italian statesman and scholar
Louis I to XVIII, kings of France
Louis I (known as Louis the Great)
(1326–82) king of Hungary 1342–82
and of Poland 1370–82
Louis-Napoleon See NAPOLEON
Louis Philippe (1773–1850) king of
France 1830–48
Ludendorff, Erich (1865–1937)
German general
Ludwig I to III, kings of Bavaria
Luthuli, Albert John (also Lutuli) (c.
1898–1967) South African political
leader
Luxemburg, Rosa (1871–1919) Polish-
born German revolutionary leader
Lysander (died 395 BC) Spartan
general
MacAlpine, Kenneth See KENNETH I
MacArthur, Douglas (1880–1964)
American general
McCarthy, Joseph R(aymond)
(1909–57) American Republican
politician
Macbeth (c. 1005–57) king of
Scotland 1040–57
Maccabaeus, Judas See JUDAS
MACCABAEUS
MacDonald, Flora (1722–90) Scottish
Jacobite heroine
MacDonald, (James) Ramsay
(1866–1937) British Labour

statesman, Prime Minister 1924,
1929–31, and 1931–5
Macdonald, Sir John Alexander
(1815–91) Scottish-born Canadian
statesman, Prime Minister 1867–73
and 1878–91
Machiavelli, Niccolò di Bernardo dei
(1469–1527) Italian statesman and
political philosopher
Mackenzie, Sir Alexander
(1764–1820) Scottish explorer of
Canada
McKinlay, John (1819–72) Scottish-
born explorer
McKinley, William (1843–1901)
American Republican statesman,
25th President of the US 1897–1901
Maclean, Donald Duart (1913–83)
British Foreign Office official and
Soviet spy
**Macmillan, (Maurice) Harold, 1st Earl
of Stockton** (1894–1986) British
Conservative statesman, Prime
Minister 1957–63
Macquarie, Lachlan (1762–1824)
Scottish-born Australian colonial
administrator
Madison, James (1751–1836)
American Democratic Republican
statesman, 4th President of the US
1809–17
Maecenas, Gaius (c. 70–8 BC) Roman
statesman
Magellan, Ferdinand (Portuguese
name Fernão Magalhães) (c.
1480–1521) Portuguese explorer
Maintenon, Marquise de (title of
Françoise d'Aubigné) (1635–1719)
mistress and later second wife of
the French king Louis XIV
Major, John (born 1943) British
Conservative statesman, Prime
Minister 1990–7
Makarios III (born Mikhail
Christodolou Mouskos) (1913–77)
Greek Cypriot archbishop and
statesman, President of the republic
of Cyprus 1960–77
Malcolm I (died 954) king of Scotland,
reigned 943–54

HISTORICAL, POLITICAL, AND MILITARY FIGURES (cont.)

Malcolm II to **IV,** kings of Scotland

Malcolm X (born Malcolm Little) (1925–65) American political activist

Malenkov, Georgy (Maksimilianovich) (1902–88) Soviet statesman, born in Russia

Mandela, Nelson (Rolihlahla) (born 1918) South African statesman, President since 1994

Mandeville, Sir John (14th century) English nobleman

Man in the Iron Mask, a mysterious prisoner held in the Bastille and other prisons in 17th-century France

Manley, Michael (Norman) (1923–97) Jamaican statesman, Prime Minister 1972–80 and 1989–92

Mao Zedong (also Mao Tse-tung) (1893–1976) Chinese statesman, chairman of the Communist Party of the Chinese People's Republic 1949–76 and head of state 1949–59

Marat, Jean Paul (1743–93) French revolutionary and journalist

Marco Polo (c. 1254–c. 1324) Italian traveller

Marcus Aurelius See AURELIUS

Margaret, Princess, Margaret Rose (born 1930) only sister of Elizabeth II

Maria de' Medici See MARIE DE MÉDICIS

Maria Theresa (1717–80) Archduchess of Austria, queen of Hungary and Bohemia 1740–80

Marie Antoinette (1755–93) French queen, wife of Louis XVI

Marie de Médicis (Italian name Maria de' Medici) (1573–1642) queen of France

Marius, Gaius (c. 157–86 BC) Roman general and politician

Mark Antony See ANTONY

Marks, Simon, 1st Baron Marks of Broughton (1888–1964) English businessman

Marlborough, 1st Duke of (title of John Churchill) (1650–1722) British general

Marshall, George C(atlett) (1880–

1959) American general and statesman

Martel, Charles See CHARLES MARTEL

Mary I (known as Mary Tudor) (1516–58) daughter of Henry VIII, reigned 1553–8

Mary II (1662–94) joint queen of England, Scotland and Ireland (1689–94)

Mary, Queen of Scots (known as Mary Stuart) (1542–87) queen of Scotland 1542–67

Mary Stuart See MARY, QUEEN OF SCOTS

Mary Tudor See MARY I

Masaryk, Tomáš (Garrigue) (1850–1937) Czechoslovak statesman, President 1918–35

Mata Hari (born Margaretha Geertruida Zelle) (1876–1917) Dutch dancer and secret agent

Matilda (known as 'the Empress Maud') (1102–67) English princess, daughter of Henry I

Maximilian (full name Ferdinand Maximilian Joseph) (1832–67) emperor of Mexico 1864–7

Mazarin, Jules (Italian name Giulio Mazzarino) (1602–61) Italian-born French statesman

Mazzini, Giuseppe (1805–72) Italian nationalist leader

Médicis, Marie de See MARIE DE MÉDICIS

Meiji Tenno (born Mutsuhito) (1852–1912) emperor of Japan 1868–1912

Meir, Golda (born Goldie Mabovich) (1898–1978) Israeli stateswoman, Prime Minister 1969–74

Melbourne, William Lamb, 2nd Viscount (1779–1848) British Whig statesman, Prime Minister 1834 and 1835–41

Mellon, Andrew W(illiam) (1855–1937) American financier and philanthropist

Mendoza, Antonio de (c. 1490–1552) Spanish colonial administrator

Menes, Egyptian pharaoh, reigned c. 3100 BC

Menzies, Sir Robert Gordon (1894–

HISTORICAL, POLITICAL, AND MILITARY FIGURES (cont.)

1978) Australian Liberal statesman, Prime Minister 1939–41 and 1949–66

Messalina, Valeria (also Messallina) (AD c. 22–48) Roman empress, third wife of Claudius

Metternich, Klemens Wenzel Nepomuk Lothar, Prince of Metternich-Winneburg-Beilstein (1773–1859) Austrian statesman

Michelin, André (1853–1931) and **Édouard** (1859–1940) French industrialists

Mihailović, Dragoljub ('Draža') (1893–1946) Yugoslav soldier

Mirabeau, Honoré Gabriel Riqueti, Comte de (1749–91) French revolutionary politician

Mithridates VI (also Mithradates VI) (c. 132–63 BC) king of Pontus 120–63

Mitterrand, François (Maurice Marie) (1916–96) French statesman, President 1981–95

Mobutu, Sese Seko (full name Mobutu Sese Seko Kuku Ngbendu Wa Za Banga) (1930–97) Zaïrean politician, President 1965–97

Molotov, Vyacheslav (Mikhailovich) (born Vyacheslav Mikhailovich Skryabin) (1890–1986) Soviet statesman

Monash, Sir John (1865–1931) Australian general

Monck, George, 1st Duke of Albemarle (1608–70) English general

Monmouth, Duke of (title of James Scott) (1649–85) English claimant to the throne of England

Monroe, James (1758–1831) American Democratic Republican statesman, 5th President of the US 1817–25

Montcalm, Louis Joseph de Montcalm-Gozon, Marquis de (1712–59) French general

Montespan, Marquise de (title of Françoise-Athénaïs de Rochechouart) (1641–1707) French noblewoman

Montezuma II (1466–1520) Aztec emperor 1502–20

Montfort, Simon de (c. 1165–1218) French soldier

Montfort, Simon de, Earl of Leicester (c. 1208–65) English soldier, born in Normandy

Montgomery, Bernard Law, 1st Viscount Montgomery of Alamein ('Monty') (1887–1976) British Field Marshal

Montrose, James Graham, 1st Marquess of (1612–50) Scottish general

Moore, Sir John (1761–1809) British general

Mortimer, Roger de, 8th Baron of Wigmore and 1st Earl of March (c. 1287–1330) English noble

Moses (fl. c. 14th–13th centuries BC) Hebrew prophet and lawgiver

Mosley, Sir Oswald (Ernald), 6th Baronet (1896–1980) English Fascist leader

Mountbatten, Louis (Francis Albert Victor Nicholas), 1st Earl Mountbatten of Burma (1900–79) British admiral and administrator

Mubarak, (Muhammad) Hosni (Said) (born 1928) Egyptian statesman, President since 1981

Mugabe, Robert (Gabriel) (born 1924) Zimbabwean statesman, Prime Minister 1980–7 and President since 1987

Muhammad, Mahathir (born 1925) Malaysian statesman, Prime Minister since 1981

Muhammad Ali (1769–1849) Ottoman viceroy and pasha of Egypt 1805–49, possibly of Albanian descent

Mujibur Rahman (known as Sheikh Mujib) (1920–75) Bangladeshi statesman, Prime Minister 1972–5 and President 1975

Muldoon, Sir Robert (David) (1921–92) New Zealand statesman, Prime Minister 1975–84

Mulroney, (Martin) Brian (born 1939)

HISTORICAL, POLITICAL, AND MILITARY FIGURES (cont.)

Canadian Progressive Conservative statesman, Prime Minister 1984–93

Murat, Joachim (c. 1767–1815) French general, king of Naples 1808–15

Murdoch, (Keith) Rupert (born 1931) Australian-born American publisher and media entrepreneur

Mussolini, Benito (Amilcaro Andrea) (known as 'Il Duce' = the leader) (1883–1945) Italian Fascist statesman, Prime Minister 1922–43

Mutsuhito See MEIJI TENNO

Nagy, Imre (1896–1958) Hungarian Communist statesman, Prime Minister 1953–5 and 1956

Nansen, Fridtjof (1861–1930) Norwegian Arctic explorer

Napoleon I (known as Napoleon; full name Napoleon Bonaparte or Buonaparte) (1769–1821) Emperor of France 1804–14 and 1815

Napoleon II (known as the King of Rome) (1811–1832) Duke of Reichstadt

Napoleon III (known as Louis-Napoleon) (1808–73) Emperor of France 1852–70

Nasser, Gamal Abdel (1918–70) Egyptian colonel and statesman, Prime Minister 1954–6 and President 1956–70

Nebuchadnezzar (c. 630–562 BC) king of Babylon 605–562 BC

Necker, Jacques (1732–1804) Swiss-born banker

Nefertiti (also Nofretete) (fl. 14th century BC) Egyptian queen, wife of Akhenaten

Nehemiah (5th century BC) Hebrew leader who supervised the rebuilding of the walls of Jerusalem (c. 444) and introduced moral and religious reforms (c. 432)

Nehru, Jawaharlal (known as Pandit Nehru) (1889–1964) Indian statesman, Prime Minister 1947–64

Nelson, Horatio, Viscount Nelson, Duke of Bronte (1758–1805) British admiral

Nero (full name Nero Claudius Caesar Augustus Germanicus) (AD 37–68) Roman emperor 54–68

Nerva, Marcus Cocceius (AD c. 30–98) Roman emperor 96–8

Netanyahu, Benjamin (born 1949) Israeli Likud statesman, Prime Minister since 1996

Neville, Richard See WARWICK

Nevsky See ALEXANDER NEVSKY

Newcastle, 1st Duke of (title of Thomas Pelham-Holles) (1693–1768) British Whig statesman, Prime Minister 1754–6 and 1757–62

Ne Win (born 1911) Burmese general and socialist statesman

Ney, Michel (1768–1815) French marshal

Ngata, Sir Apirana Turupa (1874–1950) New Zealand Maori leader and politician

Nicholas I and **II**, tsars of Russia

Nixon, Richard (Milhous) (1913–94) American Republican statesman, 37th President of the US 1969–74

Nkomo, Joshua (Mqabuko Nyongolo) (born 1917) Zimbabwean statesman

Nkrumah, Kwame (1909–72) Ghanaian statesman, Prime Minister 1957–60, President 1960–6

Nofretete See NEFERTITI

Noriega, Manuel (Antonio Morena) (born 1940) Panamanian statesman and general, head of state 1983–9

North, Frederick, Lord (1732–92) British Tory statesman, Prime Minister 1770–82

Northcliffe, 1st Viscount (title of Alfred Charles William Harmsworth) (1865–1922) British newspaper proprietor

Novotný, Antonín (1904–75) Czechoslovak Communist statesman, President 1957–68

Nyerere, Julius Kambarage (born 1922) Tanzanian statesman, President of Tanganyika 1962–4 and of Tanzania 1964–85

HISTORICAL, POLITICAL, AND MILITARY FIGURES (cont.)

Oakley, Annie (full name Phoebe Anne Oakley Mozee) (1860–1926) American markswoman

Obote, (Apollo) Milton (born 1924) Ugandan statesman, Prime Minister 1962–6, President 1966–71 and 1980–5

O'Connell, Daniel (known as 'the Liberator') (1775–1847) Irish nationalist leader and social reformer

Octavian See AUGUSTUS

Offa (died 796) king of Mercia 757–96

O'Higgins, Bernardo (c. 1778–1842) Chilean revolutionary leader and statesman, head of state 1817–23

Olaf I Tryggvason (969–1000) king of Norway, reigned 995–1000

Olaf II to V, kings of Norway

Old Hickory, nickname of Andrew Jackson

Old Pretender See STUART

Omar I (c. 581–644) Muslim caliph 634–44

Onassis, Aristotle (Socrates) (1906–75) Greek shipping magnate and businessman

Onassis, Jacqueline Lee Bouvier Kennedy (known as 'Jackie O') (1929–94) American First Lady

Orange, William of See WILLIAM

Ortega, Daniel (full surname Ortega Saavedra) (born 1945) Nicaraguan statesman, President 1985–90

Orton, Arthur (known as 'the Tichborne claimant') (1834–98) English butcher

Osman I (also Othman) (1259–1326) Turkish conqueror, founder of the Ottoman (Osmanli) dynasty and empire

Oswald, Lee Harvey (1939–63) American alleged assassin of John F. Kennedy

Othman See OSMAN I

Otho, Marcus Salvius (AD 32–69) Roman emperor January–April 69

Otto I (known as Otto the Great) (912–73) king of the Germans 936–73, Holy Roman emperor 962–73

Owen, David (Anthony Llewellyn), Baron Owen of the City of Plymouth (born 1938) British politician

Owen, Robert (1771–1858) Welsh social reformer and industrialist

Pahlavi, Muhammad Reza (also known as Reza Shah) (1919–80) shah of Iran 1941–79

Pahlavi, Reza (born Reza Khan) (1878–1944) shah of Iran 1925–41

Paisley, Ian (Richard Kyle) (born 1926) Northern Irish clergyman and politician

Palme, (Sven) Olof (Joachim) (1927–86) Swedish statesman, Prime Minister 1969–76 and 1982–6

Palmerston, Henry John Temple, 3rd Viscount (1784–1865) British Whig statesman, Prime Minister 1855–8 and 1859–65

Pandit, Vijaya (Lakshmi) (1900–90) Indian politician and diplomat

Pankhurst, Mrs Emmeline (1858–1928), **Christabel** (1880–1958), and **(Estelle) Sylvia** (1882–1960) English suffragettes

Papineau, Louis Joseph (1786–1871) French-Canadian politician

Park, Mungo (1771–1806) Scottish explorer

Park Chung Hee (1917–79) South Korean statesman, President 1963–79

Parnell, Charles Stewart (1846–91) Irish nationalist leader

Parr, Katherine (1512–48) sixth and last wife of Henry VIII

Paton, Alan (Stewart) (1903–88) South African writer and politician

Pašić, Nikola (1845–1926) Serbian statesman

Pearson, Lester Bowles (1897–1972) Canadian diplomat and Liberal statesman, Prime Minister 1963–8

Peary, Robert Edwin (1856–1920) American explorer

Peel, Sir Robert (1788–1850) British Conservative statesman, Prime

HISTORICAL, POLITICAL, AND MILITARY FIGURES (cont.)

Minister 1834–5 and 1841–6

Peisistratus See PISISTRATUS

Pelham, Henry (1696–1754) British Whig statesman, Prime Minister 1743–54

Penn, William (1644–1718) English Quaker, founder of Pennsylvania

Perceval, Spencer (1762–1812) British Tory statesman, Prime Minister 1809–12

Percy, Sir Henry (known as 'Hotspur' and 'Harry Hotspur') (1364–1403) English soldier

Peres, Shimon (Polish name Szymon Perski) (born 1923) Israeli statesman, Prime Minister 1984–6 and 1995–6

Pérez de Cuéllar, Javier (born 1920) Peruvian diplomat

Pericles (c. 495–429 BC) Athenian statesman and general

Perón, Eva (full name María Eva Duarte de Perón; known as 'Evita') (1919–52) Argentinian politician

Perón, Juan Domingo (1895–1974) Argentinian soldier and statesman, President 1946–55 and 1973–4

Pestalozzi, Johann Heinrich (1746–1827) Swiss educational reformer

Pétain, (Henri) Philippe (Omer) (1856–1951) French general and statesman, head of state 1940–2

Peter I (known as Peter the Great) (1672–1725) tsar of Russia 1682–1725

Pheidippides (5th century BC) Athenian messenger

Philby, Harold Adrian Russell ('Kim') (1912–88) British Foreign Office official and spy

Philip II of Macedon (382–336 BC) king of Macedon, father of Alexander the Great, reigned 359–336

Philip I to V, kings of Spain

Philip I to VI, kings of France

Philip, Prince, Duke of Edinburgh (born 1921) husband of Elizabeth II

Photius (c. 820–c. 891) Byzantine scholar and patriarch of

Constantinople

Pierce, Franklin (1804–69) American Democratic statesman, 14th President of the US 1853–7

Pilate, Pontius (died AD c. 36) Roman procurator of Judaea c. 26–c. 36

Pinkerton, Allan (1819–84) Scottish-born American detective

Pinochet, Augusto (full name Augusto Pinochet Ugarte) (born 1915) Chilean general and statesman, President 1974–90

Pisistratus (also Peisistratus) (c. 600–c. 527 BC) tyrant of Athens

Pitt, William, 1st Earl of Chatham (known as Pitt the Elder) (1708–78) British Whig statesman

Pitt, William (known as Pitt the Younger) (1759–1806) British statesman, Prime Minister 1783–1801 and 1804–6

Pizarro, Francisco (c. 1478–1541) Spanish conquistador

Pocahontas (c. 1595–1617) American Indian princess, daughter of Powhatan (died 1618) an Algonquian chief in Virginia

Polk, James Knox (1795–1849) American Democratic statesman, 11th President of the US 1845–9

Polo, Marco See MARCO POLO

Pol Pot (born Saloth Sar) (1925–98) Cambodian Communist leader, Prime Minister 1976–9

Pompadour, Marquise de (title of Jeanne Antoinette Poisson; known as Madame de Pompadour) (1721–64) French noblewoman

Pompey (known as Pompey the Great; Latin name Gnaeus Pompeius Magnus) (106–48 BC) Roman general and statesman

Pompidou, Georges (Jean Raymond) (1911–74) French statesman, Prime Minister 1962–8 and President 1969–74

Ponce de León, Juan (c. 1460–1521) Spanish explorer

Porsenna, Lars (also Porsena) (6th century BC) legendary

HISTORICAL, POLITICAL, AND MILITARY FIGURES (cont.)

Etruscan chieftain

Powell, (John) Enoch (1912–98) British politician

Primo de Rivera, Miguel (1870–1930) Spanish general and statesman, head of state 1923–30

Prince Albert, Prince Charles See ALBERT, PRINCE; CHARLES, PRINCE, ETC

Prince of Wales See CHARLES, PRINCE

Princes in the Tower, the young sons of Edward IV, namely **Edward, Prince of Wales** (born 1470) and **Richard, Duke of York** (born 1472), supposedly murdered in the Tower of London in or shortly after 1483

Princess Anne, Princess Diana See ANNE, PRINCESS; DIANA, PRINCESS, ETC

Profumo, John (Dennis) (born 1915) British Conservative politician

Pulitzer, Joseph (1847–1911) Hungarian-born American newspaper proprietor and editor

Pulu Tiglath-pileser III See TIGLATH-PILESER

Pyrrhus (c. 318–272 BC) king of Epirus c. 307–272

Qaddafi See GADDAFI

Rabin, Yitzhak (1922–95) Israeli statesman and military leader, Prime Minister 1974–7 and 1992–5

Radhakrishnan, Sir Sarvepalli (1888–1975) Indian philosopher and statesman, President 1962–7

Raffles, Sir (Thomas) Stamford (1781–1826) British colonial administrator

Rafsanjani, Ali Akbar Hashemi (born 1934) Iranian statesman and religious leader, President since 1989

Rahman See ABDUL RAHMAN, MUJIBUR RAHMAN

Rákosi, Mátyás (1892–1971) Hungarian Communist statesman, First Secretary of the Hungarian Socialist Workers' Party 1945–56 and Prime Minister 1952–3 and 1955–6

Raleigh, Sir Walter (also Ralegh) (c.

1552–1618) English explorer, courtier, and writer

Rameses See RAMSES

Ramses I to XI (also Rameses) Egyptian pharaohs

Ranjit Singh (known as 'the Lion of the Punjab') (1780–1839) Indian maharaja, founder of the Sikh state of Punjab

Rao, P(amulaparti) V(enkata) Narasimha (born 1921) Indian statesman, Prime Minister 1991–6

Rasputin, Grigori (Efimovich) (1871–1916) Russian monk

Ratana, Tahupotiki Wiremu (1873–1939) Maori political and religious leader

Reagan, Ronald (Wilson) (born 1911) American Republican statesman, 40th President of the US 1981–9

Red Baron, the See RICHTHOFEN

Redmond, John (Edward) (1856–1918) Irish politician

Rehoboam, king of ancient Israel c. 930–c. 915 BC

Reith, John (Charles Walsham), 1st Baron (1889–1971) Scottish politician, first director-general (1927–38) of the BBC

Revere, Paul (1735–1818) American patriot

Reynolds, Albert (born 1933) Irish Fianna Fáil statesman, Taoiseach (Prime Minister) 1992–4

Reza Shah See PAHLAVI

Rhodes, Cecil (John) (1853–1902) British-born South African statesman, Prime Minister of Cape Colony 1890–6

Ribbentrop, Joachim von (1893–1946) German Nazi politician

Richard I (known as Richard Coeur de Lion or Richard the Lionheart) (1157–99) king of England reigned 1189–99

Richard II (1367–1400) king of England, reigned 1377–99

Richard III (1452–85) king of England, reigned 1483–5

Richelieu, Armand Jean du Plessis

HISTORICAL, POLITICAL, AND MILITARY FIGURES (cont.)

(1585–1642) French cardinal and statesman

Richthofen, Manfred, Freiherr von (known as 'the Red Baron') (1882–1918) German fighter pilot

Riel, Louis (1844–85) Canadian political leader

Roberts, Frederick Sleigh, 1st Earl Roberts of Kandahar (1832–1914) British Field Marshal

Robert the Bruce (Robert I of Scotland) (1274–1329) king of Scotland, reigned 1306–29

Robespierre, Maximilien François Marie Isidore de (1758–94) French revolutionary

Robinson, Mary (Terese Winifred) (born 1944) Irish Labour stateswoman, President 1990–7

Rob Roy (born Robert Macgregor) (1671–1734) Scottish outlaw

Robsart, Amy (1532–60) English noblewoman, wife of Robert Dudley, Earl of Leicester

Rockefeller, John D(avison) (1839–1937) American industrialist and philanthropist

Rommel, Erwin (known as 'the Desert Fox') (1891–1944) German Field Marshal

Roosevelt, (Anna) Eleanor (1884–1962) American humanitarian and diplomat

Roosevelt, Franklin D(elano) (known as FDR) (1882–1945) American Democratic statesman, 32nd President of the US 1933–45

Roosevelt, Theodore ('Teddy') (1858–1919) American Republican statesman, 26th President of the US 1901–9

Rosebery, 5th Earl of (title of Archibald Philip Primrose) (1847–1929) British Liberal statesman, Prime Minister 1894–5

Ross, Sir James Clark (1800–62) British explorer

Rothschild, Meyer Amschel (1743–1812) German financier

Rowntree, Benjamin Seebolm

(1871–1954) English entrepreneur and philanthropist

Rupert, Prince (1619–82) English Royalist general, son of Frederick V, elector of the Palatinate, and nephew of Charles I

Russell, John, 1st Earl Russell (1792–1878) British Whig statesman, Prime Minister 1846–52 and 1865–6

Ryder, Sue, Baroness Ryder of Warsaw and Cavendish (born 1923) English philanthropist

Sadat, (Muhammad) Anwar al- (1918–81) Egyptian statesman, President 1970–81

Saddam Hussein See HUSSEIN

Saladin (Arabic name Salah-ad-Din Yusuf ibn-Ayyub) (1137–93) sultan of Egypt and Syria 1174–93

Salazar, Antonio de Oliveira (1889–1970) Portuguese statesman, Prime Minister 1932–68

Salisbury, Robert Arthur Talbot Gascoigne-Cecil, 3rd Marquess of (1830–1903) British Conservative statesman, Prime Minister 1885–6, 1886–92, and 1895–1902

Sanger, Margaret (Higgins) (1883–1966) American birth-control campaigner

San Martín, José de (1778–1850) Argentinian soldier and statesman

Sargon II (died 705 BC) king of Assyria 721–705

Saul (11th century BC) (in the Bible) the first king of Israel

Savage, Michael Joseph (1872–1940) New Zealand Labour statesman,

Schindler, Oskar (1908–74) German industrialist

Scipio Aemilianus (full name Publius Cornelius Scipio Aemilianus Africanus Minor) (c. 185–129 BC) Roman general and politician

Scipio Africanus (full name Publius Cornelius Scipio Africanus Major) (236–c. 184 BC) Roman general and politician

Scott, Sir Robert Falcon (1868–1912)

HISTORICAL, POLITICAL, AND MILITARY FIGURES (cont.)

English explorer and naval officer

Selcraig See SELKIRK

Selkirk, Alexander (also called Alexander Selcraig) (1676–1721) Scottish sailor

Selous, Frederick Courteney (1851–1917) English explorer, naturalist, and soldier

Senanayake, Don Stephen (1884–1952) Sinhalese statesman, Prime Minister of Ceylon 1947–52

Seneca, Lucius Annaeus (known as Seneca the Younger) (*c.* 4 BC–AD 65) Roman statesman, philosopher, and dramatist

Seneca, Marcus (*or* **Lucius**) **Annaeus** (known as Seneca the Elder) (*c.* 55 BC–*c.* AD 39) Roman rhetorician, born in Spain

Sennacherib (died 681 BC) king of Assyria 705–681

Severus, Septimius (full name Lucius Septimius Severus Pertinax) (146–211) Roman emperor 193–211

Seymour, Jane (*c.* 1509–37) third wife of Henry VIII and mother of Edward VI

Shabaka (known as Sabacon) (died 698 BC) Egyptian pharaoh of the 25th dynasty

Shackleton, Sir Ernest Henry (1874–1922) British explorer

Shaftesbury, Anthony Ashley Cooper, 7th Earl of (1801–85) English philanthropist

Shah, Reza See PAHLAVI

Shaka (also Chaka) (*c.* 1787–1828) Zulu chief

Shalmaneser III (died 824 BC) king of Assyria 859–824

Shamir, Yitzhak (Polish name Yitzhak Jazernicki) (born 1915) Israeli statesman, Prime Minister 1983–4 and 1986–92

Sharma, Shankar Dayal (born 1918) Indian statesman

Sherman, William Tecumseh (1820–91) American general

Shevardnadze, Eduard (Amvrosievich) (born 1928) Soviet

statesman and head of state of Georgia from 1992

Shivaji (also Sivaji) (1627–80) Indian raja of the Marathas 1674–80

Sihanouk, Norodom (born 1922) Cambodian king 1941–55 and since 1993

Simnel, Lambert (*c.* 1475–1525) English pretender and rebel

Simpson, Wallis (*née* Wallis Warfield) (1896–1986) American wife of Edward, Duke of Windsor (Edward VIII)

Sitting Bull (Sioux name Tatanka Iyotake) (*c.* 1831–90) Sioux chief

Sivaji See SHIVAJI

Smith, Ian (Douglas) (born 1919) Rhodesian statesman, Prime Minister 1964–79

Smuts, Jan Christiaan (1870–1950) South African statesman and soldier, Prime Minister 1919–24 and 1939–48

Sobieski, John See JOHN III

Soliman See SULEIMAN I

Solomon, king of ancient Israel *c.* 970–*c.* 930 BC

Solon (*c.* 630–*c.* 560 BC) Athenian statesman and lawgiver

Solyman See SULEIMAN I

Somoza, Anastasio (full surname Somoza García) (1896–1956) Nicaraguan soldier and statesman, President 1937–47 and 1951–6

Spartacus (died *c.* 71 BC) Thracian slave and gladiator

Speke, John Hanning (1827–64) English explorer

Stalin, Joseph (born Iosif Vissarionovich Dzhugashvili) (1879–1953) Soviet statesman

Stanhope, Lady Hester Lucy (1776–1839) English traveller

Stanley, Sir Henry Morton (born John Rowlands) (1841–1904) Welsh explorer

Stephen (*c.* 1097–1154) grandson of William the Conqueror, king of England 1135–54

Stopes, Marie (Charlotte Carmichael)

HISTORICAL, POLITICAL, AND MILITARY FIGURES (cont.)

(1880–1958) Scottish birth-control campaigner

Stuart, Charles Edward (known as 'the Young Pretender' or 'Bonnie Prince Charlie') (1720–88) pretender to the British throne, son of James Stuart

Stuart, James (Francis Edward) (known as 'the Old Pretender') (1688–1766) pretender to the British throne, son of James II (James VII of Scotland)

Stuart, John McDouall (1815–66) Scottish explorer

Stuart, Mary See MARY, QUEEN OF SCOTS

Sturt, Charles (1795–1869) English explorer

Sucre, Antonio José de (1795–1830) Venezuelan revolutionary and statesman, President of Bolivia 1826–8

Sukarno, Achmad (1901–70) Indonesian statesman, President 1945–67

Suleiman I (also Soliman or Solyman) (c. 1494–1566) sultan of the Ottoman Empire 1520–66

Sulla (full name Lucius Cornelius Sulla Felix) (138–78 BC) Roman general and politician

Sun King, nickname of Louis XIV of France

Sun Yat-sen (also Sun Yixian) (1866–1925) Chinese Kuomintang statesman, provisional President of the Republic of China 1911–12 and President of the Southern Chinese Republic 1923–5

Suzman, Helen (born 1917) South African politician, of Lithuanian Jewish descent

Sven See SWEYN I

Sweyn I (also Sven; known as Sweyn Forkbeard) (died 1014) king of Denmark c. 985–1014, ruler of England 1013–4

Taft, William Howard (1857–1930) American Republican statesman, 27th President of the US 1909–13

Talleyrand, Charles Maurice de (full surname Talleyrand-Périgord) (1754–1838) French statesman

Tambo, Oliver (1917–93) South African politician

Tamerlane (also Tamburlaine) (born Timur Lenk, 'lame Timur') (1336–1405) Mongol ruler of Samarkand 1369–1405

Tarquinius Priscus (anglicized name Tarquin) semi-legendary Etruscan king, reigned c. 616–c. 578 BC

Tarquinius Superbus (anglicized name Tarquin) semi-legendary Etruscan king reigned c. 534–c. 510 BC

Tasman, Abel (Janszoon) (1603–c. 1659) Dutch navigator

Taylor, Zachary (1784–1850) American Whig statesman, 12th President of the US 1849–50

Teng Hsiao-p'ing See DENG XIAOPING

Thatcher, Margaret (Hilda), Baroness Thatcher of Kesteven (born 1925) British Conservative stateswoman, Prime Minister 1979–90

Themistocles (c. 528–462 BC) Athenian statesman

Theodora (c. 500–48) Byzantine empress, wife of Justinian

Theodoric (known as Theodoric the Great) (c. 454–526) king of the Ostrogoths 471–526

Theodosius I (known as Theodosius the Great; full name Flavius Theodosius) (c. 346–95) Roman emperor 379–95

Thesiger, Wilfred (Patrick) (born 1910) English explorer

Thomson, Roy Herbert, 1st Baron Thomson of Fleet (1894–1976) Canadian-born British newspaper proprietor

Tiberius (full name Tiberius Julius Caesar Augustus) (42 BC–AD 37) Roman emperor AD 14–37

Tichborne claimant See ORTON

Tiglath-pileser I to **III,** kings of Assyria

Timur See TAMERLANE

HISTORICAL, POLITICAL, AND MILITARY FIGURES (cont.)

Tinbergen, Jan (1903–94) Dutch economist

Tito (born Josip Broz) (1892–1980) Yugoslav Marshal and statesman, Prime Minister 1945–53 and President 1953–80

Titus (full name Titus Vespasianus Augustus; born Titus Flavius Vespasianus) (AD 39–81) Roman emperor 79–81, son of Vespasian

Tojo, Hideki (1884–1948) Japanese military leader and statesman, Prime Minister 1941–4

Tone, (Theobald) Wolfe (1763–98) Irish nationalist

Torquemada, Tomás de (c. 1420–98) Spanish cleric and Grand Inquisitor

Toussaint L'Ouverture, Pierre Dominique (c. 1743–1803) Haitian revolutionary leader

Toynbee, Arnold (1852–83) English economist and social reformer

Trajan (Latin name Marcus Ulpius Traianus) (AD c. 53–117) Roman emperor 98–117

Trenchard, Hugh Montague, 1st Viscount of Wolfeton (1873–1956) British Marshal of the RAF

Trotsky, Leon (born Lev Davidovich Bronstein) (1879–1940) Russian revolutionary and Marxist theorist

Trudeau, Pierre (Elliott) (born 1919) Canadian Liberal statesman, Prime Minister of Canada 1968–79 and 1980–4

Trujillo, Rafael (born Rafael Leónidas Trujillo Molina; known as 'Generalissimo') (1891–1961) Dominican statesman, President of the Dominican Republic 1930–8 and 1942–52

Truman, Harry S. (1884–1972) American Democratic statesman, 33rd President of the US 1945–53

Tudor, Henry See HENRY VII of England

Tudor, Mary See MARY I of England

Turpin, Dick (1706–39) English highwayman

Tutankhamen (also Tutankhamun) (died c. 1352 BC) Egyptian pharaoh of the 18th dynasty, reigned c. 1361–c. 1352 BC

Tuthmosis III (died c. 1450 BC) Egyptian pharaoh of the 18th dynasty c. 1504–c. 1450

Tutu, Desmond (Mpilo) (born 1931) South African clergyman

Tyler, John (1790–1862) American Whig statesman, 10th President of the US 1841–5

Tyler, Wat (died 1381) English leader of the Peasants' Revolt of 1381

Ulyanov, Vladimir Ilich See LENIN

Valera, Eamon de See DE VALERA

Valerian (Latin name Publius Licinius Valerianus) (died 260) Roman emperor 253–60

Van Buren, Martin (1782–1862) American Democratic statesman, 8th President of the US 1837–41

Vancouver, George (1757–98) English navigator

Vanderbilt, Cornelius (1794–1877) American businessman and philanthropist

Vargas, Getúlio Dornelles (1883–1954) Brazilian statesman, President 1930–45 and 1951–4

Velázquez de Cuéllar, Diego (c. 1465–1524) Spanish conquistador

Verwoerd, Hendrik (Frensch) (1901–66) South African statesman, Prime Minister 1958–66

Vespasian (Latin name Titus Flavius Vespasianus) (AD 9–79) Roman emperor 69–79

Vespucci, Amerigo (1451–1512) Italian merchant and explorer

Victor Emmanuel II (1820–78) ruler of the kingdom of Sardinia 1849–61 and king of Italy 1861–78

Victor Emmanuel III (1869–1947) king of Italy 1900–46

Victoria (1819–1901) queen of Great Britain and Ireland 1837–1901 and empress of India 1876–1901

Villa, Pancho (born Doroteo Arango) (1878–1923) Mexican revolutionary

Vitellius, Aulus (15–69) Roman emperor 69

HISTORICAL, POLITICAL, AND MILITARY FIGURES (cont.)

Vivekananda, Swami (born Narendranath Datta) (1863–1902) Indian spiritual leader and reformer

Vladimir I (known as Vladimir the Great; canonized as St Vladimir) (956–1015) grand prince of Kiev 980–1015

Wade, George (1673–1748) English soldier

Waldheim, Kurt (born 1918) Austrian diplomat and statesman,

Walesa, Lech (born 1943) Polish statesman, President 1990–5

Wales, Prince of See CHARLES, PRINCE

Wallace, Sir William (*c.* 1270–1305) Scottish national hero

Wallenberg, Raoul (1912–??) Swedish diplomat

Walpole, Horace, 4th Earl of Orford (1717–97) English writer and politician

Walpole, Sir Robert, 1st Earl of Orford (1676–1745) British Whig statesman

Walsingham, Sir Francis (*c.* 1530–90) English politician

Warbeck, Perkin (1474–99) Flemish claimant to the English throne

Warren, Earl (1891–1974) American judge

Warwick, Earl of (title of Richard Neville; known as 'the Kingmaker') (1428–71) English statesman

Washington, Booker T(aliaferro) (1856–1915) American educationist

Washington, George (1732–99) American soldier and statesman, 1st President of the US 1789–97

Webb, (Martha) Beatrice (*née* Potter) (1858–1943) and **Sidney (James), Baron Passfield** (1859–1947) English socialists, economists, and historians

Weber, Max (1864–1920) German economist and sociologist

Weizmann, Chaim (Azriel) (1874–1952) Israeli statesman, President 1949–52

Wellington, 1st Duke of (title of Arthur Wellesley; also known as 'the Iron Duke') (1769–1852) British soldier and Tory statesman, Prime Minister 1828–30 and 1834

Wenceslas (also Wenceslaus) (1361–1419) king of Bohemia (as Wenceslas IV) 1378–1419

Whitlam, (Edward) Gough (born 1916) Australian Labor statesman, Prime Minister 1972–5

Whittington, Sir Richard ('Dick') (died 1423) English merchant and Lord Mayor of London

Wiesenthal, Simon (born 1908) Austrian Jewish investigator of Nazi war crimes

Wilberforce, William (1759–1833) English politician and social reformer

Wilhelm I (1797–1888) king of Prussia 1861–88 and emperor of Germany 1871–88

Wilhelm II (known as Kaiser Wilhelm) (1859–1941) emperor of Germany 1888–1918, grandson of Queen Victoria

Wilhelmina (1880–1962) queen of the Netherlands 1890–1948

Willard, Emma (1787–1870) American educational reformer

William I (known as William the Conqueror) (*c.* 1027–87) the first Norman king of England, reigned 1066–87

William I (known as William the Lion) (1143–1214) grandson of David I, king of Scotland 1165–1214

William II (Rufus) (*c.* 1056–1100) king of England 1087–1100

William III and **IV,** kings of England

William of Orange (1650–1702) joint king of Great Britain and Ireland 1689–1702

William Rufus See WILLIAM II

William the Conqueror See WILLIAM I

Wills, William John (1834–61) English explorer

Wilson, (James) Harold, Baron Wilson of Rievaulx (1916–95) British Labour statesman, Prime Minister 1964–70 and 1974–6

HISTORICAL, POLITICAL, AND MILITARY FIGURES (cont.)

Wilson, (Thomas) Woodrow
(1856–1924) American Democratic
statesman, 28th President of the US
1913–21
Windsor, Duke of, title conferred on
Edward VIII on his abdication in
1936
Wolfe, James (1727–59) British
general
Wolsey, Thomas (known as Cardinal
Wolsey) (c. 1474–1530) English
prelate and statesman
Xenophon (c. 435–c. 354 BC) Greek
historian, writer, and military leader
Xerxes I (c. 519–465 BC) son of Darius
I, king of Persia 486–465
Ximenes de Cisneros See JIMÉNEZ DE
CISNEROS
Yamamoto, Isoroku (1884–1943)
Japanese admiral
Yeltsin, Boris (Nikolaevich) (born

1931) Russian statesman, President
of the Russian Federation since
1991
Young Pretender, the See STUART
Zapata, Emiliano (1879–1919)
Mexican revolutionary
Zenobia (3rd century AD) queen of
Palmyra c. 267–272
Zhou Enlai (also Chou En-lai)
(1898–1976) Chinese Communist
statesman, Prime Minister of China
1949–76
Zhukov, Georgi (Konstantinovich)
(1896–1974) Soviet military leader,
born in Russia
Zia ul-Haq, Muhammad (1924–88)
Pakistani general and statesman,
President 1978–88
Zog I (full name Ahmed Bey Zogu)
(1895–1961) Albanian statesman
and king 1928–39

RELIGIOUS FIGURES AND THEOLOGIANS

Abelard, Peter (1079–1142) French scholar, theologian, and philosopher

Abu-Bekr (also Abu-Bakr) (573–634 AD) first caliph of Islam, companion and father-in-law of Mohammed

Abu Hanifah (700–67 AD) Muslim theologian and teacher of jurisprudence

Abduh, Muhammad (1849–1905) Egyptian Islamic scholar, jurist, and liberal reformer

Adrian IV (born Nicholas Breakspear) (c. 1100–59) Pope (1154–59) the only English Pope

Agnes, St (4th century AD) Roman virgin martyr

Aidan, St (died 651 AD) Irish missionary

Alban, St (3rd century) the first British Christian martyr

Albertus Magnus, St (known as 'Saint Albert the Great') (c. 1200–80) German bishop, philosopher, and Doctor of the Church

Alcuin (or Albinus) (c. 735–804 AD) English theologian and educator

Ali (c. 600–661 AD) fourth caliph of Islam (656–61 AD); considered the first caliph by the Shiites

Ambrose, St (c. 339–97 AD) Italian bishop and Doctor of the Church

Ananda (5th century BC) the cousin, disciple, and personal attendant of the Buddha

Andrew, St, an Apostle, the brother of St Peter

Angelic Doctor, nickname of St Thomas Aquinas

Anne, St, traditionally the mother of the Virgin Mary

Anselm of Canterbury, St (c. 1033–1109) Italian theologian and philosopher, archbishop, and Doctor of the Church

Anthony of Egypt, St (also Antony) (c. 251–356 AD) Egyptian hermit

Anthony of Padua, St (also Antony) (1195–1231) Portuguese Franciscan friar

Apollinaris Sidonius (5th century AD) Italian bishop and writer

Aquinas, St Thomas (known as 'the Angelic Doctor') (c. 1225–74) Italian Dominican theologian, scholastic philosopher, and Doctor of the Church

Asoka (died 232 BC) Indian Buddhist emperor (?273–232 BC)

Assisi, Clare of See CLARE OF ASSISI, ST

Assisi, Francis of See FRANCIS OF ASSISI, ST

Athanasius, St (296–373 AD) Egyptian bishop of Alexandria

Augustine, St (known as St Augustine of Canterbury) (died c. 604) Italian churchman, the first Archbishop of Canterbury

Augustine, St (known as St Augustine of Hippo) (354–430) Doctor of the Church

Averroës (1126–98) Spanish-Arabian philosopher

Avila, St Teresa of (1515–82) Spanish nun and religious reformer

Aylward, Gladys (May) (1902–70) English missionary

Baal Shem Tov (or Baal Shem Tob) (original name Israel ben Eliezer) (?1700–60) Jewish religious leader: founder of modern Hasidism

Bab, the, title of MIRZA ALI MOHAMMED

Baeck, Leo (1873–1956) German Jewish theologian

Baha'ullah, title of MIRZA HOSEIN ALI

Barnabas, St, a Cypriot Levite and Apostle

Barth, Karl (1886–1968) Swiss Protestant theologian

Bartholomew, St, an Apostle

Basil, St (known as St Basil the Great) (c. 330–79) Doctor of the Church

Bede, St (known as the Venerable Bede) (c. 673–735) English monk,

RELIGIOUS FIGURES AND THEOLOGIANS (cont.)

theologian, and historian

Beecher, Henry Ward (1813–87)
American clergyman, orator, and
writer

Benedict, St (*c.* 480–*c.* 550) Italian
hermit

Berkeley, George (1685–1753) Irish
philosopher and bishop

Bernadette, St (born Marie
Bernarde Soubirous) (1844–79)
French saint

Bernard of Clairvaux, St (1090–1153)
French theologian and abbot

Bernard, St (*c.* 996–*c.* 1081) French
monk

Besant, Annie (1847–1933) English
theosophist, writer, and political
campaigner

Birgitta, St See BRIDGET OF SWEDEN, ST

Blavatsky, Helena (Petrovna)
(known as Madame Blavatsky; née
Hahn) (1831–91) Russian
spiritualist, born in Ukraine

Blessed Virgin Mary See MARY

Bodhidharma (6th century AD)
Indian Buddhist monk: considered
to be the founder of Zen
Buddhism.

Bonaventura, St (born Giovanni di
Fidanza; known as 'the Seraphic
Doctor') (1221–74) Franciscan
theologian

Bonhoeffer, Dietrich (1906–45)
German Lutheran theologian and
pastor

Boniface, St (born Wynfrith; known
as 'the Apostle of Germany')
(680–754) Anglo-Saxon missionary

Booth, William (1829–1912) English
religious leader, founder and first
general of the Salvation Army

Breakspear, Nicholas See ADRIAN IV

Brendan, St (*c.* 486–*c.* 575) Irish
abbot

Bride, St See BRIDGET OF IRELAND, ST

Bridget of Ireland, St (also Bride *or*
Brigid) (6th century) Irish abbess

Bridget of Sweden, St (also Birgitta)
(*c.* 1303–73) Swedish nun and
visionary

Brigid, St See BRIDGET OF IRELAND, ST

Bruno, St (*c.* 1032–1101) German-
born French churchman

Buber, Martin (1878–1965) Israeli
religious philosopher, born in
Austria

Buddha, a title given to successive
teachers (past and future) of
Buddhism, although it usually
denotes the founder of Buddhism,
Siddhartha Gautama (*c.* 563 BC–*c.*
480 BC)

Bultmann, Rudolf (Karl) (1884–1976)
German Lutheran theologian

Caedmon (7th century) English
monk and poet

Calvin, John (1509–64) French
Protestant theologian and
reformer

Campion, St Edmund (1540–81)
English Jesuit priest and martyr

Carey, George (Leonard) (born
1935) English Anglican
churchman, Archbishop of
Canterbury since 1991

Caro, Joseph (ben Ephraim)
(1488–1575) Jewish legal scholar
and mystic

Catherine, St (known as St
Catherine of Alexandria) (died *c.*
307) early Christian martyr

Cecilia, St (2nd or 3rd century)
Roman martyr

Chrysostom, St John (*c.* 347–407)
Doctor of the Church, bishop of
Constantinople

Clare of Assisi, St (1194–1253)
Italian saint and abbess

Clement of Alexandria, St (Latin
name Titus Flavius Clemens) (*c.*
150–*c.* 215) Greek theologian

Clement, St (known as St Clement
of Rome) (1st century AD) Pope *c.*
88–*c.* 97

Columba, St (*c.* 521–97) Irish abbot
and missionary

Coverdale, Miles (1488–1568)
English biblical scholar

Cranmer, Thomas (1489–1556)
English Protestant cleric

RELIGIOUS FIGURES AND THEOLOGIANS (cont.)

and martyr

Cuthbert, St (died 687) English monk

Cyprian, St (died 258) Carthaginian bishop and martyr

Cyril of Alexandria, St (died 444) Doctor of the Church and patriarch of Alexandria

Cyril, St (826–69) Greek missionary, an 'Apostle of the Slavs'

David, St (also Dewi) (6th century) Welsh monk

Denis, St (also Denys) (died c. 250) Italian-born French bishop, patron saint of France

Dewi See DAVID, ST

Dionysius Exiguus (died c. 556) Scythian monk and scholar

Dionysius the Areopagite (1st century AD) Greek churchman

Dominic, St (Spanish name Domingo de Guzmán) (c. 1170–1221) Spanish priest and friar

Duns Scotus, John (known as 'the Subtle Doctor') (c. 1265–1308) Scottish theologian and scholar

Dunstan, St (c. 909–88) Anglo-Saxon prelate

Eddy, Mary Baker (1821–1910) American religious leader and founder of the Christian Science movement

Erastus (Swiss name Thomas Lieber; also called Liebler or Lüber) (1524–83) Swiss theologian and physician

Eusebius (known as Eusebius of Caesaria) (c. 264–c. 340 AD) bishop and Church historian

Fatima (c. 606–32 AD) youngest daughter of the prophet Muhammad and wife of the fourth caliph, Ali (died 661)

Fa Xian (or Fa-hsien; original namel: Sehi) (5th century AD) Chinese Buddhist monk

Fisher, St John (1469–1535) English churchman

Fox, George (1624–91) English preacher and founder of the Society of Friends (Quakers)

Foxe, John (1516–87) English religious writer

Francis of Assisi, St (born Giovanni di Bernardone) (c. 1181–1226) Italian monk, founder of the Franciscan order

Francis of Sales, St (1567–1622) French bishop

Francis Xavier, St See XAVIER, ST FRANCIS

Fry, Elizabeth (1780–1845) English Quaker prison reformer

Fuller, Thomas (1608–61) English cleric and historian

Gautama, Siddhartha See BUDDHA

George, St, patron saint of England

Gobind Singh, Guru (or Govind Singh) (1666–1708) Tenth and last Guru of the Sikhs

Graham, William Franklin ('Billy') (born 1918) American evangelical preacher

Gregory of Nazianzus, St (329–89) Doctor of the Church, bishop of Constantinople

Gregory of Nyssa, St (c. 330–c. 395) Doctor of the Eastern Church, bishop of Nyssa in Cappadocia

Gregory of Tours, St (c. 540–94) Frankish bishop and historian

Gregory, St (known as St Gregory the Great) (c. 540–604) Pope (as Gregory I) 590–604 and Doctor of the Church

Grosseteste, Robert (c. 1175–1253) English churchman, philosopher, and scholar

Gurdjieff, George (Ivanovich) (1877–1949) Russian spiritual leader and occultist

Gutiérrez, Gustavo (born 1928) Peruvian theologian

Hasan al-Basri (died 728 AD) Muslim religious thinker

Héloïse (1098–1164) French abbess

Herzl, Theodor (1860–1904) Austrian writer, born in Hungary; founder of the Zionist movement

Famous People

41

RELIGIOUS FIGURES AND THEOLOGIANS (cont.)

Hilary, St (c. 315–c. 367) French
bishop
Hilda, St (614–80) English abbess
Huntingdon, Selina, Countess of
(title of Selina Hastings, née
Shirley) (1707–91) English
religious leader
Huss, John (Czech name Jan Hus)
(c. 1372–1415) Bohemian religious
reformer
ibn-al-Arabi, Muhyi-I-din
(1165–1240) Muslim mystic and
poet, noted for his influence on
Sufism
Ignatius Loyola, St (1491–1556)
Spanish theologian and founder of
the Jesuits
Irenaeus, St (c. 130–c. 200 AD) Greek
theologian
Isidore of Seville, St (also called
Isidorus Hispalensis) (c. 560–636)
Spanish archbishop and Doctor of
the Church
Jalal ad-Din ar-Rumi (also called
Mawlana) (1207–73) Sufi mystic
and poet
James, St (known as St James the
Great) An Apostle, son of Zebedee
and brother of John
James, St (known as St James the
Just or 'the Lord's brother') Leader
of the early Christian Church at
Jerusalem
James, St (known as St James the
Less) An Apostle
Jansen, Cornelius Otto (1585–1638)
Flemish Roman Catholic
theologian and founder of
Jansenism
Jerome, St (c. 342–420) Doctor of
the Church
Jesus (also Jesus Christ) the central
figure of the Christian religion
John Chrysostom, St See
CHRYSOSTOM, ST JOHN
John of Damascus, St (c. 675–c.
749) Syrian theologian and Doctor
of the Church
John of the Cross, St (born Juan de
Yepis y Alvarez) (1542–91) Spanish

mystic and poet
John Paul II (born Karol Jozef
Wojtyla) (born 1920) Polish cleric,
Pope since 1978
John, St (known as St John the
Evangelist or St John the Divine)
an Apostle, son of Zebedee and
brother of James, and traditonal
author of the fourth Gospel
John the Baptist, St, Jewish
preacher and prophet, a
contemporary of Jesus
John the Evangelist, St See JOHN, ST
Joseph, St, Carpenter of Nazareth,
husband of the Virgin Mary
Josephus, Flavius (born Joseph ben
Matthias) (c. 37–c. 100) Jewish
historian, general, and Pharisee
Judah ha-Levi (?1075–1141) Jewish
poet and theological philosopher
Judas See JUDE, ST
Judas Maccabaeus (2nd century BC)
Jewish revolutionary leader
Jude, St (known as Judas) an
Apostle, supposed brother of
James
Julian of Norwich (or Juliana) (c.
1342–c. 1413) English mystic
Justin, St (known as St Justin the
Martyr) (c. 100–165) Christian
philosopher
Keble, John (1792–1866) English
churchman
Kempe, Margery (c. 1373–c. 1440)
English mystic
Kempis, Thomas à See THOMAS À
KEMPIS
Khomeini, Ruholla (known as
Ayatollah Khomeini) (1900–89)
Iranian Shiite Muslim religious
and political leader
Knox, John (c. 1505–72) Scottish
Protestant reformer
Knox, Ronald Arbuthnott
(1888–1957) English theologian
Langton, Stephen (c. 1150–1228)
English prelate
Latimer, Hugh (c. 1485–1555)
English Protestant prelate and
martyr

RELIGIOUS FIGURES AND THEOLOGIANS (cont.)

Laud, William (1573–1645) English prelate

Lawrence, St (Latin name Laurentius) (died 258) Roman martyr and deacon of Rome

Layamon (late 12th century) English poet and priest

Livingstone, David (1813–73) Scottish missionary and explorer

Luke, St, traditional author of the third Gospel

Luria, Isaac (ben Solomon) (1534–72) Jewish mystic

Luther, Martin (1483–1546) German Protestant theologian, the principal figure of the German Reformation

Lydgate, John (*c.* 1370–*c.* 1450) English poet and monk

Maimonides (born Moses ben Maimon) (1135–1204) Jewish philosopher and Rabbinic scholar, born in Spain

Maimonides (born Moses ben Maimon) (1135–1204) Jewish philosopher and Rabbinic scholar, born in Spain

Malthus, Thomas Robert (1766–1834) English economist and clergyman

Manetho (3rd century BC) Egyptian priest

Margaret, St (*c.* 1046–93) Scottish queen, wife of Malcolm III

Mark, St, an Apostle, companion of St Peter and St Paul, traditional author of the second Gospel

Marquette, Jacques (1637–75) French Jesuit missionary and explorer

Martin, St (died 397) French bishop, a patron saint of France

Mary (known as the (Blessed) Virgin Mary, or St Mary, or Our Lady), mother of Jesus

Mary Magdalene, St (in the New Testament) a woman of Magdala in Galilee

Mary, St See MARY

Matthew, St, an Apostle, a tax-gatherer from Capernaum in Galilee, traditional author of the first Gospel

Matthias, St, an Apostle, chosen by lot after the Ascension to take the place left by Judas

Mawlana See JALAL AD-DIN AR-RUMI

Melanchthon, Philipp (born Philipp Schwarzerd) (1497–1560) German Protestant reformer

Mendelssohn, Moses (1729–86) German Jewish theologian

Methodius, St (815–85) Greek missionary, an 'Apostle of the Slavs'

Mirza Ali Mohammed (1819–50) Persian religious leader: founded Babism

Mirza Hosein Ali (1817–92) Persian religious leader: founder of Baha'ism

Mohammed See MUHAMMAD

Monica, St (332–*c.* 387) mother of St Augustine of Hippo

Moon, Sun Myung (born 1920) Korean industrialist and religious leader

More, Sir Thomas (canonized as St Thomas More) (1478–1535) English scholar and statesman, Lord Chancellor 1529–32

Morton, John (*c.* 1420–1500) English prelate and statesman

Mother Teresa See TERESA, MOTHER

Muhammad (also Mohammed) (*c.* 570–632) Arab prophet and founder of Islam

Nagarjuna (*c.* 150–*c.* 250 AD) Indian Buddhist monk, founder of the Madhyamika (Middle Path) school of Mahayana Buddhism

Nanak (known as Guru Nanak) (1469–1539) Indian religious leader and founder of Sikhism

Newman, John Henry (1801–91) English prelate and theologian

Nicholas, St (4th century) Christian prelate

Niemöller, Martin (1892–1984) German Lutheran pastor

RELIGIOUS FIGURES AND THEOLOGIANS (cont.)

Ninian, St (c. 360–c. 432) Scottish bishop and missionary

Oates, Titus (1649–1705) English clergyman and conspirator

Occam, William of See WILLIAM OF OCCAM

Ockham, William of See WILLIAM OF OCCAM

Omar (or Umar) (died 644 AD) the second caliph of Islam (634–44)

Origen (c. 185–c. 254) Christian scholar and theologian, probably born in Alexandria

Oswald of York, St (died 992) English prelate and Benedictine monk

Paris, Matthew (c. 1199–1259) English chronicler and Benedictine monk

Pascal, Blaise (1623–62) French mathematician, physicist, and religious philosopher

Patrick, St (5th century) Apostle and patron saint of Ireland

Paul III (born Alessandro Farnese) (1468–1549) Italian Pope 1534–49

Paul, St (known as Paul the Apostle, or Saul of Tarsus, or 'the Apostle of the Gentiles') (died c. 64) missionary of Jewish descent

Pelagius (c. 360–c. 420) British or Irish monk

Peter, St (born Simon) an Apostle

Peter the Hermit (c. 1050–1115) French monk

Philo Judaeus (c. 20 BC–50 AD) Jewish theologian

Pius XII (born Eugenio Pacelli) (1876–1958) Pope 1939–58

Polycarp, St (c. 69–c. 155) Greek bishop of Smyrna in Asia Minor

Pusey, Edward Bouverie (1800–82) English theologian

Rabiah al-Adawiyyah (or Rabia) (c. 713–801 AD) Islamic saint

Rajneesh, Bhagwan Shree (born Chandra Mohan Jain; known as 'the Bhagwan' from a Sanskrit word meaning 'lord') (1931–90) Indian guru

Ramakrishna (born Gadadhar Chatterjee) (1836–86) Indian yogi and mystic

Ramanuja (11th century AD) Indian Hindu philosopher and theologian.

Ram Singh (1816–85) Indian leader of a puritanical Sikh sect

Ranjit Singh (the Lion of the Punjab) (1780–1839) founder of the Sikh kingdom in the Punjab

Renan, (Joseph) Ernest (1823–92) French historian, theologian, and philosopher

Ridley, Nicholas (c. 1500–55) English Protestant bishop and martyr

Sankara (8th century AD) Hindu Vedantic philosopher

Saul (also Saul of Tarsus) the original name of St Paul

Savonarola, Girolamo (1452–98) Italian preacher and religious leader

Schweitzer, Albert (1875–1965) German theologian, musician, and medical missionary

Senussi, Sidi Mohammed ibn Ali al (or Senusi) (?1787–1859) founder of the Muslim Senussi sect

Seraphic Doctor, the, nickname of St Bonaventura

Sergius, St (Russian name Svyatoi Sergi Radonezhsky) (1314–92) Russian monastic reformer and mystic

Shankaracharya (or Shankara) (9th century AD) Hindu Vedantic philosopher and teacher

Simeon Stylites, St (c. 390–459) Syrian monk

Simon, St (known as Simon the Zealot) An Apostle

Smith, Joseph (1805–44) American religious leader and founder of the Church of Jesus Christ of Latter-Day Saints (the Mormons)

Stanislaus, St (known as St Stanislaus of Cracow; Polish name Stanisław) (1030–79) Patron saint of Poland

Steiner, Rudolf (1861–1925)

RELIGIOUS FIGURES AND THEOLOGIANS (cont.)

Austrian founder of anthroposophy

Stephen, St (*c.* 977–1038) king and patron saint of Hungary, reigned 1000–38

Stephen, St (died *c.* 35) Christian martyr

Stubbs, William (1825–1901) English historian and ecclesiastic

Swedenborg, Emanuel (1688–1772) Swedish mystic, scientist, and philosopher

Swithin, St (also Swithun) (died 862) English ecclesiastic

Taylor, Jeremy (1613–67) English Anglican churchman and writer

Teresa, Mother (also Theresa) (born Agnes Gonxha Bojaxhiu) (1910–97) Roman Catholic nun and missionary, born in what is now Macedonia of Albanian parentage

Teresa of Ávila, St See AVILA, ST TERESA OF

Teresa of Lisieux, St (also Thérèse) (born Marie-Françoise Thérèse Martin) (1873–97) French Carmelite nun

Tertullian (Latin name Quintus Septimius Florens Tertullianus) (*c.* 160–*c.* 240) early Christian theologian

Thaddaeus, an apostle named in St Matthew's Gospel, traditionally identified with St Jude

Theresa, Mother See TERESA, MOTHER

Thérèse of Lisieux, St See TERESA OF LISIEUX, ST

Thomas à Kempis (born Thomas Hemerken) (*c.* 1380–1471) German theologian

Thomas Aquinas, St See AQUINAS, ST THOMAS

Thomas, St, an Apostle

Tillich, Paul (Johannes) (1886–1965) German-born American theologian and philosopher

Timothy, St (1st century AD) convert and disciple of St Paul

Titus, St (1st century AD) Greek churchman

Truth, Sojourner (previously Isabella Van Wagener) (*c.* 1797–1883) American evangelist and reformer

Tyndale, William (*c.* 1494–1536) English translator and Protestant martyr

Ulfilas (also Wulfila) (*c.* 311–*c.* 381) bishop and translator

Umar Tal (?1797–1864) African religious and military leader, who created a Muslim empire in West Africa

Usman dan Fodio (1754–1817) African mystic and revolutionary leader, who created a Muslim state in Nigeria

Uthman (died 656 AD) third caliph of Islam, who established an authoritative version of the Koran.

Varah, (Edward) Chad (1911–93) English clergyman, founder of the Samaritans

Vincent de Paul, St (1581–1660) French priest

Virgin Mary See MARY

Vitus, St (died *c.* 300) Christian martyr

Vivekananda (original name Narendranath Datta) (1862–1902) Indian Hindu religious teacher

Weil, Simone (1909–43) French mystic and philosopher

Wenceslas, St (also Wenceslaus; known as 'Good King Wenceslas') (*c.* 907–29) Duke of Bohemia and patron saint of the Czech Republic

Wesley, John (1703–91) English preacher and co-founder of Methodism

William of Occam (also Ockham) (*c.* 1285–1349) English philosopher and Franciscan friar

Wulfila See ULFILAS

Wyclif, John (also Wycliffe) (*c.* 1330–84) English religious reformer

Xavier, St Francis (known as 'the Apostle of the Indies') (1506–52) Spanish missionary

RELIGIOUS FIGURES AND THEOLOGIANS (cont.)

Xuan Zang (*or* Hsüan-tsang)
(602–664 AD) Chinese Buddhist
monk and traveller
Young, Brigham (1801–77)
American Mormon leader
Zoroaster (Avestan name

Zarathustra) (*c.* 628–*c.* 551 BC)
Persian prophet and founder of
Zoroastrianism
Zwingli, Ulrich (1484–1531) Swiss
Protestant reformer, the principal
figure of the Swiss Reformation

SCIENTISTS, INVENTORS, AND PIONEERS

Abbe, Ernst (1840–1905) German
physicist
Abel, Niels Henrik (1802–29)
Norwegian mathematician
Adams, John Couch (1819–92)
English astronomer
Addison, Thomas (1793–1860)
English physician
Adler, Alfred (1870–1937) Austrian
psychologist and psychiatrist
Agassiz, Jean Louis Rodolphe
(1807–73) Swiss-born zoologist,
geologist, and palaeontologist
Agnesi, Maria Gaetana (1718–99)
Italian mathematician and
philosopher
Airy, Sir George Biddell (1801–92)
English astronomer and
geophysicist
Alcock, Sir John William
(1892–1919) English aviator
Aldrin, Edwin Eugene (known as
'Buzz') (born 1930) American
astronaut
Alembert, Jean le Rond d' (1717–83)
French mathematician, physicist,
and philosopher
Alfvén, Hannes Olof Gösta
(1908–95) Swedish astrophysicist
Alvarez, Luis Walter (1911–88)
American physicist
Ampère, André Marie (1775–1836)
French physicist

Anderson, Carl David (1905–91)
American physicist
Anderson, Elizabeth Garrett
(1836–1917) English physician
Anderson, Philip Warren (1923–96)
American physicist
Andrews, Thomas (1813–85) Irish
physical chemist
Ångström, Anders Jonas (1814–74)
Swedish physicist and astronomer
Anthemius (known as Anthemius of
Tralles) (6th century AD) Greek
mathematician, engineer, and
artist
Apollonius (known as Apollonius of
Perga) (*c.* 261–*c.* 190 BC) Greek
mathematician
Appleton, Sir Edward Victor
(1892–1965) English physicist
Arbuthnot, John (1667–1735)
Scottish physician and writer
Archimedes (*c.* 287–*c.* 212 BC) Greek
mathematician
Aristarchus (known as Aristarchus
of Samos) (3rd century BC) Greek
astronomer
Arkwright, Sir Richard (1732–92)
English inventor and industrialist
Armstrong, Edwin Howard
(1890–1954) American electrical
engineer
Armstrong, Neil (Alden) (born 1930)
American astronaut

SCIENTISTS, INVENTORS, AND PIONEERS (cont.)

Arrhenius, Svante August (1859–1927) Swedish chemist

Aryabhata I (476–*c.* 550) Indian astronomer and mathematician

Asimov, Isaac (1920–92) Russian-born American writer and scientist

Aston, Francis William (1877–1945) English physicist

Attenborough, Sir David (Frederick) (born 1926) English naturalist and broadcaster

Audubon, John James (1785–1851) American naturalist and artist

Auer, Carl, Baron von Welsbach (1858–1929) Austrian chemist

Austin, Herbert, 1st Baron Austin of Longbridge (1866–1941) British motor manufacturer

Avogadro, Amedeo (1776–1856) Italian chemist and physicist

Baade, (Wilhelm Heinrich) Walter (1893–1960) German-born American astronomer

Babbage, Charles (1791–1871) English mathematician, inventor, and pioneer of machine computing

Babbitt, Milton (Byron) (born 1916) American composer and mathematician

Bacon, Roger (*c.* 1214–94) English philosopher, scientist, and Franciscan monk

Baer, Karl Ernest von (1792–1876) German biologist

Baeyer, Adolph Johann Friedrich Wilhelm von (1835–1917) German organic chemist

Baird, John Logie (1888–1946) Scottish pioneer of television

Bakewell, Robert (1725–95) English pioneer in scientific methods of livestock breeding and husbandry

Bakker, Robert T. (born 1945) American palaeontologst

Banks, Sir Joseph (1743–1820) English botanist

Banting, Sir Frederick Grant (1891–1941) Canadian physiologist and surgeon

Barnard, Christiaan Neethling (born 1922) South African surgeon

Barnardo, Thomas John (1845–1905) Irish-born doctor and philanthropist

Bates, Henry Walter (1825–92) English naturalist

Bateson, William (1861–1926) English geneticist and coiner of the term genetics in its current sense

Batten, Jean (1909–82) New Zealand aviator

Beckmann, Ernst Otto (1853–1923) German chemist

Becquerel, Antoine-Henri (1852–1908) French physicist

Beeching, Richard, Baron (1913–85) English businessman and engineer

Behring, Emil Adolf von (1854–1917) German bacteriologist and one of the founders of immunology

Bell, Alexander Graham (1847–1922) Scottish-born American scientist and inventor

Bell Burnell, (Susan) Jocelyn (born 1943) British astronomer

Benz, Karl Friedrich (1844–1929) German engineer and motor manufacturer

Berger, Hans (1873–1941) German psychiatrist

Bergius, Friedrich Karl Rudolf (1884–1949) German industrial chemist

Bernard, Claude (1813–78) French physiologist

Bernoulli, Daniel (1700–82) Swiss mathematician

Bernoulli, Jacques (1654–1705) Swiss mathematician

Bernoulli, Jean (1667–1748) Swiss mathematician

Bernoulli, Nicolas (1695–1726) Swiss mathematician

Berzelius, Jöns Jakob (1779–1848) Swedish analytical chemist

Bessel, Friedrich Wilhelm (1784–1846) German astronomer

SCIENTISTS, INVENTORS, AND PIONEERS (cont.)

and mathematician

Bessemer, Sir Henry (1813–98) English engineer and inventor

Best, Charles Herbert (1899–1978) American-born Canadian physiologist

Bethune, Henry Norman (1890–1939) Canadian surgeon

Binet, Alfred (1857–1911) French psychologist and pioneer of modern intelligence testing

Birdseye, Clarence (1886–1956) American businessman and inventor

Bjerknes, Vilhelm Frimann Koren (1862–1951) Norwegian geophysicist and meteorologist

Black, Joseph (1728–99) Scottish chemist

Blackett, Patrick Maynard Stuart, Baron (1897–1974) English physicist

Blanchard, Jean Pierre François (1753–1809) French balloonist

Blériot, Louis (1872–1936) French aviation pioneer

Blumenbach, Johann Friedrich (1752–1840) German physiologist and anatomist

Boas, Franz (1858–1942) German-born American anthropologist

Bohr, Niels Hendrik David (1885–1962) Danish physicist and pioneer in quantum physics

Boltzmann, Ludwig (1844–1906) Austrian physicist

Boole, George (1815–64) English mathematician

Bordet, Jules (1870–1961) Belgian bacteriologist and immunologist

Born, Max (1882–1970) German theoretical physicist and a founder of quantum mechanics

Bose, Sir Jagdis Chandra (1858–1937) Indian physicist and plant physiologist

Bose, Satyendra Nath (1894–1974) Indian physicist

Boucher de Perthes, Jacques

(1788–1868) French archaeologist

Boulton, Matthew (1728–1809) English engineer and manufacturer

Boyle, Robert (1627–91) Irish-born scientist

Bradley, James (1693–1762) English astronomer

Bragg, Sir William Henry (1862–1942) English physicist, a founder of solid-state physics

Brahe, Tycho (1546–1601) Danish astronomer

Bramah, Joseph (1748–1814) English inventor

Brassey, Thomas (1805–70) English engineer and railway contractor

Braun, Karl Ferdinand (1850–1918) German physicist

Braun, Wernher Magnus Maximilian von (1912–77) German-born American rocket engineer

Breuil, Henri (Édouard Prosper) (1877–1961) French archaeologist

Brewster, Sir David (1781–1868) Scottish physicist

Bridgman, Percy Williams (1882–1961) American physicist

Briggs, Henry (1561–1630) English mathematician

Brindley, James (1716–72) pioneer British canal builder

Brisbane, Sir Thomas Makdougall (1773–1860) Scottish soldier and astronomer

Bronowski, Jacob (1908–74) Polish-born British scientist, writer, and broadcaster

Brown, Sir Arthur Whitten (1886–1948) Scottish aviator

Browne, Sir Thomas (1605–82) English author and physician

Brunel, Isambard Kingdom (1806–59) English engineer

Brunel, Sir Marc Isambard (1769–1849) French-born British engineer

Buchan, Alexander (1829–1907) Scottish meteorologist

SCIENTISTS, INVENTORS, AND PIONEERS (cont.)

Buchner, Eduard (1860–1917)
German organic chemist
Buckland, William (1784–1856)
English geologist
**Buffon, Georges-Louis Leclerc,
Comte de** (1707–88) French
naturalist
Bunsen, Robert Wilhelm Eberhard
(1811–99) German chemist
Burbidge, Margaret (born 1922)
British astronomer
Burt, Cyril Lodowic (1883–1971)
English psychologist
Burton, Sir Richard (Francis)
(1821–90) English explorer,
anthropologist, and translator
Byron, Augusta Ada See LOVELACE,
COUNTESS OF
Calvin, Melvin (1911–97) American
biochemist
Candolle, Augustin Pyrame de
(1778–1841) Swiss botanist
Cannizzaro, Stanislao (1826–1910)
Italian chemist
Cannon, Annie Jump (1863–1941)
American astronomer
Cantor, Georg (1845–1918) Russian-
born German mathematician
Carnot, Nicolas Léonard Sadi
(1796–1832) French scientist
Carothers, Wallace Hume
(1896–1937) American industrial
chemist
Carrel, Alexis (1873–1944) French
surgeon and biologist
Carson, Rachel (Louise) (1907–64)
American zoologist
Carter, Howard (1874–1939) English
archaeologist
Cartwright, Edmund (1743–1823)
English engineer, inventor of the
power loom
Cassini, Giovanni Domenico
(1625–1712) Italian-born French
astronomer
Cauchy, Augustin Louis, Baron
(1789–1857) French mathematician
Cavendish, Henry (1731–1810)
English chemist and physicist
Cayley, Arthur (1821–95) English

mathematician and barrister
Cayley, Sir George (1773–1857)
British engineer, the father of
British aeronautics
Celsius, Anders (1701–44) Swedish
astronomer, best known for his
thermometer scale
Cerenkov See CHERENKOV
Chadwick, Sir James (1891–1974)
English physicist
Chain, Sir Ernst Boris (1906–79)
German-born British biochemist
Chamberlain, Owen (born 1920)
American physicist
Chandrasekhar, Subrahmanyan
(1910–95) Indian-born American
astronomer
Chanute, Octave (1832–1910)
French-born American aviation
pioneer
Charcot, Jean-Martin (1825–93)
French neurologist
Chauliac, Guy de (c. 1300–68)
French physician
Cherenkov, Pavel (Alekseevich)
(also Cerenkov) (1904–90) Soviet
physicist
**Cherwell, Frederick Lindemann, 1st
Viscount** (1886–1957) German-
born British physicist
Churchward, George Jackson
(1857–1933) English railway
engineer
Clausius, Rudolf (1822–88) German
physicist, one of the founders of
modern thermodynamics
Cochran, Jacqueline (1910–80)
American aviator
Cockcroft, Sir John Douglas
(1897–1967) English physicist
Cockerell, Sir Christopher Sydney
(born 1910) English engineer
Cohn, Ferdinand Julius (1828–98)
German botanist, a founder of
bacteriology
Colt, Samuel (1814–62) American
inventor
Compton, Arthur Holly (1892–1962)
American physicist
Cooke, Sir William Fothergill

SCIENTISTS, INVENTORS, AND PIONEERS (cont.)

(1806–79) English inventor

Copernicus, Nicolaus (Latinized name of Mikołaj Kopérnik) (1473–1543) Polish astronomer

Cort, Henry (1740–1800) English ironmaster

Coulomb, Charles-Augustin de (1736–1806) French military engineer

Courtauld, Samuel (1876–1947) English industrialist

Cousteau, Jacques-Yves (1910–97) French oceanographer and film director

Crawford, Osbert Guy Stanhope (1886–1957) British archaeologist

Crick, Francis Harry Compton (born 1916) English biophysicist

Crompton, Samuel (1753–1827) English inventor

Crookes, Sir William (1832–1919) English physicist and chemist

Culpeper, Nicholas (1616–54) English herbalist

Curie, Marie (1867–1934) Polish-born French physicist

Curie, Pierre (1859–1906) French physicist

Curtiss, Glenn (Hammond) (1878–1930) American air pioneer and aircraft designer

Cushing, Harvey Williams (1869–1939) American surgeon

Cuvier, Georges Léopold Chrétien Frédéric Dagobert, Baron (1769–1832) French naturalist

Daguerre, Louis-Jacques-Mandé (1789–1851) French physicist, painter, and inventor of the first practical photographic process

Daimler, Gottlieb (1834–1900) German engineer and motor manufacturer

Dale, Sir Henry Hallett (1875–1968) English physiologist and pharmacologist

Dalton, John (1766–1844) English chemist, the father of modern atomic theory

Dana, James Dwight (1813–95) American naturalist, geologist, and mineralogist

Dart, Raymond Arthur (1893–1988) Australian-born South African anthropologist and anatomist

Darwin, Charles (Robert) (1809–82) English natural historian and geologist, proponent of the theory of evolution by natural selection

Darwin, Erasmus (1731–1802) English physician, scientist, inventor, and poet

Davisson, Clinton Joseph (1881–1958) American physicist

Davy, Sir Humphry (1778–1829) English chemist, a pioneer of electrochemistry

Dawkins, Richard (born 1941) English biologist

de Broglie, Louis-Victor, Prince (1892–1987) French physicist

Debye, Peter Joseph William (1884–1966) Dutch-born American chemical physicist

Dedekind, Richard (1831–1916) German mathematician

de Duve, Christian René (born 1917) British-born Belgian biochemist

Dee, John (1527–1608) English alchemist, mathematician, and geographer

De Forest, Lee (1873–1961) American physicist and electrical engineer

de Havilland, Sir Geoffrey (1882–1965) English aircraft designer and manufacturer

de la Beche, Sir Henry Thomas (1796–1855) English geologist

Democritus (c. 460–c. 370 BC) Greek philosopher and scientist

Descartes, René (1596–1650) French philosopher, mathematician, and man of science, often called the father of modern philosophy

de Vries, Hugo (1848–1935) Dutch plant physiologist and geneticist

Dewar, Sir James (1842–1923) Scottish chemist and physicist

Diesel, Rudolf (Christian Karl)

SCIENTISTS, INVENTORS, AND PIONEERS (cont.)

(1858–1913) French-born German
engineer, inventor of the diesel
engine

Diophantus (*fl. prob. c.* 250 AD)
Greek mathematician

Dirac, Paul Adrian Maurice
(1902–84) English theoretical
physicist

Doll, Sir (William) Richard (Shaboe)
(born 1912) English physician

Donkin, Bryan (1768–1855) English
engineer

Doppler, Johann Christian (1803–53)
Austrian physicist

Dunlop, John Boyd (1840–1921)
Scottish inventor

Durkheim, Émile (1858–1917)
French sociologist

Du Vigneaud, Vincent (1901–78)
American biochemist

Earhart, Amelia (1898–1937)
American aviator

Eastman, George (1854–1932)
American inventor and
manufacturer of photographic
equipment

Eccles, Sir John Carew (1903–97)
Australian physiologist

Eddington, Sir Arthur Stanley
(1882–1944) English astronomer,
founder of the science of
astrophysics

Edison, Thomas (Alva) (1847–1931)
American inventor

**Egas Moniz, Antonio Caetano de
Abreu Freire** (1874–1955)
Portuguese neurologist

Ehrlich, Paul (1854–1915) German
medical scientist, one of the
founders of modern immunology

Eiffel, Alexandre Gustave
(1832–1923) French engineer

Eijkman, Christiaan (1858–1930)
Dutch physician

Einstein, Albert (1879–1955)
German-born American
theoretical physicist, founder of
the theory of relativity, often
regarded as the greatest scientist
of the 20th century

Einthoven, Willem (1860–1927)
Dutch physiologist

Ekman, Vagn Walfrid (1874–1954)
Swedish oceanographer

Ellis, (Henry) Havelock (1859–1939)
English psychologist and writer

Elton, Charles Sutherland (1900–91)
English zoologist

Empedocles (*c.* 493–*c.* 433 BC) Greek
philosopher, born in Sicily

Enders, John Franklin (1897–1985)
American virologist

Epicurus (341–270 BC) Greek
philosopher and scientist

Eratosthenes (*c.* 275–194 BC) Greek
scholar, geographer, and
astronomer

Ericsson, John (1803–89) Swedish
engineer

Erlanger, Joseph (1874–1965)
American physiologist

Esaki, Leo (born 1925) Japanese
physicist

Euclid (*c.* 300 BC) Greek
mathematician

Euler, Leonhard (1707–83) Swiss
mathematician

Euler, Ulf Svante von (1905–83)
Swedish physiologist, the son of
Hans Euler-Chelpin

**Euler-Chelpin, Hans Karl August
Simon von** (1873–1964) German-
born Swedish biochemist

Evans, Sir Arthur (John)
(1851–1941) English archaeologist

Evans-Pritchard, Sir Edward (Evan)
(1902–73) English anthropologist

Eysenck, Hans Jürgen (1916–97)
German-born British psychologist

Fabre, Jean Henri (1823–1915)
French entomologist

Fabricius, Johann Christian
(1745–1808) Danish entomologist

Fahrenheit, Gabriel Daniel
(1686–1736) German physicist

Faraday, Michael (1791–1867)
English physicist and chemist

Fechner, Gustav Theodor (1801–87)
German physicist and
psychologist

SCIENTISTS, INVENTORS, AND PIONEERS (cont.)

Fermat, Pierre de (1601–65) French mathematician

Fermi, Enrico (1901–54) Italian-born American atomic physicist

Ferranti, Sebastian Ziani de (1864–1930) English electrical engineer

Ferrari, Enzo (1898–1988) Italian car designer and manufacturer

Fessenden, Reginald Aubrey (1866–1932) Canadian-born American physicist and radio engineer

Feynman, Richard Phillips (1918–88) American theoretical physicist

Fibonacci, Leonardo (known as Fibonacci of Pisa) (*c.* 1170–*c.* 1250) Italian mathematician

Fischer, Emil Hermann (1852–1919) German organic chemist

Fischer, Hans (1881–1945) German organic chemist

Fisher, Sir Ronald Aylmer (1890–1962) English statistician and geneticist

FitzGerald, George Francis (1851–1901) Irish physicist

Flamsteed, John (1646–1719) English astronomer

Fleming, Sir Alexander (1881–1955) Scottish bacteriologist

Fleming, Sir John Ambrose (1849–1945) English electrical engineer

Florey, Howard Walter, Baron (1898–1968) Australian pathologist

Fokker, Anthony Herman Gerard (1890–1939) Dutch-born American pioneer aircraft designer and pilot

Foucault, Jean Bernard Léon (1819–68) French physicist

Fourier, Jean Baptiste Joseph (1768–1830) French mathematician

Franck, James (1882–1964) German-born American physicist

Franklin, Benjamin (1706–90) American statesman, inventor, and scientist

Franklin, Rosalind Elsie (1920–58) English physical chemist and molecular biologist

Fraunhofer, Joseph von (1787–1826) German optician and pioneer in spectroscopy

Frazer, Sir James George (1854–1941) Scottish anthropologist

Frege, Gottlob (1848–1925) German philosopher and mathematician, founder of modern logic

Fresnel, Augustin Jean (1788–1827) French physicist and civil engineer

Freud, Anna (1895–1982) Austrian-born British psychoanalyst, the youngest child of Sigmund Freud

Freud, Sigmund (1856–1939) Austrian neurologist and psychotherapist

Frisch, Karl von (1886–1982) Austrian zoologist

Frisch, Otto Robert (1904–79) Austrian-born British physicist

Fuchs, (Emil) Klaus (Julius) (1911–88) German-born British physicist

Fulton, Robert (1765–1815) American pioneer of the steamship

Funk, Casimir (1884–1967) Polish-born American biochemist

Gabor, Dennis (1900–79) Hungarian-born British electrical engineer

Gagarin, Yuri (Alekseevich) (1934–68) Russian cosmonaut

Galen (full name Claudios Galenos; Latin name Claudius Galenus) (129–99) Greek physician

Galileo Galilei (1564–1642) Italian astronomer and physicist, one of the founders of modern science

Galois, Évariste (1811–32) French mathematician

Galton, Sir Francis (1822–1911) English scientist

Galvani, Luigi (1737–98) Italian anatomist

Gamow, George (1904–68) Russian-born American physicist

Gassendi, Pierre (1592–1655) French astronomer and philosopher

SCIENTISTS, INVENTORS, AND PIONEERS (cont.)

Gasser, Herbert Spencer
(1888–1963) American
physiologist

Gates, William (Henry) ('Bill') (born
1955) American computer
entrepreneur

Gatling, Richard Jordan (1818–1903)
American inventor

Gauss, Karl Friedrich (1777–1855)
German mathematician,
astronomer, and physicist

Gay-Lussac, Joseph Louis
(1778–1850) French chemist and
physicist

Geber (Latinized name of Jabir ibn
Hayyan, c. 721–c. 815) Arab
chemist

Geiger, Hans (Johann) Wilhelm
(1882–1945) German nuclear
physicist

Geikie, Sir Archibald (1835–1924)
Scottish geologist

Gell-Mann, Murray (born 1929)
American theoretical physicist

Gerard, John (1545–1612) English
herbalist

Germain, Sophie (1776–1831)
French mathematician

Gibbs, Josiah Willard (1839–1903)
American physical chemist

Gilbert, William (1544–1603) English
physician and physicist

Glashow, Sheldon Lee (born 1932)
American theoretical physicist

Goddard, Robert Hutchings
(1882–1945) American physicist

Gödel, Kurt (1906–78) Austrian-born
American mathematician

Goldmark, Peter Carl (1906–77)
Hungarian-born American
inventor and engineer

Goldschmidt, Victor Moritz
(1888–1947) Swiss-born
Norwegian chemist, the founder
of modern geochemistry

Golgi, Camillo (1844–1926) Italian
histologist and anatomist

Goodall, Jane (born 1934) English
zoologist

Goodyear, Charles (1800–60)
American inventor

Gould, Stephen Jay (born 1941)
American palaeontologist

Graham, Thomas (1805–69) Scottish
physical chemist

Gray, Asa (1810–88) American
botanist

Gresley, Sir (Herbert) Nigel
(1876–1941) British railway
engineer

Grimaldi, Francesco Maria (1618–63)
Italian Jesuit physicist and
astronomer, discoverer of the
diffraction of light

Guericke, Otto von (1602–86)
German engineer and physicist

Haeckel, Ernst Heinrich (1834–1919)
German biologist and philosopher

Hahn, Otto (1879–1968) German
chemist, co-discoverer of nuclear
fission

**Haldane, J(ohn) B(urdon)
S(anderson)** (1892–1964) Scottish
mathematical biologist

Hale, George Ellery (1868–1938)
American astronomer

Hall, Charles Martin (1863–1914)
American industrial chemist

Haller, Albrecht von (1708–77)
Swiss anatomist and physiologist

Halley, Edmond (1656–1742) English
astronomer and mathematician

Hamilton, Sir William Rowan
(1806–65) Irish mathematician and
theoretical physicist

Handley Page, Frederick See PAGE

Hargreaves, James (1720–78)
English inventor

Harvey, William (1578–1657) English
discoverer of the mechanism of
blood circulation and physician to
James I and Charles I

Hawking, Stephen William (born
1942) English theoretical physicist

Haworth, Sir Walter Norman
(1883–1950) English organic
chemist

Heaviside, Oliver (1850–1925)
English physicist and electrical
engineer

SCIENTISTS, INVENTORS, AND PIONEERS (cont.)

Heisenberg, Werner Karl (1901–76)
German mathematical physicist
and philosopher, who developed a
system of quantum mechanics
based on matrix algebra

**Helmholtz, Hermann Ludwig
Ferdinand von** (1821–94) German
physiologist and physicist

Helmont, Joannes Baptista van
(1577–1644) Belgian chemist and
physician

Hero (known as Hero of Alexandria)
(1st century) Greek mathematician
and inventor

Herophilus (4th–3rd centuries BC)
Greek anatomist, regarded as the
father of human anatomy

Herschel, Caroline Lucretia
(1750–1848) German-born British
astronomer

Herschel, Sir (Frederick) William
(1738–1822) German-born British
astronomer, the father of stellar
astronomy

**Herschel, Sir John (Frederick
William)** (1792–1871) British
astronomer and physicist, son of
William Herschel

Hertz, Heinrich Rudolf (1857–94)
German physicist and pioneer of
radio communication

Hess, Victor Francis (born Victor
Franz Hess) (1883–1964) Austrian-
born American physicist

Hevesy, George Charles de
(1885–1966) Hungarian-born
radiochemist

Heyerdahl, Thor (born 1914)
Norwegian anthropologist

Hilbert, David (1862–1943) German
mathematician

Hill, Sir Rowland (1795–1879) British
educationist, administrator, and
inventor

Hinshelwood, Sir Cyril Norman
(1897–1967) English physical
chemist

Hipparchus (c. 170–after 126 BC)
Greek astronomer and
geographer, working in Rhodes

Hippocrates (c. 460–377 BC) the
most famous of all physicians, of
whom, paradoxically, almost
nothing is known

Hodgkin, Sir Alan Lloyd (born 1914)
English physiologist

Hodgkin, Dorothy (Crowfoot)
(1910–94) British chemist

Hoe, Richard March (1812–86)
American inventor and
industrialist

Hollerith, Herman (1860–1929)
American engineer

Holmes, Arthur (1890–1965) English
geologist and geophysicist

Honda, Soichiro (1906–92) Japanese
motor manufacturer

Hooke, Robert (1635–1703) English
scientist

Hooker, Sir Joseph Dalton
(1817–1911) English botanist and
pioneer in plant geography

Hopkins, Sir Frederick Gowland
(1861–1947) English biochemist,
considered the father of British
biochemistry

Howe, Elias (1819–67) American
inventor

Hoyle, Sir Fred (born 1915) English
astrophysicist, one of the
proponents of the steady-state
theory of cosmology

Hubble, Edwin Powell (1889–1953)
American astronomer

Huggins, Sir William (1824–1910)
British astronomer

**Humboldt, Friedrich Heinrich
Alexander, Baron von** (1769–1859)
German explorer and scientist

Hunter, John (1728–93) Scottish
anatomist

Hutton, James (1726–97) Scottish
geologist

Huxley, Sir Andrew Fielding (born
1917) English physiologist and
grandson of Thomas Henry
Huxley

Huxley, Sir Julian (1887–1975)
English biologist and grandson of
Thomas Henry Huxley

SCIENTISTS, INVENTORS, AND PIONEERS (cont.)

Huxley, Thomas Henry (1825–95) English biologist

Huygens, Christiaan (1629–95) Dutch physicist, mathematician, and astronomer

Hypatia (*c.* 370–415) Greek philosopher, astronomer, and mathematician

Ingenhousz, Jan (1730–99) Dutch scientist

Ipatieff, Vladimir Nikolaievich (1867–1952) Russian-born American chemist

Issigonis, Sir Alec (Arnold Constantine) (1906–88) Turkish-born British car designer

Jacobi, Karl Gustav Jacob (1804–51) German mathematician

Jeans, Sir James Hopwood (1877–1946) English physicist and astronomer

Jenner, Edward (1749–1823) English physician, the pioneer of vaccination

Jobs, Steven (Paul) (born 1955) American computer entrepreneur

Johnson, Amy (1903–41) English aviator

Joliot, Jean-Frédéric (1900–58) French nuclear physicist

Joule, James Prescott (1818–89) English physicist

Jung, Carl (Gustav) (1875–1961) Swiss psychologist

Jussieu, Antoine Laurent de (1748–1836) French botanist

Kamerlingh Onnes, Heike (1853–1926) Dutch physicist, who studied cryogenic phenomena

Kekulé, Friedrich August (full name Friedrich August Kekulé von Stradonitz) (1829–96) German chemist

Kelvin, William Thomson, 1st Baron (1824–1907) British physicist, professor of natural philosophy at Glasgow 1846–95

Kendall, Edward Calvin (1886–1972) American biochemist

Kennelly, Arthur Edwin (1861–1939) American electrical engineer

Kepler, Johannes (1571–1630) German astronomer

Kettering, Charles Franklin (1876–1958) American automobile engineer

Kinsey, Alfred Charles (1894–1956) American zoologist and sex researcher

Kirchhoff, Gustav Robert (1824–87) German physicist, a pioneer in spectroscopy

Kitzinger, Sheila (Helena Elizabeth) (born 1929) English childbirth educator

Klaproth, Martin Heinrich (1743–1817) German chemist, one of the founders of analytical chemistry

Klein, Melanie (1882–1960) Austrian-born psychoanalyst

Koch, Robert (1843–1910) German bacteriologist

Krafft-Ebing, Richard von (1840–1902) German physician and psychologist

Krebs, Sir Hans Adolf (1900–81) German-born British biochemist

Lagrange, Joseph Louis, Comte de (1736–1813) Italian-born French mathematician

Laing, R(onald) D(avid) (1927–89) Scottish psychiatrist

Lamarck, Jean Baptiste de (1744–1829) French naturalist, an early proponent of organic evolution

Landau, Lev (Davidovich) (1908–68) Soviet theoretical physicist, born in Russia

Landsteiner, Karl (1868–1943) Austrian-born American physician

Langley, Samuel Pierpont (1834–1906) American astronomer and aviation pioneer

Langmuir, Irving (1881–1957) American chemist and physicist

Laplace, Pierre Simon, Marquis de (1749–1827) French applied mathematician and

SCIENTISTS, INVENTORS, AND PIONEERS (cont.)

theoretical physicist

Lavoisier, Antoine Laurent
(1743–94) French scientist,
regarded as the father of modern
chemistry

Lawrence, Ernest Orlando (1901–58)
American physicist

Leakey, Louis (Seymour Bazett)
(1903–72) British-born Kenyan
archaeologist and anthropologist

Leary, Timothy (Francis) (1920–96)
American psychologist and drug
pioneer

Leblanc, Nicolas (1742–1806) French
surgeon and chemist

Leeuwenhoek, Antoni van
(1632–1723) Dutch naturalist

Le Verrier, Urbain (1811–77) French
mathematician

Lévi-Strauss, Claude (born 1908)
French social anthropologist

Leibniz, Gottfried Wilhelm
(1646–1716) German rationalist
philosopher, mathematician, and
logician

Liebig, Justus von, Baron (1803–73)
German chemist and teacher

Lilienthal, Otto (1848–96) German
pioneer in the design and flying of
gliders

Linacre, Thomas (c. 1460–1524)
English physician and classical
scholar

Lind, James (1716–94) Scottish
physician

Lindbergh, Charles (Augustus)
(1902–74) American aviator

Lindemann, Frederick Alexander
See CHERWELL

Linnaeus, Carolus (Latinized name
of Carl von Linné) (1707–78)
Swedish botanist, founder of
modern systematic botany and
zoology

Lippmann, Gabriel Jonas
(1845–1921) French physicist

Lister, Joseph, 1st Baron
(1827–1912) English surgeon,
inventor of antiseptic techniques
in surgery

Lobachevski, Nikolai Ivanovich
(1792–1856) Russian
mathematician

Locke, Joseph (1805–60) English
civil engineer

Lockyer, Sir (Joseph) Norman
(1836–1920) English astronomer

Lodge, Sir Oliver (Joseph)
(1851–1940) English physicist

Loewi, Otto (1873–1961) American
pharmacologist and physiologist,
born in Germany

Lorentz, Hendrik Antoon
(1853–1928) Dutch theoretical
physicist

Lorenz, Konrad (Zacharias)
(1903–89) Austrian zoologist

Lovelace, Countess of (title of
Augusta Ada King née Byron)
(1815–52) English mathematician

Lovell, Sir (Alfred Charles) Bernard
(born 1913) English astronomer
and physicist, and pioneer of radio
astronomy

Lovelock, James (Ephraim) (born
1919) English scientist

Lowell, Percival (1855–1916)
American astronomer

Lyell, Sir Charles (1797–1875)
Scottish geologist

Lysenko, Trofim Denisovich
(1898–1976) Soviet biologist and
geneticist

Mach, Ernst (1838–1916) Austrian
physicist and philosopher of
science

Macleod, John James Rickard
(1876–1935) Scottish physiologist

Malinowski, Bronisław (1884–1942)
Polish anthropologist

Malpighi, Marcello (c. 1628–94)
Italian microscopist

Mandelbrot, Benoit (born 1924)
Polish-born French mathematician

Manson, Sir Patrick (1844–1922)
Scottish physician, pioneer of
tropical medicine

Mantell, Gideon Algernon
(1790–1852) English geologist

Marconi, Guglielmo (1874–1937)

SCIENTISTS, INVENTORS, AND PIONEERS (cont.)

Italian electrical engineer, the father of radio

Maury, Matthew Fontaine (1806–73) American oceanographer

Maxwell, James Clerk (1831–79) Scottish physicist

Mayr, Ernst Walter (born 1904) German-born American zoologist

Mead, Margaret (1901–78) American anthropologist and social psychologist

Medawar, Sir Peter (Brian) (1915–87) English immunologist and author

Meitner, Lise (1878–1968) Austrian-born Swedish physicist

Mendel, Gregor Johann (1822–84) Moravian monk, the father of genetics

Mendeleev, Dmitri (Ivanovich) (1834–1907) Russian chemist

Mercator, Gerardus (Latinized name of Gerhard Kremer) (1512–94) Flemish geographer and cartographer, resident in Germany from 1552

Mesmer, Franz Anton (1734–1815) Austrian physician

Messerschmidt, Wilhelm Emil ('Willy') (1898–1978) German aircraft designer and industrialist

Messier, Charles (1730–1817) French astronomer

Meyerhof, Otto Fritz (1884–1951) German-born American biochemist

Michelson, Albert Abraham (1852–1931) American physicist

Millikan, Robert Andrews (1868–1953) American physicist

Minkowski, Hermann (1864–1909) Russian-born German mathematician

Mitchell, R(eginald) J(oseph) (1895–1937) English aeronautical engineer

Moissan, Ferdinand Frédéric Henri (1852–1907) French chemist

Monod, Jacques Lucien (1910–76) French biochemist

Montgolfier, Joseph Michel (1740–1810) and **Jacques Étienne** (1745–99) French inventors

Moog, Robert (born 1934) American inventor

Moore, Francis (1657–c. 1715) English physician, astrologer, and schoolmaster

Morgan, Thomas Hunt (1866–1945) American zoologist

Morley, Edward Williams (1838–1923) American chemist

Morse, Samuel F(inley) B(reese) (1791–1872) American inventor

Mosander, Carl Gustaf (1797–1858) Swedish chemist

Moseley, Henry Gwyn Jeffreys (1887–1915) English physicist

Muir, John (1838–1914) Scottish-born American naturalist, a pioneer of environmental conservation

Muller, Hermann Joseph (1890–1967) American geneticist

Müller, Johannes Peter (1801–58) German anatomist and zoologist

Müller, Paul Hermann (1899–1965) Swiss chemist

Napier, John (1550–1617) Scottish mathematician

Nasmyth, James (1808–90) British engineer

Needham, Joseph (1900–95) English scientist and historian

Nernst, Hermann Walther (1864–1941) German physical chemist

Nervi, Pier Luigi (1891–1979) Italian engineer and architect

Neumann, John von (1903–57) Hungarian-born American mathematician and computer pioneer

Newcomen, Thomas (1663–1729) English engineer, developer of the first practical steam engine

Newlands, John Alexander Reina (1837–98) English industrial chemist

Newton, Sir Isaac (1642–1727)

SCIENTISTS, INVENTORS, AND PIONEERS (cont.)

English mathematician and
physicist
Nightingale, Florence (1820–1910)
English nurse and medical
reformer
Nobel, Alfred Bernhard (1833–96)
Swedish chemist and engineer
Noether, Emmy (1882–1935)
German mathematician
Nostradamus (Latinized name of
Michel de Notredame) (1503–66)
French astrologer and physician
Nuffield, 1st Viscount (title of
William Richard Morris)
(1877–1963) British motor
manufacturer and philanthropist
Oersted, Hans Christian (1777–1851)
Danish physicist, discoverer of the
magnetic effect of an electric
current
Ohm, Georg Simon (1789–1854)
German physicist
Omar Khayyám (died 1123) Persian
poet, mathematician, and
astronomer
Oort, Jan Hendrik (1900–92) Dutch
astronomer
Opel, Wilhelm von (1871–1948)
German motor manufacturer
Oppenheimer, Julius Robert
(1904–67) American theoretical
physicist
Osler, Sir William (1849–1919)
Canadian-born physician and
classical scholar
Ostwald, Friedrich Wilhelm
(1853–1932) German physical
chemist
Otis, Elisha Graves (1811–61)
American inventor and
manufacturer
Otto, Nikolaus August (1832–91)
German engineer
Owen, Sir Richard (1804–92) English
anatomist and palaeontologist
Page, Sir Frederick Handley
(1885–1962) English aircraft
designer
Pappus (known as Pappus of
Alexandria) (fl. c. 300–350 AD)

Greek mathematician
Paracelsus (born Theophrastus
Phillipus Aureolus Bombastus von
Hohenheim) (c. 1493–1541) Swiss
physician
Parsons, Sir Charles (Algernon)
(1854–1931) British engineer,
scientist, and manufacturer
Pascal, Blaise (1623–62) French
mathematician, physicist, and
religious philosopher
Pasteur, Louis (1822–95) French
chemist and bacteriologist
Pauli, Wolfgang (1900–58) Austrian-
born American physicist who
worked chiefly in Switzerland
Pauling, Linus Carl (1901–94)
American chemist
Pavlov, Ivan (Petrovich) (1849–1936)
Russian physiologist
Pearson, Karl (1857–1936) English
mathematician, the principal
founder of 20th-century statistics
Pelletier, Pierre-Joseph (1788–1842)
French chemist
Perkin, Sir William Henry
(1838–1907) English chemist and
pioneer of the synthetic organic
chemical industry
Perrin, Jean Baptiste (1870–1942)
French physical chemist
Perthes, Jacques Boucher de See
BOUCHER DE PERTHES
**Petrie, Sir (William Matthew)
Flinders** (1853–1942) English
archaeologist and Egyptologist
Piaget, Jean (1896–1980) Swiss
psychologist
Pickering, William Hayward (born
1910) New Zealand-born American
engineer
**Pitt-Rivers, Augustus Henry Lane
Fox** (1827–1900) English
archaeologist and anthropologist
Planck, Max (Karl Ernst Ludwig)
(1858–1947) German theoretical
physicist, who founded the
quantum theory
Playfair, John (1748–1819) Scottish
mathematician and geologist

SCIENTISTS, INVENTORS, AND PIONEERS (cont.)

Pliny (known as Pliny the Elder; Latin name Gaius Plinius Secundus) (23–79 AD) Roman natural historian

Poincaré, Jules-Henri (1854–1912) French mathematician and philosopher of science

Poisson, Siméon-Denis (1781–1840) French mathematical physicist

Porsche, Ferdinand (1875–1952) Austrian car designer

Prandtl, Ludwig (1875–1953) German physicist

Priestley, Joseph (1733–1804) English scientist and theologian

Proust, Joseph Louis (1754–1826) French analytical chemist

Prout, William (1785–1850) English chemist and biochemist

Ptolemy (2nd century) Greek astronomer and geographer

Raman, Sir Chandrasekhara Venkata (1888–1970) Indian physicist

Ramanujan, Srinivasa Aaiyangar (1887–1920) Indian mathematician

Ramón y Cajal, Santiago (1852–1934) Spanish physician and histologist

Ramsay, Sir William (1852–1916) Scottish chemist, discoverer of the noble gases

Ray, John (1627–1705) English naturalist

Rayleigh, John William Strutt, 3rd Baron (1842–1919) English physicist

Réaumur, René Antoine Ferchault de (1683–1757) French scientist

Reed, Walter (1851–1902) American physician

Regiomontanus, Johannes (born Johannes Müller) (1436–76) German astronomer and mathematician

Renault, Louis (1877–1944) French engineer and motor manufacturer

Rennie, John (1761–1821) Scottish civil engineer

Reuter, Paul Julius, Baron von (born Israel Beer Josephat) (1816–99) German pioneer of telegraphy and news reporting

Richter, Charles Francis (1900–85) American geologist

Riemann, (Georg Friedrich) Bernhard (1826–66) German mathematician

Roe, Sir (Edwin) Alliott Verdon (1877–1958) English engineer and aircraft designer

Rolls, Charles Stewart (1877–1910) English motoring and aviation pioneer

Röntgen, Wilhelm Conrad (1845–1923) German physicist, the discoverer of X-rays

Ross, Sir Ronald (1857–1932) British physician

Royce, Sir (Frederick) Henry (1863–1933) English engine designer

Russell, Bertrand (Arthur William), 3rd Earl Russell (1872–1970) British philosopher, mathematician, and social reformer

Russell, Henry Norris (1877–1957) American astronomer

Rutherford, Sir Ernest, 1st Baron Rutherford of Nelson (1871–1937) New Zealand physicist

Ryle, Sir Martin (1918–84) English astronomer

Sagan, Carl (Edward) (1934–96) American astronomer

Saha, Meghnad (1894–1956) Indian physicist

Sakharov, Andrei (Dmitrievich) (1921–89) Russian nuclear physicist

Salam, Abdus (1926–96) Pakistani theoretical physicist

Salk, Jonas Edward (1914–95) American microbiologist

Sanger, Frederick (born 1918) English biochemist

Sapir, Edward (1884–1939) German-born American linguistics scholar and anthropologist

SCIENTISTS, INVENTORS, AND PIONEERS (cont.)

Savery, Thomas (known as 'Captain Savery') (*c.* 1650–1715) English engineer, constructor of the first practical steam engine

Scheele, Carl Wilhelm (1742–86) Swedish chemist

Schlick, Moritz (1882–1936) German philosopher and physicist

Schliemann, Heinrich (1822–90) German archaeologist

Schrödinger, Erwin (1887–1961) Austrian theoretical physicist

Schwann, Theodor Ambrose Hubert (1810–82) German physiologist

Scott, Sir Peter (Markham) (1909–89) English naturalist

Seaborg, Glenn (Theodore) (born 1912) American nuclear chemist

Sedgwick, Adam (1785–1873) English geologist

Selye, Hans Hugo Bruno (1907–82) Austrian-born Canadian physician

Semmelweis, Ignaz Philipp (born Ignác Fülöp Semmelweis) (1818–65) Hungarian obstetrician who spent most of his working life in Vienna

Shannon, Claude Elwood (born 1916) American engineer

Shapley, Harlow (1885–1972) American astronomer

Sherrington, Sir Charles Scott (1857–1952) English physiologist

Shockley, William (Bradford) (1910–89) American physicist

Siemens, Ernst Werner von (1816–92) German electrical engineer

Sikorsky, Igor (Ivanovich) (1889–1972) Russian-born American aircraft designer

Simpson, Sir James Young (1811–71) Scottish surgeon and obstetrician

Sinclair, Sir Clive (Marles) (born 1940) English electronics engineer and entrepreneur

Singer, Isaac Merrit (1811–75) American inventor

Skinner, Burrhus Frederic (1904–90) American psychologist

Sloane, Sir Hans (1660–1753) English physician and naturalist

Smith, William (1769–1839) English land-surveyor and geologist

Snow, C(harles) P(ercy), 1st Baron Snow of Leicester (1905–80) English novelist and scientist

Soddy, Frederick (1877–1956) English physicist

Sopwith, Sir Thomas (Octave Murdoch) (1888–1989) English aircraft designer

Spallanzani, Lazzaro (1729–99) Italian physiologist and biologist

Spock, Benjamin McLane (known as Dr Spock) (1903–98) American paediatrician and writer

Stanier, Sir William (Arthur) (1876–1965) English railway engineer

Starling, Ernest Henry (1866–1927) English physiologist

Steller, Georg Wilhelm (1709–46) German naturalist and geographer

Steno, Nicolaus (Danish name Niels Steensen) (1638–86) Danish anatomist and geologist

Stephenson, George (1781–1848) English engineer, the father of railways

Stirling, James (1692–1770) Scottish mathematician

Stirling, Robert (1790–1878) Scottish engineer and Presbyterian minister

Struve, Otto (1897–1963) Russian-born American astronomer

Swammerdam, Jan (1637–80) Dutch naturalist and microscopist

Swan, Sir Joseph Wilson (1828–1914) English physicist and chemist

Swedenborg, Emanuel (1688–1772) Swedish scientist, philosopher, and mystic

Sydenham, Thomas (*c.* 1624–89) English physician

Szent-Györgyi, Albert von (1893–1986) American biochemist,

SCIENTISTS, INVENTORS, AND PIONEERS (cont.)

born in Hungary

Szilard, Leo (1898–1964) Hungarian-born American physicist and molecular biologist

Talbot, (William Henry) Fox (1800–77) English pioneer of photography

Teilhard de Chardin, Pierre (1881–1955) French Jesuit philosopher and palaeontologist

Telford, Thomas (1757–1834) Scottish civil engineer

Teller, Edward (born 1908) Hungarian-born American physicist

Tereshkova, Valentina (Vladimirovna) (born 1937) Russian cosmonaut

Tesla, Nikola (1856–1943) American electrical engineer and inventor, born in what is now Croatia of Serbian descent

Thales (c. 624–c. 545 BC) Greek philosopher, mathematician, and astronomer

Theophrastus (c. 370–c. 287 BC) Greek philosopher and scientist

Thom, Alexander (1894–1985) Scottish expert on prehistoric stone circles

Thomson, Sir Joseph John (1856–1940) English physicist, discoverer of the electron

Thomson, Sir William See KELVIN

Tinbergen, Nikolaas (1907–88) Dutch zoologist

Tombaugh, Clyde William (1906–97) American astronomer

Tompion, Thomas (c. 1639–1713) English clock and watchmaker

Torricelli, Evangelista (1608–47) Italian mathematician and physicist

Townes, Charles Hard (born 1915) American physicist

Tradescant, John (1570–1638) English botanist and horticulturalist

Trevithick, Richard (1771–1833) English engineer

Tsiolkovsky, Konstantin (Eduardovich) (1857–1935) Russian aeronautical engineer

Tull, Jethro (1674–1741) English agriculturalist

Turing, Alan (Mathison) (1912–54) English mathematician

Tycho Brahe See BRAHE

Tyndall, John (1820–93) Irish physicist

Urey, Harold Clayton (1893–1981) American chemist

Van Allen, James Alfred (born 1914) American physicist

Van de Graaf, Robert Jemison (1901–67) American physicist

Vavilov, Nikolai (Ivanovich) (1887–c. 1943) Soviet plant geneticist

Vening Meinesz, Felix Andries (1887–1966) Dutch geophysicist

Verdon Roe, Sir Edwin Alliott See ROE

Vesalius, Andreas (1514–64) Flemish anatomist, the founder of modern anatomy

Vine, Frederick John (born 1939) English geologist

Virchow, Rudolf Karl (1821–1902) German physician and pathologist, founder of cellular pathology

Vitruvius (full name Marcus Vitruvius Pollio) (fl. 1st century BC) Roman architect and military engineer

Volta, Alessandro Giuseppe Antonio Anastasio, Count (1745–1827) Italian physicist

von Braun, Wernher Magnus Maximilian See BRAUN

von Neumann See NEUMANN

Waksman, Selman Abraham (1888–1973) Russian-born American microbiologist

Wallace, Alfred Russel (1823–1913) English naturalist

Wallis, Sir Barnes Neville (1887–1979) English inventor

Walton, Ernest Thomas Sinton (1903–95) Irish physicist

SCIENTISTS, INVENTORS, AND PIONEERS (cont.)

Warburg, Otto Heinrich (1883–1970) German biochemist

Watson, James Dewey (born 1928) American biologist

Watson, John Broadus (1878–1958) American psychologist, founder of the school of behaviourism

Watson-Watt, Sir Robert Alexander (1892–1973) Scottish physicist

Watt, James (1736–1819) Scottish engineer

Wegener, Alfred Lothar (1880–1930) German meteorologist and geologist

Weinberg, Steven (born 1933) American theoretical physicist

Weismann, August Friedrich Leopold (1834–1914) German biologist, one of the founders of modern genetics

Welsbach, Carl Auer, Baron von See AUER

Werner, Abraham Gottlob (1749–1817) German geologist

Werner, Alfred (1866–1919) French-born Swiss chemist, founder of coordination chemistry

Westinghouse, George (1846–1914) American engineer

Wheatstone, Sir Charles (1802–75) English physicist and inventor

Wheeler, John Archibald (born 1911) American theoretical physicist

White, Gilbert (1720–93) English clergyman and naturalist

Whitehead, A(lfred) N(orth) (1861–1947) English philosopher and mathematician

Whitney, Eli (1765–1825) American inventor

Whittle, Sir Frank (1907–96) English aeronautical engineer, test pilot, and inventor of the jet aircraft engine

Wiener, Norbert (1894–1964) American mathematician

Wilkins, Maurice Hugh Frederick (born 1916) New Zealand-born British biochemist and molecular biologist

Wilson, Charles Thomson Rees (1869–1959) Scottish physicist

Wilson, Edward Osborne (born 1929) American social biologist

Wilson, John Tuzo (1908–93) Canadian geophysicist

Winckelmann, Johann (Joachim) (1717–68) German archaeologist and art historian, born in Prussia

Windaus, Adolf (1876–1959) German organic chemist

Wöhler, Friedrich (1800–82) German chemist

Wollaston, William Hyde (1766–1828) English chemist and physicist

Woodward, Robert Burns (1917–79) American organic chemist

Woolley, Sir (Charles) Leonard (1880–1960) English archaeologist

Wright, Orville (1871–1948) and **Wilbur** (1867–1912) American aviation pioneers

Wundt, Wilhelm (1832–1920) German psychologist

Yeager, Charles E(lwood) ('Chuck') (born 1923) American pilot

Young, Thomas (1773–1829) English physicist, physician, and Egyptologist

Zeiss, Carl (1816–88) German optical instrument-maker

Zeppelin, Ferdinand (Adolf August Heinrich), Count von (1838–1917) German aviation pioneer

Zsigmondy, Richard Adolph (1865–1929) Austrian-born German chemist

Zworykin, Vladimir (Kuzmich) (1889–1982) Russian-born American physicist and television pioneer

ARTISTS, DESIGNERS, AND ARCHITECTS

Aalto, (Hugo) Alvar (Henrik) (1898–1976) Finnish architect and furniture designer

Abakanowicz, Magdalena (born 1930) Polish artist and weaver

Abbot, Berenice (1898–1991) American photographer

Adam, Robert (1728–92) Scottish architect

Adams, Ansel (Easton) (1902–84) American photographer

Albers, Josef (1888–1976) German-born American artist, designer, and teacher

Alberti, Leon Battista (1404–72) Italian architect, humanist, painter, and art critic

Allston, Washington (1779–1843) American landscape painter

Alma-Tadema, Sir Lawrence (1836–1912) Dutch-born British painter

Altdorfer, Albrecht (c. 1480–1538) German painter and architect

Andre, Carl (born 1935) American minimalist sculptor

Angelico, Fra (born Guido di Pietro, monastic name Fra Giovanni da Fiesole) (c. 1400–55) Italian painter

Anguissola, Sofonisba (c. 1535–1625) Italian painter

Annigoni, Pietro (1910–88) Italian painter

Apelles (4th century BC) Greek painter

Appel, Karel (born 1921) Dutch painter, sculptor, and graphic artist

Arbus, Diane (1923–71) American photographer

Archipenko, Aleksandr (Porfirevich) (1887–1964) Russian-born American sculptor and painter

Armani, Giorgio (born 1934) Italian fashion designer

Arp, Jean (also known as Hans Arp) (1887–1966) French painter, sculptor, and poet

Ashley, Laura (1925–85) Welsh fashion and textile designer

Auerbach, Frank (born 1931) German-born British painter

Bacon, Francis (1909–92) Irish painter

Bailey, David (born 1938) English photographer

Bakst, Léon (born Lev Samuilovich Rozenberg) (1866–1924) Russian painter and designer

Balenciaga, Cristóbal (1895–1972) Spanish couturier

Barry, Sir Charles (1795–1860) English architect

Bartholdi, Frédéric-Auguste (1834–1904) French sculptor

Bartolommeo, Fra (born Baccio della Porta) (c. 1472–1517) Italian painter

Baskerville, John (1706–75) English printer and type designer

Bateman, H(enry) M(ayo) (1887–1970) Australian-born British cartoonist

Beardsley, Aubrey (Vincent) (1872–98) English artist and illustrator

Beaton, Sir Cecil (Walter Hardy) (1904–80) English photographer

Beckmann, Max (1884–1950) German painter and graphic artist

Behrens, Peter (1868–1940) German architect and designer

Bell, Vanessa (1879–1961) English painter and designer

Bellini, Gentile (c. 1429–1507) Italian artist

Bellini, Giovanni (c. 1430–1516) Italian artist

Bellini, Jacopo (c. 1400–c. 1470) Italian artist

Bernini, Gian Lorenzo (1598–1680) Italian sculptor, painter, and architect

Beuys, Joseph (1921–86) German artist

Bewick, Thomas (1753–1828) English artist and wood engraver

Blake, Peter (born 1932) English painter

Blake, William (1757–1827) English

ARTISTS, DESIGNERS, AND ARCHITECTS (cont.)

artist and poet

Bodoni, Giambattista (1740–1813)
Italian printer and type designer

Bonnard, Pierre (1867–1947) French
painter and graphic artist

Borromini, Francesco (1599–1667)
Italian architect

Bosch, Hieronymus (c. 1450–1516)
Dutch painter

Botticelli, Sandro (born Alessandro
di Mariano Filipepi) (1445–1510)
Italian painter

Boucher, François (1703–70) French
painter and decorative artist

Bourke-White, Margaret (1906–71)
American photojournalist

Boyd, Arthur (Merric Bloomfield)
(born 1920) Australian painter,
potter, etcher, and ceramic artist

Bramante, Donato (di Angelo)
(1444–1514) Italian architect

Brancusi, Constantin (1876–1957)
Romanian sculptor, who spent
much of his working life in France

Brandt, Hermann Wilhelm ('Bill')
(1904–83) German-born British
photographer

Braque, Georges (1882–1963)
French painter

Breughel See BRUEGEL

Bronzino, Agnolo (born Agnolo di
Cosimo) (1503–72) Italian painter

Brouwer, Adriaen (c. 1605–38)
Flemish painter

Brown, Ford Madox (1821–93)
English painter

Brown, Lancelot (known as
Capability Brown) (1716–83)
English landscape gardener

Bruegel, Jan (Jan Bruegel the Elder)
(1568–1625) Flemish artist

Bruegel, Pieter (Bruegel the Elder)
(1525–69) Flemish artist

Bruegel, Pieter (Bruegel the
Younger) (?1564–?1638) Flemish
artist

Brunelleschi, Filippo (born Filippo di
Ser Brunellesco) (1377–1446)
Italian architect

Buonarroti, Michelangelo See
MICHELANGELO

Burne-Jones, Sir Edward (Coley)
(1833–98) English painter and
designer

Burra, Edward (1905–76) English
painter

Butler, Reginald Cotterell ('Reg')
(1913–81) English sculptor

Butterfield, William (1814–1900)
English architect

Caldecott, Randolph (1846–86)
English graphic artist and
watercolour painter

Calder, Alexander (1898–1976)
American sculptor and painter

Callicrates (5th century BC) Greek
architect

Cameron, Julia Margaret (1815–79)
English photographer

Canaletto (born Giovanni Antonio
Canale) (1697–1768) Italian painter

Canova, Antonio (1757–1822) Italian
sculptor

Capability Brown See BROWN,
LANCELOT

Capp, Al (born Alfred Gerald Caplin)
(1909–79) American cartoonist

Caravaggio, Michelangelo Merisi da
(c. 1571–1610) Italian painter

Cardin, Pierre (born 1922) French
couturier

Carpaccio, Vittore (c. 1455–1525)
Italian painter

Carr, Emily (1871–1945) Canadian
painter and writer

Carracci, Agostino (1557–1602)
Italian painter

Carracci, Annibale (1560–1609)
Italian painter

Carracci, Ludovico (1555–1619)
Italian painter

Carrington, Dora (de Houghton)
(1893–1932) English painter

Cartier-Bresson, Henri (born 1908)
French photographer and film
director

Caslon, William (1692–1766) English
typographer

Cassatt, Mary (1844–1926)
American painter

ARTISTS, DESIGNERS, AND ARCHITECTS (cont.)

Casson, Sir Hugh (Maxwell) (born 1910) English architect

Cellini, Benvenuto (1500–71) Italian goldsmith and sculptor

Cézanne, Paul (1839–1906) French painter

Chagall, Marc (1887–1985) Russian-born French painter and graphic artist

Chambers, Sir William (1723–96) Scottish architect

Chanel, Coco (born Gabrielle Bonheur Chanel) (1883–1971) French couturière

Chippendale, Thomas (1718–79) English furniture-maker and designer

Chirico, Giorgio de (1888–1978) Greek-born Italian painter

Claude Lorraine (also Lorrain) (born Claude Gellée) (1600–82) French painter

Clouet, Jean (c. 1485–1541) French painter

Clouet, François (c. 1516–72) French painter, son of Jean

Constable, John (1776–1837) English painter

Cooper, Susan Vera ('Susie') (1902–95) English ceramic designer and manufacturer

Copley, John Singleton (1738–1815) American painter

Corot, (Jean-Baptiste) Camille (1796–1875) French landscape painter

Correggio, Antonio Allegri da (born Antonio Allegri) (c. 1494–1534) Italian painter

Costa, Lúcio (1902–63) French-born Brazilian architect, town planner, and architectural historian

Cotman, John Sell (1782–1842) English painter

Courbet, Gustave (1819–77) French painter

Courrèges, André (born 1923) French fashion designer

Cranach, Lucas (known as Cranach the Elder) (1472–1553) German painter

Crome, John (1768–1821) English painter

Cruikshank, George (1792–1878) English painter, illustrator, and caricaturist

Dadd, Richard (1817–86) English painter

Dalcroze See JAQUES-DALCROZE

Dali, Salvador (1904–89) Spanish painter

Daubigny, Charles François (1817–78) French landscape painter

Daumier, Honoré (1808–78) French painter and lithographer

David, Jacques-Louis (1748–1825) French painter

da Vinci, Leonardo See LEONARDO DA VINCI

Degas, (Hilaire Germain) Edgar (1834–1917) French painter and sculptor

de Hooch, Pieter (also de Hoogh) (c. 1629–c. 1684) Dutch genre painter

de Kooning, Willem (1904–97) Dutch-born American painter

Delacroix, (Ferdinand Victor) Eugène (1798–1863) French painter

Delaunay, Robert (1885–1941) French painter

Delaunay-Terk, Sonia (1885–1979) Russian-born French painter and textile designer

della Francesca See PIERO DELLA FRANCESCA

della Quercia, Jacopo (c. 1374–1438) Italian sculptor

della Robbia, Andrea (1435–1525) Italian sculptor

della Robbia, Giovanni (1469–c. 1529) Italian sculptor

della Robbia, Girolamo (1488–1566) Italian sculptor

della Robbia, Lucia (1400–82) Italian sculptor

del Sarto, Andrea See SARTO

Denis, Maurice (1870–1943) French painter, designer, and art theorist

ARTISTS, DESIGNERS, AND ARCHITECTS (cont.)

Derain, André (1880–1954) French painter

Dior, Christian (1905–57) French couturier

Dobell, Sir William (1899–1970) Australian painter

Doisneau, Robert (1912–94) French photographer

Donatello (born Donato di Betto Bardi) (1386–1466) Italian sculptor

Doré, Gustave (1832–83) French book illustrator

Drysdale, Sir Russell (1912–81) British-born Australian painter

Dubuffet, Jean (1901–85) French artist

Duccio (full name Duccio di Buoninsegna) (c. 1255–c. 1320) Italian painter

Duchamp, Marcel (1887–1968) French-born painter, sculptor, and art theorist

Dufy, Raoul (1877–1953) French painter and textile designer

Du Maurier, George (Louis Palmella Busson) (1834–96) French-born cartoonist, illustrator, and novelist

Dürer, Albrecht (1471–1528) German painter and engraver

Eakins, Thomas (1844–1916) American painter and photographer

Elgin, 7th Earl of (title of Thomas Bruce) (1766–1841) British diplomat and art connoisseur

El Greco (Spanish for 'the Greek'; born Domenikos Theotokopoulos) (1541–1614) Cretan-born Spanish painter

Ensor, James (Sydney), Baron (1860–1949) Belgian painter and engraver

Epstein, Sir Jacob (1880–1959) American-born British sculptor

Ernst, Max (1891–1976) German artist

Erté (born Romain de Tirtoff) (1892–1990) Russian-born French fashion designer and illustrator

Escher, M(aurits) C(orneille) (1898–1972) Dutch graphic artist

Fabergé, Peter Carl (1846–1920) Russian goldsmith and jeweller, of French descent

Fabriano, Gentile da See GENTILE DA FABRIANO

Flaxman, John (1755–1826) English sculptor and draughtsman

Foster, Sir Norman (Robert) (born 1935) English architect

Fragonard, Jean-Honoré (1732–1806) French painter

Freud, Lucian (born 1922) German-born British painter, grandson of Sigmund Freud

Friedrich, Caspar David (1774–1840) German painter

Frink, Dame Elisabeth (1930–93) English sculptor and graphic artist

Frith, William Powell (1819–1909) English painter

Fry, Roger (Eliot) (1866–1934) English art critic and painter

Fuller, R(ichard) Buckminster (1895–1983) American designer and architect

Fuseli, Henry (born Johann Heinrich Füssli) (1741–1825) Swiss-born British painter and art critic

Gabo, Naum (born Naum Neemia Pevsner) (1890–1977) Russian-born American sculptor

Gainsborough, Thomas (1727–88) English painter

Gaudí, Antonio (full surname Gaudí y Cornet) (1853–1926) Spanish architect

Gaudier-Brzeska, Henri (1891–1915) French sculptor

Gauguin, (Eugène Henri) Paul (1848–1903) French painter

Gentile da Fabriano (c. 1370–1427) Italian painter

Gentileschi, Artemisia (c. 1597–c. 1652) Italian painter

Géricault, (Jean Louis André) Théodore (1791–1824) French painter

Ghiberti, Lorenzo (1378–1455) Italian sculptor and goldsmith

ARTISTS, DESIGNERS, AND ARCHITECTS (cont.)

Ghirlandaio (born Domenico di Tommaso Bigordi) (*c.* 1448–94) Italian painter

Giacometti, Alberto (1901–66) Swiss sculptor and painter

Gibbons, Grinling (1648–1721) Dutch-born English sculptor

Gibbs, James (1682–1754) Scottish architect

Gill, (Arthur) Eric (Rowton) (1882–1940) English sculptor, engraver, and typographer

Giorgione (also called Giorgio Barbarelli or Giorgio da Castelfranco) (*c.* 1478–1510) Italian painter

Giotto (full name Giotto di Bondone) (*c.* 1267–1337) Italian painter

Goes, Hugo van der (*fl. c.* 1467–82) Flemish painter, born in Ghent

Gorky, Arshile (1904–48) Turkish-born American painter

Gould, John (1804–81) English bird artist

Goya (full name Francisco José de Goya y Lucientes) (1746–1828) Spanish painter and etcher

Grant, Duncan (James Corrow) (1885–1978) Scottish painter and designer

Greco, El See EL GRECO

Greenaway, Catherine ('Kate') (1846–1901) English artist

Greuze, Jean-Baptiste (1725–1805) French painter

Gris, Juan (born José Victoriano Gonzales) (1887–1927) Spanish painter

Gropius, Walter (1883–1969) German-born American architect

Grosz, George (1893–1959) German painter and draughtsman

Grünewald, Mathias (born Mathis Nithardt; also called Mathis Gothardt) (*c.* 1460–1528) German painter

Guardi, Francesco (1712–93) Italian painter

Hadid, Zaha (born 1950) Iraqi architect

Hals, Frans (*c.* 1580–1666) Dutch portrait and genre painter

Hamada, Shoji (1894–1978) Japanese potter

Hamnett, Katharine (born 1952) English fashion designer

Hartnell, Sir Norman (1901–79) English couturier

Hawksmoor, Nicholas (1661–1736) English architect

Henri, Robert (1865–1929) American painter

Hepplewhite, George (died 1786) English cabinet-maker and furniture designer

Hepworth, Dame (Jocelyn) Barbara (1903–75) English sculptor

Hitchens, Ivon (1893–1979) English painter

Hobbema, Meindert (1638–1709) Dutch landscape painter

Hockney, David (born 1937) English painter and draughtsman

Hogarth, William (1697–1764) English painter and engraver

Hokusai, Katsushika (1760–1849) Japanese painter and wood-engraver

Holbein, Hans (known as Holbein the Younger) (1497–1543) German painter

Homer, Winslow (1836–1910) American painter

Hooch, Pieter de See DE HOOCH

Hopper, Edward (1882–1967) American realist painter

Horta, Victor (1861–1947) Belgian architect

Hunt, (William) Holman (1827–1910) English painter

Ictinus (5th century BC) Greek architect

Imhotep (*fl.* 27th century BC) Egyptian architect and scholar

Ingres, Jean Auguste Dominique (1780–1867) French painter

Jacopo della Quercia See DELLA QUERCIA

Jansens, Cornelius See JOHNSON

ARTISTS, DESIGNERS, AND ARCHITECTS (cont.)

Jekyll, Gertrude (1843–1932)
English horticulturalist and garden
designer

John, Augustus (Edwin)
(1878–1961) Welsh painter

John, Gwen (1876–1939) Welsh
painter

Johns, Jasper (born 1930) American
painter, sculptor, and printmaker

Johnson, Cornelius (also Jansens)
(1593–c. 1661) English-born Dutch
portrait painter

Jones, Inigo (1573–1652) English
architect and stage designer

Jordaens, Jacob (1593–1678)
Flemish painter

Kahlo, Frida (1907–54) Mexican
painter

Kandinsky, Wassily (1866–1944)
Russian painter and theorist

Kauffmann, Angelica (also
Kauffman) (1740–1807) Swiss
painter

Keene, Charles Samuel (1823–91)
English illustrator and caricaturist

Kent, William (c. 1685–1748) English
architect and landscape gardener

Kirchner, Ernst Ludwig (1880–1938)
German expressionist painter

Klee, Paul (1879–1940) Swiss
painter, resident in Germany from
1906

Klein, Calvin (Richard) (born 1942)
American fashion designer

Klimt, Gustav (1862–1918) Austrian
painter and designer

Knight, Dame Laura (1877–1970)
British painter

Kollwitz, Kathe (1867–1945) German
artist

Kooning, Willem de See DE KOONING

Lalique, René (1860–1945) French
jeweller

Landseer, Sir Edwin Henry
(1802–73) English painter and
sculptor

La Tour, Georges de (1593–1652)
French painter

Lawrence, Sir Thomas (1769–1830)
English painter

Leach, Bernard (Howell)
(1887–1979) British potter, born in
Hong Kong

Lebrun, Charles (1619–90) French
painter, designer, and decorator

Le Corbusier (born Charles Édouard
Jeanneret) (1887–1965) French
architect and town planner, born
in Switzerland

Léger, Fernand (1881–1955) French
painter

Leibovitz, Annie (born 1950)
American photographer

**Leighton, Frederic, 1st Baron
Leighton of Stretton** (1830–96)
English painter and sculptor

Lely, Sir Peter (Dutch name Pieter
van der Faes) (1618–80) Dutch
portrait painter, resident in
England from 1641

Le Nôtre, André (1613–1700) French
landscape gardener

Leonardo da Vinci (1452–1519)
Italian painter, scientist, and
engineer

Leyster, Judith (1609–60) Dutch
painter

Lichtenstein, Roy (1923–97)
American painter and sculptor

Lindsay, Norman Alfred William
(1879–1969) Australian artist

Lipchitz, Jacques (born Chaim
Jacob Lipchitz) (1891–1973)
Lithuanian-born French sculptor

Lippi, Filippino (c. 1457–1504) Italian
painter, son of Fra Filippo Lippi

Lippi, Fra Filippo (c. 1406–69) Italian
painter

Lorraine, Claude See CLAUDE LORRAINE

Lotto, Lorenzo (c. 1480–1556) Italian
painter

Low, Sir David (Alexander Cecil)
(1891–1963) British cartoonist,
born in New Zealand

Lowry, L(aurence) S(tephen)
(1887–1976) English painter

Lucas van Leyden (c. 1494–1533)
Dutch painter and engraver

Lutyens, Sir Edwin (Landseer)
(1869–1944) English architect

ARTISTS, DESIGNERS, AND ARCHITECTS (cont.)

Lysippus (4th century BC) Greek sculptor

Mabuse, Jan (Flemish name Jan Gossaert) (*c.* 1478–*c.* 1533) Flemish painter

Mackintosh, Charles Rennie (1868–1928) Scottish architect and designer

Magritte, René (François Ghislain) (1898–1967) Belgian painter

Malevich, Kazimir (Severinovich) (1878–1935) Russian painter and designer

Manet, Édouard (1832–83) French painter

Man Ray See RAY

Mansart, François (1598–1666) French architect

Mantegna, Andrea (1431–1506) Italian painter and engraver

Martini, Simone (*c.* 1284–1344) Italian painter

Masaccio (born Tommaso Giovanni di Simone Guidi) (1401–28) Italian painter

Masson, André (1896–1987) French painter and graphic artist

Matisse, Henri (Émile Benoît) (1869–1954) French painter and sculptor

Michelangelo (full name Michelangelo Buonarroti) (1475–1564) Italian sculptor, painter, architect, and poet

Michelozzo (full name Michelozzo di Bartolommeo) (1396–1472) Italian architect and sculptor

Mies van der Rohe, Ludwig (1886–1969) German-born architect and designer

Millais, Sir John Everett (1829–96) English painter

Millet, Jean (François) (1814–75) French painter

Minton, Thomas (1765–1836) English pottery and china manufacturer

Miró, Joan (1893–1983) Spanish painter

Modigliani, Amedeo (1884–1920) Italian painter and sculptor, resident in France from 1906

Moholy-Nagy, László (1895–1946) Hungarian-born American painter, sculptor, and photographer

Mondrian, Piet (born Pieter Cornelis Mondriaan) (1872–1944) Dutch painter

Monet, Claude (1840–1926) French painter

Montagna, Bartolommeo Cincani (*c.* 1450–1523) Italian painter

Moore, Henry (Spencer) (1898–1986) English sculptor and draughtsman

Morisot, Berthe (Marie Pauline) (1841–95) French painter

Morland, George (1763–1804) English painter

Morris, William (1834–96) English designer, craftsman, poet, and socialist writer

Moses, Anna Mary (known as Grandma Moses) (1860–1961) American painter

Mucha, Alphonse (born Alfons Maria) (1860–1939) Czech painter and designer

Muir, Jean (Elizabeth) (1933–95) English fashion designer

Munch, Edvard (1863–1944) Norwegian painter and engraver

Murillo, Bartolomé Esteban (*c.* 1618–82) Spanish painter

Myron (*fl. c.* 480–440 BC) Greek sculptor

Nash, John (1752–1835) English town planner and architect

Nash, Paul (1889–1946) English painter and designer

Newman, Barnett (1905–70) American painter

Nicholson, Ben (1894–1982) English painter

Niemeyer, Oscar (born 1907) Brazilian architect

Nolan, Sir Sidney Robert (1917–93) Australian painter

O'Keeffe, Georgia (1887–1986) American painter

Oldfield, Bruce (born 1950) English

ARTISTS, DESIGNERS, AND ARCHITECTS (cont.)

fashion designer

Opie, John (1761–1807) English painter

Orcagna (born Andrea di Cione) (*c.* 1308–68) Italian painter, sculptor, and architect

Ostade, Adriaen van (1610–85) Dutch painter and engraver

Palissy, Bernard (*c.* 1510–90) French potter

Palladio, Andrea (1508–80) Italian architect

Palmer, Samuel (1805–91) English painter and etcher

Paolozzi, Eduardo (Luigi) (born 1924) Scottish artist and sculptor, of Italian descent

Parmigianino (also Parmigiano) (born Girolano Francesco Maria Mazzola) (1503–40) Italian painter

Paxton, Sir Joseph (1801–65) English gardener and architect

Peeters, Clara (1594–*c.* 1660) Flemish painter

Pei, I(eoh) M(ing) (born 1917) American architect, born in China

Pevsner, Antoine (1886–1962) Russian-born French sculptor and painter

Phidias (5th century BC) Athenian sculptor

Phiz (pseudonym of Hablot Knight Browne) (1815–82) English illustrator

Piero della Francesca (1416–92) Italian painter

Piper, John (1903–92) English painter and decorative designer

Piranesi, Giovanni Battista (1720–78) Italian engraver

Pisano, Andrea (*c.* 1290–*c.* 1348) and **Nino**, his son (died *c.* 1368) Italian sculptors

Pisano, Nicola (*c.* 1220–*c.* 1278) and **Giovanni**, his son (*c.* 1250–*c.* 1314) Italian sculptors

Pissarro, Camille (1830–1903) French painter and graphic artist

Pollaiuolo, Antonio (*c.* 1432–98) and **Piero** (1443–96) Italian sculptors, painters, and engravers

Pollock, (Paul) Jackson (1912–56) American painter

Polyclitus (5th century BC) Greek sculptor

Pontormo, Jacopo da (1494–1557) Italian painter

Poussin, Nicolas (1594–1665) French painter

Praxiteles (mid-4th century BC) Athenian sculptor

Pugin, Augustus Welby Northmore (1812–52) English architect

Quant, Mary (born 1934) English fashion designer

Quercia, Jacopo della See DELLA QUERCIA

Rackham, Arthur (1867–1939) English illustrator

Raeburn, Sir Henry (1756–1823) Scottish portrait painter

Ramsay, Allan (1713–84) Scottish portrait painter

Raphael (Italian name Raffaello Sanzio) (1483–1520) Italian painter and architect

Rauschenberg, Robert (born 1925) American artist

Ray, Man (born Emmanuel Rudnitsky) (1890–1976) American photographer, painter, and film-maker

Redon, Odilon (1840–1916) French painter and graphic artist

Rembrandt (full name Rembrandt Harmensz van Rijn) (1606–69) Dutch painter

Renoir, (Pierre) Auguste (1841–1919) French painter

Repton, Humphry (1752–1818) English landscape gardener

Reynolds, Sir Joshua (1723–92) English painter

Ribera, José (*or* Jusepe) **de** (known as 'Lo Spagnoletto') (*c.* 1591–1652) Spanish painter and etcher, resident in Italy from 1616

Rie, Dame Lucie (1902–95) British potter, born in Austria

Riley, Bridget (born 1931) British

ARTISTS, DESIGNERS, AND ARCHITECTS (cont.)

Op art painter

Rodin, Auguste (1840–1917) French
sculptor

Rogers, Sir Richard (George) (born
1933) British architect

Romney, George (1734–1802)
English portrait painter

Rosa, Salvator (1615–73) Italian
painter and etcher

Rossetti, Dante Gabriel (full name
Gabriel Charles Dante Rossetti)
(1828–82) English painter

Rothko, Mark (born Marcus
Rothkovich) (1903–70) American
painter, born in Latvia

Rouault, Georges (Henri)
(1871–1958) French painter and
engraver

Rousseau, Henri (Julien) (known as
'le Douanier', 'the customs
officer') (1844–1910) French
painter

**Rousseau, (Pierre Étienne)
Théodore** (1812–67) French painter

Rowlandson, Thomas (1756–1827)
English painter, draughtsman, and
caricaturist

Rubens, Sir Peter Paul (1577–1640)
Flemish painter

Ruisdael, Jacob van (also Ruysdael)
(c. 1628–82) Dutch landscape
painter

Ruskin, John (1819–1900) English
art and social critic

Ruysch, Rachel (1664–1750) Dutch
painter

Ruysdael See RUISDAEL

Saint Laurent, Yves (Mathieu) (born
1936) French couturier

Sansovino, Jacopo Tatti
(1486–1570) Italian sculptor and
architect

Sargent, John Singer (1856–1925)
American painter

Sarto, Andrea del (born Andrea
d'Agnolo) (1486–1531) Italian
painter

Sassoon, Vidal (born 1928) English
hairstylist

Schiaparelli, Elsa (1896–1973)
Italian-born French fashion
designer

Schiele, Egon (1890–1918) Austrian
painter and draughtsman

Schulz, Charles (born 1922)
American cartoonist

Scott, Sir George Gilbert (1811–78)
English architect

Searle, Ronald (William Fordham)
(born 1920) English artist

Seurat, Georges Pierre (1859–91)
French painter

Sickert, Walter Richard (1860–1942)
British painter, of Danish and
Anglo-Irish descent

Signac, Paul (1863–1935) French
neo-impressionist painter

Sirani, Elisabetta (1638–65) Italian
painter

Sisley, Alfred (1839–99) French
impressionist painter, of English
descent

Smith, David (Roland) (1906–65)
American sculptor

Soane, Sir John (1753–1837) English
architect

Soutine, Chaim (1893–1943) French
painter, born in Lithuania

Speer, Albert (1905–81) German
architect and Nazi government
official

Spence, Sir Basil (Unwin) (1907–76)
British architect, born in India

Spencer, Sir Stanley (1891–1959)
English painter

Spode, Josiah (1755–1827) English
potter

Stella, Frank (Philip) (born 1936)
American painter

Stieglitz, Alfred (1864–1946)
American photographer

Stirling, Sir James (1926–92)
English architect

Stubbs, George (1724–1806) English
painter and engraver

Sutherland, Graham (Vivian)
(1903–80) English painter

Tange, Kenzo (born 1913) Japanese
architect

Teniers, David (known as David

ARTISTS, DESIGNERS, AND ARCHITECTS (cont.)

Teniers the Younger) (1610–90)
Flemish painter
Tenniel, Sir John (1820–1914)
English illustrator and
cartoonist
Thomson, Tom (full name Thomas
John Thomson) (1877–1917)
Canadian painter
Thorvaldsen, Bertel (also
Thorwaldsen) (c. 1770–1844)
Danish neoclassical sculptor
Tiepolo, Giovanni Battista
(1696–1770) Italian painter
Tiffany, Louis Comfort (1848–1933)
American glass-maker and interior
decorator
Tintoretto (born Jacopo Robusti)
(1518–94) Italian painter
Titian (Italian name Tiziano Vecellio)
(c. 1488–1576) Italian painter
**Toulouse-Lautrec, Henri (Marie
Raymond) de** (1864–1901) French
painter and lithographer
Turner, J(oseph) M(allord) W(illiam)
(1775–1851) English painter
Tussaud, Madame (née Marie
Grosholtz) (1761–1850) French
founder of Madame Tussaud's
waxworks, resident in Britain from
1802
Uccello, Paolo (born Paolo di Dono)
(c. 1397–1475) Italian painter
Utamaro, Kitagawa (born Kitagawa
Nebsuyoshi) (1753–1806)
Japanese painter and printmaker
Utrillo, Maurice (1883–1955) French
painter
Valadon, Suzanne (1867–1938)
French painter
Vanbrugh, Sir John (1664–1726)
English architect and dramatist
van de Velde, Adriaen (1636–72)
Dutch painter
van de Velde, Esaias (c. 1591–1630)
Dutch painter
van de Velde, Henri (Clemens)
(1863–1957) Belgian architect,
designer, and teacher
van de Velde, Willem (van de Velde
the Elder) (1611–93) Dutch painter

van de Velde, Willem (van de Velde
the Younger) (1633–1707) Dutch
painter
Van Dyck, Sir Anthony (also
Vandyke) (1599–1641) Flemish
painter
Van Eyck, Jan (c. 1370–1441)
Flemish painter
Van Gogh, Vincent (Willem)
(1853–90) Dutch painter
van Leyden, Lucas See LUCAS VAN
LEYDEN
Vasarely, Viktor (1908–97)
Hungarian-born French painter
Vasari, Giorgio (1511–74) Italian
painter, architect, and biographer
**Velázquez, Diego Rodríguez de
Silva y** (1599–1660) Spanish
painter
Velde, van de See VAN DE VELDE
Venturi, Robert (Charles) (born
1925) American architect
Vermeer, Jan (1632–75) Dutch
painter
Veronese, Paolo (born Paolo Caliari)
(c. 1528–88) Italian painter
**Vigée-Lebrun, (Marie Louise)
Elisabeth** (1755–1842) French
painter
Vignola, Giacomo Barozzi da
(1507–73) Italian architect
Vinci, Leonardo da See LEONARDO DA
VINCI
Vitruvius (Marcus Vitruvius Pollio)
(fl. 1st century BC) Roman architect
and military engineer
Vlaminck, Maurice de (1876–1958)
French painter and writer
Vuillard, (Jean) Édouard
(1868–1940) French painter and
graphic artist
Warburg, Aby (Moritz) (1866–1929)
German art historian
Warhol, Andy (born Andrew
Warhola) (c. 1928–87) American
painter, graphic artist, and film-
maker
Waterhouse, Alfred (1830–1905)
English architect
Watteau, Jean Antoine (1684– 1721)

ARTISTS, DESIGNERS, AND ARCHITECTS (cont.)

French painter, of Flemish descent

Watts, George Frederick
(1817–1904) English painter and
sculptor

Wedgwood, Josiah (1730–95)
English potter

West, Benjamin (1738–1820)
American painter, resident in
Britain from 1763

Weyden, Rogier van der (French
name Rogier de la Pasture) (*c.*
1400–64) Flemish painter

Whistler, James (Abbott) McNeill
(1834–1903) American painter and
etcher

Wilkie, Sir David (1785–1841)
Scottish painter

Winterhalter, Franz Xavier
(1806–73) German painter

Worth, Charles Frederick (1825–95)
English couturier, resident in
France from 1845

Wren, Sir Christopher (1632–1723)
English architect

Wright, Frank Lloyd (1869–1959)
American architect

Wyatt, James (1746–1813) English
architect

Yamasaki, Minoru (1912–86)
American architect

Zeuxis (*fl.* late 5th century BC) Greek
painter, born at Heraclea in
southern Italy

Zoffany, Johann (*c.* 1733–1810)
German-born painter, resident in
England from 1758

Zurbarán, Francisco de (1598–1664)
Spanish painter

COMPOSERS, MUSICIANS, SINGERS, AND INSTRUMENT MAKERS

Albinoni, Tomaso (1671–1751) Italian composer

Amati, Andrea (c. 1520–c. 1578) Italian violin maker

Amati, Antonio (c. 1550–1638) Italian violin maker

Amati, Girolamo (1551–1635) Italian violin maker

Amati, Nicolò (1596–1684) Italian violin maker

Anderson, Marian (1902–93) American operatic contralto

Armstrong, (Daniel) Louis (known as 'Satchmo') (1900–71) US jazz trumpeter and singer

Arne, Thomas (1710–78) English composer

Arnold, Sir Malcolm (Henry) (born 1921) English composer and trumpeter

Arrau, Claudio (1903–91) Chilean pianist

Ashkenazy, Vladimir (Davidovich) (born 1937) Russian-born pianist and conductor

Auric, Georges (1899–1983) French composer

Babbitt, Milton (Byron) (born 1916) American composer and mathematician

Bacewicz, Grazyna (1909–69) Polish composer and violinist

Bach, Johann Sebastian (1685–1750) German composer

Bacharach, Burt (born 1929) American writer of popular songs

Baez, Joan (born 1941) American folk-singer

Baker, Dame Janet (Abbott) (born 1933) English operatic mezzo-soprano

Barber, Samuel (1910–81) American composer

Barbirolli, Sir John (Giovanni Battista) (1899–1970) English conductor, of Franco-Italian descent

Barenboim, Daniel (born 1942) Israeli pianist and conductor, born in Argentina

Bart, Lionel (born 1930) English composer and lyricist

Bartók, Béla (1881–1945) Hungarian composer

Basie, Count (born William Basie) (1904–84) American jazz pianist, organist, and band leader

Bax, Sir Arnold (Edward Trevor) (1883–1953) English composer

Beach, Amy (1867–1944) American composer and pianist

Bechstein, Friedrich Wilhelm Carl (1826–1900) German piano-builder

Beecham, Sir Thomas (1879–1961) English conductor and impresario

Beethoven, Ludwig van (1770–1827) German composer

Beiderbecke, Bix (born Leon Bismarck Beiderbecke) (1903–31) American jazz musician and composer

Bellini, Vincenzo (1801–35) Italian composer

Bennett, Sir Richard Rodney (born 1936) English composer

Berg, Alban (Maria Johannes) (1885–1935) Austrian composer

Berio, Luciano (born 1925) Italian composer

Berkeley, Sir Lennox (Randall Francis) (1903–89) English composer

Berlin, Irving (born Israel Baline) (1888–1989) Russian-born American songwriter

Berlioz, (Louis-)Hector (1803–69) French composer

Bernstein, Leonard (1918–90) American composer, conductor, and pianist

Berry, Chuck (born Charles Edward Berry) (born 1931) American rock and roll singer, guitarist, and songwriter

Birtwistle, Sir Harrison (Paul) (born 1934) English composer and clarinettist

Bizet, Georges (born Alexandre César Léopold Bizet) (1838–75) French composer

COMPOSERS, MUSICIANS, SINGERS, AND INSTRUMENT
MAKERS (cont.)

Blakey, Arthur ('Art') (1919–90),
American jazz drummer

**Bliss, Sir Arthur (Edward
Drummond)** (1891–1975) English
composer

Bloch, Ernest (1880–1959) Swiss-
born American composer, of
Jewish descent

Boccherini, Luigi (1743–1805) Italian
composer and cellist

Borodin, Aleksandr (Porfirevich)
(1833–87) Russian composer

Boulanger, Nadia Juliette
(1887–1979) French composer and
conductor

Boulez, Pierre (born 1925) French
composer and conductor

Boult, Sir Adrian (Cedric)
(1889–1983) English conductor

Bowie, David (born David Robert
Jones) (born 1947) English rock
singer, songwriter, and actor

Bowles, Paul (Frederick) (born 1910)
American writer and composer

Boyce, William (1711–79) English
composer and organist

Brahms, Johannes (1833–97)
German composer and pianist

Brain, Dennis (1921–57) English
French-horn player

Bream, Julian (Alexander) (born
1933) English guitarist and lute-
player

Brel, Jacques (1929–78) Belgian
singer and composer

Brico, Antonia (1902–89) Dutch-born
American conductor

Bridge, Frank (1879–1941) English
composer, conductor, and
violist

**Britten, (Edward) Benjamin, Lord
Britten of Aldeburgh** (1913–76)
English composer, pianist, and
conductor

Brown, James (born 1928)
American soul and funk singer
and songwriter

Brubeck, David Warren ('Dave')
(born 1920) American jazz pianist,
composer, and band leader

Bruckner, Anton (1824–96) Austrian
composer and organist

Busoni, Ferruccio (Benvenuto)
(1866–1924) Italian composer,
conductor, and pianist

Buxtehude, Dietrich (c. 1637–1707)
Danish organist and composer

Byrd, William (1543–1623) English
composer

Caballé, Montserrat (born 1933)
Spanish operatic soprano

Cage, John (Milton) (1912–92)
American composer, pianist, and
writer

Callas, Maria (born Maria Cecilia
Anna Kalageropoulos) (1923–77)
American-born operatic soprano,
of Greek parentage

Calloway, Cab(ell) (1907–94)
American jazz singer and band
leader

Carmichael, Hoagy (born Howard
Hoagland Carmichael) (1899–1981)
American jazz pianist, composer,
and singer

Carreño, Maria Teresa (1853–1917)
Venezuelan composer and pianist

Carreras, José (born 1946) Spanish
operatic tenor

Carter, Elliott (Cook) (born 1908)
American composer

Caruso, Enrico (1873–1921) Italian
operatic tenor

Casals, Pablo (also called Pau
Casals) (1876–1973) Spanish
cellist, conductor, and composer

Cash, Johnny (born 1932) American
country music singer and
songwriter

Chaliapin, Fyodor (Ivanovich)
(1873–1938) Russian operatic bass

Chaminade, Cécile Louise
(1857–1944) French composer

Charles, Ray (born Ray Charles
Robinson) (born 1930) American
pianist and singer

Chopin, Frédéric (François) (Polish
name Fryderyk Franciszek Szopen)
(1810–49) Polish-born French
composer

COMPOSERS, MUSICIANS, SINGERS, AND INSTRUMENT MAKERS (cont.)

Clapton, Eric (born 1945) English blues and rock guitarist, singer, and composer

Cline, Patsy (born Virginia Petterson Hensley) (1932–63) American country singer

Cobain, Kurt (Donald) (1967–94) American rock singer, guitarist, and songwriter

Cochran, Eddie (born Edward Cochrane) (1938–60) American rock and roll singer and songwriter

Cole, Nat King (born Nathaniel Adams Coles) (1919–65) American singer and pianist

Coleman, Ornette (born 1930) American jazz saxophonist, trumpeter, violinist, and composer

Coltrane, John (William) (1926–67) American jazz saxophonist and composer

Copland, Aaron (1900–90) American composer, pianist, and conductor, of Lithuanian descent

Corelli, Arcangelo (1653–1713) Italian violinist and composer

Couperin, François (1668–1733) French composer, organist, and harpsichordist

Crosby, Bing (born Harry Lillis Crosby) (1904–77) American singer and actor

Czerny, Karl (1791–1857) Austrian pianist, teacher, and composer

Dallapiccola, Luigi (1904–75) Italian composer

Davies, Sir Peter Maxwell (born 1934) English composer and conductor

Davis, Miles (Dewey) (1926–91) American jazz trumpeter, composer, and band leader

Debussy, (Achille) Claude (1862–1918) French composer and critic

de Falla, Manuel See FALLA

Delibes, (Clément Philibert) Léo (1836–91) French composer and organist

Delius, Frederick (1862–1934) English composer, of German and Scandinavian descent

de Pisan, Christine (also de Pizan) (c. 1364–c. 1430) Italian composer and writer, resident in France from 1369

des Prez, Josquin (also des Prés) (c. 1440–1521) Flemish composer

Domingo, Placido (born 1941) Spanish-born tenor

Domino, Fats (born Antoine Domino) (born 1928) American pianist, singer, and songwriter

Donizetti, Gaetano (1797–1848) Italian composer

Dufay, Guillaume (c. 1400–74) French composer

Dunstable, John (c. 1390–1453) English composer

du Pré, Jacqueline (1945–87) English cellist

Durey, Louis (1888–1979) French composer

Dvořák, Antonín (1841–1904) Czech composer

Dylan, Bob (born Robert Allen Zimmerman) (born 1941) American singer and songwriter

Elgar, Sir Edward (William) (1857–1934) British composer

Ellington, Duke (born Edward Kennedy Ellington) (1899–1974) American jazz pianist, composer, and band leader

Evans, Gil (born Ian Ernest Gilmore Green) (1912–88) Canadian jazz pianist, composer, and arranger

Falla, Manuel de (1876–1946) Spanish composer and pianist

Fauré, Gabriel (Urbain) (1845–1924) French composer and organist

Fender, Leo (1907–91) American guitar-maker

Ferrier, Kathleen (1912–53) English contralto

Field, John (1782–1837) Irish composer and pianist

Fischer-Dieskau, Dietrich (born 1925) German baritone

COMPOSERS, MUSICIANS, SINGERS, AND INSTRUMENT MAKERS (cont.)

Fitzgerald, Ella (1917–96) American jazz singer

Foster, Stephen (Collins) (1826–64) American composer

Franck, César (Auguste) (1822–90) Belgian-born French composer

Franklin, Aretha (born 1942) American soul and gospel singer

Furtwängler, Wilhelm (1886–1954) German conductor

Garcia, Jerry (full name Jerome John Garcia) (1942–95) American rock singer and guitarist

Gaye, Marvin (1939–84) American soul singer and songwriter

Gershwin, George (born Jacob Gershovitz) (1898–1937) American composer and pianist, of Russian Jewish parentage

Getz, Stan (born Stanley Gayetsky) (1927–91) American jazz saxophonist

Gibbons, Orlando (1583–1625) English composer and musician

Gigli, Beniamino (1890–1957) Italian operatic tenor

Gillespie, Dizzy (born John Birks Gillespie) (1917–93) American jazz trumpet player, composer, and band leader

Gipps, Ruth (born 1921) British composer

Glanville-Hicks, Peggy (1912–90) American composer

Glass, Philip (born 1937) American composer

Glazunov, Aleksandr (Konstantinovich) (1865–1936) Russian composer

Glinka, Mikhail (Ivanovich) (1804–57) Russian composer

Gluck, Christoph Willibald von (1714–87) German composer

Gobbi, Tito (1915–84) Italian operatic baritone

Godard, Jean-Luc (born 1930) French film director

Goodman, Benjamin David ('Benny') (1909–86) American jazz clarinettist and band leader

Goossens, Sir (Aynsley) Eugene (1893–1962) English conductor, violinist, and composer, of Belgian descent

Gordy, Berry Jr (born 1929) American record producer

Górecki, Henryk (Mikołaj) (born 1933) Polish composer

Gould, Glenn (Herbert) (1932–82) Canadian pianist and composer

Gounod, Charles François (1818–93) French composer, conductor, and organist

Grainger, (George) Percy (Aldridge) (1882–1961) Australian-born American composer and pianist

Grappelli, Stephane (1908–97) French jazz violinist

Grieg, Edvard (1843–1907) Norwegian composer, conductor, and violinist

Grove, Sir George (1820–1900) English musicologist

Guarneri, Giuseppe ('del Gesù') (1687–1744) Italian violin-maker

Gurney, Ivor (Bertie) (1890–1937) English poet and composer

Guthrie, Woody (born Woodrow Wilson Guthrie) (1912–67) American folk-singer and songwriter

Haitink, Bernard (born 1929) Dutch conductor

Haley, William John Clifton ('Bill') (1925–81) American rock and roll singer

Hallé, Sir Charles (German name Karl Halle) (1819–95) German-born pianist and conductor

Hammerstein, Oscar (full name Oscar Hammerstein II) (1895–1960) American librettist

Hammond, Dame Joan (1912–96) Australian operatic soprano, born in New Zealand

Handel, George Frederick (born Georg Friedrich Händel) (1685–1759) German-born composer, resident in England

Handy, W(illiam) C(hristopher)

**COMPOSERS, MUSICIANS, SINGERS, AND INSTRUMENT
MAKERS (cont.)**

(1873–1958) American blues
musician
Harrison, George (born 1943)
English rock and pop guitarist
Hawkins, Coleman Randolph
(1904–69) American jazz
saxophonist
Haydn, Franz Joseph (1732–1809)
Austrian composer
Hendrix, Jimi (born James Marshall
Hendrix) (1942–70) American rock
guitarist and singer
Henze, Hans Werner (born 1926)
German composer and conductor
Hess, Dame Myra (1890–1965)
English pianist
Hildegard of Bingen, St (1098–1179)
German abbess, scholar,
composer, and mystic
Hindemith, Paul (1895–1963)
German composer
Holiday, Billie (born Eleanora
Fagan) (1915–59) American jazz
singer
Holly, Buddy (born Charles Hardin
Holley) (1936–59) American rock
and roll singer, guitarist, and
songwriter
Holst, Gustav (Theodore)
(1874–1934) English composer, of
Swedish and Russian descent
Honegger, Arthur (1892–1955)
French composer, of Swiss
descent
Horowitz, Vladimir (1904–89)
Russian pianist
Humperdinck, Engelbert
(1854–1921) German composer
Iglesias, Julio (born 1943) Spanish
singer
Ives, Charles (Edward) (1874–1954)
American composer
Jackson, Michael (Joe) (born 1958)
American singer and songwriter
Jagger, Michael Philip ('Mick') (born
1943) English rock singer and
songwriter
Jaques-Dalcroze, Émile (1865–1950)
Austrian-born Swiss music
teacher and composer

John, Sir Elton (Hercules) (born
Reginald Kenneth Dwight) (born
1947) English pop and rock singer,
pianist, and composer
Johnson, Robert (1911–38)
American blues singer and
guitarist
Jones, Tom (born Thomas Jones
Woodward) (born 1940) Welsh
pop singer
Joplin, Janis (1943–70) American
singer
Joplin, Scott (1868–1917) American
pianist and composer
Josquin des Prez See DES PREZ
Joyce, Eileen (1912–91) Australian
pianist
Karajan, Herbert von (1908–89)
Austrian conductor
Kenton, Stan (born Stanley
Newcomb) (1912–79) American
band leader, composer, and
arranger
Kern, Jerome (David) (1885–1945)
American composer
Khachaturian, Aram (Ilich) (1903–78)
Soviet composer, born in Georgia
King, B. B. (real name Riley B. King)
(born 1925) American blues singer
and guitarist
Klemperer, Otto (1885–1973)
German-born conductor and
composer
Kodály, Zoltán (1882–1967)
Hungarian composer
Kreisler, Fritz (1875–1962) Austrian-
born American violinist and
composer
Lambert, (Leonard) Constant
(1905–51) English composer,
conductor, and critic
Lassus, Orlande de (Italian name
Orlando di Lasso) (c. 1532–94)
Flemish composer
LeFanu, Nicola (born 1947) British
composer
Lehár, Franz (Ferencz) (1870–1948)
Hungarian composer
Lennon, John (1940–80) English
pop and rock singer, guitarist,

COMPOSERS, MUSICIANS, SINGERS, AND INSTRUMENT MAKERS (cont.)

and songwriter

Lewis, Jerry Lee (born 1935) American rock and roll singer and pianist

Liberace (full name Wladziu Valentino Liberace) (1919–87) American pianist and entertainer

Ligeti, György Sándor (born 1923) Hungarian composer

Lind, Jenny (born Johanna Maria Lind Goldschmidt) (1820–87) Swedish soprano

Liszt, Franz (1811–86) Hungarian composer and pianist

Lloyd Webber, Andrew, Baron (born 1948) English composer of musicals

Lully, Jean-Baptiste (Italian name Giovanni Battista Lulli) (1632–87) French composer, born in Italy

Lutosławski, Witold (1913–94) Polish composer

Lutyens, (Agnes) Elizabeth (1906–83) English composer

Lympany, Dame Moura (born 1916) British pianist

Lynn, Dame Vera (born Vera Margaret Lewis) (born 1917) English singer

McCartney, Sir (James) Paul (born 1942) English pop and rock singer, songwriter, and bass guitarist

Maconchy, Dame Elizabeth (1907–94) British composer

Madonna (born Madonna Louise Ciccone) (born 1958) American pop singer and actress

Mahler, Gustav (1860–1911) Austrian composer, conductor, and pianist

Marley, Robert Nesta ('Bob') (1945–81) Jamaican reggae singer, guitarist, and songwriter

Marsalis, Wynton (born 1962) American trumpeter

Martin, Sir George (Leonard) (born 1926) English record producer

Mascagni, Pietro (1863–1945) Italian composer and conductor

Melba, Dame Nellie (born Helen Porter Mitchell) (1861–1931) Australian operatic soprano

Mendelssohn, Felix (full name Jakob Ludwig Felix Mendelssohn-Bartholdy) (1809–47) German composer and pianist

Menuhin, Yehudi, Baron (born 1916) American-born British violinist

Mercury, Freddy (born Frederick Bulsara) (1946–91) British rock singer, born in Zanzibar

Messiaen, Olivier (Eugène Prosper Charles) (1908–92) French composer

Meyerbeer, Giacomo (born Jakob Liebmann Beer) (1791–1864) German composer

Milhaud, Darius (1892–1974) French composer

Miller, (Alton) Glenn (1904–44) American jazz trombonist and band leader

Mingus, Charles (1922–79) American jazz bassist and composer

Mitchell, Joni (born Roberta Joan Anderson) (born 1943) Canadian singer and songwriter

Monk, Thelonious (Sphere) (1917–82) American jazz pianist and composer

Monteverdi, Claudio (1567–1643) Italian composer

Morrison, James Douglas ('Jim') (1943–71) American rock singer

Morrison, Van (full name George Ivan Morrison) (born 1945) Northern Irish singer, songwriter, and musician

Morton, Jelly Roll (born Ferdinand Joseph La Menthe Morton) (1885–1941) American jazz pianist, composer, and band leader

Moussorgsky See MUSSORGSKY

Mozart, (Johann Chrysostom) Wolfgang Amadeus (1756–91) Austrian composer

Musgrave, Thea (born 1928) Scottish composer

Mussorgsky, Modest (Petrovich)

COMPOSERS, MUSICIANS, SINGERS, AND INSTRUMENT MAKERS (cont.)

(also Moussorgsky) (1839–81) Russian composer

Mutter, Anne-Sophie (born 1965) German violinist

Nelson, Willie (born 1933) American country singer and songwriter

Nielsen, Carl August (1865–1931) Danish composer

Nilsson, (Märta) Birgit (born 1918) Swedish operatic soprano

Norman, Jessye (born 1945) American operatic soprano

Novello, Ivor (born David Ivor Davies) (1893–1951) Welsh composer, actor, and dramatist

Nyman, Michael (born 1944) English composer

Offenbach, Jacques (born Jacob Offenbach) (1819–80) German composer, resident in France from 1833

Ono, Yoko (born 1933) American musician and artist, born in Japan

Orbison, Roy (1936–88) American singer and composer

Orff, Carl (1895–1982) German composer

Ozawa, Seiji (born 1935) Japanese conductor

Pachelbel, Johann (1653–1706) German composer and organist

Paderewski, Ignacy Jan (1860–1941) Polish pianist, composer, and statesman, Prime Minister 1919

Paganini, Niccolò (1782–1840) Italian violinist and composer

Palestrina, Giovanni Pierluigi da (c. 1525–94) Italian composer

Parker, Charles Christopher ('Charlie'; known as 'Bird' or 'Yardbird') (1920–55) American saxophonist

Parry, Sir (Charles) Hubert (Hastings) (1848–1918) English composer

Parton, Dolly (Rebecca) (born 1946) American singer and songwriter

Paul, Les (born Lester Polfus) (born 1915) American guitarist and inventor of the solid-body electric guitar

Pavarotti, Luciano (born 1935) Italian operatic tenor

Pears, Sir Peter (1910–86) English operatic tenor

Penderecki, Krzysztof (born 1933) Polish composer

Peterson, Oscar (Emmanuel) (born 1925) Canadian jazz pianist and composer

Piaf, Edith (born Edith Giovanna Gassion) (1915–63) French singer

Picasso, Pablo (1881–1973) Spanish painter, sculptor, and graphic artist, resident in France from 1904

Pisan, Christine de See DE PISAN

Pizan, Christine de See DE PISAN

Porter, Cole (1892–1964) American songwriter

Poulenc, Francis (Jean Marcel) (1899–1963) French composer

Presley, Elvis (Aaron) (1935–77) American rock-and-roll and pop singer

Previn, André (George) (born 1929) German-born American conductor, pianist, and composer

Prez, Josquin des See DES PREZ

Puccini, Giacomo (1858–1924) Italian composer

Purcell, Henry (1659–95) English composer

Rachmaninov, Sergei (Vasilevich) (1873–1943) Russian composer and pianist, resident in the US from 1917

Rameau, Jean-Philippe (1683–1764) French composer, musical theorist, and organist

Rattle, Sir Simon (Denis) (born 1955) English conductor

Ravel, Maurice (Joseph) (1875–1937) French composer

Redding, Otis (1941–67) American soul singer

Reed, Lou (full name Lewis Allan Reed) (born 1942) American rock singer, guitarist, and songwriter

Reich, Steve (born 1936) American composer

COMPOSERS, MUSICIANS, SINGERS, AND INSTRUMENT MAKERS (cont.)

Schifrin, Lalo

Reinhardt, Django (born Jean Baptiste Reinhardt) (1910–53) Belgian jazz guitarist

Respighi, Ottorino (1879–1936) Italian composer

Rice, Sir Tim(othy Miles Bindon) (born 1944) English lyricist and entertainer

Rich, Buddy (born Bernard Rich) (1917–87) American jazz drummer and band leader

Richard, Sir Cliff (born Harry Roger Webb) (born 1940) British pop singer, born in India

Rodgers, Richard (Charles) (1902–79) American composer

Romberg, Sigmund (1887–1951) Hungarian-born American composer

Ross, Diana (born 1944) American pop and soul singer

Rossini, Gioacchino Antonio (1792–1868) Italian composer

Rubbra, (Charles) Edmund (1901–86) English composer and pianist

Rubinstein, Anton (Grigorevich) (1829–94) Russian composer and pianist

Rubinstein, Artur (1888–1982) Polish-born American pianist

Saint-Saëns, (Charles) Camille (1835–1921) French composer, pianist, and organist

Salerno-Sonnenberg, Najda (born 1961) American violinist

Salieri, Antonio (1750–1825) Italian composer

Sargent, Sir (Henry) Malcolm (Watts) (1895–1967) English conductor and composer

Satie, Erik (Alfred Leslie) (1866–1925) French composer

Scarlatti, (Pietro) Alessandro (Gaspare) (1660–1725) Italian composer

Scarlatti, (Giuseppe) Domenico (1685–1757) Italian composer

Schoenberg, Arnold (1874–1951) Austrian-born American composer

Schubert, Franz (1797–1828) Austrian composer

Schumann, Clara (1819–96) German pianist and composer

Schumann, Robert (Alexander) (1810–56) German composer

Schütz, Heinrich (1585–1672) German composer and organist

Schwarzkopf, Dame (Olga Maria) Elisabeth (Friederike) (born 1915) German-born British soprano

Scriabin, Aleksandr (Nikolaevich) (also Skryabin) (1872–1915) Russian composer and pianist

Seeger, Pete (born 1919) American folk musician and songwriter

Segovia, Andrés (1893–1987) Spanish guitarist and composer

Shankar, Ravi (born 1920) Indian sitar player and composer

Sharp, Cecil (James) (1859–1924) English collector of folk-songs and folk-dances

Shostakovich, Dmitri (Dmitrievich) (1906–75) Russian composer

Sibelius, Jean (born Johan Julius Christian Sibelius) (1865–1957) Finnish composer

Simon, Paul (born 1942) American singer and songwriter

Sinatra, Frank (full name Francis Albert Sinatra) (1915–98) American singer and actor

Skryabin See SCRIABIN

Smetana, Bedrich (1824–84) Czech composer

Smith, Bessie (1894–1937) American blues singer

Smyth, Dame Ethel (1858–1944) British composer

Solti, Sir Georg (1912–97) Hungarian-born British conductor

Sondheim, Stephen (Joshua) (born 1930) American composer and lyricist

Sousa, John Philip (1854–1932) American composer and conductor

Spector, Phil (born 1940) American record producer

COMPOSERS, MUSICIANS, SINGERS, AND INSTRUMENT MAKERS (cont.)

Springsteen, Bruce (born 1949) American rock singer, songwriter, and guitarist

Stainer, Sir John (1840–1901) English composer

Stanford, Sir Charles (Villiers) (1852–1924) British composer, born in Ireland

Starr, Ringo (born Richard Starkey) (born 1940) English rock and pop drummer

Steinway, Henry (Engelhard) (born Heinrich Engelhard Steinweg) (1797–1871) German piano-builder, resident in the US from 1849

Stewart, Rod(erick David) (born 1945) English rock singer and songwriter

Stockhausen, Karlheinz (born 1928) German composer

Stokowski, Leopold (1882–1977) British-born American conductor, of Polish descent

Stradivari, Antonio (c. 1644–1737) Italian violin-maker

Strauss, Johann (known as Strauss the Elder) (1804–49) Austrian composer

Strauss, Johann (known as Strauss the Younger) (1825–99) Austrian composer

Strauss, Richard (1864–1949) German composer

Stravinsky, Igor (Fyodorovich) (1882–1971) Russian-born composer

Streisand, Barbra (Joan) (born 1942) American singer, actress, and film director

Sullivan, Sir Arthur (Seymour) (1842–1900) English composer

Sutherland, Dame Joan (born 1926) Australian operatic soprano

Tailleferre, Germaine (1892–1983) French composer and pianist

Tallis, Thomas (c. 1505–85) English composer

Tansen (c. 1500–89) Indian musician and singer

Tate, Phyllis (1911–87) British composer

Tatum, Arthur ('Art') (1910–56) American jazz pianist

Tchaikovsky, Pyotr (Ilich) (1840–93) Russian composer

Te Kanawa, Dame Kiri (Janette) (born 1944) New Zealand operatic soprano, resident in Britain since 1966

Telemann, Georg Philipp (1681–1767) German composer and organist

Theodorakis, Mikis (born 1925) Greek composer

Tippett, Sir Michael (Kemp) (1905–98) English composer

Tortelier, Paul (1914–90) French cellist

Toscanini, Arturo (1867–1957) Italian conductor

Turner, Tina (born Anna Mae Bullock) (born 1939) American rock and soul singer

Varèse, Edgar(d) (1883–1965) French-born American composer

Vaughan, Sarah (Lois) (1924–90) American jazz singer and pianist

Vaughan Williams, Ralph (1872–1958) English composer

Verdi, Giuseppe (Fortunino Francesco) (1813–1901) Italian composer

Victoria, Tomás Luis de (1548–1611) Spanish composer

Villa-Lobos, Heitor (1887–1959) Brazilian composer

Vivaldi, Antonio (Lucio) (1678–1741) Italian composer and violinist

Wagner, (Wilhelm) Richard (1813–83) German composer

Waller, Fats (born Thomas Wright Waller) (1904–43) American jazz musician and songwriter

Walton, Sir William (Turner) (1902–83) English composer

Waters, Muddy (born McKinley Morganfield) (1915–83) American blues singer and guitarist

Weber, Carl Maria von (1786–1826)

COMPOSERS, MUSICIANS, SINGERS, AND INSTRUMENT MAKERS (cont.)

German composer

Webern, Anton von (1883–1945) Austrian composer

Weill, Kurt (1900–50) German composer, resident in the US from 1935

Weir, Judith (born 1954) British composer

Williams, Hank (born Hiram King Williams) (1923–53) American country singer and songwriter

Williams, John (Christopher) (born 1941) Australian guitarist and composer

Wolf, Hugo (Philipp Jakob) (1860–1903) Austrian composer

Wonder, Stevie (born Steveland Judkins Morris) (born 1950) American singer, songwriter, and musician

Wood, Sir Henry (Joseph) (1869–1944) English conductor

Wynette, Tammy (born Tammy Wynette Pugh) (1942–98) American country singer

Xenakis, Iannis (born 1922) French composer and architect, of Greek descent

Young, Neil (Percival) (born 1945) Canadian singer, songwriter, and guitarist

Zappa, Frank (1940–93) American rock singer, musician, and songwriter

PEOPLE INVOLVED IN FILM, THEATRE, AND DANCE

Allen, Woody (born Allen Stewart Konigsberg) (born 1935) American film director, writer, and actor

Almodóvar, Pedro (born 1949) Spanish film director

Altman, Robert (born 1925) American film director

Anderson, Lindsay (Gordon) (1923–94) English film director

Andrews, Julie (born Julia Elizabeth Wells) (born 1935) English actress and singer

Antonioni, Michelangelo (born 1912) Italian film director

Artaud, Antonin (1896–1948) French actor, director, and poet

Ashcroft, Dame Peggy (Edith Margaret Emily) (1907–91) English actress

Ashton, Sir Frederick (William Mallandaine) (1904–88) British ballet-dancer and choreographer

Askey, Arthur (Bowden) (1900–82) English comedian and actor

Astaire, Fred (born Frederick Austerlitz) (1899–1987) American dancer, singer, and actor

Attenborough, Richard (Samuel), Baron Attenborough of Richmond-upon-Thames (born 1923) English film actor, producer, and director

Bacall, Lauren (born 1924) American actress

Baker, Josephine (1906–75) American dancer

Balanchine, George (born Georgi Melitonovich Balanchivadze) (1904–83) Russian-born American ballet-dancer and choreographer

Balcon, Sir Michael (1896–1977) English film producer

Ball, Lucille (1911–89) American comedienne

Bankhead, Tallulah (1903–68) American actress

Bardot, Brigitte (born Camille Javal) (born 1934) French actress

Barnum, P(hineas) T(aylor) (1810–91) American showman

Barrault, Jean-Louis (1910–94) French actor and director

Barrymore, Ethel (1879–1959) American actress

Barrymore, John (1882–1942) American actor

Barrymore, Lionel (1878–1954) American actor

Baryshnikov, Mikhail (Nikolaevich) (born 1948) American ballet-dancer, born in Latvia of Russian parents

Baylis, Lilian Mary (1874–1937) English theatre manager

Beatty, Warren (born Henry Warren Beaty) (born 1937) American actor, film director, and screenwriter

Béjart, Maurice (born Maurice Jean Berger) (born 1927) French choreographer

Benny, Jack (born Benjamin Kubelsky) (1894–1974) American comedian and actor

Bergman, (Ernst) Ingmar (born 1918) Swedish film and theatre director

Bergman, Ingrid (1915–82) Swedish actress

Berkeley, Busby (born William Berkeley Enos) (1895–1976) American choreographer and film director

Berkoff, Steven (born 1937) English dramatist, director, and actor

Bernhardt, Sarah (born Henriette Rosine Bernard) (1844–1923) French actress

Bertolucci, Bernardo (born 1940) Italian film director

Betterton, Thomas (1635–1710) English actor

Blondin, Charles (born Jean-François Gravelet) (1824–97) French acrobat

Bogarde, Sir Dirk (born Derek Niven van den Bogaerde) (born 1921) British actor and writer, of Dutch descent

Bogart, Humphrey (DeForest) (1899–1957) American actor

PEOPLE INVOLVED IN FILM, THEATRE, AND DANCE (cont.)

Boulting, John (1913–85) and **Roy** (born 1913) English film producers and directors

Bow, Clara (1905–65) American actress

Boyer, Charles (1897–1977) French-born American actor

Branagh, Kenneth (Charles) (born 1960) English actor, producer, and director

Brando, Marlon (born 1924) American actor

Bresson, Robert (born 1907) French film director

Brook, Peter (Stephen Paul) (born 1925) English theatre director

Brooks, Mel (born Melvin Kaminsky) (born 1927) American film director and actor

Bruce, Lenny (born Leonard Alfred Schneider) (1925–66) American comedian

Buffalo Bill (born William Frederick Cody) (1846–1917) American showman

Buñuel, Luis (1900–83) Spanish film director

Burbage, Richard (*c.* 1567–1619) English actor

Burns, George (born Nathan Birnbaum) (1896–1996) American comedian

Burton, Richard (born Richard Jenkins) (1925–84) Welsh actor

Cagney, James (1899–1986) American actor

Caine, Sir Michael (born Maurice Micklewhite) (born 1933) English film actor

Campbell, Mrs Patrick (*née* Beatrice Stella Tanner) (1865–1940) English actress

Campion, Jane (born 1954) New Zealand film director and screenwriter

Capra, Frank (1897–1991) Italian-born American film director

Carlyle, Robert (born 1962) Scottish actor

Carné, Marcel (1909–96) French film director

Carson, John William ('Johnny') (born 1925) American television personality

Chabrol, Claude (born 1930) French film director

Chaney, Lon (full name Alonso Chaney) (1883–1930) American actor

Chaplin, Sir Charles Spencer ('Charlie') (1889–1977) English film actor and director

Chevalier, Maurice (1888–1972) French singer and actor

Cibber, Colley (1671–1757) English actor, theatre manager, and dramatist

Clair, René (born René Lucien Chomette) (1898–1981) French film director

Cleese, John (Marwood) (born 1939) English comic actor and writer

Clift, (Edward) Montgomery (1920–66) American actor

Cochran, Sir C(harles) B(lake) (1872–1951) English theatrical producer

Cody, William Frederick See BUFFALO BILL

Collins, Joan (Henrietta) (born 1933) English actress

Connery, Sean (born Thomas Connery) (born 1930) Scottish actor

Connolly, Billy (born 1942) Scottish comedian and actor

Cook, Peter (Edward) (1937–94) English comedian and actor

Cooper, Gary (born Frank James Cooper) (1901–61) American actor

Coppola, Francis Ford (born 1939) American film director, writer, and producer

Coward, Sir Noel (Pierce) (1899–1973) English dramatist, actor, and composer

Crawford, Joan (born Lucille le

PEOPLE INVOLVED IN FILM, THEATRE, AND DANCE (cont.)

Sueur) (1908–77) American actress
Cruft, Charles (1852–1939) English
showman
Cunningham, Merce (born 1919)
American dancer and
choreographer
Cushing, Peter (1913–94) English
actor
Davis, Bette (born Ruth Elizabeth
Davis) (1908–89) American actress
Day, Doris (born Doris Kappelhoff)
(born 1924) American actress and
singer
Dean, James (born James Byron)
(1931–55) American actor
**Delfont, Bernard, Baron Delfont of
Stepney** (born Boris Winogradsky)
(1909–94) British impresario, born
in Russia
de Mille, Cecil B(lount) (1881–1959)
American film producer and
director
Dench, Dame Judi(th Olivia) (born
1934) English actress
Deneuve, Catherine (born Catherine
Dorléac) (born 1943) French
actress
De Niro, Robert (born 1943)
American actor
Depardieu, Gérard (born 1948)
French actor
De Sica, Vittorio (1901–74) Italian
film director and actor
de Valois, Dame Ninette (born Edris
Stannus) (born 1898) Irish
choreographer, ballet-dancer, and
teacher
Diaghilev, Sergei (Pavlovich)
(1872–1929) Russian ballet
impresario
Dietrich, Marlene (born Maria
Magdelene von Losch) (1901–92)
German-born American actress
and singer
Dimbleby, (Frederick) Richard
(1913–65) English broadcaster
Disney, Walter Elias ('Walt')
(1901–66) American animator and
film producer
Dolin, Sir Anton (born Sydney

Francis Patrick Chippendall
Healey-Kay) (1904–83) English
ballet-dancer and choreographer
D'Oyly Carte, Richard (1844–1901)
English impresario and producer
Duncan, Isadora (1878–1927)
American dancer and teacher
Duse, Eleonora (1858–1924) Italian
actress
Eastwood, Clint (born 1930)
American film actor and director
Eisenstein, Sergei (Mikhailovich)
(1898–1948) Soviet film director,
born in Latvia
Evans, Dame Edith (Mary)
(1888–1976) English actress
Fairbanks, Douglas (Elton) (born
Julius Ullman) (1883–1939)
American actor
Fassbinder, Rainer Werner
(1946–82) German film director
Fellini, Federico (1920–93) Italian
film director
Fields, Dame Gracie (born Grace
Stansfield) (1898–1979) English
singer and comedienne
Fields, W. C. (1880–1946) American
film actor
Flynn, Errol (born Leslie Thomas
Flynn) (1909–59) Australian-born
American actor
Fokine, Michel (born Mikhail
Mikhailovich Fokin) (1880–1942)
Russian-born American dancer
and choreographer
Fonda, Henry (1905–82) American
actor
Fonda, Jane (born 1937) American
actress
Fonda, Peter (born 1939) American
actor
Fonteyn, Dame Margot (born
Margaret Hookham) (1919–91)
English ballet-dancer
Ford, Harrison (born 1942)
American actor
Ford, John (born Sean Aloysius
O'Feeney) (1895–1973) American
film director
Forman, Milos (born 1932) Czech-

PEOPLE INVOLVED IN FILM, THEATRE, AND DANCE (cont.)

born American film director

Formby, George (born George Booth) (1904–61) English comedian

Foster, Jodie (born 1962) American film actress

Gable, (William) Clark (1901–60) American actor

Gance, Abel (1889–1991) French film director

Garbo, Greta (born Greta Gustafsson) (1905–90) Swedish-born American actress

Gardner, Ava (Lavinia) (1922–90) American actress

Garland, Judy (born Frances Gumm) (1922–69) American singer and actress

Garrick, David (1717–79) English actor, manager, and dramatist

Gibson, Mel (Columcille Gerard) (born 1956) American-born Australian actor and director

Gielgud, Sir (Arthur) John (born 1904) English actor and director

Gish, Lillian (1896–1993) American actress

Goldwyn, Samuel (born Schmuel Gelbfisz; changed to Goldfish then Goldwyn) (1882–1974) Polish-born American film producer

Grade, Lew, Baron Grade of Elstree (born Louis Winogradsky) (born 1906) British television producer and executive, born in Russia

Graham, Martha (1893–1991) American dancer, teacher, and choreographer

Grant, Cary (born Alexander Archibald Leach) (1904–86) British-born American actor

Granville-Barker, Harley (1877–1946) English dramatist, critic, theatre director, and actor

Greenaway, Peter (born 1942) English film director

Grenfell, Joyce (Irene Phipps) (1910–79) English entertainer and writer

Grierson, John (1898–1972) Scottish

film director and producer

Griffith, D(avid) W(ark) (1875–1948) American film director

Grimaldi, Joseph (1779–1837) English circus entertainer

Guinness, Sir Alec (born 1914) English actor

Gwynn, Eleanor ('Nell') (1650–87) English actress

Hancock, Tony (full name Anthony John Hancock) (1924–68) English comedian

Hanks, Tom (Thomas J.) (born 1956) American film actor

Hardy, Oliver See LAUREL AND HARDY

Harlow, Jean (born Harlean Carpenter) (1911–37) American film actress

Harrison, Sir Rex (born Reginald Carey Harrison) (1908–90) English actor

Hawks, Howard (1896–1977) American film director, producer, and screenwriter

Hay, Will(iam Thomson) (1888–1949) English actor and comedian

Hayworth, Rita (born Margarita Carmen Cansino) (1918–87) American actress and dancer

Head, Edith (1907–81) American costume designer

Helpmann, Sir Robert (Murray) (1909–86) Australian ballet-dancer, choreographer, director, and actor

Hepburn, Audrey (1929–93) British actress, born in Belgium

Hepburn, Katharine (born 1909) American actress

Herzog, Werner (born Werner Stipetic) (born 1942) German film director

Hill, Benny (born Alfred Hawthorne) (1925–92) English comedian

Hitchcock, Sir Alfred (Joseph) (1899–1980) English film director

Hoffman, Dustin (Lee) (born 1937) American actor

Hope, Bob (born Leslie Townes Hope) (born 1903) British-born

PEOPLE INVOLVED IN FILM, THEATRE, AND DANCE (cont.)

American comedian

Hopkins, Sir Anthony (Philip) (born 1937) Welsh actor

Hordern, Sir Michael (Murray) (1911–95) English actor

Houdini, Harry (born Erik Weisz) (1874–1926) Hungarian-born American magician and escape artist

Howard, Leslie (born Leslie Howard Stainer) (1893–1943) English actor

Howard, Trevor (Wallace) (1916–88) English actor

Hughes, Howard (Robard) (1905–76) American industrialist, film producer, and aviator

Humphries, (John) Barry (born 1934) Australian comedian

Huston, John (1906–87) American-born film director

Irving, Sir Henry (born Henry Brodribb) (1838–1905) English actor-manager

Ivory, James (born 1928) American film director

Jackson, Glenda (born 1936) English actress and politician

Jarman, Derek (1942–94) English film director

Jewison, Norman (born 1926) Canadian film director and producer

Jolson, Al (born Asa Yoelson) (1886–1950) Russian-born American singer, film actor, and comedian

Kapoor, (Prithvi) Raj (1924–88) Indian actor and director

Karloff, Boris (born William Henry Pratt) (1887–1969) British-born American actor

Kaye, Danny (born David Daniel Kominski) (1913–87) American actor and comedian

Kazan, Elia (born Elia Kazanjoglous) (born 1909) Turkish-born American film and theatre director

Kean, Edmund (1787–1833) English actor

Keaton, Buster (born Joseph Francis Keaton) (1895–1966) American actor and director

Kelly, Gene (born Eugene Curran Kelly) (1912–96) American dancer and choreographer

Kelly, Grace (Patricia) (also called (from 1956) Princess Grace of Monaco) (1928–82) American film actress

Kemble, John Philip (1757–1823) English actor-manager, brother of Sarah Siddons

Kemble, Frances Anne ('Fanny') (1809–93) English actress

Kieslowski, Krzysztof (1941–96) Polish film director

Korda, Sir Alexander (born Sándor Kellner) (1893–1956) Hungarian-born British film producer and director

Kubrick, Stanley (born 1928) American film director, producer, and writer

Kurosawa, Akira (1910–98) Japanese film director

Laban, Rudolf von (1879–1958) Hungarian choreographer and dancer

Lancaster, Burt(on Stephen) (1913–94) American film actor

Lang, Fritz (1890–1976) Austrian-born film director

Langtry, Lillie (born Emilie Charlotte le Breton) (1853–1929) British actress

Lauder, Sir Harry (born Hugh MacLennan Lauder) (1870–1950) Scottish music-hall performer

Laughton, Charles (1899–1962) British-born American actor

Laurel and Hardy, Stan Laurel (born Arthur Stanley Jefferson) (1890–1965) and **Oliver Hardy** (1892–1957) American comedy duo

Lean, Sir David (1908–91) English film director

Lee, Bruce (born Lee Yuen Kam) (1941–73) American actor

Lee, Christopher (Frank Carandini)

PEOPLE INVOLVED IN FILM, THEATRE, AND DANCE (cont.)

(born 1922) English actor

Lee, Gypsy Rose (born Rose Louise Hovick) (1914–70) American striptease artist

Lee, Spike (born Shelton Jackson Lee) (born 1957) American film director and actor

Leigh, Vivien (born Vivian Mary Hartley) (1913–67) British actress, born in India

Lemmon, Jack (born John Uhler) (born 1925) American actor

Littlewood, (Maud) Joan (1914–91) English theatre director

Lloyd, Harold (Clayton) (1893–1971) American film comedian

Lloyd, Marie (born Matilda Alice Victoria Wood) (1870–1922) English music-hall entertainer

Loach, Ken(neth) (born 1936) English film director

Loren, Sophia (born Sophia Scicolone) (born 1934) Italian actress

Lorre, Peter (born Laszlo Lowenstein) (1904–64) Hungarian-born American actor

Lucas, George (born 1944) American film director, producer, and screenwriter

Lugosi, Bela (born Béla Ferenc Blasko) (1884–1956) Hungarian-born American actor

Lumière, Auguste Marie Louis Nicholas (1862–1954) and **Louis Jean** (1864–1948) French inventors and pioneers of cinema

McGregor, Ewan (born 1971) Scottish actor

Malle, Louis (1932–95) French film director

Marceau, Marcel (born 1923) French mime artist

Markova, Dame Alicia (born Lilian Alicia Marks) (born 1910) English ballet-dancer

Martin, Dean (born Dino Paul Crocetti) (1917–95) American singer and actor

Martin, Steve (born 1945) American

actor and comedian

Marx, Chico (Leonard) (1886–1961) American comic actor

Marx, Groucho (Julius Henry) (1890–1977) American comic actor

Marx, Gummo (Milton) (1893–1977) American comic actor

Marx, Harpo (Adolph) (1888–1964) American comic actor

Marx, Zeppo (Herbert) (1901–1979) American comic actor

Mason, James (Neville) (1909–84) English actor

Massine, Léonide Fëdorovich (born Leonid Fëdorovich Myassin) (1895–1979) Russian-born choreographer and ballet dancer

Mayer, Louis B(urt) (born Eliezer Mayer) (1885–1957) Russian-born American film executive

Merchant, Ismail (born 1936) Indian film producer

Mercouri, Melina (born Anna Amalia Mercouri) (1925–94) Greek actress and politician

Milligan, Spike (born Terence Alan Milligan) (born 1918) British comedian and writer, born in India

Mills, Sir John (Lewis Ernest Watts) (born 1908) English actor

Mitchum, Robert (1917–97) American actor

Monroe, Marilyn (born Norma Jean Mortenson, later Baker) (1926–62) American actress

Montez, Lola (born Marie Dolores Eliza Rosanna Gilbert) Irish dancer

Moore, Dudley (Stuart John) (born 1935) English actor, comedian, and musician

Moreau, Jeanne (born 1928) French actress

Morecambe, Eric (born John Eric Bartholomew) (1926–84) English comedian

Murnau, Friedrich W. (1889–1931) German film director

Neill, Sam (born Nigel John Dermot) (born 1947) New Zealand actor

PEOPLE INVOLVED IN FILM, THEATRE, AND DANCE (cont.)

Newman, Paul (born 1925) American actor and film director

Nicholson, Jack (born 1937) American actor and director

Nijinsky, Vaslav (Fomich) (1890–1950) Russian ballet-dancer and choreographer

Niro, Robert De See DE NIRO

Noverre, Jean-Georges (1727–1810) French choreographer and dance theorist

Nureyev, Rudolf (1939–93) Russian-born ballet-dancer and choreographer

Olivier, Laurence (Kerr), Baron Olivier of Brighton (1907–89) English actor and director

O'Toole, (Seamus) Peter (born 1932) Irish-born British actor

Pacino, Al(fred) (born 1940) American film actor

Park, Nick (born 1958) English animator

Pasolini, Pier Paolo (1922–75) Italian film director and novelist

Pathé, Charles (1863–1957) French film pioneer

Pavlova, Anna (Pavlovna) (1881–1931) Russian dancer, resident in Britain from 1912

Peck, (Eldred) Gregory (born 1916) American actor

Petipa, Marius (Ivanovich) (1818–1910) French ballet-dancer and choreographer, resident in Russia from 1847

Pickford, Mary (born Gladys Mary Smith) (1893–1979) Canadian-born American actress

Poitier, Sidney (born 1924) American actor and film director

Polanski, Roman (born 1933) French film director, of Polish descent

Powell, Michael (Latham) (1905–90) English film director, producer, and screenwriter

Preminger, Otto (Ludwig) (1906–86) Austrian-born American film director

Price, Vincent (1911–93) American stage and film actor

Prokofiev, Sergei (Sergeevich) (1891–1953) Russian composer

Puttnam, Sir David (Terence) (born 1941) English film director

Rambert, Dame Marie (born Cyvia Rambam) (1888–1982) British ballet-dancer, teacher, and director, born in Poland

Rank, J(oseph) Arthur, 1st Baron (1888–1972) English industrialist and film executive, founder of the Rank Organization

Ray, Satyajit (1921–92) Indian film director

Redford, (Charles) Robert (born 1936) American film actor

Redgrave, Corin (born 1939) English actor

Redgrave, Lynn (born 1943) English actress

Redgrave, Sir Michael (1908–85) English actor

Redgrave, Vanessa (born 1937) English actress

Reed, Sir Carol (1906–76) English film director

Reinhardt, Max (born Max Goldmann) (1873–1943) Austrian theatre director and impresario

Renoir, Jean (1894–1979) French film director, son of Auguste

Resnais, Alain (born 1922) French film director

Richardson, Sir Ralph (David) (1902–83) English actor

Riefenstahl, Leni (full name Bertha Helene Amalie Riefenstahl) (born 1902) German film-maker, photographer, and Nazi propagandist

Roddenberry, Gene (full name Eugene Wesley Roddenberry) (1921–91) American television producer and scriptwriter

Roeg, Nicholas (Jack) (born 1928) English film director

Rogers, Ginger (born Virginia Katherine McMath) (1911–95) American actress and dancer

PEOPLE INVOLVED IN FILM, THEATRE, AND DANCE (cont.)

Rooney, Mickey (born Joseph Yule Jr.) (born 1920) American actor

Roscius (full name Quintus Roscius Gallus) (died 62 BC) Roman actor

Rossellini, Roberto (1906–77) Italian film director

Russell, Ken (born Henry Kenneth Alfred Russell) (born 1927) English film director

Rutherford, Dame Margaret (1892–1972) English actress

Schwarzenegger, Arnold (born 1947) Austrian-born American film actor

Scorsese, Martin (born 1942) American film director

Scott, Ridley (born 1939) English film director

Sellers, Peter (1925–80) English comic actor

Selznick, David O(liver) (1902–65) American film producer

Seymour, Lynn (born 1939) Canadian ballet-dancer

Shankar, Uday (1900–77) Indian dancer

Shearer, Moira (full name Moira Shearer King) (born 1926) Scottish ballet-dancer and actress

Siddons, Mrs Sarah (*née* Kemble) (1755–1831) English actress

Spielberg, Steven (born 1947) American film director and producer

Stanislavsky, Konstantin (Sergeevich) (born Konstantin Sergeevich Alekseev) (1863–1938) Russian theatre director and actor

Stewart, James (Maitland) (1908–97) American actor

Stone, Oliver (born 1946) American film director, screenwriter, and producer

Strasberg, Lee (born Israel Strassberg) (1901–82) American actor, director, and drama teacher, born in Austria

Streep, Meryl (born Mary Louise Streep) (born 1949) American actress

Swanson, Gloria (born Gloria May Josephine Svensson) (1899–1983) American actress

Tarantino, Quentin (Jerome) (born 1963) American film director, screenwriter, and actor

Tarkovsky, Andrei (Arsenevich) (1932–86) Russian film director

Tati, Jacques (born Jacques Tatischeff) (1908–82) French film director and actor

Taylor, Elizabeth (born 1932) American actress, born in England

Tempest, Dame Marie (born Mary Susan Etherington) (1864–1942) English actress

Temple, Shirley (latterly Shirley Temple Black) (born 1928) American child star

Terry, Dame (Alice) Ellen (1847–1928) English actress

Thompson, Emma (born 1959) English actress and screenwriter

Thorndike, Dame (Agnes) Sybil (1882–1976) English actress

Tracy, Spencer (1900–67) American actor

Truffaut, François (1932–84) French film director

Ulanova, Galina (Sergeevna) (1910–98) Russian ballet-dancer

Ustinov, Sir Peter (Alexander) (born 1921) British actor, director, and dramatist, of Russian descent

Valentino, Rudolph (born Rodolfo Guglielmi di Valentina d'Antonguolla) (1895–1926) Italian-born American actor

Valois, Dame Ninette de See DE VALOIS

Vigo, Jean (1905–34) French film director

Visconti, Luchino (full name Don Luchino Visconti, Conte di Modrone) (1906–76) Italian film and theatre director

von Sternberg, Josef (1894–1969) Austrian-born American film director

Wajda, Andrzej (born 1929) Polish

PEOPLE INVOLVED IN FILM, THEATRE, AND DANCE (cont.)

film director

Wayne, John (born Marion Michael Morrison; known as 'the Duke') (1907–79) American actor

Weissmuller, John Peter ('Johnny') (1904–84) American swimmer and actor

Welles, (George) Orson (1915–85) American film director and actor

West, Mae (1892–1980) American actress and dramatist

Wilder, Billy (born Samuel Wilder) (born 1906) American film director

and screenwriter, born in Austria

Wood, Natalie (1938–81) American actress

Zanuck, Darryl F(rancis) (1902–79) American film producer

Zeffirelli, Franco (born Gianfranco Corsi) (born 1923) Italian film and theatre director

Ziegfeld, Florenz (1869–1932) American theatre manager

Zinnemann, Fred (1907–97) Austrian-born American film director

WRITERS, PHILOSOPHERS, AND SCHOLARS

Abelard, Peter (1079–1142) French scholar, theologian, and philosopher

Achebe, Chinua (born Albert Chinualumgu) (born 1930) Nigerian novelist, poet, short-story writer, and essayist

Addison, Joseph (1672–1719) English poet, dramatist, essayist, and Whig politician

Adorno, Theodor Wiesengrund (born Theodor Wiesengrund) (1903–69) German philosopher, sociologist, and musicologist

AE, pseudonym of George William RUSSELL

Aelfric (c. 955–c. 1020) Anglo-Saxon writer

Aeschylus (c. 525–456 BC) Greek tragic dramatist

Aesop (6th century BC) Greek storyteller

Agnesi, Maria Gaetana (1718–99) Italian philosopher and mathematician

Akhmatova, Anna (pseudonym of Anna Andreevna Gorenko)

(1889–1966) Russian poet

Alain-Fournier (pseudonym of Henri-Alban Fournier) (1886–1914) French novelist

Alarcón, Pedro Antonio de (1833–91) Spanish novelist

Alarcón y Mendoza, Juan Ruiz de (1581–1639) Spanish dramatist

Albee, Edward Franklin (born 1928) American dramatist

Albertus Magnus, St (known as Saint Albert the Great) (c. 1200–80) German bishop, philosopher, and Doctor of the Church

Alcaeus (6th century BC) Greek lyric poet

Alcott, Louisa May (1832–88) American novelist

Aldiss, Brian W(ilson) (born 1925) English novelist and critic

Aldus Manutius (Latinized name of Teobaldo Manucci; also known as Aldo Manuzio) (1450–1515) Italian scholar, printer, and publisher

Algren, Nelson (Abraham) (1909–81) American novelist

Althusser, Louis (1918–90) French

WRITERS, PHILOSOPHERS, AND SCHOLARS (cont.)

philosopher

Amis, Sir Kingsley (1922–95) English
novelist and poet

Amis, Martin (Louis) (born 1949)
English novelist, son of Kingsley
Amis

Anacreon (6th century BC) Greek
lyric poet

Anaxagoras (c. 500–428 BC) Greek
philosopher

Anaximander (c. 610–c. 546 BC)
Greek philosopher

Anaximenes (6th century BC) Greek
philosopher

Andersen, Hans Christian (1805–75)
Danish writer

Andrić, Ivo (1892–1975) Serbian
writer

Angelou, Maya (born 1928)
American novelist and poet

Anouilh, Jean (1910–87) French
dramatist

Anselm of Canterbury, St (c.
1033–1109) Italian theologian and
philosopher, archbishop, and
Doctor of the Church

Apollinaire, Guillaume (pseudonym
of Wilhelm Apollinaris de
Kostrowitzki) (1880–1918) French
poet

Apollonius (known as Apollonius of
Rhodes) (3rd century BC) Greek
poet

Apuleius (2nd century AD) Roman
writer and rhetorician

Archilochus (8th or 7th century BC)
Greek poet

Arendt, Hannah (1906–75) German-
born American philosopher and
political theorist

Ariosto, Ludovico (1474–1533)
Italian poet

Aristarchus (known as Aristarchus
of Samothrace) (c. 217–145 BC)
Greek critic and grammarian

Aristippus (known as Aristippus the
Elder) (late 5th century BC), Greek
philosopher

Aristophanes (c. 450–c. 385 BC)
Greek comic dramatist

Aristotle (384–322 BC) Greek
philosopher and scientist

Arnold, Matthew (1822–88) English
poet, essayist, and social critic

Ascham, Roger (1515–68) English
scholar and writer

Asimov, Isaac (1920–92) Russian-
born American writer and scientist

Asturias, Miguel Ángel (1899–1974)
Guatemalan novelist

Atwood, Margaret (Eleanor) (born
1939) Canadian novelist, poet,
critic, and short-story writer

Aubrey, John (1626–97) English
antiquarian and author

Auden, W(ystan) H(ugh) (1907–73)
British-born poet

Austen, Jane (1775–1817) English
novelist

Austin, John (1790–1859) English
jurist

Austin, John Langshaw (1911–60)
English philosopher

Averroës (1126–98) Spanish-Arabian
philosopher

Avicenna (Arabic name ibn-Sina)
(980–1037) Persian-born Islamic
philosopher and physician

Awdry, Reverend W(ilbert) V(ere)
(born 1911) English writer of
children's stories

Ayckbourn, Sir Alan (born 1939)
English dramatist

Ayer, Sir A(lfred) J(ules) (1910–89)
English philosopher

Bagehot, Walter (1826–77) English
economist and journalist

Baldwin, James (Arthur) (1924–87)
American novelist

Ballantyne, R(obert) M(ichael)
(1825–94) Scottish writer

Ballard, J(ames) G(raham) (born
1930) British novelist and short-
story writer, born in China

Balzac, Honoré de (1799–1850)
French novelist

Barbour, John (c. 1320–95) Scottish
poet and prelate

Barker, George (Granville) (1913–91)
English poet

WRITERS, PHILOSOPHERS, AND SCHOLARS (cont.)

Barrett, Elizabeth See BROWNING

Barrie, Sir J(ames) M(atthew) (1860–1937) Scottish dramatist and novelist

Barth, John (Simmons) (born 1930) American novelist and short-story writer

Barthes, Roland (1915–80) French writer and critic

Bates, H(erbert) E(rnest) (1905–74) English novelist and short-story writer

Baudelaire, Charles (Pierre) (1821–67) French poet and critic

Baudrillard, Jean (born 1929) French sociologist and cultural critic

Baxter, James K(eir) (1926–72) New Zealand poet, dramatist, and critic

Beaumarchais, Pierre Augustin Caron de (1732–99) French dramatist

Beaumont, Francis (1584–1616) English dramatist

Beauvoir, Simone de See DE BEAUVOIR

Beckett, Samuel (Barclay) (1906–89) Irish dramatist, novelist, and poet

Beckford, William (1759–1844) English writer and collector

Beerbohm, Sir Henry Maximilian ('Max') (1872–1956) English caricaturist, essayist, and critic

Beeton, Mrs Isabella Mary (1836–65) English writer on cookery

Behan, Brendan (Francis) (1923–64) Irish dramatist and poet

Behn, Aphra (1640–89) English novelist and dramatist

Bell, Currer, Ellis, and Acton, pseudonyms used by Charlotte, Emily, and Anne BRONTË

Bell, Gertrude (1868–1926) English archaeologist and writer

Belloc, (Joseph) Hilaire (Pierre René) (1870–1953) French-born British writer, historian, and poet, of French–British descent

Bellow, Saul (born 1915) Canadian-born American novelist, of Russian Jewish descent

Bennett, Alan (born 1934) English dramatist and actor

Bennett, (Enoch) Arnold (1867–1931) English novelist, dramatist, and critic

Bentham, Jeremy (1748–1832) English philosopher and jurist

Bentley, Edmund Clerihew (1875–1956) English journalist and novelist

Bergerac See CYRANO DE BERGERAC

Bergson, Henri (Louis) (1859–1941) French philosopher

Berkeley, George (1685–1753) Irish philosopher and bishop

Berlin, Sir Isaiah (1909–97) Latvian-born British philosopher

Bertillon, Alphonse (1853–1914) French criminologist

Besant, Annie (1847–1933) English writer, theosophist, and political campaigner

Betjeman, Sir John (1906–84) English poet

Betti, Ugo (1892–1953) Italian dramatist, poet, and short-story writer

Bierce, Ambrose (Gwinnett) (1842–c. 1914) American writer

Bishop, Elizabeth (1911–79) American poet

Blackmore, R(ichard) D(oddridge) (1825–1900) English novelist and poet

Blackstone, Sir William (1723–80) English jurist

Blackwood, Algernon (Henry) (1869–1951) English writer

Blake, William (1757–1827) English poet and artist

Blixen, Karen (Christentze), Baroness Blixen-Finecke (née Dinesen; also known by the pseudonym of Isak Dinesen) (1885–1962) Danish novelist and short-story writer

Bloomfield, Leonard (1887–1949) American linguist

Blunden, Edmund (Charles) (1896–1974) English poet and critic

WRITERS, PHILOSOPHERS, AND SCHOLARS (cont.)

Blyton, Enid (1897–1968) English writer of children's fiction

Boccaccio, Giovanni (1313–75) Italian writer, poet, and humanist

Boileau, Nicholas (full surname Boileau-Despréaux) (1636–1711) French critic and poet

Boldrewood, Rolf (pseudonym of Thomas Alexander Browne) (1826–1915) Australian novelist

Böll, Heinrich (Theodor) (1917–85) German novelist and short-story writer

Bolt, Robert (Oxton) (1924–95) English dramatist and screenwriter

Bond, Edward (born 1934) English dramatist

Borges, Jorge Luis (1899–1986) Argentinian poet, short-story writer, and essayist

Borrow, George (Henry) (1803–81) English writer

Boswell, James (1740–95) Scottish author and biographer

Bowen, Elizabeth (Dorothea Cole) (1899–1973) British novelist and short-story writer, born in Ireland

Bowles, Paul (Frederick) (born 1910) American writer and composer

Boz, pseudonym used by Charles DICKENS in his *The Pickwick Papers* and contributions to the Morning Chronicle

Bradbury, Malcolm (Stanley) (born 1932) English novelist, critic, and academic

Bradbury, Ray (Douglas) (born 1920) American writer of science fiction

Braille, Louis (1809–52) French educationist

Braine, John (Gerard) (1922–86) English novelist

Brecht, (Eugen) Bertolt (Friedrich) (1898–1956) German dramatist, producer, and poet

Breton, André (1896–1966) French poet, essayist, and critic

Bridges, Robert (Seymour) (1844–1930) English poet and literary critic

Brink, André (born 1935) South African novelist, short-story writer, and dramatist

Brodsky, Joseph (born Iosif Aleksandrovich Brodsky) (1940–96) Russian-born American poet

Brontë, Charlotte (1816–55), **Emily** (1818–48), and **Anne** (1820–49), English novelists

Brooke, Rupert (Chawner) (1887–1915) English poet

Brookner, Anita (born 1928) English novelist and art historian

Brooks, Cleanth (1906–94) American teacher and critic

Browning, Elizabeth Barrett (1806–61) English poet

Browning, Robert (1812–89) English poet

Bruno, Giordano (1548–1600) Italian philosopher

Buber, Martin (1878–1965) Israeli religious philosopher, born in Austria

Buchan, John, 1st Baron Tweedsmuir (1875–1940) Scottish novelist and statesman

Buck, Pearl S(ydenstricker) (1892–1973) American writer

Bulwer-Lytton See LYTTON

Bunin, Ivan (Alekseevich) (1870–1953) Russian poet and prose-writer

Bunting, Basil (1900–85) English poet and journalist

Bunyan, John (1628–88) English writer

Burgess, Anthony (pseudonym of John Anthony Burgess Wilson) (1917–93) English novelist and critic

Burke, Edmund (1729–97) Irish politician, philosopher, and writer

Burke, John (1787–1848) Irish genealogical and heraldic writer

Burnett, Frances (Eliza) Hodgson (1849–1924) British-born American novelist

WRITERS, PHILOSOPHERS, AND SCHOLARS (cont.)

Burney, Frances ('Fanny')
(1752–1840) English novelist
Burns, Robert (1759–96) Scottish
poet
Burroughs, Edgar Rice (1875–1950)
American novelist and writer of
science fiction
Burroughs, William S(eward)
(1914–97) American novelist
Burton, Sir Richard (Francis)
(1821–90) English explorer,
anthropologist, and translator
Butler, Samuel (1835–1902) English
novelist
Butler, Samuel ('Hudibras')
(1612–80) English poet
Byatt, A(ntonia) S(usan) (born 1936)
English novelist and literary critic
Byron, George Gordon, 6th Baron
(1788–1824) English poet
Caedmon (7th century) English poet
and monk
Calderón de la Barca, Pedro
(1600–81) Spanish dramatist and
poet
Caldwell, Erskine (Preston)
(1903–87) American novelist and
short-story writer
Callimachus (c. 305–c. 240 BC) Greek
poet and scholar
Calvino, Italo (1923–87) Italian
novelist and short-story writer,
born in Cuba
Camões, Luis (Vaz) de (also
Camoëns) (c. 1524–80) Portuguese
poet
**Campbell, (Ignatius) Roy(ston
Dunnachie)** (1901–57) South
African poet
Campbell, Thomas (1777–1844)
Scottish poet
Camus, Albert (1913–60) French
novelist, dramatist, and essayist
Canetti, Elias (1905–94) Bulgarian-
born British writer
Čapek, Karel (1890–1938) Czech
novelist and dramatist
Capote, Truman (born Truman
Streckfus Persons) (1924–84)
American writer

Carlyle, Thomas (1795–1881)
Scottish historian and political
philosopher
Carnap, Rudolf (1891–1970)
German-born American
philosopher
Carr, Emily (1871–1945) Canadian
writer and painter
Carroll, Lewis (pseudonym of
Charles Lutwidge Dodgson)
(1832–98) English writer
Carter, Angela (1940–92) English
novelist and short-story writer
**Cartland, Dame (Mary) Barbara
(Hamilton)** (born 1901) English
writer
Cary, (Arthur) Joyce (Lunel)
(1888–1957) English novelist
Cather, Willa (Sibert) (1876–1974)
American novelist and short-story
writer
Catullus, Gaius Valerius (c. 84–c. 54
BC) Roman poet
Cavafy, Constantine (Peter) (born
Konstantinos Petrou Kavafis)
(1863–1933) Greek poet
Céline, Louis-Ferdinand
(pseudonym of Louis-Ferdinand
Destouches) (1894–1961) French
novelist
Cervantes, Miguel de (full surname
Cervantes Saavedra) (1547–1616)
Spanish novelist and dramatist
Champollion, Jean-François
(1790–1832) French Egyptologist
Chandler, Raymond (Thornton)
(1888–1959) American novelist
Chapman, George (c. 1560–1634)
English poet and dramatist
**Chateaubriand, François-René,
Vicomte de** (1768–1848) French
writer and diplomat
Chatterton, Thomas (1752–70)
English poet
Chaucer, Geoffrey (c. 1342–1400)
English poet
Cheever, John (1912–82) American
short-story writer and novelist
Chekhov, Anton (Pavlovich)
(1860–1904) Russian dramatist and

WRITERS, PHILOSOPHERS, AND SCHOLARS (cont.)

short-story writer

Chesterton, G(ilbert) K(eith)
(1874–1936) English essayist,
novelist, and critic

Chomsky, (Avram) Noam (born
1928) American theoretical linguist
and political activist

Chopin, Kate (O'Flaherty)
(1851–1904) American novelist
and short-story writer

Chrétien de Troyes (12th century)
French poet

Christie, Dame Agatha (1890–1976)
English writer of detective fiction

Churchill, Caryl (born 1938) English
dramatist

Cicero, Marcus Tullius (106–43 BC)
Roman statesman, orator, and
writer

Clare, John (1793–1864) English
poet

Clarke, Sir Arthur C(harles) (born
1917) English writer of science
fiction

Clarke, Marcus (Andrew Hislop)
(1846–81) British-born Australian
writer

Clemens, Samuel Langhorne See
TWAIN

Clough, Arthur Hugh (1819–61)
English poet

Cobbett, William (1763–1835)
English writer and political
reformer

Cocteau, Jean (1889–1963) French
dramatist, novelist, and film
director

Coetzee, J(ohn) M(axwell) (born
1940) South African novelist

Coleridge, Samuel Taylor
(1772–1834) English poet, critic,
and philosopher

Colette (born Sidonie Gabrielle
Claudine) (1873–1954) French
novelist

Collins, (William) Wilkie (1824–89)
English novelist

Compton-Burnett, Dame Ivy
(1884–1969) English novelist

Comte, Auguste (1798–1857) French

philosopher, one of the founders
of sociology

Conan Doyle See DOYLE

Conegliano, Emmanuele See DA
PONTE

Confucius (Latinized name of K'ung
Fu-tzu = 'Kong the master')
(551–479 BC) Chinese philosopher

Congreve, William (1670–1729)
English dramatist

Connolly, Cyril (Vernon) (1903–74)
English writer

Conrad, Joseph (born Józef Teodor
Konrad Korzeniowski) (1857–1924)
Polish-born British novelist

Cookson, Dame Catherine (Anne)
(1906–98) English writer

Cooper, James Fenimore
(1789–1851) American novelist

Corelli, Marie (pseudonym of Mary
Mackay) (1855–1924) English
writer of romantic fiction

Corneille, Pierre (1606–84) French
dramatist

Coward, Sir Noel (Pierce)
(1899–1973) English dramatist,
actor, and composer

Cowper, William (1731–1800)
English poet

Crabbe, George (1754–1832) English
poet

Crane, (Harold) Hart (1899–1932)
American poet

Crane, Stephen (1871–1900)
American writer

Croce, Benedetto (1866–1952)
Italian philosopher

Crompton, Richmal (pseudonym of
Richmal Crompton Lamburn)
(1890–1969) English writer

Cronin, A(rchibald) J(oseph)
(1896–1981) Scottish novelist

**Cudlipp, Hugh, Baron Cudlipp of
Aldingbourne** (1913–98) British
newspaper editor

cummings, e(dward) e(stlin)
(1894–1962) American poet and
novelist

Cynewulf (late 8th–9th centuries)
Anglo-Saxon poet

WRITERS, PHILOSOPHERS, AND SCHOLARS (cont.)

Cyrano de Bergerac, Savinien
(1619–55) French soldier, duellist,
and writer

Dahl, Roald (1916–90) British writer,
of Norwegian descent

Dana, Richard Henry (1815–82)
American adventurer, lawyer, and
writer

d'Annunzio, Gabriele (1863–1938)
Italian novelist, dramatist, and
poet

Dante (full name Dante Alighieri)
(1265–1321) Italian poet

Da Ponte, Lorenzo (born
Emmanuele Conegliano)
(1749–1838) Italian poet and
librettist

Daudet, Alphonse (1840–97) French
novelist and dramatist

David, Elizabeth (1913–92) British
cookery writer

Davies, W(illiam) H(enry)
(1871–1940) English poet

Davies, (William) Robertson
(1913–95) Canadian novelist,
dramatist, and journalist

Day Lewis, C(ecil) (1904–72) English
poet and critic

de Beauvoir, Simone (1908–86)
French existentialist philosopher,
novelist, and feminist

Defoe, Daniel (1660–1731) English
novelist and journalist

Deighton, Leonard Cyril ('Len')
(born 1929) English novelist

Dekker, Thomas (c. 1570–1632)
English dramatist and novelist

de la Mare, Walter (John)
(1873–1956) English poet and
novelist

de la Roche, Mazo (1879-1961)
Canadian novelist

de Maupassant, Guy See
MAUPASSANT

de Pisan, Christine (also de Pizan)
(c. 1364–c. 1430) Italian writer,
resident in France from 1369

De Quincey, Thomas (1785–1859)
English essayist and critic

Derrida, Jacques (born 1930) French
philosopher

de Sade, Marquis See SADE

Descartes, René (1596–1650) French
philosopher, mathematician, and
man of science, often called the
father of modern philosophy

de Spinoza, Baruch See SPINOZA

de Staël, Mme (née Anne Louise
Germaine Necker) (1766–1817)
French novelist and critic

de Troyes, Chrétien See CHRÉTIEN DE
TROYES

Dickens, Charles (John Huffam)
(1812–70) English novelist

Dickinson, Emily (Elizabeth)
(1830–86) American poet

Diderot, Denis (1713–84) French
philosopher, writer, and critic

Dinesen, Isak See BLIXEN

Diogenes (c. 400–c. 325 BC) Greek
philosopher

Dionysius of Halicarnassus (1st
century BC) Greek historian,
literary critic, and rhetorician

Dodgson, Charles Lutwidge See
CARROLL

Donatus, Aelius (4th century)
Roman grammarian

Donne, John (1572–1631) English
poet and preacher

Doolittle, Hilda (known as HD)
(1886–1961) American poet

Dos Passos, John (Roderigo)
(1896–1970) American novelist

Dostoevsky, Fyodor Mikhailovich
(also Dostoyevsky) (1821–81)
Russian novelist

Douglas, Lord Alfred (Bruce)
(1870–1945) English poet

Dowson, Ernest (Christopher)
(1867–1900) English poet

Doyle, Sir Arthur Conan (1859–1930)
Scottish novelist

Drabble, Margaret (born 1939)
English novelist

Draco (7th century BC) Athenian
legislator

Dreiser, Theodore (Herman Albert)
(1871–1945) American novelist

Dryden, John (1631–1700) English

WRITERS, PHILOSOPHERS, AND SCHOLARS (cont.)

poet, dramatist, and critic

Du Bois, W(illiam) E(dward) B(urghardt) (1868–1963) American writer and political activist

Du Fu See TU FU

Dumas, Alexandre (known as Dumas père) (1802–70) French novelist and dramatist

Du Maurier, Dame Daphne (1907–89) English novelist

Dunbar, William (c. 1456–c. 1513) Scottish poet

Dunne, John William (1875–1949) English philosopher

Duras, Marguerite (pseudonym of Marguerite Donnadieu) (1914–96) French novelist, film director, and dramatist

Durrell, Gerald (Malcolm) (1925–95) English zoologist and writer, brother of Lawrence Durrell

Durrell, Lawrence (George) (1912–90) English novelist, poet, and travel writer

Eco, Umberto (born 1932) Italian novelist and semiotician

Edgeworth, Maria (1767–1849) Irish novelist, born in England

Ehrenburg, Ilya (Grigorevich) (1891–1967) Russian novelist and journalist

Elia, pseudonym adopted by Charles LAMB in his *Essays of Elia* (1823) and *Last Essays of Elia* (1833)

Eliot, George (pseudonym of Mary Ann Evans) (1819–80) English novelist

Eliot, T(homas) S(tearns) (1888–1965) American-born British poet, critic, and dramatist

Éluard, Paul (pseudonym of Eugène Grindel) (1895–1952) French poet

Emerson, Ralph Waldo (1803–82) American philosopher and poet

Empson, Sir William (1906–84) English poet and literary critic

Engels, Friedrich (1820–95) German socialist and political philosopher, resident chiefly in England from 1842

Ennius, Quintus (239–169 BC) Roman poet and dramatist

Epictetus (c. 55–c. 135 AD) Greek philosopher

Erasmus, Desiderius (Dutch name Gerhard Gerhards) (c. 1469–1536) Dutch humanist and scholar

Erastus (Swiss name Thomas Lieber; also called Liebler or Lüber) (1524–83) Swiss theologian and physician

Euripides (480–c. 406 BC) Greek dramatist

Evelyn, John (1620–1706) English diarist and writer

Farquhar, George (1678–1707) Irish dramatist

Farrell, J(ames) G(ordon) (1935–79) English novelist

Farrell, J(ames) T(homas) (1904–79) American novelist

Faulkner, William (1897–1962) American novelist

Ferlinghetti, Lawrence (Monsanto) (born Lawrence Ferling) (born 1919) American poet and publisher

Feuerbach, Ludwig (Andreas) (1804–72) German materialist philosopher

Feydeau, Georges (1862–1921) French dramatist

Fichte, Johann Gottlieb (1762–1814) German philosopher

Fielding, Henry (1707–54) English novelist

Fitzgerald, Edward (1809–83) English scholar and poet

Fitzgerald, F(rancis) Scott (Key) (1896–1940) American novelist

Flaubert, Gustave (1821–80) French novelist and short-story writer

Flecker, James (Herman) Elroy (1884–1915) English poet

Fleming, Ian (Lancaster) (1908–64) English novelist

Fletcher, John (1579–1625) English dramatist

Fo, Dario (born 1926) Italian

WRITERS, PHILOSOPHERS, AND SCHOLARS (cont.)

dramatist

Ford, Ford Madox (born Ford Hermann Hueffer) (1873–1939) English novelist and editor

Ford, John (1586–c. 1639) English dramatist

Forester, C(ecil) S(cott) (pseudonym of Cecil Lewis Troughton Smith) (1899–1966) English novelist

Forster, E(dward) M(organ) (1879–1970) English novelist and literary critic

Forsyth, Frederick (born 1938) English novelist

Foucault, Michel (1926–84) French philosopher

Fowles, John (Robert) (born 1926) English novelist

Foxe, John (1516–87) English religious writer

Frame, Janet (Paterson) (born 1924) New Zealand novelist

France, Anatole (pseudonym of Jacques-Anatole-François Thibault) (1844–1924) French writer

Francis, Richard Stanley ('Dick') (born 1920) English jockey and writer

Franklin, (Stella Maria Sarah) Miles (1879–1954) Australian novelist

Frege, Gottlob (1848–1925) German philosopher and mathematician, founder of modern logic

Friedan, Betty (born 1921) American feminist and writer

Fromm, Erich (1900–80) German-born American psychoanalyst and social philosopher

Frost, Robert (Lee) (1874–1963) American poet

Fry, Christopher (Harris) (born 1907) English dramatist

Frye, (Herman) Northrop (1912–91) Canadian literary critic

Fuentes, Carlos (born 1928) Mexican novelist and writer

Fugard, Athol (born 1932) South African dramatist

Galsworthy, John (1867–1933)

English novelist and dramatist

García Lorca See LORCA

García Márquez, Gabriel (born 1928) Colombian novelist

Gardner, Erle Stanley (1899–1970) American novelist and short-story writer

Gaskell, Mrs Elizabeth (Cleghorn) (1810–65) English novelist

Gassendi, Pierre (1592–1655) French philosopher and astronomer

Gay, John (1685–1732) English poet and dramatist

Genet, Jean (1910–86) French novelist, poet, and dramatist

Geoffrey of Monmouth (c. 1100–c. 1154) Welsh chronicler

Gibbon, Edward (1737–94) English historian

Gibbon, Lewis Grassic (pseudonym of James Leslie Mitchell) (1901–35) Scottish writer

Gibran, Khalil (also Jubran) (1883–1931) Lebanese-born American writer and artist

Gide, André (Paul Guillaume) (1869–1951) French novelist, essayist, and critic

Gilbert, Sir W(illiam) S(chwenck) (1836–1911) English dramatist and librettist

Ginsberg, Allen (1926–97) American poet

Gissing, George (Robert) (1857–1903) English novelist

Gobineau, Joseph Arthur, Comte de (1816–82) French writer and anthropologist

Godwin, William (1756–1836) English social philosopher and novelist

Goethe, Johann Wolfgang von (1749–1832) German poet, dramatist, and scholar

Gogol, Nikolai (Vasilevich) (1809–52) Russian novelist, dramatist, and short-story writer, born in Ukraine

Golding, Sir William (Gerald) (1911–93) English novelist

WRITERS, PHILOSOPHERS, AND SCHOLARS (cont.)

Goldsmith, Oliver (1728–74) Irish novelist, poet, essayist, and dramatist

Goncharov, Ivan (1812–91) Russian novelist

Goncourt, Edmond de (1822–96) and **Jules de** (1830–70) French novelists and critics

Gordimer, Nadine (born 1923) South African novelist and short-story writer

Gorky, Maxim (pseudonym of Aleksei Maksimovich Peshkov) (1868–1936) Russian writer and revolutionary

Grahame, Kenneth (1859–1932) Scottish-born writer of children's stories, resident in England from 1864

Gramsci, Antonio (1891–1937) Italian political theorist and activist

Grass, Günter (Wilhelm) (born 1927) German novelist, poet, and dramatist

Graves, Robert (Ranke) (1895–1985) English poet, novelist, and critic

Gray, Thomas (1716–71) English poet

Greene, (Henry) Graham (1904–91) English novelist

Greer, Germaine (born 1939) Australian feminist and writer

Grey, Zane (born Pearl Grey) (1872–1939) American writer

Grimm, Jacob (Ludwig Carl) (1785–1863) and **Wilhelm (Carl)** (1786–1859) German philologists and folklorists

Grosseteste, Robert (c. 1175–1253) English churchman, philosopher, and scholar

Grotius, Hugo (Latinized name of Huig de Groot) (1583–1645) Dutch jurist and diplomat

Gunn, Thom (full name Thomson William Gunn) (born 1929) English poet

Habermas, Jürgen (born 1929) German social philosopher

Haeckel, Ernst Heinrich (1834–1919) German biologist and philosopher

Haggard, Sir Henry Rider (1856–1925) English novelist

Hakluyt, Richard (c. 1552–1616) English geographer and historian

Hall, (Marguerite) Radclyffe (1883–1943) English novelist and poet

Hammett, (Samuel) Dashiell (1894–1961) American novelist

Hamsun, Knut (pseudonym of Knut Pedersen) (1859–1952) Norwegian novelist

Han Suyin See SUYIN

Hardy, Thomas (1840–1928) English novelist and poet

Harris, Frank (born James Thomas Harris) (1856–1931) Irish writer

Harte, (Francis) Bret (1836–1902) American short-story writer and poet

Hartley, L(eslie) P(oles) (1895–1972) English novelist

Hauptmann, Gerhart (1862–1946) German dramatist

Hašek, Jaroslav (1883–1923) Czech novelist and short-story writer

Hawthorne, Nathaniel (1804–64) American novelist and short-story writer

Hazlitt, William (1778–1830) English essayist and critic

H. D., pseudonym of Hilda DOOLITTLE

Heaney, Seamus (Justin) (born 1939) Irish poet

Hegel, Georg Wilhelm Friedrich (1770–1831) German philosopher

Heidegger, Martin (1889–1976) German philosopher

Heine, (Christian Johann) Heinrich (1797–1856) German poet

Heller, Joseph (born 1923) American novelist

Hellman, Lillian (Florence) (1907–84) American dramatist

Hemingway, Ernest (Miller) (1899–1961) American writer

Henry, O. (pseudonym of William Sidney Porter) (1862–1910) American short-story writer

WRITERS, PHILOSOPHERS, AND SCHOLARS (cont.)

Heraclitus (*c.* 500 BC) Greek philosopher

Herbert, George (1593–1633) English metaphysical poet

Herbert, Sir A(lan) P(atrick) (1890–1970) English writer and politician

Herodotus (known as 'the Father of History') (5th century BC) Greek historian

Herrick, Robert (1591–1674) English poet

Herriot, James (pseudonym of James Alfred Wight) (1916–95) English short-story writer and veterinary surgeon

Herzl, Theodor (1860–1904) Hungarian-born journalist, dramatist, and Zionist leader

Hesiod (*c.* 700 BC) Greek poet

Hesse, Hermann (1877–1962) German-born Swiss novelist and poet

Heyer, Georgette (1902–74) English novelist

Highsmith, Patricia (born Patricia Plangman) (1921–95) American writer of detective fiction

Hite, Shere (born 1942) American feminist

Hobbes, Thomas (1588–1679) English philosopher

Hoffmann, E(rnst) T(heodor) A(madeus) (1776–1822) German novelist, short-story writer, and music critic

Hofmannsthal, Hugo von (1874–1929) Austrian poet and dramatist

Hogg, James (1770–1835) Scottish poet and novelist

Hölderlin, (Johann Christian) Friedrich (1770–1843) German poet

Holinshed, Raphael (died *c.* 1580) English chronicler

Holmes, Oliver Wendell (1809–94) American physician and writer

Homer (8th century BC) Greek epic poet

Hood, Thomas (1799–1845) English poet and humorist

Hopkins, Gerard Manley (1844–89) English poet

Horace (full name Quintus Horatius Flaccus) (65–8 BC) Roman poet of the Augustan period

Horkheimer, Max (1895–1973) German philosopher and sociologist

Hornung, Ernest William (1866–1921) English novelist

Housman, A(lfred) E(dward) (1859–1936) English poet and classical scholar

Hughes, Ted (born 1930) English poet

Hughes, (James Mercer) Langston (1902–67) American writer

Hugo, Victor(-Marie) (1802–85) French poet, novelist, and dramatist

Hume, David (1711–76) Scottish philosopher, economist, and historian

Hurston, Zora Neale (1901–60) American novelist

Husserl, Edmund (Gustav Albrecht) (1859–1938) German philosopher

Huxley, Aldous (Leonard) (1894–1963) English novelist and essayist

Hypatia (*c.* 370–415) Greek philosopher, astronomer, and mathematician

Ibsen, Henrik (1828–1906) Norwegian dramatist

Illich, Ivan (born 1926) Austrian-born American educationist and writer

Ionesco, Eugène (1912–94) Romanian-born French dramatist

Iqbal, Sir Muhammad (1875–1938) Indian poet and philosopher, generally regarded as the father of Pakistan

Irving, Washington (1783–1859) American writer

Isherwood, Christopher (William Bradshaw) (1904–86) British-born

WRITERS, PHILOSOPHERS, AND SCHOLARS (cont.)

American novelist

Ishiguro, Kazuo (born 1954)
Japanese-born British novelist

Jacobs, William Wymark
(1863–1943) English short-story
writer

Jalal ad-Din ar-Rumi (also called
Mawlana) (1207–73) Persian poet
and Sufi mystic

James, Clive (Vivian Leopold) (born
1939) Australian television
personality, writer, and critic

James, C(yril) L(ionel) R(obert)
(1901–89) Trinidadian historian,
journalist, political theorist, and
novelist

James, P(hyllis) D(orothy), Baroness
(born 1920) English writer of
detective fiction

James, Henry (1843–1916)
American-born British novelist
and critic

James, William (1842–1910)
American philosopher and
psychologist, brother of Henry
James

Jarry, Alfred (1873–1907) French
dramatist

Jean Paul (pseudonym of Johann
Paul Friedrich Richter) (1763–1825)
German novelist

Jerome, Jerome K(lapka)
(1859–1927) English novelist and
dramatist

Jespersen, (Jens) Otto (Harry)
(1860–1943) Danish philologist,
grammarian, and educationist

Johnson, Samuel (known as Dr
Johnson) (1709–84) English
lexicographer, writer, critic, and
conversationalist

Jones, Daniel (1881–1967) British
linguist and phonetician

Jong, Erica (Mann) (born 1942)
American poet and novelist

Jonson, Benjamin ('Ben')
(1572–1637) English dramatist and
poet

Joyce, James (Augustine Aloysius)
(1882–1941) Irish writer

Jubran, Khalil See GIBRAN

Juvenal (Latin name Decimus
Junius Juvenalis) (c. 60–c. 140)
Roman satirist

Kafka, Franz (1883–1924) Czech
novelist, who wrote in German

Kaiser, Georg (1878–1945) German
dramatist

Kalidasa (5th century AD) Indian poet
and dramatist

Kant, Immanuel (1724–1804)
German philosopher

Karadžić, Vuk Stefanović
(1787–1864) Serbian writer,
grammarian, lexicographer, and
folklorist

Kawabata, Yasunari (1899–1972)
Japanese novelist

Keats, John (1795–1821) English
poet

Keller, Helen (Adams) (1880–1968)
American writer, social reformer,
and academic

Keneally, Thomas (Michael) (born
1935) Australian novelist

Kerouac, Jack (born Jean-Louis
Lebris de Kérouac) (1922–69)
American novelist and poet, of
French-Canadian descent

Kesey, Ken (Elton) (born 1935)
American novelist

Kierkegaard, Søren (1813–55)
Danish philosopher

Kingsley, Charles (1819–75) English
novelist and clergyman

Kipling, (Joseph) Rudyard
(1865–1936) English novelist,
short-story writer, and poet

Knox, Ronald Arbuthnott
(1888–1957) English theologian
and writer

Koestler, Arthur (1905–83)
Hungarian-born British novelist
and essayist

Kotzebue, August von (1761–1819)
German dramatist

Kundera, Milan (born 1929) Czech
novelist

Kung Fu-tzu See CONFUCIUS

Kyd, Thomas (1558–94)

WRITERS, PHILOSOPHERS, AND SCHOLARS (cont.)

English dramatist

La Barca, Pedro Calderón de See
CALDERÓN DE LA BARCA

La Bruyère, Jean de (1645–96)
French writer and moralist

Lacan, Jacques (1901–81) French
psychoanalyst and writer

**Laclos, Pierre (-Ambroise-François)
Choderlos de** (1741–1803) French
novelist

La Fontaine, Jean de (1621–95)
French poet

Lagerlöf, Selma (Ottiliana Lovisa)
(1858–1940) Swedish novelist

Lamartine, Alphonse Marie Louis de
(1790–1869) French poet,
statesman, and historian

Lamb, Charles (1775–1834) English
essayist and critic

Lampedusa, Giuseppe Tomasi de
(1896–1957) Italian novelist

Landor, Walter Savage (1775–1864)
English poet and essayist

Langland, William (c. 1330–c. 1400)
English poet

Larkin, Philip (Arthur) (1922–85)
English poet

**La Rochefoucauld, François de
Marsillac, Duc de** (1613–80) French
writer and moralist

Laurence, (Jean) Margaret
(1926–87) Canadian novelist

Lawrence, D(avid) H(erbert)
(1885–1930) English novelist, poet,
and essayist

Lawrence, T(homas) E(dward)
(known as Lawrence of Arabia)
(1888–1935) British soldier and
writer

Layamon (late 12th century) English
poet and priest

Leacock, Stephen (Butler)
(1869–1949) Canadian humorist
and economist

Lear, Edward (1812–88) English
humorist and illustrator

Le Carré, John (pseudonym of
David John Moore Cornwell) (born
1931) English novelist

Leconte de Lisle, Charles Marie

René (1818–94) French poet

Lee, Laurie (1914–97) English writer

Lee, (Nelle) Harper (born 1926)
American novelist

Le Fanu, (Joseph) Sheridan
(1814–73) Irish novelist

Leibniz, Gottfried Wilhelm
(1646–1716) German rationalist
philosopher, mathematician, and
logician

Leonard, Elmore (John) (born 1925)
American writer of thrillers

Lerner, Alan J(ay) (1918–86)
American lyricist and dramatist

Lesage, Alain-René (1668–1747)
French novelist and dramatist

Lessing, Doris (May) (born 1919)
British novelist and short-story
writer, brought up in Rhodesia

Lessing, Gotthold Ephraim
(1729–81) German dramatist and
critic

Levi, Primo (1919–87) Italian
novelist and poet

Lewis, Cecil Day See DAY LEWIS

Lewis, C(live) S(taples) (1898–1963)
British novelist, religious writer,
and literary scholar

Lewis, (Harry) Sinclair (1885–1951)
American novelist

Lewis, (Percy) Wyndham
(1882–1957) British novelist, critic,
and painter, born in Canada

Li Bo See LI PO

Liddell Hart, Sir Basil Henry
(1895–1970) British military
historian and theorist

Li Po (also Li Bo, Li T'ai Po) (AD
701–62) Chinese poet

Li T'ai Po See LI PO

Littré, Émile (1801–81) French
lexicographer and philosopher

Livy (Latin name Titus Livius) (59
BC–AD 17) Roman historian

Llosa, Mario Vargas See VARGAS
LLOSA

Locke, John (1632–1704) English
philosopher, a founder of
empiricism and political liberalism

Lodge, David (John) (born 1935)

WRITERS, PHILOSOPHERS, AND SCHOLARS (cont.)

English novelist and academic

London, Jack (pseudonym of John Griffith Chaney) (1876–1916) American novelist

Longfellow, Henry Wadsworth (1807–82) American poet

Longinus (*fl.* 1st century AD) Greek scholar

Lorca, Federico García (1898–1936) Spanish poet and dramatist

Loti, Pierre (pseudonym of Louis Marie Julien Viaud) (1850–1923) French novelist

Lovelace, Richard (1618–57) English poet

Lowell, Amy (Lawrence) (1874–1925) American poet

Lowell, James Russell (1819–91) American poet and critic

Lowell, Robert (Traill Spence) (1917–77) American poet

Lowry, (Clarence) Malcolm (1909–57) English novelist

Lucan (Latin name Marcus Annaeus Lucanus) (AD 39–65) Roman poet, born in Spain

Lucretius (full name Titus Lucretius Carus) (*c.* 94–*c.* 55 BC) Roman poet and philosopher

Lukács, György (1885–1971) Hungarian philosopher, literary critic, and politician

Lycurgus (9th century BC) Spartan lawgiver

Lydgate, John (*c.* 1370–*c.* 1450) English poet and monk

Lyly, John (*c.* 1554–1606) English prose writer and dramatist

Lyotard, Jean-François (1924–98) French philosopher and literary critic

Lytton, 1st Baron (born Edward George Earle Bulwer-Lytton) (1803–73) British novelist, dramatist, and statesman

McCarthy, Mary (Therese) (1912–89) American novelist and critic

Macaulay, Dame (Emilie) Rose (1881–1958) English novelist and essayist

Macaulay, Thomas Babington, 1st Baron (1800–59) English historian, essayist, and philanthropist

McCullers, (Lula) Carson (1917–67) American writer

MacDiarmid, Hugh (pseudonym of Christopher Murray Grieve) (1892–1978) Scottish poet and nationalist

McGonagall, William (1830–1902) Scottish poet

Mackenzie, Sir (Edward Montague) Compton (1883–1972) English novelist, essayist, and poet

Maclean, Alistair (1922–87) Scottish novelist

McLuhan, (Herbert) Marshall (1911–80) Canadian writer and thinker

MacNeice, (Frederick) Louis (1907–63) Northern Irish poet

Maeterlinck, Count Maurice (1862–1949) Belgian poet, dramatist, and essayist

Mahfouz, Naguib (born 1911) Egyptian novelist and short-story writer

Mailer, Norman (born 1923) American novelist and essayist

Maimonides (born Moses ben Maimon) (1135–1204) Jewish philosopher and Rabbinic scholar, born in Spain

Malamud, Bernard (1914–86) American novelist and short-story writer

Malherbe, François de (1555–1628) French poet

Mallarmé, Stéphane (1842–98) French poet

Malory, Sir Thomas (?1400–1471) English writer

Malraux, André (1901–76) French novelist, politician, and art critic

Mandelstam, Osip (Emilevich) (also Mandelshtam) (1891–1938) Russian poet

Mann, Thomas (1875–1955) German novelist and essayist

Manning, Olivia (Mary) (1908–80)

WRITERS, PHILOSOPHERS, AND SCHOLARS (cont.)

English novelist

Mansfield, Katherine (pseudonym of Kathleen Mansfield Beauchamp) (1888–1923) New Zealand short-story writer

Manzoni, Alessandro (1785–1873) Italian novelist, dramatist, and poet

Marcuse, Herbert (1898–1979) German-born American philosopher

Mare, Walter de la See DE LA MARE

Marinetti, Filippo Tommaso (1876–1944) Italian poet and dramatist

Marlowe, Christopher (1564–93) English dramatist and poet

Márquez, Gabriel García See GARCÍA MÁRQUEZ

Marryat, Frederick (known as Captain Marryat) (1792–1848) English novelist

Marsh, Dame Ngaio (Edith) (1899–1982) New Zealand writer of detective fiction

Martial (Latin name Marcus Valerius Martialis) (AD c. 40–c. 104) Roman epigrammatist, born in Spain

Martineau, Harriet (1802–76) English writer

Marvell, Andrew (1621–78) English poet

Marx, Karl (Heinrich) (1818–83) German political philosopher and economist, resident in England from 1849

Masefield, John (Edward) (1878–1967) English poet and novelist

Mason, A(lfred) E(dward) W(oodley) (1865–1948) English novelist

Massinger, Philip (1583–1640) English dramatist

Matthew Paris See PARIS, MATTHEW

Maugham, (William) Somerset (1874–1965) British novelist, short-story writer, and dramatist

Maupassant, (Henri René Albert) Guy de (1850–93) French novelist and short-story writer

Mauriac, François (1885–1970) French novelist, dramatist, and critic

Mawlana See JALAL AD-DIN AR-RUMI

Mayakovsky, Vladimir (Vladimirovich) (1893–1930) Soviet poet and dramatist, born in Georgia

Meleager (fl. 1st century BC) Greek poet

Melville, Herman (1819–91) American novelist and short-story writer

Menander (c. 342–292 BC) Greek dramatist

Mencius (Latinized name of Meng-tzu or Mengzi, 'Meng the Master') (c. 371–c. 289 BC) Chinese philosopher

Mencken, H(enry) L(ouis) (1880–1956) American journalist and literary critic

Meng-tzu See MENCIUS

Mengzi See MENCIUS

Meredith, George (1828–1909) English novelist and poet

Middleton, Thomas (c. 1570–1627) English dramatist

Mill, John Stuart (1806–73) English philosopher and economist

Miller, Arthur (born 1915) American dramatist

Miller, Henry (Valentine) (1891–1980) American novelist

Millett, Katherine ('Kate') (born 1934) American feminist

Milne, A(lan) A(lexander) (1882–1956) English writer of stories and poems for children

Milton, John (1608–74) English poet

Mishima, Yukio (pseudonym of Hiraoka Kimitake) (1925–70) Japanese writer

Mitchell, Margaret (1900–49) American novelist

Mitford, Nancy (Freeman) (1904–73) and her sister **Jessica (Lucy)** (1917–96) English writers

Molière (pseudonym of Jean-Baptiste Poquelin) (1622–73)

WRITERS, PHILOSOPHERS, AND SCHOLARS (cont.)

French dramatist

Mommsen, Theodor (1817–1903) German historian

Montaigne, Michel (Eyquem) de (1533–92) French essayist

Montesquieu, Baron de La Brède et de (title of Charles Louis de Secondat) (1689–1755) French political philosopher

Montessori, Maria (1870–1952) Italian educationist

Montgomery, Lucy Maud (1874–1942) Canadian novelist

Moore, George (Augustus) (1852–1933) Irish novelist

Moore, G(eorge) E(dward) (1873–1958) English philosopher

Moore, Thomas (1779–1852) Irish poet and musician

More, Sir Thomas (canonized as St Thomas More) (1478–1535) English scholar and statesman, Lord Chancellor 1529–32

Morrison, Toni (full name Chloe Anthony Morrison) (born 1931) American novelist

Muir, Edwin (1887–1959) Scottish poet and translator

Munro, H(ector) H(ugh) See SAKI

Murdoch, Dame (Jean) Iris (born 1919) British novelist and philosopher, born in Ireland

Murray, (George) Gilbert (Aimé) (1866–1957) Australian-born British classical scholar

Musil, Robert (1880–1942) Austrian novelist

Nabokov, Vladimir (Vladimorovich) (1899–1977) Russian-born American novelist and poet

Nader, Ralph (born 1934) American lawyer and reformer

Naipaul, V(idiadhar) S(urajprasad) (born 1932) Trinidadian novelist and travel writer of Indian descent, resident in Britain since 1950

Narayan, R(asipuram) K(rishnaswamy) (born 1906) Indian novelist and short-story writer

Nash, (Frederic) Ogden (1902–71) American poet

Nashe, Thomas (1567–1601) English writer

Neill, A(lexander) S(utherland) (1883–1973) Scottish teacher and educationist

Nennius (fl. c. 800) Welsh chronicler

Neruda, Pablo (born Ricardo Eliezer Neftalí Reyes) (1904–73) Chilean poet and diplomat

Nesbit, E(dith) (1858–1924) English novelist

Newby, (George) Eric (born 1919) English travel writer

Nietzsche, Friedrich Wilhelm (1844–1900) German philosopher

Nin, Anaïs (1903–77) American writer

O'Brien, Edna (born 1932) Irish novelist and short-story writer

O'Brien, Flann (pseudonym of Brian O'Nolan) (1911–66) Irish novelist and journalist

O'Casey, Sean (1880–1964) Irish dramatist

Occam, William of See WILLIAM OF OCCAM

Ockham, William of See WILLIAM OF OCCAM

O'Connor, (Mary) Flannery (1925–64) American novelist and short-story writer

Odets, Clifford (1906–63) American dramatist

Omar Khayyám (died 1123) Persian poet, mathematician, and astronomer

Ondaatje, (Philip) Michael (born 1943) Canadian writer, born in Sri Lanka

O'Neill, Eugene (Gladstone) (1888–1953) American dramatist

Orczy, Baroness Emmusca (1865–1947) Hungarian-born British novelist

Ortega y Gasset, José (1883–1955) Spanish philosopher

Orton, Joe (born John Kingsley Orton) (1933–67) English dramatist

WRITERS, PHILOSOPHERS, AND SCHOLARS (cont.)

Orwell, George (pseudonym of Eric Arthur Blair) (1903–50) British novelist and essayist

Osborne, John (James) (1929–94) English dramatist

Otway, Thomas (1652–85) English dramatist

Ouida (pseudonym of Marie Louise de la Ramée) (1839–1908) English novelist

Overbury, Sir Thomas (1581–1613) English writer and courtier

Ovid (full name Publius Ovidius Naso) (43 BC–AD c 17) Roman poet

Owen, Wilfred (1893–1918) English poet

Paglia, Camille (Anna) (born 1947) American cultural critic

Pagnol, Marcel (1895–1974) French dramatist, film director, and writer

Paine, Thomas (1737–1809) English political writer

Palgrave, Francis Turner (1824–97) English critic and poet

Panini (lived sometime between 7th and 4th centuries BC) Indian grammarian

Paris, Matthew (c. 1199–1259) English chronicler and Benedictine monk

Parker, Dorothy (Rothschild) (1893–1967) American humorist, literary critic, short-story writer, and poet

Parmenides (fl. 5th century BC) Greek philosopher

Pascal, Blaise (1623–62) French mathematician, physicist, and religious philosopher

Pasolini, Pier Paolo (1922–75) Italian film director, poet, and novelist

Passos, John Dos See DOS PASSOS

Pasternak, Boris (Leonidovich) (1890–1960) Russian poet, novelist, and translator

Pater, Walter (Horatio) (1839–94) English essayist and critic

Patmore, Coventry (Kersey Dighton) (1823–96) English poet

Paton, Alan (Stewart) (1903–88) South African writer and politician

Pausanias (2nd century) Greek geographer and historian

Pavese, Cesare (1908–50) Italian novelist, poet, and translator

Paz, Octavio (1914–98) Mexican poet and essayist

Peacock, Thomas Love (1785–1866) English novelist and poet

Peake, Mervyn (Laurence) (1911–68) British novelist, poet, and artist, born in China

Peirce, Charles Sanders (1839–1914) American philosopher and logician

Pepys, Samuel (1633–1703) English diarist and naval administrator

Perelman, S(idney) J(oseph) (1904–79) American humorist and writer

Perrault, Charles (1628–1703) French writer

Petrarch (Italian name Francesco Petrarca) (1304–74) Italian poet

Petronius, Gaius (known as Petronius Arbiter) (died AD 66) Roman writer

Philo Judaeus (also known as Philo of Alexandria) (c. 15 BC–AD c. 50) Jewish philosopher of Alexandria

Pindar (c. 518–c. 438 BC) Greek lyric poet

Pinero, Sir Arthur Wing (1855–1934) English dramatist and actor

Pinter, Harold (born 1930) English dramatist, actor, and director

Pirandello, Luigi (1867–1936) Italian dramatist and novelist

Plath, Sylvia (1932–63) American poet

Plato (c. 429–c. 347 BC) Greek philosopher

Plautus, Titus Maccius (c. 250–184 BC) Roman comic dramatist

Pliny (known as Pliny the Younger; Latin name Gaius Plinius Caecilius Secundus) (c. 61–c. 112) Roman senator and writer

Plotinus (c. 205–70) Philosopher, probably of Roman descent, the

WRITERS, PHILOSOPHERS, AND SCHOLARS (cont.)

founder and leading exponent of
Neoplatonism

Plutarch (Latin name Lucius
Mestrius Plutarchus) (*c.* 46–*c.* 120)
Greek biographer and philosopher

Poe, Edgar Allan (1809–49)
American short-story writer, poet,
and critic

Polybius (*c.* 200–*c.* 118 BC) Greek
historian

Ponte, Lorenzo Da See DA PONTE

Pope, Alexander (1688–1744)
English poet

Popper, Sir Karl Raimund (1902–94)
Austrian-born British philosopher

Porphyry (born Malchus) (*c.*
232–303)Syrian-born neoplatonist
philosopher

Porter, Katherine Anne (1890–1980)
American short-story writer and
novelist

Porter, Peter (Neville Frederick)
(born 1929) Australian poet,
resident chiefly in England since
1951

Potter, Dennis (Christopher George)
(1935–94) English television
dramatist

Potter, (Helen) Beatrix (1866–1943)
English writer of children's stories

Pound, Ezra (Weston Loomis)
(1885–1972) American poet and
critic

Powell, Anthony (Dymoke) (born
1905) English novelist

Prévost d'Exiles, Antoine-François
(known as Abbé Prévost)
(1696–1763) French novelist

Priestley, J(ohn) B(oynton)
(1894–1984) English novelist,
dramatist, and critic

Priscian (full name Priscianus
Caesariensis) (6th century AD)
Byzantine grammarian

Pritchett, Sir V(ictor) S(awdon)
(1900–97) English writer and critic

Procopius (*c.* 500–*c.* 562) Byzantine
historian, born in Caesarea in
Palestine

Propertius, Sextus (*c.* 50–*c.* 16 BC)
Roman poet

Proudhon, Pierre Joseph (1809–65)
French social philosopher and
journalist

Proust, Marcel (1871–1922) French
novelist, essayist, and critic

Pushkin, Aleksandr (Sergeevich)
(1799–1837) Russian poet,
novelist, and dramatist

Pym, Barbara (Mary Crampton)
(1913–80) English novelist

Pynchon, Thomas (Ruggles) (born
1937) American novelist

Pyrrho (*c.* 365–*c.* 270 BC) Greek
philosopher

Pythagoras (known as Pythagoras
of Samos) (*c.* 580–500 BC) Greek
philosopher

Quasimodo, Salvatore (1901–68)
Italian poet

Queen, Ellery (pseudonym of
Frederic Dannay, 1905–82, and
Manfred Lee, 1905–71) American
writers of detective fiction

Quincey, Thomas De See DE QUINCEY

Quine, Willard Van Orman (born
1908) American philosopher and
logician

Quintilian (Latin name Marcus
Fabius Quintilianus) (AD *c.* 35–*c.*
96) Roman rhetorician

Rabelais, François (*c.* 1494–1553)
French satirist

Racine, Jean (1639–99) French
dramatist

Radcliffe, Mrs Ann (1764–1823)
English novelist

Rand, Ayn (born Alissa Rosenbaum)
(1905–82) American writer and
philosopher, born in Russia

Ransom, John Crowe (1888–1974)
American poet and critic

Ransome, Arthur (Michell)
(1884–1967) English novelist

Rattigan, Sir Terence (Mervyn)
(1911–77) English dramatist

Rawls, John (born 1921) American
philosopher

Reade, Charles (1814–84) English
novelist and dramatist

WRITERS, PHILOSOPHERS, AND SCHOLARS (cont.)

Remarque, Erich Maria (1898–1970) German-born American novelist

Renan, (Joseph) Ernest (1823–92) French historian, theologian, and philosopher

Renault, Mary (pseudonym of Mary Challans) (1905–83) British novelist, resident in South Africa from 1948

Rendell, Ruth (Barbara), Baroness (born 1930) English writer of detective fiction and thrillers

Rhys, Jean (pseudonym of Ella Gwendolen Rees Williams) (1890–1979) British novelist and short-story writer, born in Dominica

Richards, I(vor) A(rmstrong) (1893–1979) English literary critic and poet

Richardson, Samuel (1689–1761) English novelist

Richler, Mordecai (born 1931) Canadian novelist

Rilke, Rainer Maria (pseudonym of René Karl Wilhelm Josef Maria Rilke) (1875–1926) Austrian poet, born in Bohemia

Rimbaud, (Jean Nicholas) Arthur (1854–91) French poet

Robbe-Grillet, Alain (born 1922) French novelist

Rochester, 2nd Earl of (title of John Wilmot) (1647–80) English poet and courtier

Roget, Peter Mark (1779–1869) English scholar

Rolland, Romain (1866–1944) French novelist, dramatist, and essayist

Rossetti, Christina (Georgina) (1830–94) English poet

Rossetti, Dante Gabriel (full name Gabriel Charles Dante Rossetti) (1828–82) English painter and poet

Rostand, Edmond (1868–1918) French dramatist and poet

Roth, Philip (Milton) (born 1933) American novelist and short-story writer

Rousseau, Jean-Jacques (1712–78) French philosopher and writer, born in Switzerland

Rowe, Nicholas (1674–1718) English dramatist

Ruiz de Alarcón y Mendoza, Juan (1580–1639) Spanish dramatist, born in Mexico City

Runyon, (Alfred) Damon (1884–1946) American author and journalist

Rushdie, (Ahmed) Salman (born 1947) Indian-born British novelist

Russell, Bertrand (Arthur William), 3rd Earl Russell (1872–1970) British philosopher, mathematician, and social reformer

Russell, George William (known as AE) (1867–1935) Irish poet and writer

Ryle, Gilbert (1900–76) English philosopher

Saadi See SADI

Sachs, Hans (1494–1576) German poet and dramatist

Sackville-West, Vita (full name Victoria Mary Sackville-West) (1892–1962) English novelist and poet

Sade, Donatien Alphonse François, Comte de (known as the Marquis de Sade) (1740–1814) French writer and soldier

Sadi (also Saadi) (born Sheikh Muslih Addin) (*c.* 1213–*c.* 1291) Persian poet

Sagan, Françoise (pseudonym of Françoise Quoirez) (born 1935) French novelist, dramatist, and short-story writer

Said, Edward W(adi) (born 1935) American critic and writer, born in Palestine

Sainte-Beuve, Charles Augustin (1804–69) French critic and writer

Saint-Exupéry, Antoine (Marie Roger de) (1900–44) French writer and aviator

Saint-Simon, Claude-Henri de Rouvroy, Comte de (1760–1825)

WRITERS, PHILOSOPHERS, AND SCHOLARS (cont.)

French social reformer and philosopher

Saint-Simon, Louis de Rouvroy, Duc de (1675–1755) French writer

Saki (pseudonym of Hector Hugh Munro) (1870–1916) British short-story writer, born in Burma

Salinger, J(erome) D(avid) (born 1919) American novelist and short-story writer

Sallust (Latin name Gaius Sallustius Crispus) (86–35 BC) Roman historian and politician

Sand, George (pseudonym of Amandine-Aurore Lucille Dupin, Baronne Dudevant) (1804–76) French novelist

Santayana, George (born Jorge Augustin Nicolás Ruiz de Santayana) (1863–1952) Spanish philosopher and writer

Sappho (early 7th century BC) Greek lyric poet

Sartre, Jean-Paul (1905–80) French philosopher, novelist, dramatist, and critic

Sassoon, Siegfried (Lorraine) (1886–1967) English poet and writer

Saussure, Ferdinand de (1857–1913) Swiss linguistics scholar

Sayers, Dorothy L(eigh) (1893–1957) English novelist and dramatist

Scaliger, Joseph Justus (1540–1609) French scholar

Scaliger, Julius Caesar (1484–1558) Italian-born French classical scholar

Schiller, (Johann Christoph) Friedrich (von) (1759–1805) German dramatist, poet, and writer

Schlegel, August Wilhelm von (1767–1845) German poet, critic, and translator

Schopenhauer, Arthur (1788–1860) German philosopher

Schreiner, Olive (Emilie Albertina) (1855–1920) South African novelist

Scott, Sir Walter (1771–1832)

Scottish novelist and poet

Seneca, Lucius Annaeus (known as Seneca the Younger) (c. 4 BC–AD 65) Roman statesman, philosopher, and dramatist

Shakespeare, William (also known as 'the Bard (of Avon)') (1564–1616) English dramatist

Shaw, George Bernard (1856–1950) Irish dramatist and writer

Shelley, Mary (Wollstonecraft) (1797–1851) English writer, wife of Percy Bysshe Shelley

Shelley, Percy Bysshe (1792–1822) English poet

Sheridan, Richard Brinsley (1751–1816) Irish dramatist and Whig politician

Shute, Nevil (pseudonym of Nevil Shute Norway) (1899–1960) English novelist

Sidney, Sir Philip (1554–86) English poet and soldier

Sillitoe, Alan (born 1928) English writer

Simenon, Georges (Joseph Christian) (1903–89) Belgian-born French novelist

Simon, (Marvin) Neil (born 1927) American dramatist

Simonides (c. 556–468 BC) Greek lyric poet

Sinclair, Upton (Beall) (1878–1968) American novelist and social reformer

Singer, Isaac Bashevis (1904–91) Polish-born American novelist and short-story writer

Sitwell, Dame Edith (Louisa) (1887–1964) English poet

Skelton, John (c. 1460–1529) English poet

Smith, Adam (1723–90) Scottish economist and philosopher

Smith, Stevie (pseudonym of Florence Margaret Smith) (1902–71) English poet and novelist

Smith, Sydney (1771–1845) English Anglican churchman, essayist,

WRITERS, PHILOSOPHERS, AND SCHOLARS (cont.)

and wit

Smollett, Tobias (George) (1721–71)
Scottish novelist

Snorri Sturluson (1178–1241)
Icelandic historian and poet

**Snow, C(harles) P(ercy), 1st Baron
Snow of Leicester** (1905–80)
English novelist and scientist

Socrates (469–399 BC) Greek
philosopher

Solzhenitsyn, Alexander (Russian
name Aleksandr Isaevich
Solzhenitsyn) (born 1918) Russian
novelist

Sontag, Susan (born 1933)
American writer and critic

Sophocles (c. 496–406 BC) Greek
dramatist

Southey, Robert (1774–1843)
English poet and writer

Soyinka, Wole (born 1934) Nigerian
dramatist, novelist, and critic

Spark, Dame Muriel (born 1918)
Scottish novelist

Spencer, Herbert (1820–1903)
English philosopher and
sociologist

Spender, Sir Stephen (1909–95)
English poet and critic

Spengler, Oswald (1880–1936)
German philosopher

Spenser, Edmund (c. 1552–99)
English poet

Spillane, Mickey (pseudonym of
Frank Morrison Spillane) (born
1918) American writer

Spinoza, Baruch de (or Benedict)
(1632–77) Dutch philosopher, of
Portuguese Jewish descent

Staël, Mme de See DE STAËL

Statius, Publius Papinius (AD c.
45–96) Roman poet

Steele, Sir Richard (1672–1729) Irish
essayist and dramatist

Stein, Gertrude (1874–1946)
American writer

Steinbeck, John (Ernst) (1902–68)
American novelist

Steiner, Rudolf (1861–1925)
Austrian philosopher, founder

of anthroposophy

Stendhal (pseudonym of Marie
Henri Beyle) (1783–1842) French
novelist

Sterne, Laurence (1713–68) Irish
novelist

Stevens, Wallace (1879–1955)
American poet

Stevenson, Robert Louis (Balfour)
(1850–94) Scottish novelist, poet,
and travel writer

Stoker, Abraham ('Bram')
(1847–1912) Irish novelist and
theatre manager

Stoppard, Sir Tom (born Thomas
Straussler) (born 1937) British
dramatist, born in Czechoslovakia

Stowe, Harriet (Elizabeth) Beecher
(1811–96) American novelist

Strabo (c. 63 BC–AD c. 23) historian
and geographer of Greek descent

Strachey, (Giles) Lytton (1880–1932)
English biographer

Strindberg, (Johan) August
(1849–1912) Swedish dramatist
and novelist

Suckling, Sir John (1609–42) English
poet, dramatist, and Royalist
leader

Suetonius (full name Gaius
Suetonius Tranquillus) (AD c. 69–c.
150) Roman biographer and
historian

Surtees, Robert Smith (1805–64)
English journalist and novelist

Suyin, Han (pseudonym of Elizabeth
Comber) (born 1917) Chinese-born
British writer and doctor

Swedenborg, Emanuel (1688–1772)
Swedish scientist, philosopher,
and mystic

Swift, Jonathan (known as Dean
Swift) (1667–1745) Irish satirist,
poet, and Anglican cleric

Swinburne, Algernon Charles
(1837–1909) English poet and critic

Symons, Julian (Gustave) (1912–94)
English writer of detective fiction

**Synge, (Edmund) J(ohn)
M(illington)** (1871–1909) Irish

WRITERS, PHILOSOPHERS, AND SCHOLARS (cont.)

dramatist

Tacitus (full name Publius, or Gaius, Cornelius Tacitus) (AD c. 56–c. 120) Roman historian

Tagore, Rabindranath (1861–1941) Indian writer and philosopher

Tannhäuser, (c. 1200–c. 1270) German poet

Tate, Nahum (1652–1715) Irish dramatist and poet, resident in London from the 1670s

Tennyson, Alfred, 1st Baron Tennyson of Aldworth and Freshwater (1809–92) English poet

Terence (Latin name Publius Terentius Afer) (c. 190–159 BC) Roman comic dramatist

Thackeray, William Makepeace (1811–63) British novelist, born in Calcutta

Thales (c. 624–c. 545 BC) Greek philosopher, mathematician, and astronomer, of Miletus

Theocritus (c. 310–c. 250 BC) Greek poet, born in Sicily

Thespis (6th century BC) Greek dramatic poet

Thomas, Dylan (Marlais) (1914–53) Welsh poet

Thomas, (Philip) Edward (1878–1917) English poet

Thomas, R(onald) S(tuart) (born 1913) Welsh poet and clergyman

Thompson, Flora (Jane) (1876–1947) English writer

Thompson, Francis (1859–1907) English poet

Thomson, James (1700–48) Scottish poet

Thoreau, Henry David (1817–62) American essayist and poet

Thrale, Mrs Hester Lynch (latterly Hester Lynch Piozzi) (1741–1821) English writer

Thucydides (c. 455–c. 400 BC) Greek historian

Thurber, James (Grover) (1894–1961) American humorist and cartoonist

Tibullus, Albius (c. 50–19 BC) Roman

elegiac poet

Tillich, Paul (Johannes) (1886–1965) German-born American theologian and philosopher

Tolkien, J(ohn) R(onald) R(euel) (1892–1973) British novelist and academic, born in South Africa

Tolstoy, Leo (Russian name Count Lev Nikolaevich Tolstoi) (1828–1910) Russian writer

Toynbee, Arnold (Joseph) (1889–1975) English historian

Traherne, Thomas (1637–74) English prose writer and poet

Trevor, William (pseudonym of William Trevor Cox) (born 1928) Irish novelist and short-story writer

Trollope, Anthony (1815–82) English novelist

Troyes, Chrétien de See CHRÉTIEN DE TROYES

Tu Fu (AD 712–70) Chinese poet

Tulsidas (c. 1543–1623) Indian poet

Turgenev, Ivan (Sergeevich) (1818–83) Russian novelist, dramatist, and short-story writer

Twain, Mark (pseudonym of Samuel Langhorne Clemens) (1835–1910) American novelist and humorist

Tzara, Tristan (born Samuel Rosenstock) (1896–1963) Romanian-born French poet

Ulpian (Latin name Domitius Ulpianus) (died c. 228), Roman jurist, born in Phoenicia

Updike, John (Hoyer) (born 1932) American novelist, poet, and short-story writer

Uttley, Alison (1884–1976) English writer

Valéry, (Ambroise) Paul (Toussaint Jules) (1871–1945) French poet, essayist, and critic

Vanbrugh, Sir John (1664–1726) English architect and dramatist

Van der Post, Sir Laurens (Jan) (1906–96) South African explorer and writer

WRITERS, PHILOSOPHERS, AND SCHOLARS (cont.)

Vargas Llosa, (Jorge) Mario (Pedro)
(born 1936) Peruvian novelist,
dramatist, and essayist
Varro, Marcus Terentius (116–27 BC)
Roman scholar and satirist
Vaughan, Henry (1621–95) Welsh
poet
Veblen, Thorstein (Bunde)
(1857–1929) American economist
and social scientist
Vega, Lope de (full name Lope Felix
de Vega Carpio) (1562–1635)
Spanish dramatist and poet
Velleius Paterculus (c. 19 BC–AD c.
30) Roman historian and soldier
Vergil See VIRGIL
Verlaine, Paul (1844–96) French poet
Verne, Jules (1828–1905) French
novelist
Vicente, Gil (c. 1465–c. 1536)
Portuguese dramatist and poet
Vico, Giambattista (1668–1744)
Italian philosopher
Vidal, Gore (born Eugene Luther
Vidal) (born 1925) American
novelist, dramatist, and essayist
Vigny, Alfred Victor, Comte de
(1797–1863) French poet, novelist,
and dramatist
Villon, François (born François de
Montcorbier or François des
Loges) (1431–?1463) French poet
Vine, Barbara pseudonym used by
Ruth RENDELL
Virgil (also Vergil) (Latin name
Publius Vergilius Maro) (70–19 BC),
Roman poet
Voltaire (pseudonym of François-
Marie Arouet) (1694–1778) French
writer, dramatist, and poet
Vonnegut, Kurt (born 1922)
American novelist and short-story
writer
Wain, John (Barrington) (1925–94)
English writer and critic
Walker, Alice (Malsenior) (born
1944) American writer and poet
Wallace, (Richard Horatio) Edgar
(1875–1932) English novelist,
short-story writer, and journalist

Walpole, Sir Hugh (Seymour)
(1884–1941) British novelist
Walton, Izaak (1593–1683) English
writer
Ward, Mrs Humphry (née Mary
Augusta Arnold) (1851–1920)
English writer and anti-suffrage
campaigner
Warren, Robert Penn (1905–89)
American poet, novelist, and critic
Watts, Isaac (1674–1748) English
hymn-writer and poet
Waugh, Evelyn (Arthur St John)
(1903–66) English novelist
Webb, (Gladys) Mary (1881–1927)
English novelist
Weber, Wilhelm Eduard (1804–91)
German physicist
Webster, John (c. 1580–c. 1625)
English dramatist
Wedekind, Frank (1864–1918)
German dramatist
Weil, Simone (1909–43) French
essayist, philosopher, and mystic
Wells, H(erbert) G(eorge)
(1866–1946) English novelist
Welty, Eudora (born 1909) American
novelist, short-story writer, and
critic
Wesker, Arnold (born 1932) English
dramatist
West, Dame Rebecca (born Cicily
Isabel Fairfield) (1892–1983) British
writer and feminist, born in Ireland
Wharton, Edith (Newbold)
(1862–1937) American novelist
and short-story writer, resident in
France from 1907
White, Patrick (Victor Martindale)
(1912–90) Australian novelist, born
in Britain
White, T(erence) H(anbury)
(1906–64) British novelist, born in
India
Whitehead, A(lfred) N(orth)
(1861–1947) English philosopher
and mathematician
Whitman, Walt (1819–92) American
poet
Whittier, John Greenleaf (1807–92)

WRITERS, PHILOSOPHERS, AND SCHOLARS (cont.)

American poet and abolitionist

Wiesel, Elie (full name Eliezer Wiesel) (born 1928) Romanian-born American human-rights campaigner, novelist, and academic

Wilcox, Ella Wheeler (1850–1919) American poet, novelist, and short-story writer

Wilde, Oscar (Fingal O'Flahertie Wills) (1854–1900) Irish dramatist, novelist, poet, and wit

Wilder, Thornton (Niven) (1897–1975) American novelist and dramatist

William of Occam (also Ockham) (*c.* 1285–1349) English philosopher and Franciscan friar

Williams, Tennessee (born Thomas Lanier Williams) (1911–83) American dramatist

Williams, William Carlos (1883–1963) American poet, essayist, and novelist

Williamson, Henry (1895–1977) English novelist and wildlife writer

Wilson, Edmund (1895–1972) American critic, essayist, and short-story writer

Wilson, Sir Angus (Frank Johnstone) (1913–91) English novelist and short-story writer

Wittgenstein, Ludwig (Josef Johann) (1889–1951) Austrian-born philosopher

Wodehouse, Sir P(elham) G(renville) (1881–1975) British-born writer

Wolfe, Thomas (Clayton) (1900–38) American novelist

Wolfe, Tom (full name Thomas Kennerley Wolfe Jr.) (born 1931) American writer

Wollstonecraft, Mary (1759–97)

English writer and feminist, of Irish descent

Wood, Mrs Henry (*née* Ellen Price) (1814–87) English novelist

Woolf, (Adeline) Virginia (*née* Stephen) (1882–1941) English novelist, essayist, and critic

Wordsworth, Dorothy (1771–1855) English diarist, sister of William Wordsworth

Wordsworth, William (1770–1850) English poet

Wren, P(ercival) C(hristopher) (1885–1941) English novelist

Wyatt, Sir Thomas (1503–42) English poet

Wycherley, William (*c.* 1640–1716) English dramatist

Wyndham, John (pseudonym of John Wyndham Parkes Lucas Beynon Harris) (1903–69) English writer of science fiction

Xenophanes (*c.* 570–*c.* 480 BC) Greek philosopher

Xenophon (*c.* 435–*c.* 354 BC) Greek historian, writer, and military leader

Yeats, W(illiam) B(utler) (1865–1939) Irish poet and dramatist

Yevtushenko, Yevgeni (Aleksandrovich) (born 1933) Russian poet

Yourcenar, Marguerite (pseudonym of Marguerite de Crayencoeur) (1903–87) French writer

Zeno (known as Zeno of Elea) (*fl.* 5th century BC) Greek philosopher

Zeno (known as Zeno of Citium) (*c.* 335–*c.* 263 BC) Greek philosopher, founder of Stoicism

Zola, Émile (Édouard Charles Antoine) (1840–1902), French novelist and critic

SPORTSPEOPLE

Abrahams, Harold (Maurice)
(1899–1978) English athlete
Agassi, André (born 1970) American
tennis player
Agostini, Giacomo (born 1944)
Italian racing motorcyclist
Akabusi, Kriss (born 1958) Brit.
runner
Alekhine, Alexander (born
Aleksandr Aleksandrovich
Alyokhin) (1892–1946) Russian-
born French chess player
Ali, Muhammad See MUHAMMAD ALI
Andretti, Mario (Gabriele) (born
1940) Italian-born American
motor-racing driver
Aouita, Saïd (born 1960) Moroccan
runner
Ashe, Arthur (Robert) (1943–93)
American tennis player
Atherton, Michael (born 1968)
British cricketer
Ballesteros, Severiano ('Sevvy')
(born 1957) Spanish golfer
Banks, Gordon (born 1937) English
footballer
Bannister, Sir Roger (Gilbert) (born
1929) British middle-distance
runner and neurologist
Barrington, Jonah (born 1940)
British squash player
Beamon, Robert ('Bob') (born 1946)
American athlete
Beckenbauer, Franz (born 1945)
German footballer and manager
Becker, Boris (born 1967) German
tennis player
Belmonte y García, Juan
(1892–1962) Spanish matador
Berra, Yogi (born Lawrence Peter
Berra) (born 1925) American
baseball player
Best, George (born 1946) Northern
Irish footballer
Bonington, Sir Chris (born 1934)
British mountaineer
Border, Allan (Robert) (born 1955)
Australian cricketer
Borg, Björn (Rune) (born 1956)
Swedish tennis player

Bosanquet, Bernard James Tindall
(1877–1936) English all-round
cricketer
Botham, Ian (Terence) (born 1955)
English all-round cricketer
Botvinnik, Mikhail Moiseivich
(1911–95) Russian chess player
Boycott, Geoffrey (born 1940)
English cricketer
Brabham, Sir John Arthur ('Jack')
(born 1926) Australian motor-
racing driver
Bradman, Sir Donald George ('Don')
(born 1908) Australian cricketer
Bristow, Eric (born 1957) British
darts player
Broome, David (born 1940) British
show jumper
Brough, Louise (born 1923) US
tennis player
Bruno, Frank(lin Ray) (born 1961)
English boxer
Bubka, Sergey (born 1963)
Ukrainian pole-vaulter
Budge, John Donald ('Don') (born
1915) American tennis player
Bueno, Maria (Esther) (born 1939)
Brazilian tennis player
Burrell, Leroy (born 1967) American
runner
Busby, Sir Matt(hew) (1909–94)
Scottish-born footballer and
football manager
Campbell, Donald (Malcolm)
(1921–67) English motor-racing
driver and holder of world speed
records, son of Sir Malcolm
Campbell
Campbell, Sir Malcolm (1885–1948)
English motor-racing driver and
holder of world speed records
Cantona, Eric (born 1966) French
footballer
Capablanca, José Raúl (1888–1942)
Cuban chess player
Carling, Will(iam David Charles)
(born 1965) English Rugby Union
player
Carnera, Primo (1906–67) Italian
boxer

SPORTSPEOPLE (cont.)

Carpentier, Georges (1894–1975) French boxer

Carson, William Hunter Fisher ('Willie') (born 1942) Scottish jockey

Cawley, Evonne (Fay) (*née* Goolagong) (born 1951) Australian tennis player

Chappell, Gregory Stephen ('Greg') (born 1948) Australian cricketer

Chappell, Ian (born 1943) Australian cricketer

Charlton, John ('Jack') (born 1935) English footballer and manager, brother of Bobby Charlton

Charlton, Sir Robert ('Bobby') (born 1937) English footballer, brother of Jack Charlton

Chichester, Sir Francis (Charles) (1901–72) English yachtsman

Christie, Linford (born 1960) Jamaican-born British sprinter

Clay, Cassius See MUHAMMAD ALI

Coe, Sebastian (born 1956) British middle-distance runner and Conservative politician

Comaneci, Nadia (born 1961) Romanian-born American gymnast

Compton, Denis (Charles Scott) (1918–97) English cricketer

Connolly, Maureen Catherine (known as 'Little Mo') (1934–69) American tennis player

Connors, James Scott ('Jimmy') (born 1952) American tennis player

Constantine, Learie Nicholas, Baron (1902–71) West Indian cricketer

Cooper, Henry (born 1934) English boxer

Cowdrey, Sir (Michael) Colin (born 1932) British cricketer

Cruyff, Johan (born 1947) Dutch footballer and football manager

Culbertson, Ely (1891–1955) American bridge player

Curry, John (Anthony) (1949–94) English ice-skater

Dalglish, Kenneth Mathieson ('Kenny') (born 1951) Scottish footballer and manager

Davis, Joe (1901–78) and his brother, **Fred** (born 1913) English billiards and snooker players

Davis, Steve (born 1957) English snooker player

Dean, Christopher See TORVILL AND DEAN

Dempsey, William Harrison ('Jack') (1895–1983) American boxer

Devoy, Susan (born 1954) New Zealand squash player

DiMaggio, Joseph Paul ('Joe') (born 1914) American baseball player

D'Inzeo, Colonel Piero (born 1923) Italian show jumper

Di Stefano, Alfredo (born 1926) Argentinian-born Spanish footballer

D'Oliveira, Basil (Lewis) (born 1931) British cricketer and coach, born in South Africa

Duke, Geoffrey E. (born 1923) British racing motorcyclist

Edberg, Stefan (born 1966) Swedish tennis player

Edwards, Gareth (Owen) (born 1947) Welsh Rugby Union player

Edwards, Jonathan (David) (born 1966) English athlete

Eusebio (full name Ferraira da Silva Eusebio) (born 1942) Mozambican-born Portuguese footballer

Evert, Christine Marie ('Chris') (born 1954) American tennis player

Faldo, Nicholas Alexander ('Nick') (born 1957) English golfer

Fangio, Juan Manuel (1911–95) Argentinian motor-racing driver

Ferguson, Alex(ander Chapman) (born 1941) Scottish football manager and footballer

Finney, Thomas ('Tom') (born 1929) English footballer

Fischer, Robert James ('Bobby') (born 1943) American chess player

Fittipaldi, Emerson (born 1946) Brazilian motor-racing driver

Fitzsimmons, Bob (1862–1917) New

SPORTSPEOPLE (cont.)

Zealand boxer

Foreman, George (born 1948)
American boxer

Fosbury, Richard (born 1947)
American high jumper

Fraser, Dawn (born 1937) Australian
swimmer

Frazier, Joseph ('Joe') (born 1944)
American boxer

Fry, C. B. (1872–1956) British
cricketer and athlete

Gascoigne, Paul (known as 'Gazza')
(born 1967) English footballer

Gavaskar, Sunil Manohar (born
1949) Indian cricketer

Gehrig, Henry Louis ('Lou')
(1903–41) American baseball
player

Gibson, Althea (born 1927)
American tennis player

Gooch, Graham (Alan) (born 1953)
British cricketer

Grace, W(illiam) G(ilbert)
(1848–1915) English cricketer

Graf, Stephanie ('Steffi') (born 1969)
German tennis player

Greaves, James ('Jimmy') (born
1940) English footballer

Gretzky, Wayne (born 1961)
Canadian ice-hockey player

Griffith Joyner, Florence (1959–98)
American runner

Gunnell, Sally (Jane Janet) (born
1966) English athlete

Hadlee, Sir Richard (John) (born
1951) New Zealand cricketer

Hagen, Walter Charles (1892–1969)
US professional golfer

Hailwood, Mike (full name Stanley
Michael Bailey Hailwood)
(1940–81) English racing
motorcyclist

Hamilton, Sir Charles (1900–78)
New Zealand inventor and motor-
racing driver

Hammond, Wally (1903–65) British
cricketer

Hawthorn, Mike (1929–58) British
motor-racing driver

Hendry, Stephen (Gordon) (born

1969) Scottish snooker player

Heyhoe-Flint, Rachel (born 1939)
English cricketer

Higgins, Alex 'Hurricane' (born
1949) Northern Irish snooker
player

Hill, Damon (born 1960) English
motor-racing driver, son of
Graham Hill

Hill, (Norman) Graham (1929–75)
English motor-racing driver

Hillary, Sir Edmund (born 1919)
New Zealand mountaineer, first to
reach summit of Everest

Hinault, Bernard (born 1954) French
racing cyclist

Hoad, Lewis Alan (1934–94)
Australian tennis player

Hobbs, Sir John Berry ('Jack')
(1882–1963) English cricketer

Hogan, Ben (1912–97) US
professional golfer

Hunt, James (1947–93) British
motor-racing driver

Hutton, Sir Leonard ('Len')
(1916–90) English cricketer

Illingworth, Ray (born 1932) British
cricketer

Imran Khan See KHAN, IMRAN

Indurain, Miguel (born 1964)
Spanish cyclist

Jacklin, Antony ('Tony') (born 1944)
English golfer

Jackson, Colin Ray (born 1967)
British hurdler

Jeeps, Dickie (born 1931) British
Rugby Union footballer

John, Barry (born 1945) Welsh
Rugby Union player

Johnson, Earvin (known as 'Magic
Johnson') (born 1959) American
basketball player

Johnson, Jack (1878–1946)
American boxer

Jones, Robert Tyre ('Bobby')
(1902–71) American golfer

Jordan, Michael (Jeffrey) (born
1963) American basketball player

Joselito (José Gómez) (1895–1920)
Spanish matador

SPORTSPEOPLE (cont.)

Kapil Dev (full name Kapil Dev Nikhanj) (born 1959) Indian cricketer

Karpov, Anatoli (born 1951) Russian chess player

Kasparov, Gary (born Gary Weinstein) (born 1963) Azerbaijani chess player, of Armenian Jewish descent

Keegan, (Joseph) Kevin (born 1951) English footballer and manager

Khan, Hashim (born 1916) Pakistani squash player

Khan, Imran (full name Imran Ahmad Khan Niazi) (born 1952) Pakistani cricketer

Khan, Jahangir (born 1963) Pakistani squash player

King, Billie Jean (born 1943) American tennis player

Korbut, Olga (born 1955) Soviet gymnast, born in Belarus

Korchnoi, Viktor (Lvovich) (born 1931) Russian chess player

Lara, Brian (Charles) (born 1969) West Indian cricketer

Larwood, Harold (1904–95) English cricketer

Lasker, Emanuel (1868–1941) German chess player

Lauda, Nikolaus Andreas ('Niki') (born 1949) Austrian motor-racing driver

Laver, Rodney George ('Rod') (born 1938) Australian tennis player

Law, Denis (born 1940) Scottish footballer

Lendl, Ivan (born 1960) Czech-born tennis player

Lenglen, Suzanne (1899–1938) French tennis player

Leonard, Sugar Ray (real name Ray Charles Leonard) (born 1956) American boxer

Lewis, Frederick Carleton ('Carl') (born 1961) American athlete

Liddell, Eric (1902–45) British athlete and missionary, born in China

Lillee, Dennis (Keith) (born 1949) Australian cricketer

Lindwall, Raymond (born 1921) Australian cricketer

Lineker, Gary (Winston) (born 1960) English footballer

Liston, Sonny (born Charles Liston) (1932–70) American boxer

Llewellyn, Harry (born 1911) British show jumper

Lloyd, Clive (born 1944) West Indian (Guyanese) cricketer

Louis, Joe (born Joseph Louis Barrow) (1914–81) American boxer

Lyle, Sandy (born 1958) British golfer

McBride, Willie James (born 1940) Irish Rugby Union player

McEnroe, John (Patrick) (born 1959) American tennis player

Mansell, Nigel (born 1954) English motor-racing driver

Mantle, Mickey (1931–95) American baseball player

Maradona, Diego (Armando) (born 1960) Argentinian footballer

Marciano, Rocky (born Rocco Francis Marchegiano) (1923–69) American boxer

Matthews, Sir Stanley (born 1915) English footballer

May, Peter (1929–94) British cricketer

Meads, Colin Earl (born 1935) New Zealand Rugby Union player

Merckx, Eddy (born 1945) Belgian racing cyclist

Milo (late 6th century BC) Greek wrestler of legendary strength

Montana, Joe (known as 'Cool Joe') (born 1956) American football player

Moore, Robert Frederick ('Bobby') (1941–93) English footballer

Moorhouse, Adrian (1964) British swimmer

Morphy, Paul Charles (1837–84) US chess player

Moses, Ed(win Corley) (born 1955) American athlete

Moss, Stirling (born 1929) English motor-racing driver

SPORTSPEOPLE (cont.)

Muhammad Ali (born Cassius Marcellus Clay) (born 1942) American boxer

Namath, Joe (born 1943) American footballer

Navratilova, Martina (born 1956) Czech-born American tennis player

Nepia, George (1905–86) New Zealand Rugby Union player

Newcombe, John (born 1944) Australian tennis player

Nicklaus, Jack (William) (born 1940) American golfer

Norman, Gregory John ('Greg') (born 1955) Australian golfer

Nurmi, Paavo Johannes (1897–1973) Finnish middle-distance runner

Ovett, Steve (born 1955) British runner

Owens, Jesse (born James Cleveland Owens) (1913–80) American athlete

Paisley, Bob (1919–96) English footballer

Palmer, Arnold (Daniel) (born 1929) American golfer

Payton, Walter (born 1954) American footballer

Pelé (born Edson Arantes do Nascimento) (born 1940) Brazilian footballer

Perry, Frederick John ('Fred') (1909–95) British-born American tennis player

Petrosian, Tigran Vartanovich (1929–84) Soviet chess player

Piggott, Lester (Keith) (born 1935) English jockey

Player, Gary (born 1936) South African golfer

Prost, Alain (born 1955) French motor-racing driver

Puskas, Ferenc (born 1927) Hungarian footballer

Ramsey, Sir Alf(red Ernest) (born 1920) English footballer and manager

Ranjitsinhji Vibhaji, Kumar Shri, Maharaja Jam Sahib of Navanagar (1872–1933) Indian cricketer and statesman

Reardon, Ray (born 1932) Welsh snooker player

Rhodes, Wilfred (1877–1973) English cricketer

Richards, Sir Gordon (1904–86) English jockey

Richards, Viv (full name Isaac Vivian Alexander Richards) (born 1952) West Indian cricketer

Robinson, Sugar Ray (born Walker Smith) (1920–89) American boxer

Robson, Bobby (born 1933) English footballer

Robson, Bryan (born 1957) English footballer

Rosewall, Ken (born 1934) Australian tennis player

Ruth, Babe (born George Herman Ruth) (1895–1948) American baseball player

Sampras, Pete (born 1971) US tennis player

Sanchez-Vicario, Arantxa (born 1971) Spanish tennis player

Schmeling, Max (born 1905) German boxer

Schumacher, Michael (born 1969) German motor-racing driver

Scudamore, Peter (born 1958) British jockey

Seles, Monica (born 1973) American tennis player, born in Yugoslavia

Senna, Ayrton (1960–94) Brazilian motor-racing driver

Shankly, William ('Bill') (1913–81) Scottish-born football manager and footballer

Sheene, Barry (born Stephen Frank Sheene) (born 1950) English racing motorcyclist

Shilton, Peter (born 1949) English footballer

Shoemaker, Willie (born 1931) American jockey

Simpson, O(renthal) J(ames) (born 1947) American football player, actor, and celebrity

Smith, Harvey (born 1938) British

SPORTSPEOPLE (cont.)

showjumper

Sobers, Sir Garfield St Aubrun ('Gary') (born 1936) West Indian cricketer

Souness, Graeme (born 1953) Scottish footballer

Spassky, Boris (Vasilyevich) (born 1937) Russian chess player

Spitz, Mark (Andrew) (born 1950) American swimmer

Sterling, Peter (born 1960) Australian Rugby League player

Stewart, Jackie (born John Young Stewart) (born 1939) British motor-racing driver

Surtees, John (born 1934) British racing motorcyclist

Sutcliffe, Herbert (1894–1978) British cricketer

Szewinska, Irena (born 1946) Polish sprinter

Taylor, Dennis (born 1949) Irish snooker player

Tenzing Norgay (c. 1914–86) Sherpa mountaineer

Thompson, Daley (born 1958) English athlete

Todd, Mark James (born 1956) New Zealand equestrian

Torvill and Dean, Jayne Torvill (born 1957) and **Christopher (Colin) Dean** (born 1958) English ice-skaters

Trevino, Lee (Buck) (known as 'Supermex') (born 1939) American golfer

Trueman, Frederick Sewards ('Fred') (born 1931) English cricketer

Tunney, Gene (1897–1978) US boxer

Turishcheva, Ludmilla (born 1952) Soviet gymnast

Tyson, Michael Gerald ('Mike') (born 1966) American boxer

Unitas, Johnny (born 1933) American footballer

Viren, Lasse Artturi (born 1949) Finnish middle-distance runner

Wade, (Sarah) Virginia (born 1945) English tennis player

Walker, John (born 1952) New Zealand athlete

Watson, Tom (born 1949) American golfer

Weissmuller, John Peter ('Johnny') (1904–84) American swimmer and actor

Whitbread, Fatima (born 1961) British javelin thrower

Williams, J(ohn) P(eter) R(hys) (born 1949) Welsh Rugby Union player

Wills (Moody), Helen (also Helen W. Roark) (1905–98) US tennis player

Winkler, Hans Günter (born 1926) West German showjumper

Wisden, John (1826–84) English cricketer

Woods, Tiger (Eldrick Woods) (born 1975) US golfer

Worrell, Sir Frank (1924–67) West Indian (Barbadian) cricketer

Wright, William Ambrose ('Billy') (1924–94) English footballer

Zatopek, Emil (born 1922) Czech long-distance runner

ECONOMISTS

Angell, Sir Norman (1874–1967)
English economist and pacifist
Bagehot, Walter (1826–77) British
economist
Baruch, Bernard (1870–1965)
American economist
Beccaria, Cesare, Marchese di
(1738–94) Italian economist
Beveridge, William, 1st Baron
(1879–1963) British economist
Bright, John (1811–89) British
advocate of free trade
Clark, John (1884–1963) American
economist
Coase, Ronald (born 1910) British
economist
Cobden, Richard (1804–65) British
economist
Douglas, C(lifford) H(ugh)
(1879–1952) British economist
Edgeworth, Francis (1845–1926)
Irish economist
Erhard, Ludwig (1897–1977)
German economist
Friedman, Milton (born 1912)
American economist
Frisch, Ragnar (1895–1973)
Norwegian economist
Galbraith, John Kenneth
(born 1908) American economist
George, Henry (1839–97) American
economist
Hayek, Friedrich von (1899–1992)
Austrian economist
Heckscher, Eli (1879–1912) Swedish
economist
Jevons, William Stanley (1835–82)
English economist and logician
Keynes, John Maynard, 1st Baron
(1883–1946) British economist
Lindale, Erik (1891–1960) Swedish
economist
Malthus, Thomas (1766–1834)
British economist
Mansholt, Sicco Leendert (1908–95)
Dutch economist
Marx, Karl (1818–83) German
economist
Meade, James (1907–95) British
economist

Mill, James (1773–1836) Scottish
economist
Mill, John Stuart (1806–73) English
economist
Monnet, Jean (1888–1979) French
economist
Myrdal, Gunnar (1898–1987)
Swedish economist
Oresme, Nicole d' (?1320–82) French
economist
Pareto, Vilfredo (1848–1923) Italian
economist
Passy, Frédéric (1822–1912) French
economist
Quesnay, François (1694–1774)
French economist
Ricardo, David (1772–1823) British
economist
Schumacher, Ernst Friedrich
(1911–77) German economist
Schumpeter, Joseph (1883–1950)
Austrian–American economist
**Sismondi, Jean Charles Léonard
Simonde de** (1773–1842) Swiss
economist
Smith, Adam (1723–90) Scottish
economist
Tinbergen, Jan (1903–94) Dutch
economist
Toynbee, Arnold (1852–83) British
economist
Turgot, A. Robert Jacques (1727–81)
French economist and statesman
Veblen, Thorstein (1857–1929)
American economist
**Ward, Dame Barbara (Mary),
Baroness Jackson** (1914–81)
British economist
Webb, (Martha) Beatrice (née
Potter) (1858–1943) British
economic writer
**Webb, Sidney (James), Baron
Passfield** (1859–1947) British
economist, social historian, and
Fabian socialist.
Weber, Max (1864-1920) German
economist and sociologist
**Wootton, Barbara (Frances),
Baroness of Abinger** (1897–1988)
English economist

HISTORY, POLITICS, AND WAR

EMPIRES

Almoravid
Asokan
Assyrian
Athenian
Austrian
Austro-Hungarian
Aztec
Babylonian
British
Byzantine
Carthaginian
Central African
Eastern (Roman)
  Empire

Frankish
French
Fulani
German
Hittite
Holy Roman
Inca
Islamic
Khmer
Macedonian
Mali
Mayan
Median
Mogul

Mongol
Ottoman
Parthian
Phoenician
Portuguese
Roman
Russian
Songhai
Spanish
Spanish American
Venetian
Western (Roman)
  Empire

POLITICAL PHILOSOPHIES AND SYSTEMS

absolutism
anarchism
anarcho-syndicalism
authoritarianism
collectivism
communism
conservatism
democracy
egalitarianism
Eurocommunism
fascism
federalism
imperialism
individualism

laissez-faire
leftism
Leninism
liberalism
libertarianism
Maoism
Marxism
meritocracy
monarchism
nationalism
pluralism
plutocracy
populism
rightism

situationism
socialism
Sovietism
Stalinism
syndicalism
technocracy
Thatcherism
theocracy
timocracy
Titoism
totalitarianism
Trotskyism
utilitarianism
Utopianism

WARS AND BATTLES

Actium, Battle of	31 BC	Macedonian Wars	214–205 BC,
Agincourt, Battle of	1415		200–196 BC,
American Civil War	1861–5		171–168 BC,
Antietam, Battle of	1862		149–148 BC
Arbela, Battle of	331 BC	Marathon, Battle of	490 BC
Atlantic, Battle of the	1940–3	Marne, Battle of	1914
Ayacucho, Battle of	1824	Megiddo, Battle of	1469 BC,
Balaclava, Battle of	1854		1918
Balkan Wars	1912–3	Mexican War	1846–8
Boer War	1880–1,	Midway Islands,	
	1899–1902	Battle of the	1942
Bosnian Civil War	1992–5	Napoleonic Wars	1805–15
Boyne, Battle of the	1690	Nile, Battle of the	1798
Britain, Battle of	1940	Omdurman, Battle of	1898
Bulge, Battle of the	1944–5	Opium Wars	1839–42,
Bunker Hill, Battle of	1775		1856–60
Cambrai, Battle of	1917	Peloponnesian Wars	431–404 BC
Cerro Gordo,		Peninsular War	1808–14
Battle of	1847	Persian Wars	5th century
Crimean War	1853–6		BC
Culloden, Battle of	1746	Pharsalus, Battle of	48 BC
El Mansûra, Battle of	1250	Princeton, Battle of	1777
English Civil War	1642–9	Punic Wars	264–241 BC,
Erzurum, Battle of	1877, 1916		218–201
Falklands War	1982		BC, 149–
First World War	1914–8		146 BC
Franco-Prussian War	1870–1	River Plate, Battle of	
French and Indian		the	1939
War	1754–63	Russian Civil War	1918–21
French Indochina War	1946–54	Russo-Japanese War	1904–5
French Wars of		Sadowa, Battle of	1866
Religion	1562–98	Salamis, Battle of	480 BC
Gallic Wars	58–51 BC	Samnite Wars	343–341 BC,
Gettysburg, Battle of	1863		316–314
Great Northern War	1700–21		BC, 298–
Gulf War	1991		290 BC
Hastings, Battle of	1066	Second World War	1939–45
Hundred Years War	1337–1453	Seven Years War	1756–63
Iran-Iraq War	1980–8	Sino-Japanese Wars	1894–5,
Issus, Battle of	333 BC		1937–45
Jena, Battle of	1806	Six Day War	1967
Jutland, Battle of	1916	Somme, Battle of the	1916
Korean War	1950–3	Spanish-American	
Leyte Gulf, Battle of	1944	War	1898
		Spanish Civil War	1936–9

WARS AND BATTLES (cont.)

Stalingrad, Battle of	1942–3	War of the Austrian Succession	1740–8
Tannenberg, Battle of	1914	War of the Spanish Succession	1701–14
Thirty Years War	1618–48	Wars of the Roses	1455–85
Trafalgar, Battle of	1805	Waterloo, Battle of	1815
Verdun, Battle of	1916	Xuzhou, Battle of	1949
Vietnam War	1954–75	Yom Kippur War	1973
War of 1812	1812–4	Ypres, Battle of	1914, 1915, 1917
War of American Independence	1775–83		

SEVEN WONDERS OF THE ANCIENT WORLD

Pyramids of Egypt
Colossus of Rhodes
Hanging Gardens of Babylon
Mausoleum of Halicarnassus
Statue of Zeus at Olympia
Temple of Artemis at Ephesus
Pharos *or* Lighthouse of Alexandria

BRITISH RANKS OF HEREDITARY PEERAGE

(in descending order)

Duke	Duchess
Marquess	Marchioness
Earl	Countess
Viscount	Viscountess
Baron	Baroness

MILITARY RANKS

British Military Ranks

Army	Field Marshal
	General
	Lieutenant General
	Major General
	Brigadier
	Colonel
	Lieutenant Colonel
	Major
	Captain
	Lieutenant
	Second Lieutenant
Royal Navy	Admiral of the Fleet

Admiral
Vice Admiral
Rear Admiral
Commodore
Captain
Commander
Lieutenant Commander
Lieutenant
Sub Lieutenant
Midshipman

Royal Air Force	Marshal of the Royal Air Force

MILITARY RANKS (cont.)

Air Chief Marshal
Air Marshal
Air Vice-Marshal
Air Commodore
Group Captain
Wing Commander
Squadron Leader
Flight Lieutenant
Flying Officer
Pilot Officer

American Military Ranks

Army and
Air Force   Chief of Staff
General
Lieutenant General
Major General
Brigadier General
Colonel
Lieutenant Colonel

Major
Captain
First Lieutenant
Second Lieutenant

Navy   Chief of Naval
Operations
Fleet Admiral
Admiral
Vice Admiral
Rear Admiral
Captain
Commander
Lieutenant
Commander
Lieutenant
Lieutenant junior
grade (j.g.)
Ensign
Midshipman

MEDALS

Air Force Cross (AFC)
Air Force Medal (AFM)
Albert Medal (AM)
Conspicuous Gallantry Medal
(CGM)
Distinguished Flying Cross (DFC)
Distinguished Flying Medal (DFM)
Distinguished Service Cross (DSC)
Distinguished Service Medal
(DSM)
George Cross (GC)
George Medal (GM)
Medal for Distinguished Conduct
in the Field (DCM)
Military Cross (MC)
Military Medal (MM)
The Distinguished Service Order
(DSO)
Victoria Cross (VC)

PARTS OF A SUIT OF ARMOUR

beaver	nose-piece
breastplate	pauldron
coutere	poleyn
cuirass	rerebrace
cuisse	sabaton
gauntlet	solleret
gorget	taces
greave	tasset
helmet	vambrace
lance rest	ventail
neck guard	visor

WEAPONS

acoustic mine
airgun
air-to-air missile
AK-47
anti-aircraft gun
anti-ballistic-missile
anti-missile missile
anti-tank weapon
arbalest
arquebus
arrow
assault gun
assegai
atom- or A-bomb
automatic
axe
ballista
ballistic missile
battering ram
battleaxe
bayonet
bazooka
Big Bertha
bilbo
bill
blade
blockbuster
blowpipe
bludgeon
blunderbuss
Bofors gun
bolas
bolt
bombshell
boomerang
bow
bowie knife
brass cannon
brass knuckles
breech-loader
Bren gun
broadsword
Brown Bess
bullet
cannon

cannon royal
carbine
car bomb
catapult
cavalry sword
chopper
claymore
club
cluster bomb
Colt™
cordite
cosh
crossbow
cruise missile
cudgel
cutlass
dagger
dart
depth charge
dirk
double-barrelled gun
duelling pistol
dynamite
elephant gun
Enfield rifle
épée,
Exocet™
falchion
falconet
field gun
firebomb
flare
fléchette
flick knife
flintlock
flying bomb
foil
fowling piece
fragmentation bomb
fusil
Garand rifle or M-1
gas shell
Gatling gun
gelignite
gisarme

grenade
guided missile
gun
gun cotton
gunpowder
hackbut
halberd
hand grenade
handgun
hanger
harpoon
hatchet
heavy gun
howitzer
hydrogen- or H-bomb
incendiary bomb
intercontinental
    ballistic missile
javelin
jerid
kalashnikov
knife
knobkerrie
knuckleduster
kris
kukri
lance
landmine
lathi
letter bomb
Lewis gun
light machine-gun
limpet mine
longbow
lyddite
M-60 machine-gun
mace
machete
machine-gun
magazine rifle
magnetic mine
mangonel
matchlock
Maxim gun
Mills bomb

WEAPONS (cont.)

mine
mine-thrower
Minuteman
MIRV (multiple
  independently-
  targeted re-entry
  vehicle)
Molotov cocktail
mortar
musket
muzzle-loader
napalm
neutron bomb
nitroglycerine
nuclear bomb
panga
parang
partisan
Patriot™
pellet
petard
petrol bomb
pike
pistol
pistolet
plastic explosive
Polaris
poleaxe
pom-pom
quarterstaff

rapier
repeating rifle
Research Department
  Explosive *or* RDX
revolver
rifle
rocket
sabre
sawn-off shotgun
scimitar
Scud™ missile
semi-automatic
Semtex™
shell
shillelagh
shotgun
shrapnel
sidewinder
siege gun
single-barrelled gun
six-shooter
skean-dhu
sling
smoke bomb
smoothbore
spear
staff
star shell
stave
Sten gun

stick
stiletto
subgun
sub-machine gun
surface-to-air missile
surface-to-surface
  missile
swivel
sword
swordstick
throw-stick
time bomb
toledo
tomahawk
tommy-gun
torpedo
trebuchet
Trident
trinitrotoluene (TNT)
truncheon
Uzi
V-1
V-2
whiz-bang
Winchester™
woomera
woomerang
yataghan

HERALDIC TERMS

accrued
allusive arms
amethyst
annulated cross
argent
armed
aversant
azure

bar
barrulet
baton sinister
bearing
bend
bendlet
bevel
bezant

billet
blazon
bordure
brisure
cabré
canton
chaplet
charge

chevron
chief
cordon
couchant
courant
crest
delf
dexter

HERALDIC TERMS (cont.)

ecartelé
entire
ermine
etoile
fess point
fimbriated
gorged
guardant
gules
honour point
impaled

lined
lodged
lozenge
main
moline
mullet
naissant
or
ordinary
orle
passant

pheon
pile
point
potent
proper
purpure
quadrate
quartered
rampant
rayoné
regardent

reversed
rustre
sable
saltire
sanguine
shield
sinister
tawney
tincture
vair
vert

RELIGION AND MYTHOLOGY

RELIGIONS AND MAJOR DENOMINATIONS

Adventism
Amish
Anabaptism
ancestor-worship
Anglicanism
animism
Bahaism
Baptism
Brahmanism
Buddhism
cabbalism
cargo cult
Christianity
Christian Science
Confucianism
Congregationalism
Conservative Judaism
Druidism
Dutch Reformed
  Church
Eleusinianism
Evangelism
Gideons
Hare Krishna
Hasidism
Hinduism
Humanism
Islam
Ismaili Islam

Jainism
Jehovah's Witnesses
Judaism
Lamaism
Lutheranism
Mahayana Buddhism
Mazdaism
Messianic Judaism
Methodism
Mithraism
Moravianism
Norse
Orphism
Orthodox Judaism
Paganism
Parseeism
Pharisaism
Plymouth Brethren
Protestantism
Presbyterianism
Puritanism
Quakers
Rabbinism
Rastafarianism
Reconstructionism
Reform Judaism
Roman Catholicism
Sabaism
Saktism

Salvationism
Scientology™
Seventh Day
  Adventism
Shaktism
Shamanism
Shia Islam
Shintoism
Sikhism
Sivaism
Spiritualism
Sufism
Sunni Islam
Tantrism
Taoism
Theravada Buddhism
Totemism
Unitarianism
Vedantism
Vishnuism
Voodoo
Wahabism
Yogism
Zande
Zen Buddhism
Zionism
Zoroastrianism

RELIGIOUS FESTIVALS

(with religion and date)

Epiphany	Christian	Jan.
Imbolc	Pagan	Jan.
New Year	Chinese traditional religions	Jan., Feb.
Shrove Tuesday	Christian	Feb., Mar.
Ash Wednesday	Christian	Feb., Mar.
Purim	Jewish	Feb., Mar.
Mahashivaratri	Hindu	Feb., Mar.
Holi	Hindu	Feb., Mar.
Easter	Christian	Mar., Apr.
Passover	Jewish	Mar., Apr.
Holi Mohalla	Sikh	Mar., Apr.
Rama Naumi	Hindu	Mar., Apr.
Ching Ming	Chinese traditional religions	Mar., Apr.
Baisakhi	Sikh	Apr.
Beltane	Pagan	Apr.
Lailat ul-Isra wal Mi'raj	Islamic	Apr., May
Lailat ul-Bara'h	Islamic	Apr., May
Vesak	Buddhist	Apr., May
Shavuoth	Jewish	May, June
Lailat ul-Qadr	Islamic	May, June
Eid ul-Fitr	Islamic	May, June
Martyrdom of Guru Arjan	Sikh	May, June
Dragon Boat Festival	Chinese traditional religions	June
Summer Solstice	Pagan	June
Dhammacakka	Buddhist	July
Eid ul-Adha	Islamic	July
Raksha Bandhan	Hindu	Aug.
Lammas	Pagan	Aug.
Janmashtami	Hindu	Aug., Sept.
Moon Festival	Chinese traditional religions	Sept.
Rosh Hashana	Jewish	Sept., Oct.
Yom Kippur	Jewish	Sept., Oct.
Succoth	Jewish	Sept, Oct.
Dusshera	Hindu	Oct.
Samhain	Pagan	Oct.
Diwali	Hindu, Sikh	Oct., Nov.
Guru Nanak's Birthday	Sikh	Nov.
Bodhi Day	Buddhist	Nov.
Christmas	Christian	Dec.
Hanukkah	Jewish	Dec.
Winter Festival	Chinese traditional religions	Dec.
Winter Solstice	Pagan	Dec.
Birthday of Guru Gobind Singh	Sikh	Dec., Jan.
Martyrdom of Guru Tegh Bahadur	Sikh	Dec., Jan.

SAINTS

(with feast dates)

Agnes of Bohemia	Mar. 2	Cyprian	Sept. 16, 26
Agnes of Rome	Jan. 21		
Aidan	Aug. 31	Cyril	Feb. 14
Alban	June 22	Cyril of Alexandria	Feb. 9
Albertus Magnus	Nov. 15	David	Mar. 1
Alexander Nevsky	Aug. 30, Nov. 23	Denis	Oct. 9
		Dominic	Aug. 8
Aloysius	June 21	Dunstan	May 19
Ambrose	Dec. 7	Edmund	Nov. 16
Andrew	Nov. 30	Edmund the Martyr	Nov. 20
Anne	July 26	Edward the Confessor	Oct. 13
Anselm	Apr. 21	Edward the Martyr	Mar. 18
Anthony	Jan. 17	Elizabeth	Nov. 5
Anthony of Padua	June 13	John Fisher	June 22
Athanasius	May 2	Francis of Assisi	Oct. 4
Augustine (of Canterbury)	May 26	Francis of Sales	Jan. 24
		Francis Xavier	Dec. 3
Augustine (of Hippo)	Aug. 28	Geneviève	Jan. 3
Barnabas	June 11	George	Apr. 23
Bartholomew	Aug. 24	Giles	Sept. 1
Basil	Jan. 2, June 14	Gregory of Nazianzus	Jan. 25 and 30 *E. Ch.*, Jan. 2 *W. Ch.*
Bede	May 27	Gregory of Nyssa	Mar. 9
Benedict	July 11	Gregory of Tours	Nov. 17
Bernadette of Lourdes	Feb. 18	Gregory the Great	Mar. 12
Bernard	Aug. 20	Helena	May 21 *E. Ch.*, Aug. 18 *W. Ch.*
Birgitta	Oct. 8	Hilary	Jan. 13, Jan. 14 *R.C. Ch.*
Bonaventura	July 15		
Boniface	June 5	Ignatius Loyola	July 31
Bridget of Ireland	July 23	Irenaeus	Aug. 23 *E. Ch.*, June 28 *W. Ch.*
Bridget of Sweden	Feb. 1		
Bruno	Oct. 6	Isidore of Seville	Apr. 4
Campion	Dec. 1	James the Great	July 25
Catherine (of Alexandria)	Nov. 25	James the Just	May 1
		James the Less	Oct. 9 *E. Ch.*, May 1 *W. Ch.*
Catherine of Siena	Apr. 29		
Cecilia	Nov. 22	Jerome	Sept. 30
John Chrysostom	Jan. 27	Joan of Arc	May 30
Clare of Assisi	Aug. 11	John of Damascus	Dec. 4
Clement of Alexandria	Dec. 5	John of the Cross	Dec. 14
Clement (of Rome)	Nov. 23	John the Baptist	June 24
Columba	June 9	John the Evangelist	Dec. 27
Crispin	Oct. 25	Joseph	Mar. 19
Cuthbert	Mar. 20	Joseph of Arimathea	Mar. 17

SAINTS (cont.)

(with feast dates)

Jude	Oct. 28	Sergius	Sept. 25
Justin	June 1	Simeon Stylites	Jan. 5
Ladislaus I	June 27	Simon	Oct. 28
Lawrence	Aug. 10	Stanislaus	Apr. 11
Leo I	Feb. 18 *E.*	Stephen	Dec. 26
	Ch., Apr. 11 *W. Ch.*		*W. Ch.*, Dec. 27 *E. Ch.*
Louis	Aug. 25	Stephen of Hungary	Sept. 2
Lucy	Dec. 13	Swithin	July 15
Luke	Oct. 18	Teresa of Ávila	Oct. 15
Margaret	Nov. 16	Thérèse	Oct. 3
Mark	Apr. 25	Thomas	Dec. 21
Martha	July 29	Thomas à Becket	Dec. 29
Martin	Nov. 11	Thomas Aquinas	Jan. 28
Mary	Jan. 1	Thomas More	June 22
R.C. Ch., Mar. 25, Aug. 15, Sept. 8		Timothy	Jan. 26,
Mary Magdalene	July 22		Jan. 22
Matthew	Sept. 21	Titus	Aug. 23
Matthias	May 14		*E. Ch.*, Feb. 6 *W. Ch.*
	W. Ch., Aug. 9 *E. Ch.*	Ursula	Oct. 21
Michael	Sept. 29	Valentine	Feb. 14
Monica	Aug. 27	Vincent de Paul	July 19
Nicholas	Dec. 6	Vitus	June 15
Olaf II	July 29	Vladimir I	July 15
Oliver Plunket	July 11	Wenceslas	Sept. 28
Oswald of York	Feb. 28	Wilfrid	Oct. 12
Patrick	Mar. 17		
Paul	June 29		
Peter	June 29	*E. Ch.* = *Eastern Church*	
Philip	June 6	*R.C. Ch.* = *Roman Catholic Church*	
Polycarp	Feb. 23	*W. Ch.* = *Western Church*	
Sebastian	Jan. 20		

THE TWELVE TRIBES OF ISRAEL

Asher	Levi
Benjamin	Manasseh
Dan	Naphtali
Gad	Reuben
Issachar	Simeon
Judah	Zebulun

ORDERS OF ANGELS

angels	principalities
archangels	seraphim
cherubim	thrones
dominations	virtues
powers	

BIBLICAL CHARACTERS

Aaron (OT)
Abel (OT)
Abraham (OT)
Absalom (OT)
Adam (OT)
*Andrew (NT)
Baal (OT)
Barabas (NT)
Barabbas (NT)
*Bartholomew or
  Nathaniel (NT)
Bathsheba (OT)
Belshazzar (OT)
Benjamin (OT)
Caiaphas (NT)
Cain (OT)
Daniel (OT)
David (OT)
Delilah (OT)
Elijah (OT)
Elisha (OT)
Enoch (OT)
Ephraim (OT)
Esau (OT)
Esther (OT)
Eve (OT)
Ezekiel (OT)
Gabriel (NT)
Gideon (OT)
Goliath (OT)
Herod Agrippa (NT)
Herod Agrippa II (NT)
Herod Antipas (NT)
Herod the Great (NT)
Hezekiah (OT)
Isaac (OT)

Isaiah (OT)
Ishmael (OT)
Israel (OT)
Jacob (OT)
James (NT)
*James the Greater
  (NT)
*James the Less (NT)
Jeremiah (OT)
Jesus (NT)
Jezebel (OT)
Job (OT)
*John (NT)
John the Baptist (NT)
Jonah (OT)
Jonathan (OT)
Joseph (NT)
Joseph of Arimathea
  (NT)
Joseph (OT)
Joshua (OT)
Judah (OT)
*Jude or Thaddeus
  (NT)
*Judas Iscariot (NT)
Lazarus (NT)
Lot (OT)
Luke (NT)
Mark (NT)
Martha (NT)
Mary Magdalene (NT)
Mary (NT)
Mary the Holy Mother
  (NT)
*Matthew or Levi (NT)
Matthias (NT)

Methuselah (OT)
Michael (NT)
Miriam (OT)
Moses (OT)
Nathan (OT)
Nebuchadnezzar (OT)
Nicodemus (NT)
Noah (OT)
Paul (Saul) (NT)
*(Simon) Peter (NT)
*Philip (NT)
Pontius Pilate (NT)
Rachel (OT)
Rebekah (OT)
Ruth (OT)
Salome (NT)
Samson (OT)
Samuel (OT)
Sarah (OT)
Saul (Paul) (NT)
Saul (OT)
Simon (NT)
Simon of Cyrene (NT)
*Simon the Canaanite
  (NT)
Solomon (OT)
Stephen (NT)
*Thomas (NT)
Timothy (NT)
Titus (NT)

* *Indicates the twelve
  apostles.*
NT = *New Testament*
OT = *Old Testament*

BOOKS OF THE BIBLE

Old Testament
Genesis
Exodus
Leviticus
Numbers
Deuteronomy
Joshua
Judges
Ruth
Samuel I
Samuel II
Kings I
Kings II
Chronicles I
Chronicles II
Ezra
Nehemiah
Esther
Job
Psalms
Proverbs
Ecclesiastes
Song of Solomon
Isaiah
Jeremiah
Lamentations
Ezekiel
Daniel
Hosea
Joel

Amos
Obadiah
Jonah
Micah
Nahum
Habakkuk
Zephaniah
Haggai
Zechariah
Malachi

New Testament
Matthew
Mark
Luke
John
Acts
Romans
Corinthians I
Corinthians II
Galatians
Ephesians
Philippians
Colossians
Thessalonians I
Thessalonians II
Timothy I
Timothy II
Titus

Philemon
Hebrews
James
Peter I
Peter II
John I
John II
John III
Jude
Revelation

Apocrypha
Esdras I
Esdras II
Tobit
Judith
Additions to the Book
  of Esther
Wisdom of Solomon
Ecclesiasticus
Baruch
Letter of Jeremiah
Song of the Three
  Holy Children
Susanna
Bel and the Dragon
Prayer of Manasses
Maccabees I
Maccabees II

MONASTIC ORDERS

Antonians
Augustinian Hermits
Austin Friars
Barnabites
Benedictines
Bernardines
Black Friars
Black Monks
Blue Nuns
Bonhommes
Brethren of the
  Common Life
Brigittines
Brothers Hospitallers
Camaldolites
Canons Regular
Capuchins
Carmelites
Carthusians
Christian Brothers
Cistercians
Conceptionists
Conventuals

Culdees
Doctrinarians
Dominicans
Franciscans
Friars Minor
Friars Preachers
Gilbertines
Grey Friars
Grey Nuns
Hieronymites
Hospitallers
Ignorantines
Jacobins
Jesuits
Knights Templar
Marianists
Marists
Minims
Minorites
Norbertines
Oratorians
Passionists
Paulines

Piarists
Poor Clares
Poor Soldiers of the
  Temple
Praemonstratensians
Salesians
Servites
Sisters of Charity
Sisters of the Love of
  God
Sisters of the Sacred
  Cross
Somascans
Studites
Sylvestrines
Theatines
Trappists
Trinitarians
Ursulines
Visitandines
White Friars

CHRISTIAN ECCLESIASTICAL OFFICERS

acolyte
almoner
archbishop
beadle
bishop
canon
cantor
cardinal
chaplain
churchwarden
cleric
clerk in holy orders

confessor
curate
deacon
deaconess
dean
elder
father
minister
Monsignor
parson
pastor
patriarch

pope
precentor
prelate
priest
primate
rector
sexton
succentor
thurifer
verger
vicar

NAMES OF GOD

Allah (Islam)
Almighty God
Almighty, the
Alpha and
  Omega
Creator, the
Deity, the
Divine Being
Eternal, the
Everlasting
  Father
Father, Son,
  and Holy
  Ghost
Father, the
First Cause
God Almighty
Godhead, the
God the Father
God the Son
Holy Ghost, the

Holy One, the
Holy Spirit
Holy Trinity, the
Jah
Jehovah
King of Kings
Lord of Lords
Lord, the
Maker, the
Our Father
Our Maker
Prime Mover,
  the
primum mobile
Spirit of God
Supreme
  Being, the
Trinity, the
Yahweh
  (Judaism)

NAMES FOR THE DEVIL

Abbadon
Arch-fiend, the
Auld Thief
Beelzebub
Belial
deil
Deuce
dickens
Evil One, the
Foul Fiend
His Satanic
  Majesty
Lord of the
  Flies
Lucifer
Mephisto

Mephistopheles
Moloch
Old Clootie
old gentleman
  (in black)
Old Harry
Old Hornie
Old Nick
Old One
Old Scratchy
Prince of
  Darkness
Satan
Tempter, the
Wicked One

SEVEN VIRTUES

faith
fortitude
hope
justice
love or charity
prudence
temperance

SEVEN DEADLY SINS

anger
covetousness
envy
gluttony
lust
pride
sloth

PARTS OF A CHURCH

aisle
ambulatory
apse
baptistery
blind-story
buttress
chancel
chevet

choir
clerestory or
  clearstory
conch
crossing
crypt
dome
flèche

flying buttress
font
galilee
narthex
nave
rood-screen
sacristy
spire

steeple
transept
tribune gallery
triforium
vaulting
vestry
westwork

GREEK GODS AND GODDESSES

(with Roman equivalent)

Aphrodite	Venus	Hecate	
Apollo		Helios	Sol
Ares	Mars	Hephaestus	Vulcan
Artemis	Diana	Hera	Juno
Asclepius	Aesculapius	Hermes	Mercury
Athene	Minerva	Hestia	Vesta
Charites *or* Graces	Aglaia, Euphrosyne, Thalia	Hypnos	Somnus
		Iris	
		Nemesis	
Cronos	Saturn	Nike	Victoria
Demeter	Ceres	Ouranos	Uranus
Dionysus	Bacchus	Pan	Faunus
Eos	Aurora	Persephone	Proserpine
Eros	Cupid	Poseidon	Neptune
Eumenides *or* Furies		Rhea	Cybele
		Selene	Luna
Gaia	Ge	Thanatos	Mors
Hades *or* Dis	Pluto	Tuche	Fortuna
Hebe	Juventas	Zeus	Jupiter

ROMAN GODS AND GODDESSES

(with Greek equivalent)

Aesculapius	Asclepius	Luna	Selene
Apollo		Mars	Ares
Aurora	Eos	Mercury	Hermes
Bacchus	Dionysus	Minerva	Athene
Ceres	Demeter	Mors	Thanatos
Cupid	Eros	Neptune	Poseidon
Cybele	Rhea	Pluto	Hades
Diana	Artemis	Proserpine	Persephone
Faunus	Pan	Saturn	Cronos
Fortuna	Tuche	Sol	Helios
Ge	Gaia	Somnus	Hypnos
Graces	Charites	Uranus	Ouranos
Hecate	Hecate	Venus	Aphrodite
Juno	Hera	Vesta	Hestia
Jupiter	Zeus	Victoria	Nike
Juventas	Hebe	Vulcan	Hephaestus
Lares and Penates			

THE THREE FATES

Lachesis (assigns a person's destiny)
Clotho (spins the thread of life)
Atropos (cuts the thread of life)

THE NINE MUSES

Calliope (eloquence, epic poetry)
Clio (history)
Erato (lyric and love poetry)
Euterpe (music)
Melpomene (tragedy)
Polyhymnia (singing, rhetoric)
Terpsichore (dancing)
Thalia (comic and pastoral poetry)
Urania (astronomy)

CHARACTERS FROM GREEK AND ROMAN MYTHOLOGY

Achilles	Chiron	Horae *or* Hours	Pasiphae
Actaeon	Chloe	Hydra	Patroclus
Adonis	Circe	Icarus	Pegasus
Aegisthus	Clytemnestra	Io	Penelope
Aeneas	Creon	Iphicles	Perseus
Aeolus	Cyclops	Iphigenia	Phaethon
Agamemnon	Daedalus	Jason	Philoctetes
Ajax	Daphnis	Jocasta	Pollux
Alcestis	Dido	Lamia	Polynices
Amazon	Dryads	Lapiths	Polyphemus
Andromache	Electra	Maenads	Priam
Andromeda	Endymion	Medea	Prometheus
Antigone	Eteocles	Medusa	Remus
Arachne	Europa	Menelaus	Rhea Silvia
Ariadne	Eurydice	Midas	Romulus
Atalanta	Ganymede	Minotaur	Satyrs
Atlas	Gorgons	Naiads	Scylla
Atreus	(Euryale,	Narcissus	Sibyls
Bellerophon	Medusa,	Nestor	Sirens
Boreas	Stheno)	Niobe	Sisyphus
Calypso	Hamadryads	Nymphs	Tantalus
Cassiopeia	Harpies	Odysseus	Telemachus
Castor	Hector	Oedipus	Theseus
Centaurs	Hecuba	Olympus	Thetis
Cepheus	Helen of Troy	Oreads	Thyestes
Cerberus	Heracles	Orestes	Ulysses
Charon	(Hercules)	Orion	
Charybdis	Hermaphro-	Orpheus	
Chimera	ditus	Pandora	

THE LABOURS OF HERCULES

The Augean stables
The capture of Cerberus
The cattle of Geryon
The Ceryneian hind
The Cretan bull
The girdle of Hippolyte
The golden apples of the
    Hesperides
The Lernaean hydra
The mares of Diomedes
The Nemean lion
The Stymphalian birds
The wild boar of Erymanthus

RIVERS OF HADES

Acheron
Lethe
Phlegethon
Styx

EGYPTIAN GODS AND GODDESSES

Ament	Harmakhis	Min	Sebek
Ammon	Haroeris	Mont	Seker
Amon-Ra	Harsaphes	Mut	Sekhmet
Anhur	Harsiesis	Nefertum	Selket
Anquet	Hathor	Neheh	Sesheta
Anubis	Heket	Nekhebit	Seth or Set
Aten	Horus	Nephthys	Shai
Atum	Imhotep	Nun	Shu
Bast	Isis	Nut	Taueret
Behdety	Khensu	Osiris	Tefnut
Bes	Khepera	Ptah	Thoth
Buto	Khnum	Ra	Upuaut
Geb	Maat	Renenet	
Hapi	Mertseger	Renpet	
Harakhtes	Meskhent	Sati	

HINDU GODS AND GODDESSES

Aditi	Kama	Radha	Tvashtar
Agni	Kartikeya	Rama	Uma
Bhairavi	Krishna	Ravana	Ushas
Brahma	Kurma	Rudra	Vamana
Devi	Lakshmi	Sakti *or* Shakti	Varaha
Durga	Mara	Sarasvati	Varuna
Ganesha	Matsya	Savitar	Vata
Hanuman	Mitra	Shiva *or* Siva	Vishnu
Indra	Narasinha	Sita	Yama
Jagannatha *or*	Parvati	Skanda	
Juggernaut	Prajapati	Soma	
Kali	Puchan	Surya	

CELTIC GODS, GODDESSES, AND HEROES

Boann	Epona	Manannan
Boanna, the	Finn MacCool	Nuada
Bran	Fomors	Ogma
Brigit	Gobniu	Ossian
Cernunnos	Lêr	Pwyll
Dagda, the	Ludd *or* Nudd	Rhiannon
Dana *or* Danu *or* Anu	Lugh	Tuatha Dé Dannan
Dian Cecht	Macha	

NORSE GODS, GODDESSES, AND OTHER MYTHOLOGICAL FIGURES

Aesir	tribe of gods	Mjollnir	Thor's hammer
Alfheim	region of Asgard	Muspelheim	realm of fire
Asgard	home of the gods	Niflheim	home of the dead
Ask	first man	Njord or	
Audumla	primeval cow	Njorth	leader of the Vanir
Aurgelmir	primeval giant	Norns (Urth, Verthandi,	
Balder	god of the sun	Skuld)	Fates
Bifrost	rainbow bridge	Odin or	
Brynhild	leader of the Valkyries	Wotan	chief god
		Ragnarok	final battle between gods and giants
Buri	grandfather of Odin		
Draupnir	Odin's magic ring	Sif	wife of Thor
Embla	first woman	Skidbladnir	magic ship
Fenrir	wolf	Sleipnir	Odin's eight-legged horse
Freyja	goddess of love		
Freyr	protector of living things	Surt	lord of Muspelheim
		Thor	god of thunder
Frigga	wife of Odin	Tyr	god of war
Gerd	wife of Freyr	Valhalla	hall of the gods in Asgard
Gungnir	Odin's spear		
Heimdal	guardian of Bifrost	Valkyries	nine warrior goddesses
Hel	goddess of death		
Hoder	blind god	Vanir	gods of fertility
Jörmungand	serpent	Vidar	son of Odin
Kvasir	god whose death created poetry	Wayland Smith	lord of the elves
Loki	trickster god	Yggdrasil	the Cosmic Tree
Midgard or		Ymir	giant from whose body the world
Mannaheim	world of men		

ARTHURIAN LEGEND

Arthur	legendary British king	Lancelot or Launcelot	knight
Avalon	paradise	Lot	father of Gawain
Camelot	capital of Arthur's kingdom	Merlin	magician
Elaine	mother of Galahad	Modred or Mordred	son of Morgan Le Fay
Excalibur	Arthur's sword		
Fisher King	custodian of the Holy Grail	Morgan Le Fay	magician; Arthur's sister
Galahad	knight		
Gawain	knight	Nineve	Lady of the Lake
Guinevere	Arthur's wife	Percival or Perceval	knight
Holy Grail	used by Christ at the Last Supper	Tristram	knight
Iseult	lover of Tristram	Uther	
Kay	Arthur's foster brother	Pendragon	Arthur's father

MONSTERS AND DEMONS

afanc	Godzilla	mormo
afreet	golem	ngarara
basilisk	Gorgon	Ogopogo
behemoth	Grendel	ogre
bogey	griffin	orc
bunyip	harpy	Ravana
Caliban	hippocampus	sciapod
centaur	hippogriff	Scylla
Cerberus	hobgoblin	sphinx
Charybdis	Hydra	succubus
chimera	incubus	taniwha
cockatrice	King Kong	tao-tieh
dragon	kraken	Tityrus
fire-drake	lamia	troll
Frankenstein's monster	leviathan	vampire
	Lilith	werewolf
ghoul	manticore	wyvern
gnome	Medusa	zombie
goblin	Minotaur	

GEOGRAPHY

COUNTRIES OF THE WORLD

(with capital cities)

Afghanistan	Kabul
Albania	Tirana
Algeria	Algiers
Andorra	Andorra la Vella
Angola	Luanda
Antigua and Barbuda	St John's
Argentina	Buenos Aires
Armenia	Yerevan
Aruba	Oranjestad
Australia	Canberra
Austria	Vienna
Azerbaijan	Baku
Bahamas, The	Nassau
Bahrain	Manama
Bangladesh	Dhaka
Barbados	Bridgetown
Belarus	Minsk
Belgium	Brussels
Belize	Belmopan
Benin	Porto Novo
Bhutan	Thimphu
Bolivia	La Paz
Bosnia-Herzegovina	Sarajevo
Botswana	Gaborone
Brazil	Brasilia
Brunei	Bandar Seri Begawan
Bulgaria	Sofia
Burkina Faso	Ouagadougou
Burundi	Bujumbura
Cambodia	Phnom Penh
Cameroon	Yaoundé
Canada	Ottawa
Cape Verde Islands	Praia
Central African Republic	Bangui
Chad	N'Djamena
Chile	Santiago
China	Beijing or Peking
Colombia	Bogota
Comoros	Moroni
Congo	Brazzaville
Congo, Democratic Republic of – formerly Zaïre	Kinshasa
Costa Rica	San José
Croatia	Zagreb
Cuba	Havana
Cyprus	Nicosia
Czech Republic	Prague
Denmark	Copenhagen
Djibouti	Djibouti
Dominica	Roseau
Dominican Republic	Santo Domingo
Ecuador	Quito
Egypt	Cairo
El Salvador	San Salvador
Equatorial Guinea	Malabo
Eritrea	Asmara
Estonia	Tallinn
Ethiopia	Addis Ababa
Fiji	Suva
Finland	Helsinki
France	Paris
Gabon	Libreville
Gambia, The	Banjul

COUNTRIES OF THE WORLD (cont.)

(with capital cities)

Georgia	Tbilisi	Madagascar	Antananarivo
Germany	Berlin	Malawi	Lilongwe
Ghana	Accra	Malaysia	Kuala Lumpur
Greece	Athens	Maldives	Male
Grenada	St George's	Mali	Bamako
Guatemala	Guatemala City	Malta	Valletta
Guinea	Conakry	Marshall Islands	Majuro
Guinea-Bissau	Bissau	Mauritania	Nouakchott
Guyana	Georgetown	Mauritius	Port Louis
Haiti	Port-au-Prince	Mexico	Mexico City
Honduras	Tegucigalpa	Micronesia	Kolonia
Hungary	Budapest	Moldova	Chişinău
Iceland	Reykjavik	Monaco	
India	New Delhi	Mongolia	Ulan Bator
Indonesia	Djakarta	Montenegro	Podgorica
Iran	Tehran	Morocco	Rabat
Iraq	Baghdad	Mozambique	Maputo
Ireland, Republic		Myanmar – formerly	
of	Dublin	Burma	Rangoon or
Israel	Jerusalem – de		Yangon
	facto	Namibia	Windhoek
Italy	Rome	Nauru	
Ivory Coast	Yamoussoukro	Nepal	Kathmandu
Jamaica	Kingston	Netherlands, The	Amsterdam
Japan	Tokyo	New Zealand	Wellington
Jordan	Amman	Nicaragua	Managua
Kazakhstan	Akmola	Niger	Niamey
Kenya	Nairobi	Nigeria	Abuja
Kiribati	Bairiki	Norway	Oslo
Korea, North	Pyongyang	Oman	Muscat
Korea, South	Seoul	Pakistan	Islamabad
Kuwait	Kuwait City	Palau	Koror
Kyrgyzstan	Bishkek	Panama	Panama City
Laos	Vientiane	Papua New	
Latvia	Riga	Guinea	Port Moresby
Lebanon	Beirut	Paraguay	Asunción
Lesotho	Maseru	Peru	Lima
Liberia	Monrovia	Philippines	Manila
Libya	Tripoli	Poland	Warsaw
Liechtenstein	Vaduz	Portugal	Lisbon
Lithuania	Vilnius	Qatar	Doha
Luxembourg	Luxembourg	Romania	Bucharest
Macedonia, Former Yugoslav		Russia	Moscow
Republic of	Skopje	Rwanda	Kigali

COUNTRIES OF THE WORLD (cont.)

(with capital cities)

St Kitts and Nevis	Basseterre
St Lucia	Castries
St Vincent and the Grenadines	Kingstown
Samoa – formerly Western Samoa	Apia
San Marino	San Marino
São Tomé and Principe	São Tomé
Saudi Arabia	Riyadh
Senegal	Dakar
Serbia	Belgrade
Seychelles,The	Victoria
Sierra Leone	Freetown
Singapore	Singapore
Slovakia	Bratislava
Slovenia	Ljubljana
Solomon Islands	Honiara
Somalia	Mogadishu
South Africa	Pretoria
Spain	Madrid
Sri Lanka	Colombo
Sudan	Khartoum
Suriname	Paramaribo
Swaziland	Mbabane
Sweden	Stockholm
Switzerland	Berne
Syria	Damascus
Taiwan	Taipei
Tajikistan	Dushanbe
Tanzania	Dodoma
Thailand	Bangkok
Togo	Lomé
Tonga	Nuku'alofa
Trinidad and Tobago	Port of Spain
Tunisia	Tunis
Turkey	Ankara
Turkmenistan	Ashgabat
Tuvalu	Funafuti
Uganda	Kampala
Ukraine	Kiev
United Arab Emirates	Abu Dhabi
UK	London
USA	Washington, D.C.
Uruguay	Montevideo
Uzbekistan	Tashkent
Vanuatu	Vila
Vatican City	
Venezuela	Caracas
Vietnam	Hanoi
Yemen	Sana'a
Yugoslavia	*see* Serbia, Montenegro, etc.
Zambia	Lusaka
Zimbabwe	Harare

CAPITAL CITIES

(with countries)

Abu Dhabi	United Arab Emirates	Bucharest	Romania
		Budapest	Hungary
Abuja	Nigeria	Buenos Aires	Argentina
Accra	Ghana	Bujumbura	Burundi
Addis Ababa	Ethiopia	Cairo	Egypt
Akmola	Kazakhstan	Canberra	Australia
Algiers	Algeria	Caracas	Venezuela
Amman	Jordan	Castries	St Lucia
Amsterdam	Netherlands, The	Chişinău	Moldova
		Colombo	Sri Lanka
Andorra la Vella	Andorra	Conakry	Guinea
Ankara	Turkey	Copenhagen	Denmark
Antananarivo	Madagascar	Dakar	Senegal
Apia	Samoa – formerly Western Samoa	Damascus	Syria
		Dhaka	Bangladesh
Ashgabat	Turkmenistan	Djakarta	Indonesia
Asmara	Eritrea	Djibouti	Djibouti
Asunción	Paraguay	Dodoma	Tanzania
Athens	Greece	Doha	Qatar
Baghdad	Iraq	Dublin	Ireland, Republic of
Bairiki	Kiribati		
Baku	Azerbaijan	Dushanbe	Tajikistan
Bamako	Mali	Freetown	Sierra Leone
Bandar Seri Begawan	Brunei	Funafuti	Tuvalu
		Gaborone	Botswana
Bangkok	Thailand	Georgetown	Guyana
Bangui	Central African Republic	Guatemala City	Guatemala
		Hanoi	Vietnam
Banjul	Gambia, The	Harare	Zimbabwe
Basseterre	St Kitts and Nevis	Havana	Cuba
		Helsinki	Finland
Beijing or Peking	China	Honiara	Solomon Islands
Beirut	Lebanon		
Belgrade	Serbia	Islamabad	Pakistan
Belmopan	Belize	Jerusalem – de facto	Israel
Berlin	Germany		
Berne	Switzerland	Kabul	Afghanistan
Bishkek	Kyrgyzstan	Kampala	Uganda
Bissau	Guinea-Bissau	Kathmandu	Nepal
Bogota	Colombia	Khartoum	Sudan
Brasilia	Brazil	Kiev	Ukraine
Bratislava	Slovakia	Kigali	Rwanda
Brazzaville	Congo	Kingston	Jamaica
Bridgetown	Barbados	Kingstown	St Vincent and the Grenadines
Brussels	Belgium		

CAPITAL CITIES (cont.)
(with countries)

Kinshasa	Congo, Democratic Republic of – formerly Zaïre	Nicosia	Cyprus
		Nouakchott	Mauritania
		Nuku'alofa	Tonga
		Oranjestad	Aruba
		Oslo	Norway
Kolonia	Micronesia	Ottawa	Canada
Koror	Palau	Ouagadougou	Burkina Faso
Kuala Lumpur	Malaysia	Panama City	Panama
Kuwait City	Kuwait	Paramaribo	Suriname
La Paz	Bolivia	Paris	France
Libreville	Gabon	Phnom Penh	Cambodia
Lilongwe	Malawi	Podgorica	Montenegro
Lima	Peru	Port-au-Prince	Haiti
Lisbon	Portugal	Port Louis	Mauritius
Ljubljana	Slovenia	Port Moresby	Papua New Guinea
Lomé	Togo		
London	UK	Port of Spain	Trinidad and Tobago
Luanda	Angola		
Lusaka	Zambia	Porto Novo	Benin
Luxembourg	Luxembourg	Prague	Czech Republic
Madrid	Spain	Praia	Cape Verde Islands
Majuro	Marshall Islands		
		Pretoria	South Africa
Malabo	Equatorial Guinea	Pyongyang	Korea, North
		Quito	Ecuador
Male	Maldives	Rabat	Morocco
Managua	Nicaragua	Rangoon or Yangon	
Manama	Bahrain		Myanmar – formerly Burma
Manila	Philippines		
Maputo	Mozambique	Reykjavik	Iceland
Maseru	Lesotho	Riga	Latvia
Mbabane	Swaziland	Riyadh	Saudi Arabia
Mexico City	Mexico	Rome	Italy
Minsk	Belarus	Roseau	Dominica
Mogadishu	Somalia	Sana'a	Yemen
Monrovia	Liberia	San José	Costa Rica
Montevideo	Uruguay	San Marino	San Marino
Moroni	Comoros	San Salvador	El Salvador
Moscow	Russia	Santiago	Chile
Muscat	Oman	Santo Domingo	Dominican Republic
Nairobi	Kenya		
Nassau	Bahamas, The	São Tomé	São Tomé and Principe
N'Djamena	Chad		
New Delhi	India	Sarajevo	Bosnia-Herzegovina
Niamey	Niger		

CAPITAL CITIES (cont.)

(with countries)

Seoul	Korea, South
Singapore	Singapore
Skopje	Macedonia, Former Yugoslav Republic of
Sofia	Bulgaria
St George's	Grenada
St John's	Antigua and Barbuda
Stockholm	Sweden
Suva	Fiji
Taipei	Taiwan
Tallinn	Estonia
Tashkent	Uzbekistan
Tbilisi	Georgia
Tegucigalpa	Honduras
Tehran	Iran
Thimphu	Bhutan
Tirana	Albania
Tokyo	Japan
Tripoli	Libya
Tunis	Tunisia
Ulan Bator	Mongolia
Vaduz	Liechtenstein
Valletta	Malta
Victoria	Seychelles, The
Vienna	Austria
Vientiane	Laos
Vila	Vanuatu
Vilnius	Lithuania
Warsaw	Poland
Washington, DC	USA
Wellington	New Zealand
Windhoek	Namibia
Yamoussoukro	Ivory Coast
Yaoundé	Cameroon
Yerevan	Armenia
Zagreb	Croatia

ADMINISTRATIVE DIVISIONS OF ENGLAND

(with administrative centres)

*Avon — Bristol
Barking and Dagenham
Barnet
Barnsley
Bath and North East
  Somerset — Bath
Bedfordshire — Bedford
*Berkshire — Reading
Bexley
Birmingham
Bolton
Bournemouth
Bradford
Brent
Brighton and Hove
Bristol
Bromley
Buckinghamshire — Aylesbury
Bury
Calderdale
Cambridgeshire — Cambridge
Camden
Cheshire — Chester
City of London
Cornwall — Truro
Coventry
Croydon
*Cumberland — Carlisle
Cumbria — Carlisle
Darlington
Derby
Derbyshire — Matlock
Devon — Exeter
Doncaster
Dorset — Dorchester
Dudley
Durham — Durham
Ealing
East Riding of Yorkshire
Enfield
Essex — Chelmsford
Gateshead
Gloucestershire — Gloucester
Greenwich
Hackney

Hammersmith and Fulham
*Hampshire — Winchester
Haringey
Harrow
Hartlepool
Havering
*Hereford and Worcester — Worcester
Herefordshire — Hereford
Hertfordshire — Hertford
Hillingdon
Hounslow
*Humberside — Beverley
*Huntingdonshire — Huntingdon
Islington
Kensington and Chelsea
Kent — Maidstone
Kingston upon Hull
Kingston-upon-Thames
Kirklees
Knowsley
Lambeth
Lancashire — Preston
Leeds
Leicester
Leicestershire — Leicester
Lewisham
Lincolnshire — Lincoln
Liverpool
Luton
Manchester
Merton
Middlesbrough
Milton Keynes
Newcastle upon Tyne
Newham
Norfolk — Norwich
Northamptonshire — Northampton
North-East Lincolnshire
North Lincolnshire
North Somerset
North Tyneside — Wallsend
Northumberland — Morpeth
North Yorkshire — Northallerton
Nottinghamshire — Nottingham

ADMINISTRATIVE DIVISIONS OF ENGLAND (cont.)

(with administrative centres)

Oldham		Sussex, East	Lewes
Oxfordshire	Oxford	Sussex, West	Chichester
Poole		*Sutton*	
Portsmouth		Swindon	
Redbridge		Tameside	
Redcar and		*Tower Hamlets*	
Cleveland	Redcar	Trafford	
Richmond Upon Thames		Wakefield	
Rochdale		Walsall	
Rotherham		*Waltham Forest*	
Rutland	Oakham	Wandsworth	
St Helens		Warwickshire	Warwick
Salford		*Westminster*	
Sandwell		*Westmorland	Kendal
Sefton		Wigan	
Sheffield		Wight, Isle of	Newport, IOW
Shropshire	Shrewsbury	Wiltshire	Trowbridge
Solihull		Wirral	
Somerset	Taunton	Wolverhampton	
Southampton		Worcestershire	Worcester
South Gloucestershire		York	
South Tyneside		*Yorkshire	
Southwark			
Staffordshire	Stafford		
Stockport			
Stockton-on-Tees			
Stoke-on-Trent		*Former or historic county.*	
Suffolk	Ipswich	*Greater London unitary authorities*	
Sunderland		*are shown in italics.*	
Surrey	Kingston	*Where no administrative centre is*	
	Upon	*given, its name is identical to that*	
	Thames	*of the authority it serves.*	

WELSH COUNTIES AND COUNTY BOROUGHS

(with administrative centres)

Anglesey	Llangefni	Neath and Port Talbot	Port Talbot
Blaenau Gwent	Ebbw Vale	Newport	
*Breconshire	Brecon	Pembrokeshire	Haverfordwest
Bridgend		Powys	Llandrindod Wells
*Caernarfonshire	Caernarfon		
Caerphilly	Hengoed	*Radnorshire	Llandrindod Wells
Cardiff			
*Cardiganshire	Aberystwyth	Rhondda-Cynon-Taff	Tonypandy
Carmarthenshire	Carmarthen	*South Glamorgan	Cardiff
Ceredigion	Aberaeron	Swansea	
*Clwyd	Mold	Torfaen	Pontypool
Conwy		Vale of Glamorgan	Barry
Denbighshire	Ruthin	*West Glamorgan	Swansea
*Dyfed	Carmarthen	Wrexham	
Flintshire	Mold		
*Glamorgan	Cardiff		
*Gwent	Cwmbran		
Gwynedd	Caernarfon		
*Merionethshire	Dolgellau		
Merthyr Tydfil			
*Mid Glamorgan	Cardiff		
Monmouthshire	Cwmbran		
*Montgomeryshire	Welshpool		

Former or historic county.
Where no administrative centre is given, its name is identical to that of the authority it serves.

SCOTTISH COUNCIL AREAS

(with administrative centres)

Aberdeen		*Dumfries	
Aberdeenshire	Aberdeen	Dundee City	
Angus	Forfar	East Ayrshire	Kilmarnock
Argyll and Bute	Lochgilphead	East Dumbartonshire	Glasgow
*Argyll	Lochgilphead	East Lothian	Haddington
*Ayr		East Renfrewshire	Glasgow
*Banff		Falkirk	
*Berwick	Duns	Fife	Glenrothes
*Bute	Rothesay	Glasgow City	
*Caithness	Wick	*Grampian	Aberdeen
*Central	Stirling	Highland	Inverness
City of Edinburgh		Inverclyde	Greenock
Clackmannanshire	Alloa	*Inverness	
*Dumbarton	Dumbarton	*Kincardine	Stonehaven
Dumfries and Galloway	Dumfries	*Kinross	

SCOTTISH COUNCIL AREAS (cont.)

(with administrative centres)

*Kirkcudbright		Shetland Islands	Lerwick
*Lanark	Hamilton	South Ayrshire	Ayr
*Lothian	Edinburgh	South Lanarkshire	Hamilton
Midlothian	Dalkeith	*Stirling	Stirling
Moray	Elgin	*Strathclyde	Glasgow
*Nairn	Nairn	*Sutherland	Golspie
North Ayrshire	Irvine	*Tayside	Dundee
North Lanarkshire	Motherwell	West	
Orkney Islands	Kirkwall	Dumbartonshire	Dumbarton
*Peebles		Western Isles	Stornaway
Perth and Kinross		West Lothian	Livingston
*Perth		*Wigtown	Stranraer
*Renfrew	Paisley	*Zetland	Lerwick
Renfrewshire	Paisley		
*Ross and			
Cromarty	Dingwall		
*Roxburgh	Newtown St. Boswells	*Former administrative division.	
Scottish Borders	Melrose	Where no administrative centre is	
*Selkirk		given, its name is identical to that	
		of the authority it serves.	

COUNTIES AND DISTRICTS OF NORTHERN IRELAND

(with administrative centres)

Antrim		Fermanagh	Enniskillen
Antrim, County	Belfast	Fermanagh, County	Enniskillen
Ards	Newtonards	Larne	
Armagh		Limavady	
Armagh, County	Armagh	Lisburn	
Ballymena		Londonderry, County	Londonderry
Ballymoney		Magherafelt	
Banbridge		Moyle	Ballycastle
Belfast City		Newry and Mourne	Newry
Carrickfergus		Newtownabbey	Ballyclare
Castlereagh	Belfast	North Down	Bangor
Coleraine		Omagh	
Cookstown		Strabane	
Craigavon		Tyrone, County	Omagh
Derry City			
Down	Downpatrick	Where no administrative centre is	
Down, County	Downpatrick	given, its name is identical to that	
Dungannon		of the authority it serves.	

COUNTIES AND PROVINCES OF THE REPUBLIC OF IRELAND
(with county towns)

Connacht
 Galway
 Leitrim — Carrick-on-Shannon
 Mayo — Castlebar
 Roscommon
 Sligo

Leinster
 Carlow
 Dublin
 Kildare — Naas
 Kilkenny
 Laoighis or Laois or Leix — Portlaoighise or Portlaoise
 Longford
 Louth — Dundalk
 Meath — Trim
 Offaly — Tullamore
 Westmeath — Mullingar
 Wexford
 Wicklow

Munster
 Clare — Ennis
 Cork
 Kerry — Tralee
 Limerick
 Tipperary — Clonmel
 Waterford

Ulster
 *Antrim — Belfast
 *Armagh
 Cavan
 Donegal — Lifford
 *Down — Downpatrick
 *Fermanagh — Enniskillen
 *Londonderry
 Monaghan
 *Tyrone — Omagh

*Indicates a county of Northern Ireland; unmarked counties constitute the Republic of Ireland. Where no county town is given, its name is identical to that of the county it serves.

STATES OF THE USA
(with abbreviations and capitals)

Alabama	AL or Ala	Montgomery
Alaska	AK or Alas	Juneau
Arizona	AZ or Ariz	Phoenix
Arkansas	AR or Ark	Little Rock
California	CA or Cal	Sacramento
Colorado	CO or Colo	Denver
Connecticut	CT or Conn	Hartford
Delaware	DE or Del	Dover
Florida	FL or Fla	Tallahassee
Georgia	GA	Atlanta
Hawaii	HA	Honolulu
Idaho	ID or Ida	Boise
Illinois	IL or Ill	Springfield

STATES OF THE USA (cont.)

(with abbreviations and capitals)

Indiana	IN *or* Ind	Indianapolis
Iowa	IA	Des Moines
Kansas	KS *or* Kan	Topeka
Kentucky	KY *or* Ken	Frankfort
Louisiana	LA	Baton Rouge
Maine	ME	Augusta
Maryland	MD	Annapolis
Massachusetts	MA *or* Mass	Boston
Michigan	MI *or* Mich	Lansing
Minnesota	MN *or* Minn	St Paul
Mississippi	MS *or* Miss	Jackson
Missouri	MO	Jefferson City
Montana	MT *or* Mont	Helena
Nebraska	NE *or* Nebr	Lincoln
Nevada	NV *or* Nev	Carson City
New Hampshire	NH	Concord
New Jersey	NJ	Trenton
New Mexico	NM *or* N Mex	Santa Fe
New York	NY	Albany
North Carolina	NC	Raleigh
North Dakota	ND *or* N Dak	Bismarck
Ohio	OH	Columbus
Oklahoma	OK *or* Okla	Oklahoma City
Oregon	OR *or* Oreg	Salem
Pennsylvania	PA	Harrisburg
Rhode Island	RI	Providence
South Carolina	SC	Columbia
South Dakota	SD *or* S Dak	Pierre
Tennessee	TN *or* Tenn	Nashville
Texas	TX *or* Tex	Austin
Utah	UT	Salt Lake City
Vermont	VT	Montpelier
Virginia	VA	Richmond
Washington	WA *or* Wash	Olympia
West Virginia	WV *or* W Va	Charleston
Wisconsin	WI *or* Wis	Madison
Wyoming	WY *or* Wyo	Cheyenne

District

District of Columbia	DC	

STATES AND TERRITORIES OF AUSTRALIA

(with capitals)

New South Wales	Sydney
Queensland	Brisbane
South Australia	Adelaide
Tasmania	Hobart
Australian Capital Territory	Canberra – federal capital
Northern Territory	Darwin
Victoria	Melbourne
Western Australia	Perth

PROVINCES AND TERRITORIES OF CANADA

(with capitals)

Alberta	Edmonton
British Columbia	Victoria
Manitoba	Winnipeg
New Brunswick	Fredericton
Newfoundland and Labrador	St John's
Northwest Territories	Yellowknife
Nova Scotia	Halifax
Ontario	Toronto
Prince Edward Island	Charlottetown
Quebec	Quebec
Saskatchewan	Regina
Yukon Territory	Whitehorse

PROVINCES OF NEW ZEALAND

North Island
Auckland
Bay of Plenty
Gisborne
Hawkes Bay
Manawatu-Wanganui
Northland
Taranaki
Waikato
Wellington

South Island
Canterbury
Marlborough
Nelson
Otago
Southland
Tasman
West Coast

Islands
Stewart Islands
Chatham Islands

PROVINCES OF SOUTH AFRICA

(with capitals)

Eastern Cape	Bisho
Free State	Bloemfontein
Gauteng	Johannesburg
KwaZulu/Natal	Ulundi
Mpumalanga	Nelspruit
Northern	Pietersburg
Northern Cape	Kimberley
North-West	Mafikeng
Western Cape	Cape Town

CITIES

Aachen
Aalborg
Aalen
Aalst
Aarhus
Aba
Abadan
Abbottabad
Abéché
Aberdeen
Abidjan
Abilene
Åbo
Abu Dhabi
Abuja
Abydos
Acapulco
Accra
Adana
Adapazari
Addis Ababa
Adelaide
Adiyaman
Ado-Ekiti
Adrianopole
Afyon
Agadir
Agra
Ahlen
Ahmadabad
Ahmadnagar
Aintab
Aix-en-
  Provence
Ajmer
Akashi
Akita
Akkad
Aksu
Alameda
Albacete
Albany
Albuquerque
Alcalá de
  Guadaira

Alcalá de
  Henares
Aleksandrovsk-
  Sakhalinskiy
Aleppo
Alessandria
Alexandria
Alexandrou-
  polis
Algeciras
Algiers
Alhambra
Aligarh
Alkmaar
Allahabad
Allentown
Almaty
Almelo
Almirante
  Brown
Almoravid
Alost
Alphen aan den
  Rijn
Alton
Altoona
Alwar
Amagasaki
Amaravati
Amarillo
Ambala
Ambato
Amberg
Amersfoort
Amman
Amol
Amoy
Amravati
Amritsar
Amsterdam
Anaheim
Anápolis
Anchorage
Anda
Anderson

Andijon
Angarsk
Angers
Angostura
Ankara
Annaba
Ann Arbor
Anniston
Anqing
Anshan
Anshun
Antakya
Antalya
Antananarivo
Antioch
Anuradhapura
Anvers
Anyang
Aosta
Aphrodisias
Apollonia
Appleton
Aqmola
Aqtau
Aqtöbe
Aquila
Aracajú
Arad
Arak
Ardabil
Arecibo
Arequipa
Arezzo
Argolis
Argos
Arles
Arlington
Armagh
Armavir
Armidale
Arnsberg
Arta
Arthur's Seat
Asahikawa
Asansol

Aschaffenburg
Aschersleben
Asheville
Ashgabat
Ashquelon
Assyria
Astana
Astrakhan
Asunción
Aswan
Asyut
Athens
Athínai
Atlanta
Attleboro
Auburn
Auckland
Augsburg
Aurora
Austin
Avignon
Avlona
Ayacucho
Baalbek
Babel
Babol
Babylon
Bacolod
Baghdad
Baguio
Bahamas
Bahawalpur
Baicheng
Bakersfield
Balkh
Baltimore
Bamberg
Bandar
  Lampung
Bandung
Bangalore
Bangkok
Bangor
Baniyas
Baoding

CITIES (cont.)

Baoji	Benxi	Bordeaux	Bugis
Baoshan	Berezniki	Borujerd	Bujumbura
Baotou	Bergama	Bose	Bukhara
Baracaldo	Bergen	Bosra	Bulawayo
Baranavichiy	Bergisch	Bossier City	Burbank
Barcelona	Gladbach	Boston	Burgas
Bareilly	Berkeley	Botou	Burgos
Barinas	Berlin	Bottrop	Burlington
Barquisimeto	Berne	Bouaké	Burnsville
Barrie	Berry	Boulder	Bushehr
Barysaw	Bethlehem	Bowling Green	Buzau
Basle	Beverly Hills	Bradford	Byblos
Bastille	Bhagalpur	Braga	Bytom
Batman	Bhiwandi	Braganza	Byzantium
Batna	Bhopal	Braila	Cabimas
Baton Rouge	Bialystok	Brandon	Cabinda
Battambang	Bielefeld	Brantford	Cáceres
Batticaloa	Bikaner	Brasov	Cadiz
Battle Creek	Bilbao	Bratislava	Caen
Baurú	Billings	Bratsk	Cagayan de Oro
Bayamo	Binghamton	Brazzaville	Cagliari
Bayamón	Binzhou	Bremen	Caguas
Bayonne	Birmingham	Brescia	Cairo
Baytown	Biscayne Bay	Brest	Calcutta
Beaverton	Bishkek	Bridgeport	Calgary
Bei'an	Blackfoot	Brisbane	Cali
Beihai	Blagovesh-	Bristol	Caloocan
Beirut	chensk	Brno	Calvary
Bejaïa	Blantyre	Brockton	Camagüey
Belaya Tserkov	Blida	Broken Arrow	Camarillo
Belém	Bloomington	Bromberg	Cambridge
Belfast	Blumenau	Brookline	Campagna di
Belfort	Bobo-Dioulasso	Brooklyn Park	Roma
Belgaum	Bochum	Brownsville	Campina
Belgorod	Bodrum	Bruges	Grande
Bellary	Bogotá	Brunswick	Campinas
Bellevue	Bohemia	Brussels	Campos
Bellflower	Boise	Bryansk	Canandaigua
Bellingham	Bokaro Steel	Brzeg	Candia
Belo Horizonte	City	Bucaramanga	Cangzhou
Belovo	Bolan Pass	Bucharest	Canterbury
Beltsy	Bologna	Budapest	Canton
Bengbu	Bombay	Buena Park	Cape Coral
Benha	Bonampak	Buenos Aires	Capua
Benoni	Bonn	Buffalo	Caracas

CITIES (cont.)

Caracol
Carcassonne
Carchemish
Cariacica
Carniola
Carolina
Carthage
Casablanca
Castellón de la
 Plana
Catania
Caxias do Sul
Cebu
Cedar Rapids
Celaya
České
 Budějovice
Chalcedon
Champs
 Elysées
Chan Chan
Chandigarh
Chandler
Chang'an
Changchun
Changde
Changji
Changzhi
Changzhou
Chaohu
Chaoyang
Charikar
Chärjew
Charleroi
Charlesbourg
Charleston
Charlotte
Chattanooga
Chaudière Falls
Chavín de
 Huántar
Cheapside
Cheju
Chelmno
Chelyabinsk

Chemnitz
Chengde
Chengdu
Cherepovets
Cherkassy
Chernigov
Chernivtsi
Chernobyl
Chesapeake
Chester
Chiangmai
Chiba
Chicago
Chiclayo
Chicopee
Chicoutimi
Chifeng
Chigasaki
Chihuahua
Chillán
Chinatown
Chita
Choibalsan
Cholula
Chongqing
Chorzów
Christchurch
Chula Vista
Chuxiong
Chuzhou
Cicero
Cienfuegos
Cincinnati
Ciudad Bolivar
Ciudad
 Guayana
Ciudad Madero
Ciudad
 Obregón
Ciudad Victoria
Clarksville
Clearwater
Clermont-
 Ferrand
Cleveland

Cleveland
 Heights
Clifton
Clovis
Cluj-Napoca
Coblenz
Coburg
Cochabamba
Cognac
Coimbatore
Coimbra
College Station
Cologne
Colombo
Colón
Colonia
Colorado
 Springs
Colossae
Columbia
Columbus
Comilla
Concepción
Concord
Constantine
Constantinople
Constanza
Coon Rapids
Copán
Coral Springs
Córdoba
Corinth
Cork
Corona
Costa Mesa
Cotonou
Cottbus
Council Bluffs
Coventry
Cracow
Craiova
Ctesiphon
Cuenca
Cuiabá
Curitiba

Cuzco
Czestochowa
Dachau
Dali
Dallas
Damanhur
Damascus
Dan
Da Nang
Danbury
Danjiangkou
Danville
Daqing
Darbhanga
Darkhan
Dashhowuz
Daugavpils
Davangere
Davao
Davenport
David
Daxian
Dayton
Daytona Beach
Dearborn
Debrecen
Decatur
Dehra Dun
Delhi
Delmenhorst
Denison
Denton
Denver
Derbent
Derby
Des Moines
Dessau
Detroit
Deventer
Deyang
Dezhou
Dhaka
Dhanbad
Dharwar
Dijon

CITIES (cont.)

Dinajpur	El Minya	Fullerton	Gwalior
Dispura	El Paso	Fürth	Györ
Dodge City	Ely	Gaborone	Haarlemmer-
Doha	Elyria	Gabrovo	meer
Donetsk	Encinitas	Gainesville	Habikino
Dongchuan	Enschede	Galena	Hachinohe
Dongguang	Enshi	Galveston	Hachioji
Dongying	Enugu	Garden Grove	Hadano
Dordrecht	Ephesus	Gary	Haeju
Dortmund	Epidaurus	Gastonia	Hagen
Douala	Erfurt	Gath	Haicheng
Downey	Erie	Gaya	Haining
Dresden	Erlangen	Gera	Hamadan
Dubbo	Erode	Germiston	Hamamatsu
Dubrovnik	Escondido	Gerona	Hamburg
Dubuque	Espoo	Gharyan	Hamhung
Dukou	Essen	Ghaziabad	Hami
Duluth	Esslingen	Ghent	Hamilton
Dum Dum	Euclid	Gifu	Hamm
Dundee	Eugene	Gijón	Hammond
Dunedin	Evansville	Glasgow	Hampton
Dunfermline	Ezhou	Glendale	Hancheng
Dunhua	Fairbanks	Gloucester	Handan
Duque de	Fairfield	Godoy Cruz	Hanzhong
Caxias	Faisalabad	Gómez Palacio	Harappa
Durban	Fargo	Gorakhpur	Hardwar
Düren	Faridabad	Gordium	Hasselt
Durgapur	Fayetteville	Gorlovka	Hastings
Durham	Feira de	Gotha	Haverhill
Dushanbe	Santana	Granada	Hawthorne
Düsseldorf	Flint	Grand Prairie	Hayward
Duyun	Florianópolis	Grand Rapids	Hebi
Dzerzhinsk	Fontana	Graz	Hechi
East Orange	Forest Lawn	Great Falls	Heerlen
Eau Claire	Fort Lauderdale	Greeley	Hegang
Ech Chlef	Fort Smith	Greensboro	Heidelberg
Ede	Fort Wayne	Greenville	Heilbronn
Edmond	Fort Worth	Gresham	Helwan
El Cajon	Fountain Valley	Groznyy	Henderson
Elea	Frankenthal	Guatemala City	Hengshui
Elgin	Fredericksburg	Guayaquil	Hengyang
Elis	Fremont	Guimarães	Herat
Elizabeth	Fresno	Gujrat	Hereford
El Kef	Fujisawa	Gulbarga	Herne
El Mansura	Fuling	Guntur	Herning

CITIES (cont.)

Hervey Bay
Heshan
Hesperia
Heze
Hialeah
Higashimura-
  yama
High Point
Hikone
Hildesheim
Himeji
Hino
Hirakata
Hiratsuka
Hirosaki
Hitachi
Ho Chi Minh
  City
Hollywood
  Bowl
Hoorn
Huaibei
Huaihua
Huainan
Huaiyin
Huambo
Huancayo
Huangshi
Hubli
Hué
Huizhou
Hull
Hunjiang
Huntington
Huntington
  Beach
Huntington
  Park
Huntsville
Hyderabad
Ibadan
Ibaraki
Ichihara
Ichikawa
Ichinomiya

Ife
Ikeda
Ikeja
Ilam
Ilesha
Ilorin
Imperatriz
Imperia
Independence
Indore
Ingolstadt
Innsbruck
Insein
Invercargill
Inverness
Iowa City
Ipoh
Irapuato
Irbid
Iruma
Irvine
Irving
Isesaki
Istanbul
Itami
Itanagar
Ivanovo
Iwaki
Iwakuni
Iwatsuki
Iwo
Izmit
Jabalpur
Jaboatão
Jacobabad
Jalalabad
Jamalpur
Jambi
Jamnagar
Janesville
Jersey City
Jessore
Jhansi
Jiamusi
Ji'an

Jiangmen
Jiaojiang
Jiaozou
Jiaxing
Jiayuguan
Jinchang
Jincheng
Jingmen
Jinhua
Jining
Jinshi
Jinzhou
Jishou
Jiujiang
Jixi
João Pessoa
Joensuu
Johannesburg
Joinville
Joliet
Jujuy
Jundiaí
Kaduna
Kaesong
Kafr el Dauwar
Kafr el Sheikh
Kagoshima
Kaifeng
Kaili
Kairouan
Kaiyuan
Kakamigahara
Kakogawa
Kalamazoo
Kalisz
Kaluga
Kalyan
Kanazawa
Kano
Kaposvar
Karaj
Karaklis
Karakorum
Karamay
Karbala

Kariya
Karviná
Kashihara
Kashiwa
Kassel
Kasugai
Kasukabe
Kasur
Katowice
Katsuta
Kaunas
Kawachinagano
Kawagoe
Kawanishi
Kawasaki
Kazan
Kecskemét
Kediri
Kemerovo
Kenner
Kenosha
Kerman
Kettering
Key West
Khorramabad
Khulna
Kielce
Kimberley
Kingston
Kirkuk
Kirovohad
Kiryu
Kisangani
Kisarazu
Kislovodsk
Kitakyushu
Kitami
Kitchener
Kitwe
Kladno
Klagenfurt
Klerksdorp
Knossos
Knoxville
Kochi

CITIES (cont.)

Kodaira	Laramie	Longview	Matsue
Kofu	Largo	Longyan	Matsumoto
Koganei	Larkana	Lorain	Matsuyama
Kohima	Las Cruces	Los Angeles	Mayapan
Kokubunji	Las Vegas	Los Mochis	Mazar-e-Sharif
Kolhapur	Launceston	Loudi	Medan
Kolomna	Laval	Louisville	Medellín
Komaki	Lawrence	Lowell	Medicine Hat
Komatsu	Lawton	Lower Hutt	Meerut
Konin	Leeds	Luanda	Meissen
Koriyama	Lefkosia	Lubbock	Mei Xian
Korla	Leicester	Lublin	Meknès
Koshigaya	Leipzig	Lubumbashi	Melbourne
Kosice	Lengshuijiang	Lucknow	Memphis
Kostroma	Lengshuitan	Ludhiana	Mendoza
Koszalin	León	Lund	Merced
Kota	Leshan	Luohe	Mérida
Kovrov	Leverkusen	Lusaka	Mesa
Kragujevac	Levittown	Luzhou	Metz
Kramatorsk	Lexington	Lynchburg	Miami
Kumagaya	Liaocheng	Lynn	Mianyang
Kumasi	Liaoyang	Lynwood	Miass
Kunming	Liaoyuan	Ma'anshan	Michurinsk
Kurashiki	Liberec	Macheng	Midland
Kure	Lille	Machida	Midwest City
Kurgan	Lima	Macon	Mildura
Kursk	Limoges	Madrid	Miletus
Kurume	Lincoln	Madurai	Milpitas
Kutaisi	Linfen	Magdeburg	Minatitlán
Kuytun	Linhai	Mahabad	Minden
Kyongju	Linhe	Mahilyou	Minneapolis
Kyoto	Linqing	Mainz	Minoo
Lafayette	Linxia	Malegaon	Minsk
Lagos	Linyi	Malmö	Mirzapur
La Habra	Linz	Manaus	Mishima
Lahti	Lishui	Manizales	Miskolc
Laiwu	Livermore	Manta	Mission Viejo
Lake Charles	Liverpool	Manzhouli	Mississauga
Lakeland	Livonia	Maoming	Mitaka
Lakewood	Lodi	Maramba	Mitla
La Mesa	Łodz	Mari	Miyakonojo
Lancaster	London	Marib	Mmabatho
Landshut	Londrina	Matamoros	Mobile
Langfang	Long Beach	Mathura	Modena
Laohekou	Longmont	Matsubara	Modesto

CITIES (cont.)

Moe	Nantes	Norwalk	Oshkosh
Mogi das	Nanyang	Nova Iguaçu	Oshogbo
Cruzes	Naperville	Novgorod	Osijek
Mohenjo-Daro	Narbonne	Novi Sad	Öskmen
Mombasa	Nashua	Novokuznetsk	Osnabrück
Mönchen-	Nashik	Novomoskovsk	Ostia
gladbach	National City	Novosibirsk	Ostrava
Monclova	Nawabganj	Nuevo Laredo	Ota
Monroe	Nawabshah	Numazu	Otaru
Montebello	Ndola	Oak Ridge	Ouagadougou
Monterey	Nellore	Oberhausen	Oujda
Monterey Park	Nelson	Obihiro	Oxford
Monterrey	Neubranden-	Oceanside	Oxnard
Montes Claros	burg	Odawara	Paderborn
Montpellier	Neuquén	Odessa	Palembang
Monza	Neuss	Ogaki	Palm Bay
Mopti	Newark	Ogbomosho	Palmdale
Moradabad	New Britain	Ogden	Palmyra
Morelia	Newcastle upon	Okara	Palo Alto
Mostar	Tyne	Okayama	Palu
Mosul	New Orleans	Okazaki	Pamplona
Moundou	Newport Beach	Olathe	Panihati
Mountain View	Newport News	Olinda	Pasay
Mount Gambier	New Rochelle	Olomouc	Paterson
Mount Vernon	Newton	Olsztyn	Patiala
Mozir	New York	Omaha	Pavia
Mudanjiang	Nicaea	Omdurman	Pavlodar
Multan	Nice	Ome	Pawtucket
Muncie	Nicomedia	Omiya	Pécs
Münster	Nicopolis	Omsk	Pegu
Murom	Nieuwegein	Omuta	Pella
Mycenae	Nikopol	Onomichi	Pembroke Pines
Mykolayiv	Nîmes	Opole	Penza
Naga City	Nimrud	Oral	Pereira
Nagaoka	Nineveh	Orange	Perm
Nagasaki	Nishinomiya	Örebro	Pernik
Nagercoil	Nizhnevartovsk	Orem	Perpignan
Nagoya	Nizhniy	Orenburg	Persepolis
Nagpur	Novgorod	Orizaba	Perugia
Nakuru	Noda	Orlando	Petaling Jaya
Nalchik	Noginsk	Orsk	Peterborough
Namangan	Norilsk	Oruro	Petra
Nanchong	Norman	Osasco	Petrópolis
Nanded	Norrköping	Osh	Pforzheim
Nanping	North Bay	Oshawa	Philadelphia

CITIES (cont.)

Phoenix
Pico Rivera
Pietermaritz-
  burg
Pine Bluff
Pingdingshan
Pingxiang
Pinsk
Piracicaba
Pisa
Pittsburgh
Plantation
Pleasanton
Pleven
Ploiesti
Podolsk
P'ohang
Poitiers
Poltava
Pompano
  Beach
Ponce
Pontiac
Popayán
Port Arthur
Port St. Lucie
Portsmouth
Posadas
Potosí
Potsdam
Prato
Priština
Prokopyevsk
Provo
Pskov
Puente Alto
Putian
Puyang
Pyatigorsk
Qaraghandy
Qinzhou
Qitaihe
Quanzhou
Quezon City
Qufu

Quilpué
Qum
Quzhou
Racine
Radom
Raipur
Rajahmundry
Rajkot
Rancagua
Rangpur
Rapid City
Rasht
Ratisbon
Ravenna
Rawalpindi
Redlands
Rennes
Reno
Resita
Rialto
Richardson
Richland
Rio Branco
Rio Cuarto
Riverside
Rizhao
Roanoke
Rochester
Rockford
Rosetta
Rotorua
Rotterdam
Royal Oak
Rubtsovsk
Rudnyy
Ryazan
Rybinsk
Sabadell
Sagamihara
Saginaw
Saharanpur
Saidpur
Saigon
St. Albans
St. Catherines

Sainte-Foy
Saint John
St. Joseph
Saint-Laurent
St. Louis
St. Petersburg
Sakai
Sakura
Salamanca
Salavat
Salem
Salford
Salt Lake City
Salvador
Salzgitter
Samara
Samaria
Samarra
Sanandaj
San Angelo
San Antonio
San Bernardino
San Bernardo
San Diego
San Francisco
San Jose
San Luis
San Mateo
San Miguel
Sanming
Santa Ana
Santa Clara
Santarém
Santa Rosa
Santiago del
  Estero
Santos
Sanya
São Goncalo
Sapporo
Sarajevo
Sarapul
Saratoga
  Springs
Saratov

Sardis
Sargodha
Sarh
Sasebo
Saskatoon
Satu Mare
Savannah
Schenectady
Schwerin
Scranton
Seattle
Segovia
Semarang
Sendai
Sétif
Seto
Severodonetsk
Severodvinsk
Shakhty
Shangqiu
Shangrao
Shaoguan
Shaowu
Shaoxing
Shaoyang
Shashi
Sheffield
Shenzhen
Shepparton
Sherbrooke
Shihezi
Shimizu
Shimoga
Shiraz
Shishou
Shiyan
Shizuishan
Shreveport
Shuangyashan
Shymkent
Sialkot
Siena
Silistra
Simbirsk
Simi Valley

CITIES (cont.)

Sinuiju	Tamale	Tupelo	Volzhskiy
Sioux City	Tambov	Tuscaloosa	Vorkuta
Sioux Falls	Tangail	Tver	Voronezh
Siping	Tangshan	Tyler	Votkinsk
Slavyansk	Tanis	Tyumen	Waco
Slupsk	Tanta	Uberaba	Walnut Creek
Smolensk	Tapachula	Uberlândia	Waltham
Soka	Tarnów	Udaipur	Wanxian
Solingen	Tarsus	Uddevalla	Warangal
Sorocaba	Tartu	Ujjain	Waterloo
Sosnowiec	Tegucigalpa	Ulanhot	Waukegan
Southampton	Tel Aviv	Ulan Ude	Waukesha
South Bend	Tempe	Ulhasnagar	Weihai
Spokane	Temuco	Ulm	Weinan
Stakhanov	Terre Haute	Ur	Wells
Staryy Oskal	Thousand Oaks	Uruapán	Wenzhou
Stendal	Thunder Bay	Utica	West Covina
Sterlitamak	Tianshui	Utrecht	West Palm
Stockton	Tiefa	Utsunomiya	Beach
Stralsund	Tieling	Vacaville	Wheaton
Stuttgart	Tikal	Valencia	Whittier
Subotica	Tilburg	Valera	Windsor
Sudbury	Tiraspol	Valledupar	Witten
Suihua	Tivoli	Vallejo	Wolfsburg
Suita	Tlemcen	Vancouver	Wonsan
Suizhou	Toledo	Vanderbijlpark	Worcester
Sumy	Tomsk	Vantaa	Wuhai
Sunderland	Tongchuan	Venlo	Wuppertal
Surgut	Tonghua	Ventura	Würzburg
Susa	Tongliao	Vereeniging	Wuxi
Suzuka	Tongling	Vicenza	Wuzhong
Syracuse	Torrance	Vicksburg	Wuzhou
Syzran	Torreón	Victoria	Xiangfan
Tábor	Toulouse	Vila Velha	Xiangtan
Taegu	Tours	Villavicencio	Xianning
Tai'an	Toyota	Vineland	Xianyang
Taichung	Traralgon	Virginia Beach	Xiaogan
Tainan	Trieste	Visalia	Xichang
Taipei	Tromsø	Vitoria da	Xigaze
Taiping	Troy	Conquista	Xilinhot
Taiyuan	Truro	Vitsyebsk	Xingtai
Ta'iz	Tucson	Vladikavkaz	Xintai
Takaoka	Tula	Volgodonsk	Xinxiang
Takasaki	Tumen	Volgograd	Xinyang
Takatsuki	Tunxi	Vologda	Xinyu

CITIES (cont.)

Xinzhou	Yichang	Yuncheng	Zhaotong
Xuchang	Yingtan	Yuxi	Zhdanov
Yakeshi	Yining	Yuyao	Zhoukou
Yakima	Yiyang	Zabrze	Zhuhai
Yamagata	Yokkaichi	Zahedan	Zhumadian
Yamaguchi	Yongzhou	Zalantun	Zhuzhou
Yamato	Yonkers	Zamora	Zigong
Yambol	York	Zanjan	Zlatoust
Yangquan	Yoshkar-Ola	Zaria	Zunyi
Yanji	Yuci	Zhambyl	Zwickau
Yazd	Yueyang	Zhangye	
Yelets	Yulin	Zhangzhou	
Yibin	Yuma	Zhaodong	

TOWNS

Aalsmeer	Albertville	Amesbury	Arundel
Äänekoski	Albi	Amityville	Arusha
Abbeville	Albufeira	Amroha	Arzamas
Abbot's	Albury	Amstetten	Asamankese
Langley	Alcobaça	Anaconda	Ashby-de-la-
Aberdare	Alcobendas	Anadarko	Zouch
Abergele	Alcoy	Anantapur	Ashford
Aberystwyth	Aldeburgh	Andover	Ashington
Abilene	Aldershot	Andújar	Aspen
Abingdon	Aleksinac	Aného	Assisi
Abomey	Alfortville	Anniston	Athlone
Abydos	Alloa	Ansbach	Atlantic City
Achinsk	Almadén	Antequera	Aubervilliers
Adoni	Almetyevsk	Antigonish	Auchterarder
Adria	Alnwick	Antony	Auchtermuchty
Agadez	Altamira	Antsirabe	Augusta
Agrinion	Altamura	Anzhero-	Aurangabad
Aigues-Mortes	Altay	Sudzhensk	Aviemore
Airdrie	Altenburg	Apeldoorn	Avranches
Aix-la-Chapelle	Alton	Aranjuez	Axminster
Aix-les-Bains	Altötting	Ararat	Aylesbury
Ajka	Altrincham	Arlington	Aylesford
Akjoujt	Amalfi	Heights	Ayr
Aksum	Ambleside	Armentières	Ayutthaya
Albany	Amersham	Arrah	Baabda
Albena	Ames	Artigas	Baalbek

TOWNS (cont.)

Babahoyo
Bacau
Baccarat
Baden
Baden-Baden
Badulla
Baeza
Bafoussam
Baharampur
Bahraich
Baikonur
Baiyin
Bajram Curri
Bakewell
Bakhchisarai
Balakovo
Balashikha
Balboa
Balbriggan
Balkh
Ballina
Bamburgh
Bamenda
Banbury
Bangor
Banja Luka
Banqiao
Barcelos
Bardolino
Bar-le-Duc
Barnsley
Barnstaple
Barrow
Basildon
Batala
Batalha
Batangas City
Bath
Bathurst
Battle
Bat Yam
Bayeux
Bayreuth
Beaconsfield
Bearsden

Beaumaris
Beaumes de
  Venise
Beaune
Bebington
Béchar
Beckenham
Bedford
Bedlington
Bedworth
Beenleigh
Beersheba
Beipiao
Belize City
Bellagio
Belleville
Bendigo
Berchtesgaden
Berenice
Berkhamsted
Bernkastel
Berwick-upon-
  Tweed
Bhadravati
Bhamo
Bharatpur
Bhatpara
Bhiwani
Bhusawal
Bicester
Bideford
Bijapur
Bilaspur
Billund
Binche
Bingerville
Birchington
Birkenhead
Biskra
Bjorneborg
Blackburn
Blagoevgrad
Blantyre
Blois
Boa Vista

Boca Raton
Bodmin
Bodrum
Bofors
Bognor Regis
Bogor
Bole
Bolsover
Bolton
Bongor
Boston
Botosani
Boulder
Bourg-en-
  Bresse
Bournemouth
Bracknell
Braintree
Brampton
Breda
Brentwood
Bridgend
Bridgwater
Bridlington
Brighouse
Brighton
Bristol
Brive-la-
  Gaillarde
Brixham
Broken Hill
Bromsgrove
Browning
Buckingham
Bude
Bukavu
Bukittinggi
Bundaberg
Bundoran
Burnley
Burton upon
  Trent
Bury
Bury St.
  Edmunds

Buxton
Caerphilly
Cairns
Cajamarca
Calama
Caltanisetta
Calvi
Camberley
Camborne
Cambridge
Cana
Capua
Cardigan
Carefree
Carlisle
Carlsbad
Carmel
Carrara
Cashel
Casper
Cassino
Castlebar
Catanzaro
Celje
Cerignola
Cesena
Cessnock
Cetinje
Chalatenango
Chambéry
Chamonix
Changshu
Chantilly
Charlestown
Chartres
Château-Thierry
Chatham
Cheb
Chelles
Chelmsford
Chesham
Chesterfield
Chichester
Chieti
Chinon

TOWNS (cont.)

Cholula	Darlington	East Kilbride	Famagusta
Chorley	Darmstad	East Lansing	Farnborough
Christchurch	Dartford	Ebbw Vale	Farnham
Cîmpulung	Dartmouth	Eccles	Farrukhabad
Cirencester	Dawson Creek	Edam	Fátima
Cleethorpes	Deal	Eger	Feldkirch
Clonakilty	Deauville	Eidsvoll	Ferrara
Cloncurry	Dehiwala	Eilat	Fianarantsoa
Clonmel	Delft	Eisenach	Fier
Cluny	Denbigh	Ekibastuz	Firozabad
Coalport	Deolali	Elbasan	Flagstaff
Coatbridge	Deva	El Centro	Flin Flon
Cockermouth	Dewsbury	Elche	Flint
Coff's Harbour	Dhahran	Elda	Flores
Colchester	Dharamsala	El Djem	Foggia
Colditz	Dhule	Elektrostal	Fontainebleau
Coleraine	Diekirch	El Escorial	Forlì
Colwyn Bay	Dinant	Elgin	Forster-
Comayagua	Dinard	El Jadida	Tuncurry
Coober Pedy	Dindigul	Elvas	Fort Collins
Cookstown	Dingwall	Ennis	Fort William
Cooktown	Diredawa	Ensenada	Francistown
Cootamundra	Divinópolis	Entebbe	Frascati
Copiapó	Dobrich	Épernay	Frauenfeld
Corby	Dolores Hidalgo	Epping	Freiberg
Cornwall	Doncaster	Epsom	Gadag
Corozal	Dongsheng	Epworth	Gafsa
Cosenza	Dornbirn	Esch-sur-Alzette	Gaillac
Cowes	Douai	Escuintla	Galashiels
Cox's Bazar	Douglas	Esquipulas	Gällivare
Craigavon	Downend	Essaouira	Galt
Cranbourne	Downpatrick	Estoril	Gamlakarleby
Crawley	Droitwich	Esztergom	Gander
Cremona	Duffel	Etawah	Gandhinagar
Crewe	Dumfries	Etruria	Ganganagar
Cristobál	Dundalk	Evesham	Garoua
Cuddapah	Dunhuang	Évora	Gateshead
Cuernavaca	Dun Laoghaire	Évreux	Gattinara
Cuneo	Dunmow	Exmouth	Genk
Curepipe	Duras	Faenza	Getafe
Curicó	Durg	Faizabad	Gettysburg
Dakhla	Durham	Falaise	Ghardaïa
Dalandzadgad	Earlston	Falkirk	Ghazni
Dalkeith	Eastbourne	Fall River	Gillingham
Dangriga	East Dereham	Falmouth	Gitega

TOWNS (cont.)

Glace Bay	Harlow	Jena	Kilifi
Glastonbury	Harpers Ferry	Jihlava	Kilkís
Glenrothes	Hartlepool	Jijiga	Killarney
Gneizeno	Hastings	Jinja	Kilmarnock
Godalming	Hatfield	Jipijapa	Kineshma
Godhavn	Havant	Jiuquan	King's Lynn
Gomorrah	Hawick	Joliette	Kinross
Gondar	Heihei	Jonquière	Kirkcaldy
Gondia	Heinola	Jos	Kirkcudbright
Gorazde	Helensburgh	Kajaani	Kirkenes
Gorgan	Hengelo	Kalgoorlie	Kirkwall
Görlitz	Herculaneum	Kalulushi	Kirriemuir
Gosport	High Wycombe	Kamakura	Kiruna
Göttingen	Hillerod	Kampen	Kitty Hawk
Gouda	Hilversum	Kankan	Klosterneuburg
Gourock	Hitchin	Kansk	Korhogo
Grafton	Hof	Kanye	Koudougou
Gramsh	Holguin	Kapfenberg	Kourou
Grangemouth	Hospet	Karaikkudi	Kouvola
Grantham	Hotan	Kardhítsa	Kralendijk
Grasse	Houma	Kariba	Kraljevo
Gravesend	Hove	Karlovac	Kranj
Great Malvern	Hradec Králové	Karlsruhe	Krefeld
Great Yarmouth	Huancavelica	Karlstad	Krosno
Greifswald	Huangshan	Karnal	Krugersdorp
Grevená	Huánuco	Karshi	Krusevac
Grootfontein	Huddersfield	Kashan	Kusadasi
Guarda	Huntingdon	Kastoriá	Kyustendil
Guaymas	Hwange	Kateríni	La Ciotat
Gubbio	Idlib	Katihar	Ladysmith
Guelph	Igualada	Kaufbeuren	Lagos
Guéret	Ilkley	Kavieng	Laguna Beach
Guildford	Imatra	Keetmanshoop	La Jolla
Guise	Interlaken	Kendal	La Laguna
Haddington	Ioánnina	Kenilworth	Lambersart
Ha'il	Ipswich	Kerava	Laon
Hailar	Iringa	Kerkrade	La Oroya
Hakone	Irvine	Keswick	Laredo
Halabja	Iznik	Kettering	Larnaca
Halden	Jackson	Khandwa	Larne
Halesowen	Jalgaon	Kharagpur	La Roche-sur-
Halifax	Jalna	Khaylitsa	Yon
Hamilton	Jarrow	Khiva	La Serena
Hammamet	Järvenpää	Khouribga	Latacunga
Hapur	Jedburgh	Kidderminster	Latina

TOWNS (cont.)

Latur	Lourdes	Medina	Nabeul
Lausanne	Lowestoft	Mégara	Nablus
Le Cannet	Lubango	Mejicanos	Nadiad
Lecce	Lucca	Melitopol	Nampula
Le Creusot	Lüderitz	Melk	Napa
Legnica	Lugano	Melton	Navan
Leh	Lugo	Melton	Nazareth
Leiria	Lushnjë	Mowbray	Neath
Le Lamentin	Luton	Melun	Nerja
Le Mans	Lytham Saint	Mende	Newbury
Lens	Anne's	Meriden	Newcastle
Leoben	Macapá	Merthyr Tydfil	under Lyme
Leonding	Macclesfield	Meru	Newmarket
Les Abymes	Macerata	Miami Beach	New Plymouth
Les Mureaux	Machakos	Middlesbrough	Newport
Letchworth	Machala	Milagro	Newquay
Lethbridge	Mafra	Milton Keynes	Newton Abbot
Leticia	Magenta	Mödling	Newton Aycliffe
Lewes	Mahalapye	Mohács	Newton St.
Leyland	Maidenhead	Mold	Boswells
Lichfield	Maidstone	Molepolole	Newtownabbey
Lifford	Maiduguri	Monastir	Neyshabur
Likasi	Maikop	Moncton	Ngaoundéré
Limassol	Maitland	Montbéliard	Nijmegen
Limbe	Malmédy	Montélimar	Nitra
Limoux	Malmesbury	Montreux	Nizamabad
Linares	Mandurah	Monywa	Nkongsamba
Linlithgow	Mandya	Moose Jaw	Nokia
Linköping	Mantua	Morecambe	Nome
Lisburn	Manzini	Morogoro	Northallerton
Lisdoonvarna	Maradi	Morpeth	Northampton
Lismore	Marbella	Morristown	North Little
Llandudno	Maroochydore	Morwell	Rock
Llanelli	Maroua	Moshi	North Shields
Llangollen	Marsala	Motala	Norwich
Lobatse	Masaya	Moulay Idriss	Nottingham
Lockerbie	Mascara	Moulins	Novara
Logroño	Massa	Mount Isa	Nuneaton
Loja	Masvingo	Mount Prospect	Nyiregyháza
Long Eaton	Matera	Mullingar	Oak Lawn
Lons-le-Saunier	Matlock	Mutare	Oak Park
Lorca	Maun	Muzzaffarnagar	Oakville
Loreto	Mazatenango	Muzzaffarpur	Odienné
Los Alamos	Mbeya	Mwanza	Oldenburg
Loughborough	Mdina	Naas	Oldham

TOWNS (cont.)

Olmos	Pontefract	Redondo Beach	Santa Maria
Omagh	Pontypool	Reigate	Sarasota
Onitsha	Pontypridd	Remscheid	Saumur
Orange	Poole	Reus	Sausalito
Orange Walk	Porbandar	Richmond	Savannakhet
Orapa	Portalegre	Richmond Hill	Savona
Oristano	Port Dickson	Ringkøbing	Sayama
Orlova	Port el Kantaoui	Ringsted	Scarborough
Örnsköldsvik	Port Macquarie	Riobamba	Schwabach
Orvieto	Portmeirion	Río Tinto	Schweinfurt
Osorno	Portoviejo	Rivera	Scunthorpe
Otavalo	Port Sunlight	Rochdale	Sedan
Ottery St. Mary	Port Talbot	Rochester	Seinäjoki
Overland Park	Potenza	Rockingham	Seixal
Paarl	Prešov	Ronda	Selby
Pagan	Preston	Rosenheim	Selebi-Phikwe
Paignton	Préveza	Rosyth	Sensuntepeque
Pailin	Prince George	Rotherham	Seraing
Paisley	Princeton	Rothesay	Sergiyev Posad
Pakse	Privas	Rotorua	Serowe
Palm Beach	Prizren	Rottweil	Sevenoaks
Palmerston	Prome	Roubaix	Sharpeville
North	Pucallpa	Rovaniemi	Sheerness
Panipat	Puerto Plata	Rugby	Shibin el Kom
Paphos	Pula	Runcorn	Shrewsbury
Parbhani	Puno	Rustavi	Siauliai
Paris-Plage	Punta Gorda	Sagar	Sidi-bel-Abbès
Pasig	Puri	St. Andrews	Siegen
Passau	Purnia	St. Charles	Sikasso
Patan	Qazvin	St. Émilion	Silver City
Pau	Qena	St. Helens	Simferopol
Pavlograd	Queluz	St. Helier	Sincelejo
Pazardzhik	Rabaul	Saint-Hubert	Sintra
Peć	Raichur	St-Malo	Sion
Penzance	Rajapalayam	St-Nazaire	Sitka
Pervouralsk	Rambouillet	St. Peter Port	Skegness
Pesaro	Rampur	St-Quentin	Skellefteå
Peterlee	Ramsgate	Salinas	Skelmersdale
Pirmasens	Randers	Salisbury	Skokie
Pitesti	Ratlam	Sambalpur	Slavonsky Brod
Plauen	Rauma	Sambhal	Sliema
Plymouth	Reading	Sangli	Slough
Point-à-Pitre	Redcar	Sankt Pölten	Smederovo
Polonnaruwa	Redding	San Sebastian	Sneek
Ponferrada	Redditch	Santa Barbara	Sohag

TOWNS (cont.)

Solihull
Solikamsk
Sondrio
Sonoma
Sonsonate
Sopron
Soria
Sorrento
Southport
South Shields
Soyapango
Sozopol
Spa
Spanish Town
Sparks
Spoleto
Stafford
Staines
Stamford
Stavanger
Stellenbosch
Stevenage
Steyr
Stockport
Stockton-on-
  Tees
Stornoway
Strabane
Stretford
Stroud
Struga
Strumica
Suceava
Suhl
Sukhotal
Sunbury
Sundsvall
Swakopmund
Swindon
Szekszárd
Szolnok
Tahoua
Tamworth
Taree
Tarija

Taroudant
Tatabánya
Taunton
Tauranga
Taza
Telde
Telford
Tennant Creek
Teresina
Terni
Tetovo
Tewantin
Thane
Thetford
Thimphu
Thionville
Thun
Tiberias
Tighina
Tijuana
Timimoun
Tindouf
Tiruppur
Tokaj
Tombstone
Torquay
Tourcoing
Tralee
Traun
Travnik
Trim
Troon
Trowbridge
Tskhinvali
Tübingen
Tumkur
Turpan
Tuticorin
Tuzla
Tychy
Udhagaman-
  dalam
Udine
Ulundi
Urbino

Vác
Valenciennes
Varadero
Varaždin
Varese
Varna
Vaslui
Veliko Turnovo
Vellore
Vénissieux
Vercelli
Verdun
Versailles
Verviers
Veszprém
Viborg
Vichy
Vidin
Viedma
Vila do Conde
Villach
Viña del Mar
Viseu
Viterbo
Wadi Halfa
Wakefield
Wallasey
Wallsend
Walsall
Wangaratta
Wantage
Warrington
Warrnambool
Warwick
Washington
Waterbury
Waterloo
Watford
Weimar
Welkom
Wels
Welwyn Garden
  City
West Bromwich
Westerham

West Orange
Wethersfield
Weymouth
Whitby
Whyalla
Wichita Falls
Wick
Widnes
Wiener
  Neustadt
Wigan
Williamsburg
Wilton
Winchester
Windsor
Winnetka
Winona
Winterthur
Wisbech
Wittenberg
Woking
Wokingham
Wolfsberg
Woodstock
Worksop
Worms
Worthing
Wrexham
Xánthi
Xochimilco
Yeovil
Yorktown
Youghal
Zaanstad
Zadar
Zagazig
Zalaegerszeg
Zielona Gora
Zinder
Zlin
Zoetermeer
Zouerate
Zrenjanin
Zwolle

VILLAGES

Aberfoyle
Abu Simbel
Agincourt
Aihole
Albarracin
Aldermaston
Aldwinkle
Alloway
Annapolis
  Royal
Assen
Avebury
Ayia Napa
Ayot St.
  Lawrence
Badminton
Balaclava
Ballymahon
Ballymote
Balquhidder
Baniyas
Bannockburn
Barbizon
Battenberg
Beaulieu
Belsen
Bergamo
Bishopsbourne
Bisley
Blarney
Blenheim
Bodhgaya
Bogazköy
Borodino
Borstal
Bournville
Boys Town
Braemar
Bramber
Bray
Buchenwald
Caesarea
  Philippi
Callanish
Camembert

Camperdown
Capernaum
Capo di Monte
Caprese
  Michelangelo
Carnac
Catskill
Cawdor
Cerne Abbas
Certaldo
Chablis
Chavín de
  Huántar
Chawton
Cheddar
Churchill
Clifden
Clouds Hill
Clovelly
Cockburnspath
Crécy
Crosthwaite
Culloden
Dettingen
Dien Bien Phu
Down Ampney
Downe
Dunmow
Dunwich
East Bergholt
East Budleigh
East Coker
Eastwood
Ecclefechan
Elis
Elstow
Eversley
Farndon
Flodden
Folsom
Fort Raleigh
Fotheringhay
Ganvie
Glamis
Glynde

Gorgonzola
Gort
Gotham
Grasmere
Greenwich
  Village
Gretna Green
Gruyère
Hallstatt
Harlech
Hattusas
Hell
Helpston
Higher Walton
Hillsborough
Holne
Jerash
John o' Groats
Karnak
King's Cliffe
Kinnesswood
Lassa
Laxton
Lidice
Lipizza
Llanfairpwll-
  gwyngyllgo-
  gerychwyrn-
  drobwllllanty-
  siliogogogoch
Longmen
Malplaquet
Marengo
Matmata
Mayerling
Maynooth
Monbazillac
Naseby
Oberammergau
Oystermouth
Palenque
Panmunjom
Passchendaele
Pattaya
Peenemunde

Piltdown
Plassey
Pompadour
Port Arthur
Prestonpans
Quatre Bras
Ramillies
Rocamadour
Roquefort-sur-
  Soulzon
Rouffignac
Rydal
San Simeon
Scone
Selborne
Serowe
Shaoshan
Silchester
Skara Brae
Solferino
St. David's
Steventon
Stilton
Sutton
  Courtenay
Ticonderoga
Tintagel
Tolpuddle
Tordesillas
Tremadoc
Uffington
Waitangi
Walsingham
Warnham
Waterloo
West Malvern
Westward Ho
Widecombe-in-
  the-Moor
Woburn
Yattenden
Zelazowa Wola

OCEANS AND SEAS

Adriatic Sea
Aegean Sea
Andaman Sea
Antarctic Ocean
Arabian Sea
Arafura Sea
Aral Sea
Arctic Ocean
Atlantic Ocean
Azov, Sea of
Baltic Sea
Banda Sea
Barents Sea
Beaufort Sea
Bering Sea
Black Sea

Caribbean Sea
Caspian Sea
China Sea
Coral Sea
Dead Sea
East China Sea
Galilee, Sea of
Greenland Sea
Indian Ocean
Inland Sea
Ionian Sea
Irish Sea
Japan, Sea of
Java Sea
Kara Sea
Laptev Sea

Ligurian Sea
Marmara, Sea of
Mediterranean Sea
North Sea
Okhotsk, Sea of
Pacific Ocean
Red Sea
Ross Sea
Sargasso Sea
Savu Sea
South China Sea
Tasman Sea
Weddell Sea
White Sea
Yellow Sea

LAKES, LOCHS, AND LOUGHS
(with location)

Albert	Uganda, Democratic Republic of Congo	
Aral Sea	Kazakhstan, Uzbekistan	
Athabasca	Canada	
Awe	Scotland	
Baikal	Russia	
Balaton	Hungary	
Bala	Wales	
Balkhash	Kazakhstan	
Bangweulu	Zambia	
Bassenthwaite	England	
Bear	USA	
Becharof	USA	
Belfast	Northern Ireland	
Breydon	England	
Buttermere	England	
Caspian Sea	Iran, Russia, Azerbaijan, Kazakhstan, Turkmenistan	
Celyn	Wales	
Central Park Lake	USA	
Chad	Chad, Niger, Nigeria, Cameroon	
Champlain	USA	
Chiemsee	Germany	
Clark	USA	
Clywedog	Wales	
Como	Italy	
Coniston	England	
Constance	Germany	
Corrib	Republic of Ireland	
Cwellyn	Wales	
Dall	USA	
Derg	Republic of Ireland	
Derwent Water	England	

LAKES, LOCHS, AND LOUGHS (cont.)

(with location)

Dongting	China	Lomond	Scotland
Edward	Uganda, Democratic Republic of Congo	Lop Nur or Lop Nor	China
		Lucerne	Switzerland
Ennerdale	England	Maggiore	Italy, Switzerland
Ericht	Scotland	Malawi	Malawi, Tanzania, Mozambique
Erie	Canada, USA		
Erne	Northern Ireland	Manitoba	Canada
Esthwaite	England	Maracaibo	Venezuela
Eyre	Australia	Maree	Scotland
Flathead	USA	Martin	USA
Foyle	Ireland	Mask	Republic of Ireland
Garda	Italy		
Geneva	Switzerland, France	Menindee	Australia
		Michigan	USA
Grasmere	England	Mille Lacs	USA
Great Lake	USA, Canada; Australia	Mobutu	Uganda, Democratic Republic of Congo
Great Bear	Canada		
Great Salt Lake	USA		
Great Slave	Canada	Moosehead	USA
Hawes Water	England	Naknek	USA
Hickling Broad	England	Nasser	Egypt
Huron	USA, Canada	Natron	Tanzania
Ijsselmeer or		Neagh	Northern Ireland
Ysselmeer	The Netherlands	Nemi	Italy
Iliamna	USA	Ness	Scotland
Issyk-kul	Kyrgyzstan	Neusiedl	Austria, Hungary
Kara-Bogaz-Gol	Turkmenistan	Nicaragua	Nicaragua
Kariba	Zambia, Zimbabwe	Nipigon	Canada
		Nu Jiang	China, Myanmar – formerly Burma
Katrine	Scotland		
Kivu	Democratic Republic of Congo, Rwanda	Nyasa or Nyassa	Malawi, Tanzania, Mozambique
Koko Nor	China	Okeechobee	USA
Kyoga or Kioga	Uganda	Onega	Russia
Ladoga	Russia	Ontario	Canada, USA
Lake of the		Oulton Broad	England
Woods	Canada	Padarn	Wales
Leech	USA	Pend Oreille	USA
Léman	Switzerland, France	Peipus	Russia, Estonia
		Pontchartrain	USA
		Poyang or P'o-yang	China
Leven	Scotland		
Lochy	Scotland	Pyramid	USA

LAKES, LOCHS, AND LOUGHS (cont.)

(with location)

Qinghai Hu	China	Titicaca	Peru, Bolivia
Rainy	USA	Tonle Sap	Cambodia
Rannoch	Scotland	Torrens	Australia
Red Tarn	England	Trasimeno	Italy
Ree	Republic of Ireland	Tsana	Ethiopia
		Tungting or	
Reindeer	Canada	Tung-t'ing	China
Rudolf	Kenya, Ethiopia	Turkana	Kenya, Ethiopia
Rutland	England	Tustumena	USA
Rydal Water	England	Ugashik	USA
Saimaa	Finland	Ullswater	England
St Clair	USA, Canada	Upper Klamath	USA
St James's Park Lake	England	Urmia	Iran
		Utah	USA
Salton Sea	USA	Van	Turkey
Serpentine, The	England	Vänern	Sweden
Strangford	Northern Ireland	Victoria	Uganda, Tanzania, Kenya
Superior	USA, Canada		
Tahoe	USA	Vierwald-	
Tana	Ethiopia	stättersee	Switzerland
Tanganyika	Democratic Republic of Congo, Burundi, Tanzania, Zambia	Volta	Ghana
		Vyrnwy	Wales
		Wast Water	England
		Windermere	England
Taupo	New Zealand	Winnebago	USA
Tay	Scotland	Winnibigoshish	USA
Tegid	Wales	Winnipeg	Canada
Teshekpuk	USA	Winnipegosis	Canada
Thirlmere	England	Yellowstone	USA

RIVERS

(with location)

Adda	Italy	Churchill	Canada
Adige	Italy	Cherwell	England
Adur	England	Clutha	New Zealand
Ain	France	Clyde	Scotland, Canada
Aire	England; France	Colne	England
Aisne	France	Coln	England
Allan	Scotland; Syria	Colorado	USA
Aller	Spain; Germany	Columbia	USA
Allier	France	Congo	Congo, Democratic Republic of Congo
Aln	England		
Amazon	Peru, Brazil		
Amu Darya	Turkmenistan, Uzbekistan	Cooper	Australia
		Coppermine	Canada
Amur	Mongolia, Russia, China	Coquet	England
		Crouch	England
Angara	Russia	Damodar	India
Annan	Scotland	Danube	Germany, Austria, Romania, Hungary, Slovakia, Bulgaria
Araguaia	Brazil		
Arkansas	USA		
Arno	Italy		
Arun	Nepal		
Assiniboine	Canada	Darling	Australia
Athabasca	Canada	Dart	England
Aube	France	Dee	Scotland; Wales, England
Avon	England		
Bann	Northern Ireland	Demerara	Guyana
Beas	India	Derwent	England
Benue	Nigeria	Dnepr	Russia, Belarus, Ukraine
Bermejo	Argentina		
Bío-Bío	Chile	Dnestr	Ukraine, Moldova
Brahmaputra	Tibet, India	Don	Russia, Scotland, England, France Australia
Brent	England		
Bug	Ukraine, Poland, Germany		
		Doon	Scotland
Bure	England	Dordogne	France
Camel	England	Doubs	France, Switzerland
Cam	England		
Canadian	USA	Douro	Spain, Portugal
Cauvery	India	Dove	England
Chang Jiang	China	Dovey	Wales
Chao Phraya	Thailand	Drava	Italy, Austria, Yugoslavia, Hungary
Charente	France		
Chari	Cameroon, Chad		
Chenab	Pakistan	Duero	Spain
Cher	France	Durance	France

RIVERS (cont.)
(with location)

Dvina	Russia	James	USA, Australia
Ebro	Spain	Japurá	Brazil
Eden	England, Scotland	Jordan	Israel, Jordan
Elbe	Germany, Czech	Juba	Ethiopia, Somalia
	Republic	Jumna	India
Emba	Kazakhstan	Juruá	Brazil
Ems	Germany, The	Kafue	Zambia
	Netherlands	Kama	Russia
Escaut	Belgium, France	Kasai	Angola, Demo-
Esk	Australia		cratic Republic
Essequibo	Guyana		of Congo
Euphrates	Iraq	Kolyma	Russia
Exe	England	Kuban	Russia
Fal	England	Kura	Turkey, Georgia,
Fly	Papua New		Azerbaijan
	Guinea	Kwa	Democratic
Forth	Scotland		Republic of
Fraser	Canada		Congo
Frome	Australia	Lachlan	Australia
Gambia	The Gambia,	Lagan	Northern Ireland
	Senegal	Lahn	Germany
Ganges	India	Lea	England
Garonne	France	Lech	Germany, Austria
Gironde	France	Lee	Republic of
Glomma	Norway		Ireland
Godavari	India	Lena	Russia
Great Ouse	England	Liffey	Republic of
Guadalquivir	Spain		Ireland
Han	China	Limpopo	South Africa,
Hawkesbury	Australia		Zimbabwe,
Helmand	Afghanistan		Mozambique
Hooghly	India	Lippe	Germany
Hsi Chiang	China	Loddon	Australia, England
Huang Ho	China	Loire	France
Hudson	USA	Lot	France
Hunter	Australia	Lualaba	Democratic
Indus	India, Pakistan,		Republic of
	China		Congo
Irrawaddy	Myanmar –	Lune	England
	formerly Burma	Lüne	Germany
Irtysh	China,	Maas	Netherlands
	Kazakhstan,	Mackenzie	Australia
	Russia	Madeira	Brazil
Isis	England	Magdalena	Colombia
Itchen	England	Main	Germany

RIVERS (cont.)

(with location)

Mamoré	Brazil, Bolivia	Ouse	England
Manawatu	New Zealand	Oxus	Turkmenistan,
Marañón	Brazil, Peru		Uzbekistan
Maritsa	Bulgaria	Paraguay	Paraguay
Marne	France	Paraná	Brazil
Maros	Indonesia	Peace	Canada, USA
Medina	USA	Pearl	USA, China
Medway	England	Pechora	Russia
Mekong	Laos, China	Pecos	USA
Menderes	Turkey	Peel	Australia, USA
Mersey	England	Piave	Italy
Meuse	France, Belgium	Platte	USA
Minho	Spain, Portugal	Po	Italy
Miño	Spain	Potomac	USA
Mississippi	USA	Purus	Brazil
Missouri	USA	Putumayo	Ecuador
Mole	England	Rance	France
Monnow	England, Wales	Ravi	India, Pakistan
Moselle	Germany	Rede	England
Mureş	Romania,	Red	USA
	Hungary	Rhine	Switzerland,
Murray	Australia, Canada		Germany, The
Murrumbidgee	Australia		Netherlands
Neckar	Germany	Ribble	England
Negro	Spain; Brazil,	Río Bravo	Mexico
	Argentina,	Río de la Plata	Argentina,
	Bolivia,		Uruguay
	Paraguay,	Rio Grande	Jamaica
	Uruguay,	Ruhr	Germany
	Venezuela	Rur	Germany
Neisse	Poland, Germany	Rye	England
Neman	Belarus, Lithuania	Saale	Germany
Niger	Nigeria, Mali,	Saar	Germany,
	Guinea		France
Nile	Sudan, Egypt	Saguenay	Canada
Ob	Russia	Salado	Argentina, Cuba,
Oder	Germany, Czech		Mexico
	Republic, Poland	Salween	Myanmar –
Ogooué	Gabon		formerly Burma,
Ohio	USA		China
Oise	France	Saône	France
Orange	South Africa	Saskatchewan	Canada
Orontes	Syria	Scheldt	Belgium
Orwell	England	Seine	France
Otter	England	Senegal	Senegal

RIVERS (cont.)

(with location)

Severn	England	Tugela	South Africa
Shannon	Republic of Ireland	Tunguska	Russia
Shatt al-Arab	Iran, Iraq	Tweed	England, Scotland
Shenandoah	USA	Tyne	Scotland, England
Slave	Canada	Ural	Russia, Kazakhstan
Snake	USA	Ure	England
Somme	France	Uruguay	Uruguay, Brazil
Songhua	Vietnam, China	Usk	Wales, England
Spey	Scotland	Ussuri	China, Russia
St John	Liberia, USA	Vaal	South Africa
St Lawrence	USA	Vienne	France
Stour	England	Vistula	Poland
Sungari	China	Vltava	Czech Republic
Susquehanna	USA	Volga	Russia, USA
Sutlej	Pakistan, India, China	Volta	Ghana
Swale	England	Volturno	Italy
Swannee or		Wabash	USA
Suwannee	USA	Waikato	New Zealand
Syr Darya	Uzbekistan, Kazakhstan	Wansbeck	England
		Wear	England
Taff	Wales	Weaver	England
Tagus	Portugal, Spain	Weser	Germany
Tajo	Spain	Wey	England
Tamar	England	Windrush	England
Tarn	France	Wye	Wales, England
Tawe	Wales	Xi Jiang	China
Tawi	India	Xingu	Brazil
Tay	Scotland	Yangtze	China
Tees	England	Yare	England
Tejo	Brazil	Yellow	China, USA, Papua New Guinea
Tennessee	USA		
Test	England	Yellowstone	USA
Thames	England	Yenisei	Russia
Tiber	Italy	Yeo	England
Ticino	Italy, Switzerland	Zambezi	Zambia, Angola, Zimbabwe, Mozambique
Tigris	Iraq, Turkey		
Torridge	England		
Trent	England		

WATERFALLS
(with location)

Angel	Venezuela	Kegon	Japan
Augrabies	South Africa	Mardalsfossen	Norway
Cauvery	India	Niagara	Canada, USA
Cuquenán	Venezuela	Ruacana	Angola
Della	Canada	Sutherland	New Zealand
Grande Cascade	France	Takakkaw	Canada
Iguaçu	Argentina, Brazil	Tugela	South Africa
Jog	India	Victoria	Zimbabwe,
Kabalega	Uganda		Zambia
Kalambo	Tanzania, Zambia	Wallaman	Australia
Kapachira	Malawi	Yosemite	USA

MOUNTAINS
(with location)

Aconcagua	Argentina	Kilimanjaro	Tanzania
Annapurna	Nepal	Kinabalu	Malaysia
Ararat	Turkey	Logan	Canada
Ben Nevis	Scotland	McKinley	USA
Bonete	Argentina	Makalu I	Nepal, Tibet
Carrantuohill	Republic of	Margherita	Democratic Re-
	Ireland		public of Congo,
Chimborazo	Ecuador		Rwanda
Citlaltépetl	Mexico	Matterhorn	Switzerland, Italy
Communism		Mont Blanc	France, Italy
Peak	Tajikistan	Muztag	China
Cotopaxi	Ecuador	Nanga Parbat	Pakistan
Damavand	Iran	Ojos del Salado	Argentina, Chile
Dufourspitze	Switzerland	Pissis	Argentina
Dykh-Tau	Russia	Pobedy	Kyrgyzstan
Elbrus	Russia	Popocatépetl	Mexico
Etna	Italy	Ras Dashen	Ethiopia
Everest	Nepal, Tibet	St Elias	USA, Canada
Fujiyama	Japan	Scafell Pike	England
Huascarán	Peru	Slieve Donard	Northern Ireland
Jaya	Indonesia	Snowdon	Wales
K2 or Godwin-		Tirich Mir	Pakistan
Austen	India	Tupungato	Argentina, Chile
Kanchenjunga	Nepal, India	Weisshorn	Switzerland
Kenya	Kenya		

MOUNTAIN RANGES

(with location)

Alps	France, Switzerland, Italy, Austria, Liechtenstein
Altai	Kazakhstan, China, Mongolia
Andes	Venezuela, Colombia, Ecuador, Peru, Bolivia, Argentina, Chile
Apennine Hills	Italy
Appalachians	USA
Atlas Mountains	Morocco, Algeria, Tunisia
Balkan Mountains	Bulgaria
Bernese Alps	Switzerland
Black Mountains	Wales
Blue Mountains	Australia
Blue Ridge Mountains	USA
Brecon Beacons	Wales
Cairngorms	Scotland
Cambrian Mountains	Wales
Cantabrian Mountains	Spain
Carpathians	Czech Republic, Slovakia, Poland, Romania, Ukraine
Caucasus Mountains	Russia, Georgia, Azerbaijan, Armenia
Cévennes	France
Coast Mountains	Canada
Cumbrian Mountains	England
Dolomites	Italy
Drakensberg Mountains	South Africa, Lesotho
Flinders Range	Australia
Ghats Range	India
Golan Heights	Israel
Grampian Mountains	Scotland
Hamersley Range	Australia
Harz Mountains	Germany
Himalayas	China, India, Pakistan, Nepal, Bhutan
Hindu Kush	Afghanistan, Pakistan
Hoggar Mountains	Algeria
Jura Mountains	France, Switzerland
Kaikoura Ranges	New Zealand
Karakoram Range	Afghanistan, Pakistan, China, India
Kunlun Shan	China
Ladakh Range	India, Pakistan, China
MacDonnell Ranges	Australia
Middleback Ranges	Australia
Macgillicuddy's Reeks	Republic of Ireland
Mourne Mountains	Northern Ireland
Musgrave Ranges	Australia
North West Highlands	Scotland

MOUNTAIN RANGES (cont.)

(with location)

Olympic Mountains	USA
Pamir Mountains	Tajikistan, China, Afghanistan
Pennines	England
Pindus Mountains	Greece, Albania
Pyrenees	France, Spain
Rocky Mountains *or* Rockies	USA, Canada
Sayan Mountains	Russia
Sierra Madre Range	Mexico
Sierra Morena Range	Spain
Sierra Nevada Range	USA
Smoky Mountains *or* Smokies	USA
Snowy Mountains	Australia
Taurus Mountains	Turkey
Tien Shan	Kyrgyzstan, China, Mongolia
Ural Mountains	Russia
Zagros Mountains	Iran

VOLCANOES

(with location)

Acatenango	Guatemala	Coseguina	Nicaragua
Agung	Indonesia	Cotacachi	Ecuador
Alcedo	Galapagos Islands, Ecuador	Cotopaxi	Ecuador
		Demavend	Iran
Ambrim	Vanuatu	Dempo	Indonesia
Amburombu	Indonesia	Didicas	Philippines
Asama	Japan	Dukono	Indonesia
Askja	Iceland	El Misti	Peru
Aso	Japan	Erebus	Antarctica
Atitlan	Guatemala	Etna	Sicily, Italy
Awu	Indonesia	Fogo	Cape Verde
Bandai-san	Japan	Fonualei	Tongas
Bárcena	Mexico	Fuego	Guatemala
Bogoslof	USA	Fujiyama	Japan
Buleng	Indonesia	Galeras	Colombia
Bulusan	Philippines	Gamkonora	Indonesia
Cameroon	Cameroon	Gede	Indonesia
Capelinhos	Azores	Great Sitkin	USA
Cerro Negro	Nicaragua	Grimsvötn	Iceland
Chances Peak	Montserrat	Guallatiri	Chile
Chimborazo	Ecuador	Hekla	Iceland
Cleveland	USA	Hibok Hibok	Philippines
Colima	Mexico	Huainaputina	Peru

VOLCANOES (cont.)

(with location)

Hualalai	USA	Osorno	Chile
Izalco	El Salvador	Pacaya	Guatemala
Jorullo	Mexico	Paloe	Indonesia
Kaba	Indonesia	Paricutin	Mexico
Katla	Iceland	Pavlof	USA
Katmai	USA	Pelée	Caribbean
Kerintji	Indonesia	Pinatubo	Indonesia
Kilauea	USA	Poas	Costa Rica
Kilimanjaro	Tanzania	Popocatapetl	Mexico
Krakatau	Indonesia	Puracé	Colombia
Krakatoa	Indonesia	Puyehue	Chile
Laki	Iceland	Rindjani	Indonesia
Lascar	Chile	Rininahue	Chile
La Soufrière	Montserrat	Ruapehu	New Zealand
Lassen	USA	Sabrina	Azores
Llaima	Chile	Sangay	Ecuador
Long Island	Papua New Guinea	Sangeang	Indonesia
		Santa Maria	Guatemala
Lopevi	Vanuatu	Santorini	Greece
Manam	Papua New Guinea	Semeru	Indonesia
		Shishaldin	USA
Marapi	Indonesia	Siau	Indonesia
Martin	USA	Slamat	Indonesia
Mauna Kea	Hawaii, USA	Soputan	Indonesia
Mauna Loa	Hawaii, USA	Spurr	USA
Mayon	Philippines	Stromboli	Italy
Meakan	Japan	Surtsey	Iceland
Merapi	Indonesia	Taal	Philippines
Mihara	Japan	Tacana	Guatemala
Miyakejima	Japan	Tarawera	New Zealand
Momotombo	Nicaragua	Ternate	Indonesia
Mount Saint Helens	USA	Tjareme	Indonesia
		Tokachi	Japan
Myozin-syo	Japan	Tongariro	New Zealand
Ngauruhoe	New Zealand	Torbert	USA
Nila	Indonesia	Trident	USA
Niuafo'ou	Tonga	Tungurahua	Ecuador
Noyoe	Iceland	Tupungatito	Chile
Nyamiagira	Democratic Republic of Congo	Unauna	Indonesia
		Vesuvius	Italy
Nyiragongo	Democratic Republic of Congo	Villarrica	Chile
		Vulcano	Italy
Okmok	USA	White Island	New Zealand
Ometepe	Nicaragua	Yakedake	Japan
O'shima	Japan		

MAJOR DESERTS

(with location)

Arabian	Egypt	Namib	Namibia
Atacama	Chile	Negev	Israel
Chihuahuan	USA, Mexico	Nubian	Sudan
Colorado	USA	Painted	USA
Gibson	Australia	Patagonian	Argentina
Gobi	Mongolia, China	Rub' al Khali	Saudi Arabia, Oman, Yemen, United Arab Emirates
Great Basin	USA		
Great Sandy	Australia		
Great Victoria	Australia		
Kalahari	South Africa, Namibia, Botswana	Sahara	North Africa
		Simpson	Australia
Kara Kum	Turkmenistan	Sonoran	USA, Mexico
Kyzyl Kum	Kazakhstan, Uzbekistan	Sturt	Australia
		Syrian	Syria, Iraq, Jordan, Saudi Arabia
Libyan	Libya		
Lut	Iran		
Mojave	USA	Taklimakan	China
Nafud	Saudi Arabia	Thar	India, Pakistan

MAJOR EARTHQUAKES

(with location and date)

Antioch	Syria	526 AD	Iran		1978
Shaanxi	China	1556	Mexico City		1985
Hokkaido	Japan	1730	Armenia		1988
Calcutta	India	1737	San Francisco	USA	1906, 1989
Messina	Italy	1908			
Gansu	China	1920, 1932	India		1993
Yokohama	Japan	1923	Los Angeles	USA	1994
Chimbote	Peru	1970	Kobe	Japan	1995
Guatemala City	Guatemala	1976	Iran		1997
Tangshan	China	1976	Afghanistan		1997, 1998

BRIDGES
(with location)

Akashi Kaikyo Bridge	Japan	Oland Island Bridge	Sweden
Angostura		Pinang Bridge	Malaysia
Suspension Bridge	Venezuela	Rio-Niteroi Bridge	Brazil
Bendorf Bridge	Germany	Second Narrows Bridge	
Bosporus Bridge	Turkey		Canada
Bridge of Sighs	Italy	Seven Mile Bridge	USA
Forth Bridge	UK	Severn Bridge	UK
Gladesville Bridge	Australia	Storebaelt *or*	
Golden Gate Bridge	USA	East Bridge	Denmark
Hooghly River Bridge	India	Sunshine Skyway	USA
Huang Ho Bridge	China	Zarate-Brazo Largo	Argentina
Humber Bridge	UK		

DAMS
(with location)

Akosombo	Ghana	Grand Coulee		Mangla	Pakistan
Aswan High			USA	Mauvoisin	Switzer-
Dam	Egypt	Grand Dixence			land
Atatürk	Turkey		Switzer-	Mica	Canada
Bonneville	USA		land	Nurek	Tajikistan
Chicoasén	Mexico	Guri	Venezuela	Oroville	USA
Chivor	Colombia	Hoover	USA	Rogun	Tajikistan
El Cajón	Honduras	Iguri	Georgia	Supung	Korea
Fengman	China	Itaipú	Paraguay	Tarbela	Pakistan
Fort Peck	USA	Kariba	Zambia,	Tucuruí	Brazil
			Zimbabwe	Vaiont	Italy

CANALS
(with location)

All-American Canal	USA	Gulf Intracoastal	
Atlantic Intracoastal		Waterway	USA
Waterway	USA	Manchester Ship Canal	UK
Cauvery Delta System	India	Moscow Canal	Russia
Corinth Canal	Greece	Panama Canal	Panama
Gezira Canals	Sudan	St Lawrence Seaway	Canada
Grand Canal	China	Suez Canal	Egypt
Grand Canal	Venice, Italy	Thal Canal	Pakistan
Grand Union Canal	UK	Western Yamuna	
		Canal	India

TRANSPORT

MOTOR VEHICLES

ambulance
armoured car
articulated lorry
automatic
automobile
beach buggy
bloodmobile
  Am.
bookmobile
  Am.
bowser
bubble car
bulldozer
bus
cab
cabriolet
camper
car
carryall Am.
car transporter
Caterpillar™
charabanc
coach
convertible
coupé
crash wagon
  Am.
crawler tractor
delivery truck

digger
Dormobile™
double-decker
  bus
dragster
DUKW or duck
dune buggy
dustcart
electric car
estate
fire engine
float
fork-lift truck
four-wheel
  drive car
garbage truck
  Am.
go-kart
golf cart
gritter
hackney cab
half-track
hard top
hatchback
hearse
HGV
hot hatch
hot rod
JCB™

Jeep™
juggernaut
kart
Land Rover™
limousine
lorry
low-loader
mammy wagon
milk float
Mini™
mobile home
motor caravan
off-roader
omnibus
open top
people carrier
  or mover
public service
  vehicle or PSV
racing car
rally car
recreational
  vehicle or RV
  Am.
refrigerated van
removal van
roadster
runabout
saloon

sedan Am.
semitrailer
shooting brake
single-decker
  bus
snowmobile
snowplough
soft top
sports car
station wagon
steamroller
stock car
streetcar
stretch
  limousine
tanker
taxi
tourer
tracklayer
tractor
trailer
tram
transporter
trolleybus
truck
van
wagon or
  waggon

MOTORLESS VEHICLES

barouche
bicycle
brake
break
britzka
brougham
buckboard
buggy
cab
calash
Cape cart
carriage
carriole
carry-all
cart
chaise
chariot

clarence
coach
coach-and-four
Conestoga
  wagon
covered wagon
curricle
dog cart
drag
dray
droshky
equipage
fiacre
fly
four-in-hand
gharry
gig

hackney
hansom
hay-cart
haywain
herdic
jaunting car
landau
oxcart
phaeton
post-chaise
prairie
  schooner
rickshaw
rig
rockaway
spider phaeton
stagecoach

sulky
surrey
tarantass
tilbury
trap
tricycle
trishaw
tumbril
Victoria
vis-à-vis
wagon
wagonette
wain
wheelbarrow

VEHICLE PARTS

accelerator
alternator
anti-lock brake
anti-roll bar
automatic
  choke
automatic
  transmission
axle
bench seat
blinker
bodywork
bonnet
boot
brake
brake drum
brake light
bucket seat
bumper

camshaft
carburettor
catalytic
  converter
chassis
clutch
connecting rod
cowl
crank
crankcase
cruise control
cylinder
cylinder head
dashboard or
  dash
differential gear
disc brake
distributor
driving wheel

drum brake
fender *Am.*
filler cap
fluid drive
flywheel
four-wheel
  drive
freewheel
gate
gauge
gear
gearbox
gear lever
generator
grille
hazard warning
  light
headlight
hood *Am.*

horn
hydraulic brake
hydraulic
  suspension
hypoid gear
ignition
ignition key
indicator
manifold
mileometer
monocoque
muffler
number plate
odometer *Am.*
oil gauge
overrider
overrun brake
piston
pneumatic tyre

VEHICLE PARTS (cont.)

power brakes
power steering
propeller shaft
rack-and-pinion
radial tyre
radiator
radius rod
reach
reflector
reverse

running board
shaft
shift *Am.*
shock absorber
sidelight
silencer
solenoid
spark plug
speedometer
splashboard

sprag
starter
starter motor
steering
  column
steering gear
steering wheel
stick
stick shift *Am.*
stop light

suspension
tachograph
tailpipe
tail wheel
top gear
tow bar
track rod
transmission
winker
wing

INTERNATIONAL CAR REGISTRATIONS

(with countries)

A	Austria	DK	Denmark
AFG	Afghanistan	DOM	Dominican Republic
AL	Albania	DY	Benin
AND	Andorra	DZ	Algeria
AUS	Australia	E	Spain
B	Belgium	EAK	Kenya
BD	Bangladesh	EAT	Tanzania
BDS	Barbados	EAU	Uganda
BG	Bulgaria	EC	Ecuador
BH	Belize	ES	El Salvador
BR	Brazil	ET	Egypt
BRN	Bahrain	ETH	Ethiopia
BRU	Brunei	EW	Estonia
BS	Bahamas	F	France
BUR	Myanmar (Burma)	FIN	Finland
C	Cuba	FJI	Fiji
CDN	Canada	FL	Liechtenstein
CH	Switzerland	FR	Faroe Islands
CI	Ivory Coast	GB	Great Britain
CL	Sri Lanka	GCA	Guatemala
CO	Colombia	GH	Ghana
CR	Costa Rica	GR	Greece
CS	Czech Republic	GUY	Guyana
CY	Cyprus	H	Hungary
D	Germany	HKJ	Jordan

INTERNATIONAL CAR REGISTRATIONS (cont.)
(with countries)

I	Italy	RI	Indonesia
IL	Israel	RIM	Mauritania
IND	India	RL	Lebanon
IR	Iran	RM	Madagascar
IRL	Republic of Ireland	RMM	Mali
IRQ	Iraq	RN	Niger
IS	Iceland	RO	Romania
J	Japan	ROK	South Korea
JA	Jamaica	ROU	Uruguay
K	Cambodia	RP	Philippines
KWT	Kuwait	RSM	San Marino
L	Luxembourg	RU	Burundi
LAO	Laos	RUS	Russia
LAR	Libya	RWA	Rwanda
LB	Liberia	S	Sweden
LS	Lesotho	SD	Swaziland
LT	Lithuania	SGP	Singapore
LV	Latvia	SME	Surinam
M	Malta	SN	Senegal
MA	Morocco	SWA	Namibia
MAL	Malaysia	SY	Seychelles
MC	Monaco	SYR	Syria
MEX	Mexico	T	Thailand
MS	Mauritius	TG	Togo
MW	Malawi	TN	Tunisia
N	Norway	TR	Turkey
NIC	Nicaragua	TT	Trinidad and Tobago
NL	Netherlands	USA	United States of
NZ	New Zealand		America
P	Portugal	VN	Vietnam
PA	Panama	WAG	Gambia
PE	Peru	WAL	Sierra Leone
PK	Pakistan	WAN	Nigeria
PL	Poland	WD	Dominica
PNG	Papua New Guinea	WG	Grenada
PY	Paraguay	WL	St Lucia
RA	Argentina	WS	Samoa
RB	Botswana	WV	St Vincent and the
RC	Taiwan		Grenadines
RCA	Central African	YV	Venezuela
	Republic	Z	Zambia
RCB	Congo	ZA	South Africa
RCH	Chile	ZW	Zimbabwe
RH	Haiti		

FAMOUS LOCOMOTIVES AND TYPES OF LOCOMOTIVE

Aerotrain
American Standard
Beyer-Garrett
Big Boy
Blücher
Bullet train
Capitole
Catch-Me-Who-Can
Consolidation
Flying Scotsman

Fuel Foiler
Le Lyonnais
Le Shuttle
Locomotion
Mikado
Mistral
Mogul
New Castle
Novelty
Orient Express

Pioneer
Puffing Billy
Rocket
Royal George
Sans Pareil
Super C
Train à Grande
    Vitesse *or* TGV

SHIPS AND BOATS

amphibious
    landing craft
barge
battleship
botel
bulk carrier
bumboat
cabin cruiser
cable ship
canal boat
canoe
cargo ship
coal ship
collier
container ship
coracle
crabber
cruiser
cruise ship
dinghy
dory
dredger
drifter

DUKW *or* duck
E-boat
factory ship
flagship
flat boat
freighter
galley
gig
gondola
houseboat
hovercraft
hydrofoil
ice-boat
ice-breaker
Indiaman
inflatable
    dinghy
jet-boat
kayak
keelboat
launch
lifeboat
lighter

longboat
mailboat
monkey-boat
mosquito boat
motor-boat
narrow boat
oil tanker
outboard
outrigger
paddle boat
paddle steamer
passenger ship
pilot boat
pinnace
pirogue
pontoon
powerboat
punt
Q-ship
raft
randan
revenue cutter
roll-on roll-off

rowing boat
sailing ship
sampan
school-ship
sculler
shell
ship's boat
side-wheeler
speedboat
steamboat
steamship
sternwheeler
supertanker
surfboat
tanker
tender
torpedo boat
tramp steamer
trawler
troop carrier
tugboat
whaleboat
wherry

SAILING SHIPS AND BOATS

barque
barquentine
brigantine
caique
caravel
carrack
catamaran
catboat
clipper
cutter
dhow
dinghy
dragon boat
dromond
felucca
frigate
full-rigger
gaff cutter
galleass
galleon
galley
galliot

hermaphrodite brig
hooker
in-rigger
jolly boat
junk
ketch
lateen
lighter
longboat
long-ship
lugger
man-of-war
merchantman
merchant ship
monohull
multihull
nuggar
outrigger
pink
pinnace
polacre
proa

razee
rigger
sabot
schooner
scow
shallop
skiff
skipjack
sloop
sloop of war
smack
snekkja
square-rigger
tall ship
tartan
trimaran
windjammer
xebec
yacht
yawl

NAUTICAL TERMS

aback
abaft
abeam
about-ship
admiral
Admiralty mile
aft
ahoy
alee
aloft
alow
amidships
apeak

aport
astern
athwartships
atrip
avast
awash
aweather
aweigh
ballast
batten down
beam
becket
belay

berth
bilge
bitt
boltrope
boom
boomkin
bosun *or* bo's'n
bouse
bow
bowsprit
boxhaul
bridge
Bristol fashion

NAUTICAL TERMS (cont.)

bulkhead
bulwark
bunker
bunt
burgee
burton
cable
caulk
clew
companion
companion-
  ladder
coxswain
crowfoot
crow's nest
Davy Jones'
  locker
deadlights
deadweight
dog watch
dolphin striker
downhaul
easting
euphroe
fathom
fid
first watch

fore
fore-and-aft
forecastle *or*
  fo'c'sle
frap
freeboard
futtock
gaff
galley
gam
gangway
garboard
grapnel
gunwale
gybe
halyards
hatch
hawse
hawser
hold
horse latitudes
hull
jib
kedge
keel
killick
knot

landlubber
lanyard
larboard
league
lee
lubber's hole
marlinespike
mate
middle watch
moorings
nautical mile
orlop
outhaul
pitching
plimsoll line
pontoon
poop
poppet
port
prow
purser
quarter
quarterdeck
quartermaster
ratlines
rig
Roaring Forties

scuppers
scuttle
sea mile
shroud
splice
starboard
stem
stern
sundowner
superstructure
taffrail
tonnage
transom
truck
vang
veer
vigia
wake
warp
watch
windlass
windward
yardarm
yawing

PORTS

Aabenraa
Aalborg
Aalesund
Abadan
Abidjan
Abu Dhabi
Acapulco
Acre
Adamstown

Adelaide
Aden
Adria
Agadir
Aigues-Mortes
Ajaccio
Akashi
Akita
Akranes

Akrotiri
Akureyri
Albany
Aleksandrovsk-
  Sakhalinskiy
Alexandretta
Alexandria
Alexandrou-
  polis

Algeciras
Algiers
Alicante
Alleppey
Almeria
Amalfi
Ambon
Ancona
Angoulême

PORTS (cont.)

Angra do
  Heroismo
Annaba
Antalya
Antibes
Antofagasta
Antseranana
Antwerp
Anzio
Aomori
Aqaba
Aracajú
Arbroath
Archangel
Ardrossan
Arecibo
Arendal
Arica
Arkhangelsk
Arklow
Arrecife
Aschaffenburg
Ashdod
Assab
Astrakhan
Asunción
Aveiro
Avilés
Babruysk
Bahía Blanca
Baku
Balikpapan
Balkhash
Ballina
Baltimore
Bamberg
Bandar Abbas
Bandar
  Lampung
Banff
Bangkok
Bangor
Banjarmasin
Banten
Bar

Barahona
Barcelona
Bari
Barisal
Barletta
Barran-
  cabermeja
Barranquilla
Barrow-in-
  Furness
Basra
Bassein
Basse-Terre
Bastia
Bata
Batumi
Bay City
Bayonne
Beaumont
Beihai
Beira
Bejaïa
Belém
Belfast
Belgrade
Belize City
Belle-Ile
Benguela
Benin
Berbera
Berdyansk
Berenice
Bergen
Bharuch
Bhavnagar
Biarritz
Bideford
Bilbao
Birkenhead
Bismarck
Bissau
Bizerta
Bluefields
Bodø
Boma

Bombay
Bône
Bonny
Bootle
Bordeaux
Boulogne
Bratislava
Brazzaville
Brega
Bremen
Bremerhaven
Brest
Bridgeport
Bridgetown
Bridlington
Brindisi
Brisbane
Bristol
Brownsville
Buchanan
Buenaventura
Buffalo
Bunbury
Bundaberg
Burgas
Burnie
Bushehr
Bydgoszcz
Cadiz
Caesarea
Cagliari
Cagnes-sur-Mer
Cairo
Calabar
Calais
Calamata
Callao
Calvi
Camagüey
Camden
Campeche
Canea
Cap Haïtien
Carrickfergus
Cartagena

Casablanca
Castellón de la
  Plana
Castries
Catania
Cayenne
Cebu
Châlon-sur-
  Saône
Changsha
Charlestown
Charlotte
  Amalie
Châtellerault
Cheboksary
Cherkassy
Chernigov
Chetumal
Chicago
Chilung
Chimbote
Chittagong
Christiansted
Chukot
Cienfuegos
Cirebon
Ciudad Bolivar
Civitavecchia
Cleveland
Coatzacoalcos
Cóbh
Cochin
Cologne
Colombo
Colón
Comodoro
  Rivadavia
Conakry
Concepción
Concordia
Constanza
Cooktown
Copenhagen
Coquimbo
Corinto

PORTS (cont.)

Corpus Christi
Corrientes
Corunna
Cox's Bazar
Cuddalore
Cuttack
Dahlak Islands
Dakar
Dalian
Damietta
Da Nang
Dandong
Danzig
Dar es Salaam
Darmstad
Dartmouth
Davao
Dhahran
Dieppe
Díli
Dinard
Dingle
Djajapura
Djibouti
Dniprodzer-
 zhinsk
Dnipropetrovsk
Dordrecht
Dortmund
Douala
Dover
Drammen
Drogheda
Drouzhba
Dubai
Dublin
Dubrovnik
Dundee
Dunedin
Durban
Durrës
East London
Eilat
Elblag
Elizabeth

Ellesmere Port
Encarnación
Erie
Esjberg
Esmeraldas
Essaouira
Esztergom
Exmouth
Fall River
Falmouth
Famagusta
Fao
Fargo
Faro
Fécamp
Felixstowe
Fiume
Flensburg
Flushing
Folkestone
Fortaleza
Frankfurt
Fray Bentos
Fredericia
Frederiksted
Fredrikstad
Fremantle
Freeport
Fremantle
Fujairah
Fukuoka
Fukuyama
Funchal
Gabès
Galatz
Galle
Galveston
Galway
Gao
Garoua
Gävle
Gdańsk
Gdynia
Geelong
Genoa

Georgetown
George Town
Geraldton
Ghent
Gijón
Gisborne
Giurgiu
Gladstone
Gomera
Gonaïves
Gorzów
 Wielkopolski
Gothenburg
Gourock
Grangemouth
Great Yarmouth
Greenock
Greenville
Grevenmacher
Grimsby
Guayaquil
Guaymas
Hachinohe
Haeju
Haifa
Haikou
Haiphong
Hakodate
Halden
Halifax
Halmstad
Hamburg
Hamilton
Hamina
Hammerfest
Hanau
Handa
Hanko
Härnösand
Hartlepool
Harwich
Havana
Heilbronn
Helsingborg
Helsinki

Heraklion
Hilo
Hobart
Ho Chi Minh
 City
Hodeida
Holyhead
Honiara
Honolulu
Hook of Holland
Horsens
Horta
Hrodna
Hsinchu
Hué
Huelva
Hull
Hydra
Ibiza
Ifni
Imabari
Immingham
Inchon
Inhambane
Ipswich
Iquique
Iquitos
Irún
Iskenderun
Istanbul
Izmir
Izmit
Jacksonville
Jaffa
Jaffna
Jakobstad
Jamestown
Jamnagar
Jarrow
Jayapura
Jeddah
Jervis Bay
 Territory
Jiaojiang
Jilin

PORTS (cont.)

Juneau	Kotka	Lübeck	Miami
Jyväskylä	Krasnodar	Ludwigshafen	Middlesbrough
Kagoshima	Kristiansand	Luleå	Milford Haven
Kaliningrad	Kristiansund	Lüshun	Milwaukee
Kaluga	Kuching	Lyons	Minneapolis
Kampot	Kurashiki	Macao	Miyazaki
Kamyshin	Kusadasi	Maceió	Mocha
Kankan	Kushiro	Machilipatnam	Mogadishu
Kaohsiung	Kuwait City	Madras	Mohács
Karachi	Kyrenia	Magdeburg	Mokpo
Karlskrona	La Ceiba	Magwe	Mombasa
Karlsruhe	Lae	Mahajanga	Monastir
Kaunas	Lagos	Mahón	Montego Bay
Kaválla	La Paz	Makhachkala	Montevideo
Kazan	La Plata	Malabo	Montreal
Keelung	Larache	Málaga	Morecambe
Keflavik	Laredo	Maldonado	Mossel Bay
Kelang	Larne	Malindi	Mostaganem
Kemi	La Rochelle	Malmö	Moulmein
Kenitra	Larvik	Manado	Mukalla
Kenosha	Las Palmas	Manama	Münster
Kerch	La Spezia	Manaus	Murmansk
Key West	Latakia	Mandalay	Murom
Kherson	Lax	Mangalore	Muscat
Khorramshahr	Leeuwarden	Mannheim	Mykonos
Kiel	Leghorn	Manzini	Mymensingh
Kiev	Lerwick	Maracaibo	Mytilene
Kigoma	Leticia	Mar del Plata	Nacala
Kimberley	Libreville	Mariehamn	Naestved
Kimchaek	Liège	Mariupol	Nagasaki
Kineshma	Liepaja	Marsala	Nagoya
King's Lynn	Limassol	Marseilles	Naha
Kingston	Limón	Maryborough	Nakhodka
Kirkcaldy	Linea de la	Masan	Nakhon Sawan
Kirkwall	Concepción	Massawa	Namibe
Kismayu	Liverpool	Matamoros	Nampo
Kitakyushu	Lobito	Matanzas	Nanaimo
Klaipeda	Lomé	Matsuyama	Nantes
Knoxville	London	Mazatlán	Napier
Kobe	Londonderry	Mbandaka	Naples
Kochi	Lorain	Mbini	Narayanganj
Kompong	Lorient	Memphis	Narbonne
Cham	Lowestoft	Mersin	Narvik
Kompong Som	Loyalty Islands	Messina	Nashville
Kota Kinabalu	Luanda	Mexicali	Nassau

PORTS (cont.)

Natal
Nauplia
Návpaktos
N'Djamena
Negombo
Neijiang
Nellore
Nelson
Newark
New Bedford
New Caledonia
Newcastle
New Hampshire
Newhaven
New Orleans
New Plymouth
Newport News
New
  Providence
Newry
New York
Niamey
Niigata
Niihama
Ningbo
Niterói
Nizhniy
  Novgorod
Nobeoka
Norrköping
Nouadhibou
Nouakchott
Novorossiysk
Nuuk
Nyborg
Nykøbing
Nykøping
Oakland
Oban
Odense
Odessa
Oldenburg
Olympia
Omsk
Oporto

Oran
Orange
Oranjestad
Ordu
Osaka
Osijek
Ostend
Ostia
Otaru
Ouidah
Oulu
Owendo
Padang
Pago Pago
Palembang
Palermo
Panaji
Panchevo
Paramaribo
Paraná
Patras
Paysandú
Pegu
Pekanbaru
Pelotas
Pemba
Pembroke
Pensacola
Peoria
Perth
Pesaro
Peterhead
Petropavlovsk
Petrozavodsk
Philadelphia
Phnom Penh
Phuket
Piacenza
Pietarsaari
Piraeus
Plock
Ponce
Ponta Delgada
Pontevedra
Pontianak

Poole
Porbandar
Pori
Port Arthur
Port Augusta
Port-au-Prince
Port Bell
Port Blair
Port Elizabeth
Port-Gentil
Port Hedland
Port Kelang
Portland
Port Louis
Pôrto Alegre
Porto Novo
Port Pirie
Port Rashid
Port Said
Portsmouth
Port Sudan
Port
  Sweetenham
Praia
Prince Rupert
Prome
Pucallpa
Puerto Barrios
Puerto Cortés
Puerto Montt
Pula
Puntarenas
Pusan
Pyrgos
Qiqihar
Quebec
Queen
  Charlotte
  Islands
Quilon
Rabat
Rabaul
Rajshahi
Ramsgate
Randers

Rangoon
Rashid
Rawson
Recife
Rethymnon
Reykjavik
Rhodes
Richmond
Riga
Rijeka
Rio Gallegos
Rio Grande
Rivne
Rochefort-sur-
  Mer
Rochester
Rockhampton
Rockingham
Rosario
Roscoff
Roskilde
Rosslare
Rostock
Rostov-on-Don
Rota
Rotterdam
Rouen
Ruse
Ryazan
Rybinsk
Safi
Saint-Denis
St. George's
Saint John
St. Louis
St-Malo
St-Nazaire
St. Petersburg
St. Tropez
Salem
Salerno
Salvador
Samara
Samsun
Sandakan

PORTS (cont.)

San Diego
San Juan
San Nicolas
San Sebastian
Santa Cruz de
  Tenerife
Santa Fe
Santander
Santarém
Santiago de
  Cuba
Santo Domingo
Santos
São Luis
Sarapul
Sasebo
Savannah
Seattle
Sebastapol
Ségou
Semarang
Semey
Seria
Sète
Setúbal
Seville
Shanghai
Shantou
Sharjah
Sheerness
Šibenik
Shimizu
Shizuoka
Sidon
Silistra
Sines
Sinop
Sinuiju
Sittwe
Skien
Skikda
Sligo
Smederovo
Smolensk
Sochi

Sousse
Southampton
South Shields
Stanley
Stavanger
Sterlitamak
Stockholm
Stockton
Stranraer
Strasbourg
Stuttgart
Suez
Sunderland
Sundsvall
Surat
Suva
Swakopmund
Swansea
Sydney
Syracuse
Szczecin
Szeged
Szolnok
Tacoma
Taganrog
Taichung
Takamatsu
Talcahuano
Tallinn
Tampa
Tampico
Tanga
Tangier
Tarragona
Tauranga
Tekirdag
Tel Aviv
Tema
Thessaloníki
Thunder Bay
Thurso
Tianjin
Tilbury
Timaru
Toamasina

Tobruk
Togliatti
Tokushima
Tokyo
Tomakomai
Tomsk
Tonkin
Torre del Greco
Toruń
Tottori
Toulon
Townsville
Trabzon
Tralee
Trapani
Trieste
Tripoli
Trois-Rivières
Tromsø
Trondheim
Tulsa
Tunis
Turku
Tuticorin
Tver
Tyre
Uddevalla
Ugarit
Ujung Pandang
Ullapool
Ulsan
Umeå
Ushuaia
Vaasa
Vác
Valdez
Valencia
Vallejo
Valletta
Vancouver
Varna
Västerås
Veracruz
Viana do
  Castelo

Vicksburg
Victoria
Vidin
Vientiane
Villahermosa
Visakhapatnam
Vitória
Volgograd
Volos
Vyatka
Walvis Bay
Wanganui
Weihai
Wellington
Wenzhou
Whangarei
Whitby
Willemstadt
Wilmington
Windsor
Wismar
Wollongong
Wonsan
Workington
Wroclaw
Wuhan
Wuhu
Xiamen
Yakutsk
Yalta
Yambol
Yantai
Yaroslavl
Yingkou
Yokkaichi
Yokohama
Yokosuka
Zadar
Zamboanga
Zeebrugge
Zhanjiang
Ziguinchor
Zonguldak
Zrenjanin

AIRCRAFT

aerodyne	cyclogiro	helicopter	multiplane
Airbus™	dive bomber	interceptor	night fighter
airliner	drone	jet plane	pusher
amphibian	fighter	jumbo jet	seaplane
autogiro	fighter-bomber	jump jet	swing-wing
biplane	flying boat	microlight	taxiplane
bomber	freighter	multirole	triplane
canard	glider	combat	turbofan
Concorde	gyrocopter	aircraft	turbojet
convertiplane	gyrodyne	(MRCA)	turboprop

INTERNATIONAL AIRPORTS
(with countries)

Arlanda	Stockholm	La Guardia	New York
Ataturk	Istanbul	Leonardo da Vinci	
Barajas	Madrid	(Fiumicino)	Rome
Charles De Gaulle	Paris	Linate	Milan
Changi	Singapore	Lindbergh Field	San Diego
Chiang Kai-Shek	Taipei	Logan	Boston
Cointrin	Geneva	Luis Muñoz Marin	San Juan
Dallas-Fort Worth	Dallas	McCarran	Las Vegas
Dorval	Montreal	Mirabel	Montreal
Douglas	Charlotte	Narita	Tokyo
Dulles	Washington	Ninoy Aquino	Manila
Echterdingen	Stuttgart	O'Hare	Chicago
Findel	Luxembourg	Okecie	Warsaw
Fornebu	Oslo	Orly	Paris
Gatwick	London	Pearson	Toronto
Hartsfield	Atlanta	St Paul	Minneapolis
Heathrow	London	Schiphol	Amsterdam
Helsinki-Vantaa	Helsinki	Sheremetyevo	Moscow
Hongqiao	Shanghai	Sky Harbor	Phoenix
Hopkins	Cleveland	Soekarno Hatta	Jakarta
John F. Kennedy	New York	Stansted	London
(Benito) Juarez	Mexico City	Subang	Kuala Lumpur
Kimpo	Seoul	Tegel	Berlin
King Khaled	Riyadh	Tullamarine	Melbourne
Kingsford Smith	Sydney	Wayne County	Detroit

SCIENCE AND TECHNOLOGY

UNITS OF MEASUREMENT

acre
air mile
ampere
amu
angstrom
are
astronomical unit
atmosphere
atomic mass unit
barleycorn
barrel
baud
becquerel
bel
bit
Board of Trade Unit
British thermal unit
bushel
butt
byte
cable
calorie
candela
candle
carat
cental
centiare
centner
chain
chronon
circular mil
cord
coulomb
cup
curie
cusec

cycle
dalton
daraf
darcy
day
decibel
degree
degree-day
denier
dioptre
dyne
electronvolt
em
en
epoch
erg
farad
faraday
fathom
fermi
firkin
foot
fresnel
furlong
gal
gallon
gamma
gauss
gilbert
gill
grade
grain
gram-atomic weight
gram *or* gramme
gram-molecular
    weight

gray
hank
henry
hertz
hogshead
Hoppus foot
horsepower
hour
hundredweight
inch
jansky
joule
kelvin
kilderkin
kilocycle
kilogram *or*
    kilogramme
kilometre
kiloton
kilowatt-hour
kip
knot
last
lea
league
light year
line
link
litre
lumen
lux
Mach number
magneton
maxwell
megaton
metre

UNITS OF MEASUREMENT (cont.)

mho	perch	second
micrometre	phon	siemens
micron	phot	sievert
mil	pica	slug
mile	pint	span
millibar	pipe	steradian
millimicron	point	stilb
minim	poise	stokes
minute	pole	stone
mole	pound	tesla
morgan	poundal	therm
nail	puncheon	tog
nautical mile	quart	ton
neper	quarter	tonne
newton	quartern	torr
nit	quintal	troy ounce
noggin	rad	var
oersted	radian	volt
ohm	rod	watt
okta *or* octa	roentgen *or* röntgen	weber
ounce	rood	x-unit
parsec	rutherford	yard
pascal	sabin	year
peck	scruple	

ELEMENTARY PARTICLES

antielectron	fermion	muon	proton
antineutron	gluon	neutrino	psi particle
antiproton	hadron	neutron	quark
antiquark	kaon	nucleon	tau particle
baryon	lambda particle	photon	
boson	lepton	pion	
electron	meson	positron	

CHEMICAL ELEMENTS

(with symbols)

actinium	Ac	hafnium	Hf	praseodymium	Pr
aluminium	Al	hahnium	Ha	promethium	Pm
americium	Am	hassium	Hs	protactinium	Pa
antimony	Sb	helium	He	radium	Ra
argon	Ar	holmium	Ho	radon	Rn
arsenic	As	hydrogen	H	rhenium	Re
astatine	At	indium	In	rhodium	Rh
barium	Ba	iodine	I	rubidium	Rb
berkelium	Bk	iridium	Ir	ruthenium	Ru
beryllium	Be	iron	Fe	rutherfordium	Rf
bismuth	Bi	krypton	Kr	samarium	Sm
bohrium	Bh	lanthanum	La	scandium	Sc
boron	B	lawrencium	Lr	seaborgium	Sg
bromine	Br	lead	Pb	selenium	Se
cadmium	Cd	lithium	Li	silicon	Si
caesium	Cs	lutetium	Lu	silver	Ag
calcium	Ca	magnesium	Mg	sodium	Na
californium	Cf	manganese	Mn	strontium	Sr
carbon	C	meitnerium	Mt	sulphur	S
cerium	Ce	mendelevium	Md	tantalum	Ta
chlorine	Cl	mercury	Hg	technetium	Tc
chromium	Cr	molybdenum	Mo	tellurium	Te
cobalt	Co	neodymium	Nd	terbium	Tb
copper	Cu	neon	Ne	thallium	Tl
curium	Cm	neptunium	Np	thorium	Th
dubnium	Db	nickel	Ni	thulium	Tm
dysprosium	Dy	niobium	Nb	tin	Sn
einsteinium	Es	nitrogen	N	titanium	Ti
erbium	Er	nobelium	Nb	tungsten or	
europium	Eu	osmium	Os	wolfram	W
fermium	Fm	oxygen	O	uranium	U
fluorine	F	palladium	Pd	vanadium	V
francium	Fr	phosphorus	P	xenon	Xe
gadolinium	Gd	platinum	Pt	ytterbium	Yb
gallium	Ga	plutonium	Pu	yttrium	Y
germanium	Ge	polonium	Po	zinc	Zn
gold	Au	potassium	K	zirconium	Zr

MATHEMATICAL TERMS

abscissa
addition
algebra
algorithm
aliquot part
analysis
antilogarithm
Apollonius' theorem
Argand diagram
arithmetic mean
arithmetic
  progression
array
associative law
asymptote
Banach space
base
Bayes' theorem
Bernoulli numbers
Bessel functions
binomial
binomial theorem
Boolean algebra
Briggsian logarithms
calculus
Cantor set
cardinal number
Cartesian coordinates
catastrophe theory
Cauchy sequence
chaos theory
Chinese remainder
  theorem
coefficient
common denominator
commutative law
complex number
conjugate
coordinate geometry
cosecant
cosine
cotangent
cube
cube root
decimal point

definite integral
de Moivre's formula
denominator
derivative
determinant
difference
differential calculus
differential equation
differentiation
digit
Diophantine equation
Dirichlet series
distributive law
division
divisor
eigenfunction
eigenvalue
eigenvector
equation
Eratosthenes, sieve of
Euclidean geometry
Euclid's axioms
Euler's constant
Euler's formula
expansion
exponent
exponential function
extrapolation
factor
factorial
Fermat's last theorem
Fibonacci numbers
field
formula
four-colour theorem
Fourier analysis
Fourier series
fractal
fractal set
fraction
function
fuzzy set
Galois group
game theory
Gaussian distribution

Gauss's theorem
geometric mean
geometric
  progression
Gödel numbers
googol
googolplex
gradient
Green's theorem
group
group theory
harmonic progression
Hermitian matrix
highest common
  factor
Hilbert space
Hilbert's problems
hyperbolic cosine
hyperbolic sine
hyperbolic tangent
identity
imaginary number
improper fraction
indefinite integral
inequality
infinitesimal calculus
integer
integral calculus
integrand
integration
intercept
interpolation
inverse
irrational number
iteration
Julia set
Klein bottle
Lagrange's theorem
Laplace operator
least squares method
Legendre polynomials
Leibniz's theorem
L'Hôpital's rule
Lie group
limit

MATHEMATICAL TERMS (cont.)

linear equation
Lobachevskian
  geometry
locus
logarithm
long division
lowest common
  denominator
lowest common
  multiple
Maclaurin series
magic square
Mandelbrot set
Markov chain
matrix
mean
median
Mersenne numbers
midpoint theorem
Möbius strip
modulus
Monte Carlo method
multiple
multiplicand
multiplication
multiplier
Napierian logarithm
natural logarithm
natural numbers
Newton method
node
null hypothesis
number theory
numerator
operator
ordinal number
origin

parameter
partial derivative
Pascal's triangle
percentile
perfect number
perfect square
permutation
point of inflection
Poisson distribution
polar coordinates
polynomial
power
power series
prime number
product
proof
proper fraction
Pythagoras' theorem
quaternion
queuing theory
quotient
ratio
rational number
real number
reciprocal
recurring decimal
recursion
remainder
remainder theorem
repeating decimal
Riemannian geometry
ring
root
root-mean-square
Russell's paradox
scalar
secant

series
set
set theory
significant figure
Simpson's rule
simultaneous
  equations
sine
solution
square
square number
square root
stationary point
Stirling's
  approximation
Stokes' theorem
sub-group
subset
substitution
subtraction
sum
surd
tangent
Taylor series
tensor
transcendental
  function
transfinite number
transform
trigonometric function
unity
unknown
variable
vector
Venn diagram
vulgar fraction
whole number

BRANCHES OF ENGINEERING

aerodynamics
aeronautical engineering
aerospace engineering
agricultural engineering
astronautics
automotive engineering
chemical engineering
civil engineering
cosmonautics
electrical engineering

electronics
environmental engineering
ergonomics
fluid dynamics
hydraulics
mechanical engineering
mining engineering
naval engineering
nuclear engineering
production engineering

COMPUTER PROGRAMMING LANGUAGES

Ada
Algol
APL
B
Basic
BCPL
C

C++
Cobol
COMAL
CORAL
CPL
Forth
Fortran

JAVA
JOVIAL
Lisp
Logo
Modula
Pascal
PL/I

POP
Prolog
SIMULA
Smalltalk
SNOBOL
Visual Basic

COMPUTER PARTS AND PERIPHERALS

acoustic coupler
arithmetic and logic unit (ALU)
bar-code reader
buffer
bus
cache memory
cartridge
cassette
CD-ROM
console

central processing unit (CPU)
control unit
digitizer
disk
diskette
dynamic RAM (DRAM)
drum scanner
dynamic memory
erasable programmable read-only
  memory (EPROM)

COMPUTER PARTS AND PERIPHERALS (cont.)

fax modem
firmware
fixed disk
flash memory
flat-bed plotter
flat-bed scanner
floppy disk
hard disk
hardware
input-output device
input-output port
joystick
keyboard
light-pen
magnetic-tape unit (MTU)
main memory
maths coprocessor
memory
microfloppy
microprocessor
minidisk *or* minidiskette
modem
monitor
motherboard
mouse
non-volatile memory
optical disk

plotter
port
primary memory
printer
processor
random access memory (RAM)
register
read only memory (ROM)
removable disk
scanner
secondary memory
semiconductor memory
software
solid-state memory
sound card
static RAM (SRAM)
tape streamer
terminal
trackerball
video card
visual display unit (VDU)
voice synthesizer
wand
Winchester disk
zip disk
zip drive

ROCKS AND MINERALS

Sedimentary Rocks
arenite
argillite
breccia
chalk
chert
claystone
coal
conglomerate
diatomaceous earth
dolomite
flint
ironstone
limestone
marl
mudstone
oolite
radiolarite
rag
rudite
sandstone
shale
siltstone
tillite

Metamorphic Rocks
amphibolite
eclogite
epidiorite
epidosite
gneiss
granulite
hornfels
marble
phyllite

psammite
pyroxenite
quartzite
schist
slate
verdite

Igneous Rocks
amygdaloid
andesite
anorthosite
aplite
basalt
diorite
dolerite
dunite
felsite
gabbro
granite
kimberlite
lamprophyre
lava
monzonite
obsidian
pegmatite
peridotite
phonolite
picrite
porphyry
pumice
rhyolite
syenite
tephrite
tonalite
trachyte
trap
tuff
variolite

vitrophyre

Minerals
anhydrite
anorthoclase
apatite
asbestos
augite
beryl
biotite
blackjack
borax
cassiterite
chalcopyrite
Chile saltpetre
chrysoberyl
cinnabar
corundum
diamond
dolomite
emery
euxenite
feldspar
fluorspar
fool's gold
fulgurite
galena
garnet
gypsum
haematite
halite
harmotome
hornblende
hyacinth
illite
ilmenite
kaolinite
lapis lazuli
malachite

marcasite
massicot
meerschaum
mica
molybdenite
mullite
oligoclase
opal
orthoclase
periclase
pitchblende
plagioclase
polybasite
pyrite
pyrites
quartz
realgar
rutile
saponite
sapphirine
scolecite
serpentine
siderite
sodalite
sphalerite
stannite
talc
thorite
topaz
tourmaline
tungstite
turquoise
vesuvianite
water sapphire
wolframite
zeolite
zincite
zircon

METAL ORES

anglesite	chromite	magnetite
argentite	copper pyrites	mispickel
arsenopyrite	cinnabar	pitchblende
bauxite	galena	siderite
carnotite	haematite	smithsonite
cassiterite	ironstone	stibnite
cerrusite	limonite	tinstone
chalcocite	litharge	zinc blende
chalcopyrite	lodestone	zincite

GEOLOGICAL AGES, ERAS, PERIODS, AND EPOCHS

Cambrian period	Palaeocene epoch
Carboniferous period	Palaeozoic era
Cenozoic era	Permian period
Cretaceous period	Phanerozoic era
Devonian period	Pleistocene epoch
Eocene epoch	Pliocene epoch
Holocene epoch	Precambrian era
Jurassic period	Quaternary period
Mesozoic era	Silurian period
Miocene epoch	Tertiary period
Oligocene epoch	Triassic period
Ordovician period	

GALAXIES

Andromeda Galaxy	Small Magellanic Cloud *or*
Black-eye Galaxy	Nubecular Minor
Cartwheel Galaxy	Sombrero Galaxy
Helix Galaxy	Spindle Galaxy
Large Magellanic Cloud *or*	Sunflower Galaxy
Nubecular Major	Triangulum Galaxy
Milky Way Galaxy	Whirlpool Galaxy
Pinwheel Galaxy	

CONSTELLATIONS
(with common names)

Andromeda		Gemini	Twins
Antlia	Air Pump	Grus	Crane
Apus	Bird of Paradise	Hercules	
		Horologium	Clock
Aquarius	Water Bearer	Hydra	Sea Serpent
Aquila	Eagle	Hydrus	Water Snake
Ara	Altar	Indus	Indian
Aries	Ram	Lacerta	Lizard
Auriga	Charioteer	Leo	Lion
Boötes	Herdsman *or* Bear Driver	Leo Minor	Little Lion
		Lepus	Hare
Caelum	Chisel	Libra	Balance *or* Scales
Camelopardalis	Giraffe		
Cancer	Crab	Lupus	Wolf
Canes Venatici	Hunting Dogs	Lynx	
Canis Major	Great Dog	Lyra	Lyre
Canis Minor	Little Dog	Mensa	Table
Capricornus	Goat *or* Sea Goat	Microscopium	Microscope
		Monoceros	Unicorn
Carina	Keel	Musca	Fly
Cassiopeia		Norma	Level *or* Rule
Centaurus	Centaur	Octans	Octant
Cepheus		Ophiuchus	Serpent Bearer
Cetus	Whale	Orion	Hunter
Chamaeleon	Chameleon	Pavo	Peacock
Circinus	Compasses	Pegasus	
Columba	Dove	Perseus	
Coma Berenices	Berenice's Hair	Phoenix	
Corona Australis	Southern Crown	Pictor	Painter's Easel
		Pisces	Fishes
Corona Borealis	Northern Crown	Piscis Austrinus	Southern Fish
		Puppis	Stern *or* Poop
Corvus	Crow	Pyxis	Compass Box
Crater	Cup	Reticulum	Net
Crux (Australis)	Southern Cross	Sagitta	Arrow
Cygnus	Swan	Sagittarius	Archer
Delphinus	Dolphin	Scorpius	Scorpion
Dorado	Swordfish *or* Goldfish	Sculptor	
		Scutum	Shield
Draco	Dragon	Serpens	Serpent
Equuleus	Little Horse *or* Foal	Sextans	Sextant
		Taurus	Bull
Eridanus	River	Telescopium	Telescope
Fornax	Furnace	Triangle	Triangulum

CONSTELLATIONS (cont.)

(with common names)

Triangulum		Ursa Minor	Little Bear
Australe	Southern	Vela	Sails
	Triangle	Virgo	Virgin
Tucana	Toucan	Volans	Flying Fish
Ursa Major	Great Bear	Vulpecula	Fox

PLANETS AND THEIR SATELLITES

Mercury	
Venus	
Earth	Moon
Mars	Phobos, Deimos
Jupiter	Metis, Adrastea, Amalthea, Thebe, Io, Europa, Ganymede, Callisto, Leda, Himalia, Lysithea, Elara, Ananke, Carme, Pasiphae, Sinope
Saturn	Pan, Atlas, Prometheus, Pandora, Epimetheus, Janus, Mimas, Enceladus, Tethys, Telesto, Calypso, Dione, Helene, Rhea, Titan, Hyperion, Iapetus, Phoebe
Uranus	Cordelia, Ophelia, Bianca, Cressida, Desdemona, Juliet, Portia, Rosalind, Belinda, Puck, Miranda, Ariel, Umbriel, Titania, Oberon
Neptune	Naiad, Thalassa, Despina, Galatea, Larissa, Proteus, Triton, Nereid
Pluto	Charon

COMETS

Arend–Roland	Faye	Pons–Brooks
Bennett	Giacobini–Zinner	Pons–Winnecke
Biela	Grigg–Skjellerup	Schaumasse
Borrelly	Hale–Bopp	Shoemaker–Levy
Bronsen–Metcalf	Halley	Stephan–Oterma
Comas Solá	Kohoutek	Tuttle
Crommelin	Kopff	West
Daylight Comet	Lexell	Westphal
Encke	Olbers	Whipple

WINDS
(with locations)

bise	Central Europe	meltemi	E Mediterranean
bora	Central Europe	mistral	Mediterranean
buran	Central Asia	monsoon	S Asia
Cape doctor	South Africa	nor'wester	New Zealand
chinook	Rocky Mountains, USA	simoom or samiel	N Africa
etesian	E Mediterranean	sirocco	N Africa
Föhn or Foehn	Central Europe	southerly	
ghibli or gibli	N Africa	buster	SE Australia
harmattan	W Africa	tramontana	W Mediterranean
khamsin	Egypt	wet chinook	NW USA
levanter	W Mediterranean	williwaw	USA, Canada

CLOUDS

altocumulus	cumulonimbus	noctilucent cloud
altostratus	cumulostratus	rain cloud
anvil cloud	cumulus	storm cloud
cirrocumulus	lenticular cloud	stratocumulus
cirrostratus	nimbostratus	stratus
cirrus	nimbus	thundercloud

MEDICINE AND THE HUMAN BODY

HUMAN BONES

ankle-bone
anvil
astragalus
backbone
breastbone
calcaneus
carpal
cheekbone
clavicle
collarbone
costa
cranium
cuboid
ethmoid
femur
fibula
floating rib
frontal bone
funny bone

hallux
hammer
heel bone
humerus
hyoid
ilium
incus
innominate
  bone
ischium
jawbone
kneecap
lunate bone
malleus
mandible
maxilla
metacarpal
metatarsal
nasal bone

navicular bone
occipital bone
parietal bone
patella
pelvis
phalanx
pisiform bone
pubis
rachis
radius
rib
sacrum
scaphoid
scapula
sesamoid bone
shin bone
shoulder blade
skull
sphenoid

spinal column
spine
stapes
sternum
stirrup
talus
tarsal
temporal
  bone
thigh bone
tibia
ulna
vertebra
vertebral
  column
vomer
wrist-bone
zygomatic bone

PARTS OF THE HUMAN EAR

auditory canal
auditory nerve
auricle *or* pinna
basilar membrane
cochlea
endolymph
Eustachian tube
hair cell

incus *or* anvil
inner ear
malleus *or* hammer
middle ear
organ of Corti
outer ear
perilymph
pinna *or* auricle

saccule
semicircular canal
stapes *or* stirrup
tectorial membrane
tympanic membrane
  or eardrum
utricle
vestibule

HUMAN GLANDS

Endocrine Glands

adrenal gland
corpus luteum
islets of
  Langerhans
ovary
parathyroid
  gland
pineal gland
pituitary gland
testis
thyroid gland

Exocrine Glands

Bartholin's gland
breast
Brunner's gland
buccal gland
Cowper's *or*
  bulbo-urethral
  gland

gastric gland
lacrimal gland
Lieberkühn's
  gland
liver
mammary gland
meibomian *or*
  tarsal gland
pancreas
parotid gland
preputial gland
prostate gland
salivary gland
sebaceous gland
sublingual gland
submandibular
  or submaxillary
  gland
sweat gland

PARTS OF THE HUMAN EYE

aqueous
  humour
blind spot
choroid
ciliary
  body
cone
conjunctiva
cornea

extrinsic
  muscle
eyeball
eyelash *or*
  cilium
eyelid *or*
  blepharon *or*
  palpebra
fovea

iris
lens
limbus
optic foramen
optic nerve
orbit
retina
rod
sclera

stroma
suspensory
  ligament
tarsal plate
tear glands
  (lacrimal
  glands)
vitreous
  humour

HUMAN MUSCLES

abdominal
muscles
biceps
deltoid
gastrocnemius

gluteus
pectoral muscle
peroneal
muscle
psoas

quadriceps
rhomboideus
sartorius
scalenus
soleus

splenius
trapezius
triceps

MEDICAL SPECIALITIES

anaesthetics
brain surgery
cardiology
chiropractic
chiropody
dentistry
dermatology
diagnostics
endocrinology
endodontics
ENT (ear, nose, &
   throat) medicine
epidemiology
exodontics
forensic pathology
gastroenterology
geriatrics

gerontology
gynaecology
haematology
heart surgery
immunology
nephrology
neurology
neurosurgery
nosology
obstetrics
oncology
ophthalmology
orthodontics
orthopaedics
osteology
otolaryngology
otology

otorhinolaryngology
paediatrics
paedodontics
pathology
periodontics
plastic surgery
podiatry
prosthodontics
radiology
radiotherapy
rheumatology
serology
surgery
teratology
urology
venereology

TYPES OF MEDICATION AND DRUG

anaesthetic
analgesic
antacid
anthelmintic
antibiotic
antibacterial
anticoagulant
anticonvulsant
antidepressant
antidote
antiemetic
antiepileptic
antifungal

antihistamine
anti-inflammatory
antipsychotic
antipyretic
antiseptic
antitussive
appetite suppressant
beta blocker
bronchodilator
decongestant
depressant
diuretic
emetic

expectorant
fungicide
immunosuppressive
laxative
muscle relaxant
sedative
steroid
stimulant
tonic
tranquillizer
vasoconstrictor
vasodilator

DISEASES AND MEDICAL CONDITIONS

acromegaly
actinomycosis
Addison's
 disease
AIDS
Alzheimer's
 disease
anaemia
angina
anorexia
 nervosa
appendicitis
arthritis
asbestosis
Asperger's
 syndrome
asthma
autism
avitaminosis
beriberi
bilharzia
Bright's disease
bronchitis
brucellosis
bulimia nervosa
cancer
candidiasis
Chagas'
 disease
chickenpox
cholera
cirrhosis
clinical
 depression
coeliac disease
colitis
common cold
coronary heart
 disease
Crohn's disease
Cushing's
 disease
cyanosis
cystic fibrosis
cystitis

dengue
dermatitis
dhobi itch
diabetes
diphtheria
dysentery
Ebola fever
eczema
elephantiasis
emphysema
encephalitis
epilepsy
food poisoning
gastroenteritis
German
 measles
glandular fever
glaucoma
goitre
gonorrhoea
gout
Graves' disease
haemophilia
hepatitis
herpes
Hodgkin's
 disease
Huntington's
 chorea
hyperthyroid-
 ism
impetigo
influenza
jaundice
kala-azar
Kaposi's
 sarcoma
Kawasaki
 disease
kwashiorkor
laryngitis
Lassa fever
legionnaires'
 disease
leprosy

leptospirosis
leukaemia
listeriosis
lupus
Lyme disease
malaria
measles
Ménière's
 disease
meningitis
motor neurone
 disease
multiple
 sclerosis
mumps
Münchhausen's
 syndrome (by
 proxy)
muscular
 dystrophy
myalgic
 encephalitis
 (ME)
myasthenia
 gravis
narcolepsy
nephritis
osteoporosis
Paget's disease
Parkinson's
 disease
pellagra
peritonitis
phenylketonuria
plague
pneumoconiosis
pneumonia
poliomyelitis
porphyria
psittacosis
psoriasis
psychosis
rabies
Raynaud's
 disease

rheumatic fever
rheumatoid
 arthritis
rickets
ringworm
rubella
 (German
 measles)
St Vitus's dance
salmonella
scarlet fever
schizophrenia
scurvy
shingles
sickle-cell
 anaemia
silicosis
sinusitis
sleeping
 sickness
sleepy sickness
smallpox
spina bifida
sweating-
 sickness
Sydenham's
 chorea
syphilis
tetanus
thalassaemia
tonsillitis
toxic shock
 syndrome
toxoplasmosis
trachoma
tuberculosis
typhoid fever
typhus
venereal
 disease
Weil's disease
whooping
 cough
yaws
yellow fever

SURGICAL OPERATIONS
(with description)

adenoidectomy	removal of adenoids
angioplasty	repair of blood vessel
appendicectomy *or* appendectomy	removal of appendix
arteriotomy	incision of artery
cheiloplasty	repair of lips
cholecystectomy	removal of gall bladder
cholecystotomy	incision of gall bladder
colectomy	removal of colon
colostomy	opening of colon
craniotomy	incision of skull
cystectomy	removal of bladder
cystoplasty	repair of bladder
cystostomy	opening of bladder
cystotomy	incision of bladder
dermatoplasty	repair of skin
embolectomy	removal of blood clot
enterostomy	opening of small intestine
enterotomy	incision of intestine
episiotomy	incision of vaginal opening
gastrectomy	removal of whole or part of stomach
gastroplasty	repair of stomach
gastrostomy	opening of stomach
gastrotomy	incision of stomach
glossectomy	removal of all or part of tongue
haemorrhoidectomy	removal of haemorrhoids
hepatectomy	removal of all or part of liver
hepaticostomy	opening of bile duct
hysterectomy	removal of womb
hysterotomy	incision of womb
laparotomy	incision of abdomen
laryngectomy	removal of larynx
laryngotomy	incision of larynx
lithotomy	removal of kidney stone
lobectomy	removal of lobe of an organ
lobotomy	incision of nerve fibres from frontal lobe of brain
lumpectomy	removal of breast tumour
mammaplasty	reshaping of breast
mastectomy	removal of breast
myotomy	incision of muscle
nephrectomy	removal of kidney
nephrostomy	opening of kidney
nephrotomy	incision of kidney
neurectomy	removal of nerve
neurotomy	incision of nerve
oesophagectomy	opening of oesophagus
oophorectomy	removal of ovary
orchidectomy	removal of testis
orchidotomy	incision of testis
ostectomy	removal of bone
osteotomy	incision of bone
ovariectomy	removal of ovary
ovariotomy	incision of ovary
palatoplasty	repair of cleft palate

SURGICAL OPERATIONS (cont.)

(with description)

pancreatectomy	removal of pancreas	thoracoplasty	repair of thorax
pericardiectomy *or*		thoracotomy	incision of chest cavity
pericardectomy	removal of all or part of membrane around heart	thrombectomy	removal of blood clot
		thymectomy	removal of thymus gland
pericardiotomy	incision of membrane around heart	thyroidectomy	removal of all or part of thyroid gland
perineoplasty	repair of vaginal opening	tonsillectomy	removal of tonsils
phalloplasty	repair of penis	tonsillotomy	incision of tonsil
pharyngectomy	removal of pharynx	tracheostomy	opening of windpipe
phlebotomy	incision of vein	tracheotomy	incision of windpipe
pleurotomy	incision of pleural membrane	ureterectomy	removal of ureter
		ureterostomy	opening of ureter
pneumonectomy	removal of lung	ureterotomy	incision of ureter
polypectomy	removal of polyp	urethroplasty	repair of urethra
prostatectomy	removal of prostate gland	urethrotomy	incision of urethra
rhinoplasty	repair of nose	vagotomy	incision of vagus nerve
salpingectomy	removal of fallopian tube	valvotomy	incision of heart valve
salpingostomy	opening of fallopian tube	varicotomy	excision of varicose vein
splenectomy	removal of spleen	vasectomy	removal of all or part of vas deferens
tenotomy	incision of tendon		

THERAPIES

acupuncture
aromatherapy
art therapy
aversion therapy
balneotherapy
behaviour therapy
chiropractic
cognitive therapy
colour therapy
confrontation therapy
crystal therapy
drama therapy
electroconvulsive
   therapy
electroshock therapy
electrotherapy
family therapy

Gerson cure
Gestalt therapy
group therapy
homoeopathy
humanistic therapy
hydrotherapy
hypnotherapy
insulin shock therapy
mechanotherapy
megavitamin therapy
metrazol shock
   therapy
music therapy
narcotherapy
naturopathy
occupational therapy
osteopathy

play therapy
primal therapy
psychotherapy
rational-emotive
   therapy
recreational therapy
reflexology
regression therapy
relaxation therapy
release therapy
Rogerian therapy
sex therapy
shiatsu
shock therapy
sleep therapy
sound therapy

BRANCHES OF PSYCHOLOGY

abnormal psychology
Adlerian psychology
analytical psychology
animal psychology
apperceptionism
applied psychology
associationism
behaviourism
child psychology
clinical psychology
cognitive psychology
comparative
   psychology
configurationism
developmental
   psychology
educational
   psychology
ethology
experimental
   psychology

Freudianism
gestalt psychology
group psychology
Horneyan psychology
humanistic
   psychology
industrial and organi-
   zational psychology
introspection
   psychology
Jungian psychology
Lacanian psychology
metapsychology
neuropsychology
occupational
   psychology
parapsychology
Pavlovian psychology
physiological
   psychology
psychoanalysis

psychobiochemistry
psychobiography
psychobiology
psychodynamics
psychogenetics
psychography
psycholinguistics
psychometry
psychopathology
psychopharmacology
psychophysiology
Reichian psychology
Skinnerian
   psychology
social psychology
structuralism
Watsonian
   psychology

PHOBIAS

air travel	aerophobia
American people and things	Americophobia
animals	zoophobia
bacteria	bacteriophobia
beards	pogonophobia
beating	mastigophobia
bed	clinophobia
bees	apiphobia
birds	ornithophobia
Black people and things	Negrophobia
blood	haemophobia
blushing	erythrophobia
body odour	bromidrosiphobia
bridges	gephyrophobia
bullets	ballistophobia
cancer	carcinophobia
cats	ailurophobia
childbirth	tocophobia
children	paedophobia
Chinese people and things	Sinophobia
church	ecclesiophobia
clouds	nephophobia
coitus	coitophobia
cold	cheimaphobia
colour	chromophobia
comets	cometophobia
constipation	coprostasophobia
corpses	necrophobia
correspondence	epistolophobia
crowds	demophobia or ochlophobia
dampness	hygrophobia
darkness	scotophobia
dawn	eosophobia
death	thanatophobia
depth	bathophobia
dirt	mysophobia
disease	pathophobia or nosophobia
dogs	cynophobia
drink	potophobia
drugs	pharmacophobia
dust	koniophobia
electricity	electrophobia
enclosed places	claustrophobia
English people and things	Anglophobia
everything	panophobia or pantophobia
eyes	ommetaphobia
faeces	coprophobia
failure	kakorrhaphiaphobia
fatigue	kopophobia
fear	phobophobia
feathers	pteronophobia
fever	febriphobia
fire	pyrophobia
fish	ichthyophobia
floods	antlophobia
flowers	anthophobia
fog	homichlophobia
food	cibophobia or sitophobia
foreigners	xenophobia
freedom	eleutherophobia
French people and things	Francophobia or Gallophobia
fur	doraphobia
German people and things	Germanophobia or Teutophobia
germs	spermophobia or bacteriophobia
ghosts	phasmophobia
giving birth to monsters	teratophobia
God	theophobia
gold	crysophobia or aurophobia
hair	trichophobia
heart disease	cardiophobia
heat	thermophobia
heaven	uranophobia
hell	hadephobia or stygiophobia

PHOBIAS (cont.)

heredity	patroiophobia
high buildings	batophobia
high places	acrophobia *or*
	hypsophobia
home	oikophobia
homosexuals	homophobia
horses	hippophobia
ice	cryophobia
ideas	ideophobia
idleness	thassophobia
illness	nosophobia
imperfection	atelophobia
infinity	apeirophobia
injury	traumatophobia
inoculation	trypanophobia *or*
	vaccinophobia
insanity	lyssophobia *or*
	maniphobia
insects	entomophobia
insect stings	cnidophobia
Italian people and	
things	Italophobia
itching	acarophobia
jealousy	zelotypophobia
Jewish people and	
things	Judaeophobia
justice	dikephobia
lakes	limnophobia
leprosy	leprophobia
lice	pediculophobia
light	photophobia
lightning	astrapophobia
lists	pinaciphobia *or*
	katastichophobia
loneliness	autophobia *or*
	ermitophobia
machinery	mechanophobia
magic	rhabdophobia
marriage	gametophobia
men	androphobia
metal	metallophobia
mice	musophobia
microbes	bacillophobia *or*
	microbiophobia
mirrors	eisoptrophobia

mites	acarophobia
mobs	ochlophobia
money	chrematophobia
monsters	teratrophobia
motion	kinetophobia
music	musicophobia
names	onomatophobia
narrowness	anginophobia
needles	belonephobia
new things	neophobia
night	nyctophobia
open places	agoraphobia
pain	algophobia
parasites	parasitophobia
people	anthropophobia
philosophy	philosophobia
pins	enetophobia
places	topophobia
pleasure	hedonophobia
poison	toxiphobia
politics	politicophobia
The Pope	papaphobia
poverty	peniaphobia
precipices	cremnophobia
priests	hierophobia
punishment	poinephobia
rabies	hydrophobo-
	phobia
rail travel	sidero-
	dromophobia
religious works of	
art	iconophobia
reptiles	batrachophobia
responsibility	hypegiaphobia
ridicule	katagelophobia
rivers	potamophobia
robbers	harpaxophobia
ruin	atephobia
Russian people and	
things	Russophobia
saints	hagiophobia
Satan	Satanophobia
scabies	scabiophobia
Scottish people and	
things	Scotophobia

PHOBIAS (cont.)

sea	thalassophobia	symmetry	symmetrophobia
sex	erotophobia	taste	geumatophobia
shadows	sciophobia	technology	technophobia
sharpness	acrophobia	teeth	odontophobia
shock	hormephobia	telephone	telephonophobia
sin	hamartophobia	thinking	phronemophobia
skin disease	dermatosiophobia	thirteen	triskaidekaphobia
	or dermato-pathophobia	thunder	brontophobia *or* tonitrophobia *or* keraunophobia
sleep	hypnophobia		
slime	blennophobia	time	chronophobia
small things	microphobia	touch	haptophobia
smell	olfactophobia *or* osmophobia	travel	hodophobia
		tuberculosis	phthisiophobia
snakes	ophidiophobia	tyrants	tyrannophobia
snow	chionophobia	vehicles	ochophobia
sound	acousticophobia	venereal	
sourness	acerophobia	disease	syphilophobia
speech	lalophobia *or* glossophobia *or* phonophobia	voids	kenophobia
		vomiting	emetophobia
		water	hydrophobia
speed	tachophobia	waves	cymophobia
spiders	arachnophobia	weakness	asthenophobia
standing	stasophobia	wind	anemophobia
stars	siderophobia	women	gynophobia
stealing	kleptophobia	words	logophobia
string	linonophobia	work	ergophobia
sun	heliophobia	worms	helminthophobia
swallowing	phagophobia	writing	graphophobia

ANIMALS, PLANTS, AND AGRICULTURE

COLLECTIVE NAMES FOR ANIMALS AND BIRDS

army of caterpillars
bale of turtles
band of gorillas
bask of crocodiles
bellowing of bullfinches
bevy of roe deer *or* quails *or* larks
  or pheasants
bloat of hippopotami
brood of chickens
bury of rabbits
busyness of ferrets
cete of badgers
charm of finches
chattering of choughs
cloud of gnats
clowder of cats
congregation of plovers
covey of partridges
crash of rhinoceros
cry of hounds
descent of woodpeckers
desert of lapwings
dout of wild cats
down of hares
drift of swine
drove of horses *or* bullocks
erst of bees
exaltation of larks
flock of sheep
fluther of jellyfish
gaggle of geese on land
gam of whales
gang of elk
herd of cattle *or* elephants
hive of bees

hover of trout
kennel of dogs
kindle of kittens
knot of toads
labour of moles
leap *or* lepe of leopards
litter of kittens *or* pigs
mob of kangaroos
murder of crows
murmuration of starlings
muster of peacocks *or* penguins
mute of hares
obstinacy of buffalo
pace of asses
pack of hounds *or* grouse
paddling of ducks on water
pandemonium of parrots
parade of elephants
parcel of penguins
parliament of owls
pod of seals
pride of lions
rafter of turkeys
rookery of rooks
safe of ducks
sawt of lions
school of whales *or* dolphins *or*
  porpoises
siege of herons
shoal of fish
shrewdness of apes
skein of geese in flight
skulk of foxes
sloth of bears
smack of jellyfish

COLLECTIVE NAMES FOR ANIMALS AND BIRDS (cont.)

span of mules
spring of teal
stare of owls
string of horses
stud of mares
swarm of flies *or* bees
tiding of magpies
trip of goats
troop of baboons
turmoil of porpoises
turn of turtles
unkindness of ravens

watch of nightingales
yoke of oxen
zeal of zebras

*Many of these are fanciful or
humorous terms that probably
never had any real currency.
They were taken up by Joseph
Sturt in* Sports & Pastimes of
England (1801) *and by other
antiquarian writers.*

ADJECTIVES RELATING TO ANIMALS AND BIRDS

anguilliform	eel	chelonian	terrapin *or* tortoise *or* turtle
anguine	snake		
anserine	goose	colubrine	snake
apian	bee	columbine	dove
aquiline	eagle	corvine	crow
arachnoid	spider	crustacean *or* crustaceous	crab *or* lobster *or* shrimp
asinine	donkey		
avian	bird	elephantine	elephant
batrachian	frog *or* toad	equine	horse
bovine	cow	feline	cat
canine	dog	gallinaceous	fowl
caprine	goat	hircine	goat
cervid *or* cervine	deer	hirundine	swallow
cetacean *or* cetaceous	dolphin *or* porpoise *or* whale	leonine	lion
		leporine	hare
		lupine	wolf
		murine	mouse *or* rat

ADJECTIVES RELATING TO ANIMALS AND BIRDS (cont.)

musteline	ferret *or* skunk *or* weasel	sciurine	chipmunk *or* marmot *or* squirrel
ophidian	snake		
oscine	songbird	serpentine	snake
otarid	sea lion *or* seal	simian	monkey
		taurine	bull
ovine	sheep	turdine	thrush
passerine	sparrow	ursine	bear
phocine	seal	vermiform	worm
piscine	fish	viperine *or* viperous	viper
porcine	pig		
psittacine	parrot	viverrine	civet *or* mongoose
saurian	lizard		
		vulpine	fox

NAMES FOR MALE AND FEMALE ANIMALS

antelope	buck	doe	hare	buck	doe
badger	boar	sow	hartebeest	bull	cow
bear	boar	sow	horse	stallion	mare
bobcat	tom	lioness	impala	ram	ewe
buffalo	bull	cow	jackrabbit	buck	doe
camel	bull	cow	kangaroo	buck	doe
caribou	stag	doe	leopard	leopard	leopardess
cat	tom	queen	lion	lion	lioness
cattle	bull	cow	lobster	cock	hen
chicken	cock	hen	moose	bull	cow
cougar	tom	lioness	ox	bullock	cow
coyote	dog	bitch	peacock	peacock	peahen
deer	stag	doe	pheasant	cock	hen
dog	dog	bitch	pig	boar	sow
donkey	jackass	jennyass	rhinoceros	bull	cow
duck	drake	duck	seal	bull	cow
elephant	bull	cow	sheep	ram	ewe
ferret	jack	jill	swan	cob	pen
fish	cock	hen	tiger	tiger	tigress
fox	fox	vixen	weasel	boar	cow
giraffe	bull	cow	whale	bull	cow
goat	billygoat	nannygoat	wolf	dog	bitch
goose	gander	goose	zebra	stallion	mare

YOUNG OF ANIMALS

calf	buffalo *or* camel *or* cattle *or* elephant *or* elk *or* giraffe *or* hartebeest *or* rhinoceros *or* seal *or* whale	fawn	caribou *or* deer
		filly	horse
		foal	horse *or* zebra
		fry	fish
		gosling	goose
cheeper	grouse *or* quail *or* partridge	joey	kangaroo
		kid	antelope *or* goat *or* roedeer
chick	chicken *or* hawk *or* pheasant		
		kit	beaver *or* fox *or* weasel
colt	horse	kitten	bobcat *or* cat *or* cougar *or* jackrabbit *or* skunk
cub	badger *or* bear *or* fox *or* leopard *or* lion *or* tiger *or* walrus *or* wolf		
		lamb	sheep
		leveret	hare
cygnet	swan	piglet	pig
duckling	duck	puppy	coyote *or* dog
eaglet	eagle	tadpole	frog *or* toad
elver	eel	squab	pigeon
eyas	hawk	whelp	dog *or* wolf

MAMMALS

aardvark	aye-aye	blue whale	caribou
aardwolf	babirusa	boar	cat
agouti	baboon	bobcat	catamount
ai	Bactrian camel	bongo	cattle
alpaca	badger	bottlenose	cavy
angwantibo	banteng	brown bear	chamois
anoa	barbastelle	buffalo	cheetah
ant bear	barking deer	bushbaby	chevrotain
anteater	bat	bushbuck	chickaree
antelope	bear	cachalot	chimpanzee
aoudad	beaver	cacomistle	chinchilla
ape	bettong	camel	Chinese water deer
Arctic fox	bighorn	cane rat	
Arctic hare	binturong	Cape buffalo	chipmunk
armadillo	bison	capuchin monkey	chiru
ass	black bear		chital
aurochs	blackbuck	capybara	cinnamon bear
axis deer	blue fox	caracal	civet

MAMMALS (cont.)

clouded
  leopard
coati
coatimundi
colobus
colugo
cony
cottontail
cougar
cow
coyote
coypu
crabeater seal
deer
deer mouse
desert rat
desman
dhole
dik-dik
dingo
dog
dolphin
donkey
dormouse
douroucouli
drill
dromedary
dugong
duiker
dziggetai
eland
elephant
elephant seal
elk
entellus
ermine
European bison
eyra
fallow deer
fennec
ferret
fieldmouse
fisher
flying fox
flying lemur

flying squirrel
fossa
foumart
fox
fruit bat
galago
gaur
gayal
gazelle
gelada
gemsbok
genet
gerbil
gerenuk
gibbon
giraffe
glutton
gnu
goat
goat antelope
golden cat
golden mole
gopher
goral
gorilla
grampus
grass monkey
grey squirrel
grey wolf
grison
grizzly bear
groundhog
ground squirrel
guanaco
guenon
guinea pig
gymnure
hairy hedgehog
hamadryas
hamster
harbour seal
hare
hartebeest
harvest mouse
hedgehog

hinny
hippopotamus
hippo
hog
honey badger
honey bear
hooded seal
horse
horseshoe bat
howler monkey
humpback
  whale
hutia
hyena
hyrax
ibex
impala
Indian elephant
indri
jackal
jackrabbit
jaguar
jaguarundi
jerboa
jumping mouse
kangaroo rat
kiang
killer whale
kinkajou
kit fox
klipspringer
kob
Kodiak bear
kudu
langur
lemming
lemur
leopard
leopard seal
liger
linsang
lion
llama
loris
lynx

macaque
manatee
mandrill
mangabey
mara
margay
markhor
marmoset
marmot
marten
meerkat
mink
mole
mole rat
mona monkey
mongoose
monkey
moon rat
moose
mouflon
mountain
  beaver
mountain cat
mountain goat
mountain lion
mountain
  sheep
mouse
mouse deer
mule
mule deer
muntjac
musk deer
musk ox
muskrat
musquash
narwhal
New World
  monkey
nilgai
noctule
nyala
ocelot
okapi

MAMMALS (cont.)

Old World
  monkey
olingo
onager
orang-utan
oribi
oryx
otter
otter shrew
ounce
ox
paca
pack rat
Pallas's cat
palm civet
pampas cat
panda
pangolin
panther
patas monkey
peccary
Père David's
  deer
pig
pika
pilot whale
pine marten
pipistrelle
pocket gopher
pocket mouse
polar bear
polecat
porcupine
porpoise
potto
pouched rat
prairie dog
prairie wolf
proboscis
  monkey
pronghorn
puma

pygmy hippo-
  potamus
rabbit
raccoon or
  racoon
raccoon dog
rat
ratel
red deer
red fox
red squirrel
reedbuck
reindeer
rhesus monkey
rhinoceros
rhino
right whale
roan antelope
Rocky
  Mountain
  goat
roe deer
rorqual
royal antelope
sable
sable antelope
sabre-toothed
  tiger
saiga
saki
sambar
scaly anteater
scaly-tailed
  squirrel
sea cow
sea elephant
seal
sea lion
sea otter
sei whale
serotine bat
serow
serval

sheep
shrew
siamang
sifaka
sika
silver fox
sitatunga
skunk
sloth
sloth bear
snow leopard
snowshoe hare
solenodon
souslik
spectacled bear
sperm whale
spider monkey
spiny
  dormouse
springbok
springhaas
squirrel
squirrel
  monkey
steinbok
stoat
stone marten
sun bear
suslik
swine
tahr
tailless tenrec
takin
talapoin
tamandua
tamarin
tamarou
tapir
tarsier
tayra
tenrec
tiger
tigon

timber wolf
titi
tree shrew
unau
urus
vampire bat
vervet
vicuña
Virginia deer
viscacha
vole
walrus
wapiti
warthog
waterbuck
water buffalo
water rat
water shrew
water vole
weasel
whale
white
  rhinoceros
white whale
wild boar
wildcat
wild dog
wildebeest
wisent
wolf
wolverine
woodchuck
wood rat
woolly monkey
woolly
  rhinoceros
woolly spider
  monkey
yak
zebra
zebu
zorilla

MARSUPIALS

bandicoot
bilby
cuscus
dalgyte
dasyure
flying phalanger
hare wallaby
honey mouse
kangaroo
koala bear
marsupial mole

marsupial mouse
marsupial rat
mouse opossum
numbat
opossum
pademelon
phalanger
planigale
quokka
rabbit bandicoot
rat kangaroo

rat opossum
rock wallaby
Tasmanian devil
thylacine
Tasmanian wolf
tree kangaroo
wallaby
wombat
yapok

BIRDS

adjutant bird
albatross
amadavat
anhinga
antbird
Arctic tern
auk
auklet
avocet
babbler
bald eagle
Baltimore oriole
barbet
barnacle goose
barn owl
bateleur eagle
bee-eater
bellbird
bird of paradise
bittern
blackbird
blackcap
black swan
blue-bill
bluebird

blue tit
boat-bill
bobolink
bobwhite
booby
bowerbird
brambling
brent-goose
broad-bill
brush turkey
budgerigar
bulbul
bullfinch
bunting
burrowing owl
bush tit
bush wren
bustard
butcher-bird
buzzard
Canada goose
canary
canvas-back
caracara
cardinal

carrion crow
cassowary
catbird
chaffinch
chat
chickadee
chicken
chiffchaff
chipping
 sparrow
chough
coal tit
cockatiel
cockatoo
coly
condor
coot
cormorant
corncrake
cowbird
crake
crane
crested tit
crocodile bird
crossbill

crow
cuckoo
cuckoo shrike
curassow
curlew
dabchick
darter
demoiselle
 crane
diamond-bird
dipper
diver
dove
duck
dunlin
dunnock
eagle
eagle owl
egret
eider duck
emperor
 penguin
emu
emu-wren
erne

BIRDS (cont.)

fairy penguin
falcon
fantail
fernbird
fieldfare
finch
finfoot
firecrest
fish owl
flamingo
flicker
flower-pecker
flycatcher
francolin
friar-bird
frigate bird
frogmouth
fulmar
gadwall
gallinule
gannet
garganey
gnat-catcher
godwit
goldcrest
golden eagle
golden-eye
goldfinch
gooney bird
goosander
goose
goshawk
grackle
grassfinch
great tit
grebe
greenfinch
greenshank
greylag goose
griffon vulture
grosbeak
grouse
guillemot
gull
gyrfalcon

hammerhead
harlequin duck
harpy eagle
harrier
Hawaiian goose
hawfinch
hawk
hawk-owl
hedge sparrow
hen
heron
herring gull
hobby
honeycreeper
honeyeater
honeyguide
hooded crow
hoopoe
hoot owl
hornbill
horned owl
house martin
house sparrow
huia
hummingbird
ibis
jabiru
jacamar
jacana
jackdaw
jay
junco
kagu
kakapo
kea
kestrel
killdeer
kingbird
kingfisher
kinglet
kite
kittiwake
kiwi
knot
kookaburra

lammergeier
lanner
lapwing
lark
laughing
  jackass
laughing owl
laverock *Scot.*
lily-trotter
linnet
little owl
long-tailed tit
lorikeet
lory
lovebird
lyre-bird
macaw
magpie
mallard
manakin
mandarin duck
marabou stork
marsh harrier
martin
meadowlark
megapode
merganser
merlin
minivet
mistle thrush
mockingbird
Montagu's
  harrier
moorhen
Mother Carey's
  chicken
motmot
mourning dove
mousebird
Muscovy duck
mute swan
muttonbird
mynah bird
nene
nighthawk

night heron
nightingale
nightjar
noddy
notornis
nutcracker
nuthatch
oil-bird
oriole
ortolan
osprey
ostrich
ouzel
ovenbird
owl
owlet-
  frogmouth
oxpecker
oystercatcher
parakeet
parrot
partridge
peacock
peafowl
peewee
peewit
pelican
penguin
peregrine
  falcon
petrel
phalarope
pheasant
phoebe
pigeon
pigeon-hawk
pilot bird
pintail
pipit
pipiwharauroa
plains-
  wanderer
plover
pochard
ptarmigan

BIRDS (cont.)

puffin
pukeko
quetzal
rail
raven
razorbill
redhead
redpoll
redshank
redstart
redwing
reed-bird
reedling
reed warbler
rhea
rhinoceros bird
rice-bird
rifle bird
ring-dove
ring-necked
  pheasant
ring ouzel
roadrunner
robin
rock-dove
roller
rook
rosella
ruddy duck
ruff
saddleback
sanderling
sand martin
sandpiper

sapsucker
scaup
scops owl
screamer
screech owl
scrub turkey
seagull
secretary bird
seriema
serin
shag
shearwater
sheathbill
shelduck
shoebill
shoveler duck
shrike
siskin
skimmer
skua
skylark
smew
snake bird
snipe
snow bunting
snow goose
snowy owl
song thrush
sparrow
sparrowhawk
spoonbill
starling
stonechat
stone curlew

stork
storm petrel
sunbird
sun bittern
swallow
swan
swiftlet
tailor-bird
takahe
tanager
tawny owl
teal
tern
thickhead
thornbill
thrasher
thrush
tinamou
titlark
titmouse
toucan
touraco
towhee
tragopan
treecreeper
trogon
tropicbird
tui
turkey
turkey vulture
turnstone
turtle-dove
twite

tyrant
  flycatcher
umbrella bird
vulture
wagtail
wallcreeper
warbler
wattlebird
waxbill
waxwing
weaver-bird
weaver finch
wheatear
whimbrel
whinchat
whip bird
whippoorwill
whistler
whitethroat
whooping
  crane
whydah
willet
willow warbler
woodchat
woodcock
woodcreeper
wood-duck
woodpecker
wren
wrybill
wryneck
yellowhammer
yellowhead

REPTILES

adder
agama
alligator
alligator lizard
ameira
amphisbaena
anaconda
anole
asp
bandy-bandy
basilisk
bearded dragon
black snake
blind snake
blindworm
bloodsucker
boa constrictor
boomslang
box turtle
brown snake
bull snake
bushmaster
carpet python
caiman *or*
  cayman
chameleon
chuckwalla
cobra
cooter
copperhead
coral snake
corn snake
cottonmouth
crocodile

death adder
diamondback
  rattlesnake
diamondback
  terrapin
egg-eating
  snake
fence lizard
fer-de-lance
flying lizard
flying snake
frilled lizard
Gaboon viper
Galapagos
  giant tortoise
garter snake
gecko
gharial
giant tortoise
Gila monster
glass lizard
glass snake
goanna
gopher snake
grass snake
green turtle
harlequin snake
hawksbill turtle
hognose snake
horned toad
horned viper
iguana
Indian python
Indigo snake

jungle runner
king cobra
king snake
Komodo
  dragon
krait
leatherback
legless lizard
legless skink
lizard
loggerhead
  turtle
mamba
mangrove
  snake
matamata
milk snake
moccasin
moloch
monitor lizard
mugger
Nile crocodile
pit viper
pond turtle
puff-adder
python
racer
rainbow boa
rat snake
rattlesnake
reticulated
  python
ribbon snake
rinkhals

rock python
royal python
Russell's viper
sand lizard
scalyfoot
sea snake
sidewinder
skink
slider
slow-worm
smooth snake
snake
snapping turtle
soft-shelled
  turtle
spitting cobra
taipan
terrapin
tiger snake
tokay
tortoise
tree snake
tuatara
turtle
vine snake
viper
viviparous
  lizard
wall lizard
wart snake
water moccasin
water snake
whip snake
worm lizard

AMPHIBIANS

axolotl
bullfrog
caecilian
clawed toad
Congo eel
crested newt
fire-bellied newt
fire-bellied toad
fire salamander
frog

giant toad
Goliath frog
hairy frog
hellbender
horned toad
midwife toad
mud puppy
natterjack toad
newt
olm

platanna
poison-arrow frog
salamander
siren
smooth newt
spade-foot toad
Suriname toad
Tiger Salamander
toad
tree frog

FISH

albacore
alewife
allis shad
amberjack
anchovy
anemone fish
angelfish
angel shark
angler fish
arapaima
archer fish
argentine
bandfish
barbel
barracuda
barramundí
bass
batfish
beluga
bib
bichir
billfish
bitterling
blackfish
bleak
blenny

blindfish
blowfish
bluefish
blue shark
boarfish
Bombay duck
bonefish
bonito
bonnethead
bonnetmouth
bowfin
boxfish
bream
brill
brisling
buffalo fish
bullhead
bummalo
burbot
butterfish
butterfly fish
butterfly ray
candiru
candlefish
capelin
carp

carpet shark
catfish
cavefish
char
characin
chimaera
chub
chum salmon
cichlid
cisco
climbing perch
clingfish
coalfish
cobia
cod
coelacanth
conger eel
cornetfish
crappie
croaker
crucian carp
cusk
cutlass fish
dab
dace
damselfish

danio
darter
dealfish
devil ray
discus
dogfish
dolphin-fish
dorado
dory
dragonet
dragonfish
drum
eagle ray
eel
eelpout
electric eel
electric ray
elephant-snout
  fish
fighting fish
filefish
firefish
flatfish
flat-head
flounder
fluke

FISH (cont.)

flying fish	kingfish	orfe	sargassum fish
flying gurnard	kingklip	paddlefish	sauger
four-eyed fish	knifefish	parrotfish	saury
frogfish	koi carp	pearlfish	sawfish
garfish	labyrinth fish	perch	scad
garpike	lake trout	pickerel	scat
glassfish	lamprey	pike	scorpion fish
globe-fish	lancetfish	pikeperch	sculpin
goatfish	lantern fish	pilchard	scup
goby	leatherjacket	pilot fish	sea bass
goldfish	lemon sole	pipefish	sea bream
goose-fish	ling	piranha	sea horse
gourami	livebearer	plaice	sea perch
grayling	lizardfish	pollack	searobin
grenadier	loach	pollan	sea trout
groper	lumpsucker	pomfret	sergeant-fish
grunion	lungfish	pompano	shad
grunt	mackerel	pope	shanny
gudgeon	madtom	porbeagle	shark
guitarfish	mako	porcupine fish	sharksucker
gulper eel	manta	porgy	sheatfish
gunnel	marlin	pout	sheepshead
guppy	menhaden	powan	shovelhead
gurnard	midshipman	puffer fish	shovelnose
gwyniad	miller's thumb	pumpkinseed	shubunkin
haddock	minnow	rabbitfish	silverside
hagfish	molly	rainbow trout	skate
hake	monkfish	ratfish	skipjack tuna
half-beak	moonfish	ray	skipper
halibut	Moorish idol	redfin	smelt
hammerhead	moray eel	redfish	smooth hound
shark	mosquitofish	remora	snake mackerel
hatchetfish	mudfish	requiem shark	snapper
herring	mudminnow	ribbonfish	snipe fish
hogfish	mudskipper	roach	snook
horse mackerel	mullet	rockling	sockeye salmon
houting	mummichog	roughy	sole
humpback	Murray cod	rudd	sparling
salmon	muskellunge	ruffe	spadefish
ice fish	needlefish	sailfish	spearfish
ide	nurse shark	saithe	sprat
jack	oarfish	salmon	stargazer
jewfish	oilfish	sand eel	sterlet
John Dory	old wife	sandfish	stickleback
killifish	opah	sardine	stingray

FISH (cont.)

stone bass
stonefish
sturgeon
sucker
sunfish
surgeon fish
swordfish
swordtail
tarpon
tautog
tench
tetra
thornback

threadfin
thresher shark
tigerfish
tiger shark
toadfish
tomcod
tommy ruff
toothcarp
tope
topminnow
torpedo ray
trevally
triggerfish

trout
trunkfish
tuna
turbot
twaite shad
vendace
viperfish
wahoo
walleye
weakfish
weatherfish
weever
whale shark

whitebait
whitefish
white shark
whiting
wirrah
wolffish
wrasse
x-ray fish
yellow jack
yellowtail
zander
zebra fish

INSECTS AND ARACHNIDS

alder fly
amazon ant
ambrosia beetle
ant
ant-lion
aphid
army ant
army worm
assassin bug
backswimmer
bark beetle
bedbug
bee
bee fly
beetle
bird-eating
  spider
black beetle
blackfly
black widow
blister beetle
bloodworm
blowfly
bluebottle

body louse
boll-weevil
bombardier
  beetle
booklouse
bookworm
borer
bot fly
bristletail
buffalo gnat
bug
bumble-bee
burying beetle
bush cricket
butterfly
cabbage root
  fly
caddis-fly
camel spider
capsid bug
cardinal spider
carpenter bee
carpet beetle
chafer

chigger
chinch bug
cicada
click beetle
cockchafer
cockroach
Colorado
  potato beetle
corn borer
cotton stainer
crab louse
crane-fly
cricket
croton bug
cuckoo-spit
  insect
cutworm
daddy longlegs
damselfly
darkling beetle
death-watch
  beetle
deer fly

devil's coach-
  horse
diadem spider
digger wasp
diving beetle
dobsonfly
dor-beetle
dragonfly
driver ant
drosophila
dung-beetle
earwig
elm bark beetle
false scorpion
fire ant
firebrat
firefly
flea
flea beetle
fly
froghopper
fruit fly
funnel-web
  spider

INSECTS AND ARACHNIDS (cont.)

gadfly
gall midge
gall wasp
giant water bug
glow-worm
Goliath beetle
grain weevil
grasshopper
greenbottle
greenfly
ground beetle
ground bug
harlequin bug
harvestman
harvest mite
head louse
Hercules beetle
honey ant
honey bee
hornet
horntail
horsefly
housefly
hoverfly
hunting spider
huntsman
  spider
ichneumon
itch mite
jockey spider
June bug
katipo
katydid
ked
kissing bug
lacewing

lac insect
ladybird
lantern-fly
leaf beetle
leafcutter ant
leafcutter bee
leafhopper
leaf insect
leatherjacket
locust
louse
mason bee
May-bug
mayfly
mealworm
mealy bug
midge
mite
mole cricket
money spider
mosquito
moth
mygale
oil beetle
orb weaver
phylloxera
plant bug
plant hopper
pond-skater
potato beetle
potter wasp
praying mantis
raft spider
red ant
red-back
red bug

red spider mite
retiary spider
rhinoceros
  beetle
robber fly
rove beetle
sandfly
sawfly
scale insect
scarab
scorpion
scorpion fly
scorpion spider
screw-worm
sexton beetle
sheep ked
sheep tick
shield bug
silverfish
slave-making
  ant
snakefly
soldier beetle
Spanish fly
spider
spider mite
spider wasp
spittlebug
springtail
squash bug
stag beetle
stick insect
stink bug
stonefly
stylops
sun spider

tarantula
termite
thrips
tick
tiger beetle
tortoise beetle
trapdoor spider
tree hopper
tsetse fly
violin spider
warble fly
wasp
water beetle
water-boatman
water bug
water scorpion
water spider
water strider
webspinner
weevil
whip scorpion
whirligig
white ant
whitefly
white-tailed
  spider
wind scorpion
wireworm
wolf spider
wood borer
wood tick
woodwasp
woodworm

BUTTERFLIES AND MOTHS

Adonis blue
angle shades
apollo
argus
atlas moth
bagworm moth
birdwing
blue
brimstone
  butterfly
brown
burnet
burnished brass
cabbage white
Camberwell
  Beauty
cecropia moth
cinnabar moth
clearwing moth
clothes-moth
clouded yellow
codling moth
comma
copper
dagger

death's head
  hawkmoth
drinker
eggar
emerald
emperor moth
ermine
fritillary
fruit moth
gatekeeper
geometrid
goat moth
grayling
gypsy moth
hairstreak
hawkmoth
heath
io moth
lackey
lappet
large blue
leopard moth
lobster moth
luna moth
magpie moth

marbled white
meadow brown
merveille du
  jour
milkweed
monarch
morpho
Mother Shipton
mourning cloak
noctuid
nymphalid
oak eggar
orange-tip
owlet moth
painted lady
papilionid
peacock
  butterfly
peppered moth
plume moth
prominent
pug
purple emperor
puss moth
pyralid

red admiral
ringlet
satyrid
silk moth
silkworm moth
silver Y
skipper
speckled wood
sulphur
swallowtail
  butterfly
swift moth
tiger moth
tineid
tortoiseshell
tortrix
tussock moth
underwing
vapourer
wall brown
wax moth
white admiral
winter moth
yellow-tail

INVERTEBRATES

abalone
annelid worm
argonaut
ark shell
arrow worm
auger shell
bamboo worm
beard worm
blood fluke
bootlace worm
bristle worm
Cestoda
chiton

clam
coat-of-mail
  shell
cockle
conch
cone shell
cone worm
cowrie
cuttlefish
earthworm
eelworm
elephant's-tusk
  shell

eyeworm
fanworm
feather duster
filaria
flatworm
fluke
geoduck
giant clam
guinea worm
hairworm
hard-shell
heartworm
helmet shell

hookworm
horsehair worm
keyhole limpet
kidney worm
leech
limpet
liver fluke
lugworm
lungworm
mitre shell
money cowrie
murex
mussel

INVERTEBRATES (cont.)

nautilus
nematode
nudibranch
octopus
olive shell
oyster
paddleworm
palolo worm
paper nautilus
parchment
  worm
peacock worm
peanut worm
pearly nautilus
periwinkle

piddock
pinworm
planarian
platyhelminth
pogonophoran
proboscis
  worm
quahog
ragworm
razor shell
ribbonworm
roundworm
scaleworm
scallop
schistosome

sea butterfly
sea hare
sea lemon
sea mouse
sea slug
shipworm
slipper shell
slit shell
slug
snail
soft-shell clam
spider conch
squid
tapeworm
teredo

threadworm
tiger cowrie
tooth shell
top shell
triton shell
tubifex
tusk shell
venus clam
volute
wentletrap
whelk
whipworm
winkle
worm shell

SEASHELLS

abalone
angel wing
ark shell
auger
basket shell
bonnet
bubble shell
canoe shell
carpet shell
carrier shell
cask shell
chambered
  nautilus
chank
clam
coat-of-mail
cockle
cock's-comb
  oyster

conch
cone
cowrie
cup-and-saucer
date mussel
dog whelk
dove shell
drill
drupe
ear shell
fig shell
fighting conch
file shell
flamingo
  tongue
frog shell
furrow shell
gaper
giant clam

hard clam
harp
heart cockle
helmet
hoof shell
horn shell
horse mussel
jewel box
jingle shell
junonia
keyhole limpet
lima
limpet
lion's paw
lucine
marginella
mitre
money cowrie
moon shell

murex
mussel
nautilus
necklace shell
nerite
Noah's ark
nutmeg shell
nut shell
olive
ormer
otter shell
oyster
oyster drill
partridge shell
pearly nautilus
pelican's foot
pen shell
periwinkle
pheasant shell

SEASHELLS (cont.)

piddock
pyramid shell
quahog
queen scallop
razor-shell
rock shell
saddle oyster
scallop
sea snail
slipper limpet
slit limpet
slit shell

spider conch
spindle shell
spire shell
staircase shell
sundial
sunset shell
tellin
thorny oyster
tiger cowrie
tooth shell
top-shell
tower shell

triton
triton's trumpet
trough shell
trumpet shell
tulip shell
tun
turban
turkey wing
turret shell
tusk shell
umbrella shell
vase shell

venus
Venus clam
violet sea snail
volute
wedge shell
wentletrap
whelk
wing oyster
winkle
worm shell
zebra mussel

TREES AND SHRUBS

acacia
alder
almond
apple
araucaria
arbutus
ash
aspen
assegai
balsa
banksia
banyan
baobab
bay tree
bebeeru
beech
belah
birch
blackthorn
bo tree
bottle-brush
bottle tree
box
buckthorn
cacao

calabash
camphor tree
cassia
cedar
champac
chestnut
coco-de-mer
coffee tree
coolabah
coral tree
corkwood
cornel
cypress
deodar
dhak
divi-divi
dogwood
dragon tree
eaglewood
ebony
elder
elm
eucalyptus
fever tree
fir

firethorn
flame tree
frangipani
fringe tree
Gaboon
gidgee
ginkgo
gomuti
guaiacum
guayule
gum tree
hawthorn
hazel
hickory
holly
hornbeam
iroko
ironwood
ivorywood
jacaranda
jarrah
jelutong
jojoba
Joshua tree
Judas tree

juniper
kaffirboom
kahikatea
kalmia
kamala
karri
kauri
kawakawa
kiaat
kingwood
koa
kowhai
kurrajong
lacquer tree
lantana
larch
laurel
lemonwood
lilac
lilly-pilly
lime
linden
logwood
macrocarpa
madroño

TREES AND SHRUBS (cont.)

magnolia
mahogany
maidenhair tree
mako
mangrove
manna-ash
maple
matai
maté
may
mesquite
mimosa
mock orange
monkey puzzle
mulberry
myrtle
ngaio
nipa
nux vomica
oak
ocotillo
oleander
osier
pagoda tree
palm
palmyra
paulownia
peepul

pepper tree
pine
plane
pohutukawa
poplar
privet
pyinkado
pyracantha
quassia
quebracho
rain tree
redbud
redwood
rewarewa
rhododendron
ribbonwood
robinia
rosewood
rowan
rubber plant
sandalwood
sandarac
sandbox tree
sapele
sappanwood
saskatoon
sassafras
savin

sequoia
seringa
service tree
shagbark
shea
silk-cotton tree
simarouba
sneezewood
snowball tree
soapbark
sorb
sorrel tree
sourwood
spindle
spruce
stinkwood
strawberry tree
styrax
sumach or
   sumac
sycamore
tallow tree
tallow wood
tamarack
tamarind
tamarisk
tawa
teak

tea-tree
terebinth
thorn tree
thuja
toothache tree
totara
traveller's joy
tupelo
turpentine
   tree
umbrella tree
varnish tree
walnut
wandoo
wattle
wayfaring tree
wellingtonia
whitebeam
wilga
willow
wine palm
witch hazel
yarran
yaupon
yew
ylang-ylang
yucca
zebrawood

FLOWERS

acanthus
acidanthera
aconite
African violet
agrimony
alkanet
alyssum
amaryllis
anemone
arrowroot
arum lily
asphodel
aspidistra
aster
aubrietia
avens
azalea
balsam
bedstraw
begonia
belladonna
bellflower
bindweed
bittersweet
black-eyed
  Susan
bladderwort
bleeding heart
bluebell
borage
bramble
broom
bryony
buddleia
bugle
bugloss
burdock
burnet
busy Lizzie
buttercup
butterwort
cactus
camellia
camomile
campion

candytuft
cardinal flower
carnation
carrion flower
catchfly
catmint
catnip
celandine
cheese plant
chickweed
Chinese lantern
chrysanth-
  emum
cinquefoil
clematis
clove pink
clover
coltsfoot
columbine
comfrey
coneflower
convolvulus
cornflower
cotoneaster
cow parsley
cowpea
cowslip
cranesbill
crocus
crowfoot
cuckoo pint
cyclamen
daffodil
dahlia
daisy
dandelion
deadly
  nightshade
dead nettle
delphinium
dock
dropwort
duckweed
edelweiss
eglantine

evening
  primrose
eyebright
figwort
flax
fleabane
forget-me-not
forsythia
foxglove
freesia
fritillary
fuchsia
furze *or* gorse
gardenia
gentian
geranium
gillyflower
gladiolus
globe thistle
golden rod
goosefoot
groundsel
harebell
hawkweed
heather
hellebore
helleborine
hemlock
henbane
herb
  Christopher
herb Gerard
herb Paris
herb Robert
hibiscus
hogweed
hollyhock
honesty
honeysuckle
hop
houseleek
hyacinth
hydrangea
iris
japonica

jasmine
jonquil
kingcup
knapweed
knotgrass
laburnum
lady's finger
lady's slipper
lady's smock
lady's tresses
larkspur
lavender
lemon balm
lily
lily of the valley
lobelia
loosestrife
lords and ladies
lotus
lupin
mallow
marigold
may-apple
mayflower
mayweed
meadow
  saffron
meadowsweet
mignonette
milkwort
mint
mistletoe
moccasin
  flower
monkshood
montbretia
moonflower
morning glory
motherwort
mullein
narcissus
nasturtium
nettle
nightshade
orchid

FLOWERS (cont.)

oxlip
pansy
pasque flower
passion flower
pennyroyal
peony
peppermint
petunia
phlox
pimpernel
pink
pitcher plant
plantain
poinsettia
polyanthus
poppy
primrose
primula
ragged robin
ragwort
rhododendron

rock rose
rose
rosebay
rue
sage
St John's wort
salvia
samphire
saxifrage
scabious
shamrock
slipperwort
snakeroot
snapdragon
snowdrop
soapwort
Solomon's seal
sorrel
speedwell
spider plant
spikenard

spurge
stitchwort
stock
stonecrop
sundew
sunflower
sweet pea
sweet william
tansy
teasel
thistle
thorn apple
thyme
tiger lily
toadflax
touch-me-not
tradescantia
trefoil
tulip
twayblade
valerian

Venus flytrap
verbena
veronica
vervain
vetch
violet
wallflower
water lily
willowherb
wintergreen
wisteria
witchweed
wolfbane
wood sorrel
wormwood
woundwort
yarrow
yellow
  archangel
yucca
zinnia

PARTS OF A FLOWER

androecium
anther
bract
bractede
calyx
capitulum
carpel
carpophore
catkin
corolla
corymb
cyathium
cyme

filament
floret
glume
gynoecium
hypanthium
involucel
involucre
ladicule
lemma
lip
monochasium
nectary
nucellus

ovary
ovule
palea
panicle
pedicel
peduncle
petal
placenta
pollen
pollen grain
pollinium
raceme
receptacle

rhachis
sepal
spadix
spathe
spike
spikelet
spur
stamen
stigma
style
tepal
umbel

FRUITS AND NUTS

acorn
alligator pear
almond
ananas
apple
apricot
areca nut
avocado
babaco
bael
bakeapple
banana
barberry
bayberry
bearberry
beechnut
bergamot
betel-nut
bilberry
bitternut
blackberry
blackcurrant
blueberry
boysenberry
Brazil nut
breadfruit
breadnut
bullace
burrawang nut
butternut
candlenut
carambola
carob
cashew
cherimoya
cherry
chestnut
chinaberry
chincapin
chokeberry
citron
clementine
cob-nut
coc-de-mer

coconut or
  cocoanut
coffee nut
cola nut
conker
coquilla nut
costard
crab apple
cranberry
crowberry
currant
damson
date
dewberry
durian
dwarf chestnut
earth-nut
elderberry
feijoa
fig
filbert
geebung
genipap
gooseberry
gourd
granadilla
grape
grapefruit
greengage
groundnut
grugru nut
guava
gum nut
hackberry
hazelnut
hickory nut
hognut
horse chestnut
huckleberry
ivory-nut
jaboticaba
jackfruit
jujube
kaki
kiwi fruit

kumquat
lemon
lime
lingonberry
litchi nut
loganberry
longan
loquat
lychee
macadamia nut
mandarin
mango
mangosteen
manzanilla
medlar
melon
minneola
mockernut
mombin
monkey-nut
mulberry
muscat
musk melon
myrobalan
nectarine
nipa
olive
orange
palm nut
passion fruit
pawpaw
peach
peanut
pear
pecan
persimmon
pignut
pineapple
pine nut
pippin
pistachio
plantain
plum
pomegranate
pomelo

prickly pear
quandong
Queensland nut
quince
rambutan
raspberry
redcurrant
salmonberry
sal nut
saouari nut
sapodilla
satsuma
service-berry
sharon fruit
sloe
sour cherry
sour gourd
sour orange
sour plum
soursop
spice-berry
star-apple
star fruit
strawberry
sweet chestnut
sweetsop
tamarillo
tamarind
tangelo
tangerine
tayberry
tomato
tree tomato
Ugli fruit™
walnut
water chestnut
watermelon
white currant
white walnut
whortleberry
winter cherry
youngberry

VEGETABLES

artichoke
asparagus
aubergine
avocado pear
bamboo shoots
bean
beet
beetroot
breadfruit
broccoli
Brussels sprout
cabbage
calabrese
capsicum
cardoon
carrot
cassava
cauliflower
celeriac
celery
chard

chayote
chervil
chicory
Chinese
  cabbage
Chinese leaves
aard
corn on the cob
courgette
cress
cucumber
curly kale
dishcloth gourd
eggplant
endive
fennel
gherkin
gourd
gumbo
Jerusalem
  artichoke

kale
kohlrabi
leek
lentil
lettuce
mangetout
manioc
marrow
marrow squash
mustard
okra
onion
orache
oyster plant
pak-choi
parsnip
pepper
pimiento
potato
pumpkin
radish

rutabaga
salsify
savoy
scallion
scorzonera
sea kale
shallot
spinach
spinach beet
squash
succory
swede
sweet corn
sweet potato
taro
tomato
turnip
water chestnut
watercress
yam
zucchini *Am.*

GRASSES, SEDGES, AND RUSHES

bamboo
barley
beach grass
beard grass
bent
Bermuda grass
bluegrass
bristle grass
brome
broomcorn
buffalo grass
bulrush
bunch grass
canary grass
China grass

cocksfoot
cordgrass
corn
cotton grass
couch grass
crabgrass
cutgrass
darnel
dog's-tail
durra
elephant grass
esparto
feather grass
fescue
finger grass

fiorin
fog
foxtail
gama grass
hair-grass
herd's-grass
Indian corn
Indian rice
Kentucky
  bluegrass
lemon grass
lyme grass
maize
marram grass
meadow grass

melick
millet
oat
oat-grass
orchard grass
paddy
pampas grass
panic
papyrus
quack grass
quaking grass
quitch
redtop
reed
reed grass

GRASSES, SEDGES, AND RUSHES (cont.)

reed mace
rice
rush
rye
ryegrass
sedge
sorghum
spartina

spear grass
spelt
spinifex
squirrel-tail
  grass
star grass
sugar cane
switch grass

sword grass
tef
teosinte
timothy grass
tussock grass
twitch grass
vernal grass
wheat

wild oat
wild rice
wire grass
woodrush
Yorkshire fog
zoysia

FUNGI AND ALGAE

agaric
amanita
amethyst
  deceiver
anabaena
anise cap
artist's fungus
bay bolete
beefsteak
  fungus
bird's-nest
  fungus
black bulgar
bladderwrack
blewit
blusher
blushing
  bracket
bolete
boletus
bonnet
bootlace fungus
bracket fungus
brain fungus
bulgar
bull kelp
butter cap

Caesar's
  mushroom
cage fungus
candle snuff
  fungus
carrageen
caterpillar
  fungus
cauliflower
  fungus
cep
Ceylon moss
champignon
chanterelle
chicken of the
  woods
chlorella
clouded agaric
club foot
club fungus
conferva
coral fungus
coral-spot
cow-pat
  toadstool
cramp balls

dead men's
  fingers
death cap
deceiver
desmid
destroying
  angel
devil's bolete
diatom
dinoflagellate
dog stinkhorn
dryad's saddle
dulse
ear fungus
ear pick fungus
earth ball
earth fan
earthstar
earth tongue
elf-cup
ergot
euglena
fairy button
fairy cakes
fairy club
fairy-ring
  mushroom

false
  chanterelle
false death cap
false morel
field mushroom
fire fungus
flame fungus
fly agaric
fucoid
fucus
funnel cap
ghost fungus
giant puffball
grisette
gulfweed
hedgehog
  fungus or
  mushroom
herald of the
  winter
honey fungus
horn of plenty
horsehair
  toadstool or
  mushroom
horse
  mushroom

FUNGI AND ALGAE (cont.)

ink cap
jelly babies
jelly fungus
jelly tongue
jew's ear
kelp
King Alfred's
  cakes
laminaria
laver
lawyer's wig
  mushroom
liberty cap
lorchel
meadow
  mushroom
milk cap
milk drop
miller
morel
nostoc
nullipore
oarweed
old man of the
  woods

orange-peel
  fungus
oyster
  mushroom
panther cap
parasol
  mushroom
parrot toadstool
peacock's tail
penny bun
plums and
  custard
poached egg
  fungus
poison pie
polypore
porcelain
  fungus
prince
puffball
redware
rockweed
russet shank
russula
sac fungus
saffron milkcap

St George's
  mushroom
sargassum
scarlet elf-cup
scarlet hood
sea lace
sea lettuce
sea tangle
seaware
sea wrack
shaggy inkcap
shaggy parasol
sickener
slippery jack
spike cap
spirogyra
spring amanita
stag's-horn
  fungus
stinkhorn
stinking parasol
stonewort
sulphur fungus
sulphur tuft
tawny grisette
toadstool

tough shank
truffle
tuckahoe
velvet cap
velvet foot
velvet shank
wax cap
weeping widow
witches' butter
wood blewit
wood
  hedgehog
wood
  mushroom
wood witch
wood
  woollyfoot
wrack
yellow brain
  fungus
yellow-staining
  mushroom *or*
  yellow stainer

TYPES OF FARMING

arboriculture
arable farming
dairy farming
extensive farming
factory farming
fish farming
floriculture
forestry
horticulture
husbandry
hydroponics

intensive farming
livestock farming
market gardening
mixed farming
organic farming
sharecropping
share farming
silviculture
subsistence farming
viticulture

BREEDS OF HORSE AND PONY

Andalusian
Anglo-Arab
Appaloosa
Arab
Ariègois
Asiatic Wild Horse
Barb
Bardigiano
Bashkir
Basuto pony
Breton
brumby
Budenny
Camargue
Caspian
Cleveland Bay
Clydesdale
Colorado Ranger
Comtois
Conestoga
Connemara pony
criollo
Czechoslovakian
  warmblood
Dales pony
Danish warmblood
Dartmoor pony
Dutch draught
Dutch warmblood
Exmoor pony
Falabella
Fell pony
Fjord
Friesian
Galiceño
Galloway
Gelderlander
Gotland
Hackney

Haflinger
Hanoverian
Highland pony
Holsteiner
Huçul
Hunter
Iceland pony
Indian Half-bred
Irish draught
Irish hunter
Jutland
Kabardin
Karabakh
Kathiawari
Kazakh
Konik
Landais
Lippizaner
Lokai
Lundy Island
Mangalarga
Manipur pony
Mérens pony
miniature Shetland
Missouri fox-trotting
  horse
Morgan
Murgese
mustang
New Forest pony
Nonius
Noriker
Norwegian racing
  trotter
Oldenburger
Orlov trotter
Palomino
Paso Fino
Percheron

Peruvian Paso
Pinto
Pinzgauer
Plateau Persian
polo pony
pony of the Americas
Pottok
Quarter Horse
Rhinelander
Russ
Russian heavy
  draught
Russian warmblood
Sable Island
Saddlebred
Salerno
Schleswig
Shales horse
Shetland pony
Shire horse
Standardbred
Suffolk Punch
Swedish warmblood
Tarpan
Tartar pony
Tennessee walking
  horse
Tersk thoroughbred
Timor
Trakehner
trotter
Viatka
Waler warmblood
Welsh cob
Welsh Mountain pony
Württemberger
Yorkshire coach horse

POINTS OF A HORSE

cannon bone	feathers	hoof	ribs
cheek	fetlock	knee	shank
chest	fetlock joint	loin	sheath
chestnut	flank	mane	shoulder
chin groove	forearm	navicular	splint bone
coffin bone	forelock	bone	stifle
coronet	frog	pastern	tail
crest	gaskin	pedal bone	tendon
croup	gullet	point of hip	windpipe
dock	heel	point of	withers
elbow	hind quarters	shoulder	
ergot	hock	poll	

BREEDS OF CATTLE

Aberdeen Angus	Durham	N'Dama
Africander	Friesian	Pinzgauer
Andalusian	Galician Blond	Polled Hereford
Australian Illawarra Shorthorn	Galloway	Polled Welsh Black
Ayrshire	German Yellow	Red-and-White Friesian
Bangus	Guernsey	Red Poll
Barrosã	Hereford	Red Ruby Devon
Beefalo	Highland	Romagnola
Beef Shorthorn	Holstein-Friesian	Santa Gertrudis
Belgian Blue	Irish Moiled	Shetland
Belted Galloway	Jamaica Hope	Shorthorn
Belted Welsh	Jersey	Simmental
Blonde d'Aquitaine	Kerry	South Devon
Brahman	Kyloe	Sussex
British White	Limousin	Swedish Red-and-White
Brown Swiss	Lincoln Red	Texas Longhorn
Charolais	Longhorn	Welsh Black
Chianina	Luing	West Highland
Danish Red	Maine Anjou	White Galloway
Devon	Meuse-Rhine-Ijssel	White Park
Dexter	Miranda	
Droughtmaster	Mongolian	
	Murray Grey	

BREEDS OF SHEEP

Abyssinian
Africander
Altai
Askanian
Australian Merino
Awassi
Berber
Bergamo
Beulah Speckled Face
Biella
Blackface
Blackhead Persian
Black Welsh Mountain
Bluefaced Leicester
Border Leicester
Bosnian Mountain
Brazilian Woolless
Campanian Barbary
Cannock Chase
Castlemilk Moorit
Caucasian
Cheviot
Chios
Clun Forest
Colbred
Columbia
Corriedale
Cotswold
Dales-Bred
Dartmoor
Derbyshire Gritstone
Devon Closewool
Devon Longwool
Dorper
Dorset Down
Dorset Horn
Dubrovnik
English Longwool
Exmoor Horn
French Blackheaded
Galway
Greek Zackel
Hampshire Down
Hebridean
Herdwick

Hill Radnor
Icelandic
Ile-de-France
Island Pramenka
Jacob
Karakachan
Karakul
Kent
Kerry Hill
Kivircik
Lacaune
Lacho
Lamon
Leicester
Lincoln Longwool
Llanwenog
Lleyn
Lonk
Lourdes
Manech
Manx Loghtan
Masai
Merino
Mongolian
Mug
Norfolk Horn
North Country
   Cheviot
North Ronaldsay
Old Norwegian
Orkney
Oxford Down
Panama
Poll Dorset
Polwarth
Portland
Précoce
Radnor
Rambouillet
Red Karaman
Rhiw Hill
Romanov
Romeldale
Romney Marsh
Rough Fell

Ryeland
Sardinian
Scottish Blackface
Shetland
Shropshire
Sicilian
Soay
South Devon
Southdown
South Wales
   Mountain
Spanish Merino
Suffolk
Swaledale
Swiss White Alpine
Swiss White
   Mountain
Talavera
Targhee
Teeswater
Texel
Tibetan
Tsigai
Tyrol Mountain
Welsh Mountain
Wensleydale
Whiteface Dartmoor
Whiteface Woodlands
Wicklow Mountain
Wiltshire Horn

Wild Sheep
aoudad
argali
barbary sheep
bharal
bighorn
blue sheep
dall sheep
mouflon
mountain sheep
urial
white sheep

BREEDS OF FOWL

Ancona	chicken	Muscovy	duck
Andalusian	chicken	Nankin	bantam
Australorp	chicken	Narragansett	turkey
Aylesbury	duck	New Hampshire Red	chicken
Black East Indian	duck	Nicholas	turkey
Black Norfolk	turkey	Norfolk Grey	chicken
Booted	bantam	North Holland Blue	chicken
Bourbon Red	turkey	Old English Game	bantam
Brahma	chicken	Old English Pheasant	
Brecon Buff	goose	Fowl	chicken
Bresse	chicken	Orloff	chicken
Broad-Breasted Bronze	turkey	Orpington	chicken
Broad-Breasted White	turkey	Orpington	duck
Cambridge Bronze	turkey	Pearl Grey	guinea fowl
Campine	chicken	Phoenix	chicken
Cayuga	duck	Pilgrim	goose
Chinese	goose	Plymouth Rock	chicken
Cochin	chicken	Poland	chicken
Crested	duck	Redcap	chicken
Crèvecour	chicken	Rhode Island Red	chicken
Croad Langshan	chicken	Roman	goose
Dorking	chicken	Rosecomb	bantam
Embden	goose	Rouen	duck
Faverolle	chicken	Rumpless	bantam
Frizzles	bantam	Scots Dumpy	chicken
Hamburgh	chicken	Scots Grey	chicken
Houdan	chicken	Sebastopol	goose
Indian Game	chicken	Sebright	bantam
Indian Runner	duck	Sicilian Buttercup	chicken
Ixworth	chicken	Silkie	chicken
Jersey Giant	chicken	Spanish	chicken
Jubilee Indian Game	chicken	Sultan	chicken
Khaki Campbell	duck	Sumatra Game	chicken
La Fleche	chicken	Sussex	chicken
Lakenfelder	chicken	Toulouse	goose
Lavender	guinea fowl	Transylvanian Naked	
Leghorn	chicken	Neck	chicken
Magpie	duck	Welsh Harlequin	duck
Malay	chicken	Welsummer	chicken
Malines	chicken	Whalesbury	duck
Mammoth Bronze	turkey	White	guinea fowl
Marans	chicken	White Austrian	turkey
Marsh Daisy	chicken	White Holland	turkey
Modern Game	chicken	Wyandotte	chicken
Modern Langshan	chicken	Yokohama	chicken

BREEDS OF DOG

Aberdeen terrier
affenpinscher
Afghan
Airedale terrier
akita
Alaskan malamute
Alsatian
Australian terrier
basenji
basset hound
beagle
Bearded Collie
Bedlington terrier
Belgian malinois
Bernese mountain dog
Bichon Frise
Black and Tan Coonhound
Blenheim spaniel
bloodhound
Border collie
borzoi
Boston terrier
Bouvier des Flandres
boxer
Briard
Brussels griffon
bulldog
bullmastiff
bull terrier
cairn terrier
Cavalier King Charles spaniel
chihuahua
chow

Clumber spaniel
cocker spaniel
collie
coonhound
corgi
dachshund
Dalmatian
Dandie Dinmont terrier
deerhound
Dobermann pinscher
elk-hound
English setter
Eurasier
field spaniel
Finnish spitz
foxhound
fox terrier
Giant Schnauzer
golden retriever
Gordon setter
Great Dane
Great Pyrenees
greyhound
griffon
Groenendael
harrier
Hovawart
husky
Ibicencan hound
Ibizan hound
Irish setter
Irish terrier
Irish wolfhound
Ivicene
Istrian pointer
Jack Russell terrier
keeshond
kelpie

Kerry blue terrier
King Charles spaniel
Komondor
Kuvasz
Labrador retriever
laika
Lakeland terrier
Leonberger
Lhasa apso
Malamute
Maltese dog *or* terrier
Manchester terrier
mastiff
Mexican hairless
Newfoundland
Norfolk terrier
Norwegian elkhound
Norwich terrier
Old English sheepdog
otter hound
papillon
Pekinese
Pharaoh hound
pit bull terrier
pointer
Pomeranian
poodle
pug
puli
Pyrenean mountain dog
Pyrenean sheepdog
Pyrenean wolfhound
retriever

Rhodesian ridgeback
Rottweiler
St Bernard
saluki
Samoyed
schipperke
schnauzer
Scottish deerhound
Scottish terrier
Sealyham terrier
setter
Shetland sheepdog
shih-tzu
Siberian husky
Skye terrier
spaniel
spitz
springer spaniel
Staffordshire bull terrier
staghound
terrier
Tervuren
Tibetan Terrier
tosa
vizsla
Weimaraner
Welsh corgi
Welsh hound
Welsh terrier
West Highland terrier
whippet
wirehaired fox terrier
Yorkshire terrier

BREEDS OF CAT

Abyssinian
American Shorthair
American Wirehair
Balinese
Birman
Blue Burmese
blue-pointed
Bombay
British Blue
British Spotted
Burmese
Cameo
Chartreuse
Chinchilla
chocolate-pointed
Colourpoint Shorthair
Cornish Rex
Cream
Cymric
Devon Rex

domestic longhair
domestic tabby
Egyptian Mau
European Shorthair
Exotic Shorthair
Havana
Himalayan
Japanese Bobtail
Javanese
Kashmir
Korat
lilac-pointed
Maine Coon Cat
Malayan
Manx
Norwegian Forest Cat
Ocicat
Oriental Shorthair
Persian
red-pointed

Rex
Russian Blue
Scottish Fold
seal-pointed
Siamese
Singapura
Smoke
Snowshoe
Somali
Sphynx
Tabby
tabby-pointed
Tiffany
Tonkinese
Tortoiseshell
tortoiseshell-pointed
Turkish Angora
Turkish Van

THE ARTS

ARTISTIC TERMS

abstract
academy
acrylic paint
air-brush
alla prima
allegory
anamorphosis
ancients
anti-cerne
aquarelle
aquatint
archaic
architectonic
armature
arricciato
arriccio
art nouveau
ashcan
assemblage
atelier
autograph
automatism
avantgarde
bamboccanti
barbizon
baroque
bauhaus
biedermeier
biomorphic
bistre
bitumen
bodegón
body
bozzetto
brush

brushwork
burin
bust
byzantine
cabinet
camaïeu
canvas
capriccio
caricature
carolingian
cartoon
caryatid
cast
chalk
charcoal
chiaroscuro
cire-perdue
cloisonnisme
collage
colourist
conté crayon
contrapposto
cosmati
counterproof
craquelure
cubism
dada
diptych
distemper
divisionism
drawing
drôlerie
drypoint
easel
eclecticism

ecorché
emulsion
engraving
etching
expressionism
fec
fecit
fête champêtre
fixative
florentine
fresco
frottage
futurism
gesso
glaze
gothic
gouache
graffiti
grisaille
grotesque
ground
hatching
herm
illumination
illusionism
impasto
impressionism
imprimatura
inc
incidit
intaglio
intimisme
intonaco
kit-cat
kitsch

kore
kouros
landscape
limner
linocut
lithography
lost wax
maestà
mahlstick
mandorla
maquette
masterpiece
maulstick
medium
metalpoint
mezzotint
miniature
mobile
model
modello
monochrome
montage
morbidezza
mosaic
naive
naturalism
oil
op
palette
papiers collés
pastel
pastiche
patina
pencil
pentimento

ARTISTIC TERMS (cont.)

perspective
picturesque
pietà
pigment
pleurant
pochade
pointillism
polyptych
pop
portraiture
pouncing
precisionism
predella
primitive
provenance
purism
putto
quadratura
quattrocento

realism
relief
renaissance
repoussé
repoussoir
retroussage
rococo
romanesque
salon
school
sculp
sculpsit
sculpture
scumble
secco
sepia
sfumato
sinopia
size

sketch
staffage
still life
stippling
stucco
style
stylization
stylus
superrealism
suprematism
surrealism
swag
symbolism
synthetism
tachisme
tempera
tenebrism
term
tesserae

tondo
trecento
triptych
trompe l'oeil
turpentine
tuscan
vanitas
varnish
veduta
venetian
verism
vorticism
wash
watercolour
woodcut
xylography

ART SCHOOLS AND STYLES

abstract art
abstract
  expressionism
action painting
Aesthetic Movement
art brut
art deco
arte povera
art informel
art nouveau
Arts and Crafts
  Movement
avant-garde
baroque
Blaue Reiter
Byzantine art
Camden School
classicism
cloisonnism

conceptual art
concrete art
constructivism
cubism
Dada
De Stijl
divisionism
environmental art
expressionism
fauvism
figurative art
Florentine school
folk art
futurism
grand manner
High Renaissance art
impressionism
International Gothic
intimisme

Islamic art
Jugendstil
junk art
kinetic art
kitsch
land art
magic realism
mannerism
metaphysical painting
minimalism
Minoan art
Mogul art
mozarabic art
naive art
naturalism
neoclassicism
neoexpressionism
neoimpressionism
neoromanticism

ART SCHOOLS AND STYLES (cont.)

Neue Sachlichkeit
op art
orphism
Ottoman art
performance art
photorealism
plein-air painting
pointillism
pop art
postimpressionism
postmodernism
precisionism

Pre-Raphaelitism
primitive art
purism
Rayonism
realism
regionalism
Renaissance art
representational art
rococo
romanticism
Sienese school
socialist realism

social realism
suprematism
surrealism
symbolism
synchronism
synthetism
tachism
transavant-garde
Venetian school
verism
vorticism

ARCHITECTURAL TERMS

abacus
acanthus
annulet
anthemion
apophyge
architrave
Art Deco
Art Nouveau
astragal
atlas
baguette
banderole
baroque
bas-relief
Bauhaus
beaux-arts
billet
boss
brutalist
Byzantine
calotte
canephorae
capstone

Carolingian
cartouche
caryatid
cavetto
chevron
Churriguer-
  esque
cinquecento
cinquefoil
classical
colossal
composite
congé
copestone
cordon
Corinthian
cornice
corona
coving
crocket
crownpiece
cusp
Cyclopean

cyma
dancette
Deconstructioni
  sm
dentil
De Stijl
dog-tooth
Doric
Early English
Early
  Renaissance
echinus
ectype
egg and anchor
egg and dart
egg and tongue
Egyptian
Empire
epistyle
facet
fascia
Federation
festoon

fillet
finial
flamboyant
flute
foil
foliation
fret
frieze
frontispiece
functional
gadroon
gorgerin
Gothic
Gothic Revival
Graeco-Roman
Grecian
Greek Revival
guilloche
gutta
head mould
headpiece
helix
herm

ARCHITECTURAL TERMS (cont.)

hood mould
hypotrachelium
Ionic
Islamic
lierne
listel
mannerist
medallion
medieval
Mesopotamian
metope
modernist
modillion
Moorish
Moresque
moulding
Mozarabic

Mudéjar
mullion
mutule
neck-mould
neoclassical
Norman
ogee
ovolo
Palladian
pendant
Perpendicular
polychromy
postmodernist
putto
quarter-round
quatrefoil
quattrocento

quirk
quoin
reed
reglet
Renaissance
respond
rococo
Roman
Romanesque
rustication
Saracen
Saxon
scotia
scroll
splay
stria
stucco

taenia
talon
terminal
torus
tracery
transitional
transom
trefoil
triglyph
Tuscan
tympanum
vaulting
vernacular
vignette
volute
zigzag

TYPES OF BUILDING

amphitheatre
aqueduct
arena
basilica
castle
cathedral
chapel
church
convent
cottage
dagoba
dome

folly
fort
fortress
geodesic dome
house
igloo
insula
keep
mansion
mausoleum
monastery
mosque

pagoda
pavillion
Portakabin™
prison
pyramid
rath
sepulchre
skyscraper
stadium
stockade
stupa
talayot

temple
thermae
tholos
tope
tower
townhouse
triumphal arch
vault
villa
warehouse
windmill
ziggurat

FAMOUS BUILDINGS

(with location)

Acropolis	Athens
Alhambra	Granada, Spain
Blenheim Palace	Woodstock, England
British Museum	London
Blue Mosque	Istanbul
Buckingham Palace	London
Canary Wharf	London
Casa Milá	Barcelona
Chartres Cathedral	France
Chrysler Building	New York
Cologne Cathedral	Germany
Colosseum	Rome
Crystal Palace	London
Dome of the Rock	Jerusalem
Edinburgh Castle	Scotland
Eiffel Tower	Paris
Empire State Building	New York
Erechtheum *or* Erechtheion	Athens
Florence Cathedral	Italy
Forum Romanum	Rome
Galleria Vittorio Emanuele II	Milan
Golden Temple	Amritsar, India
Guggenheim Museum	New York
Hall of Supreme Harmony	Beijing
Hermitage, The	St Petersburg
Horyu-ji	Nara, Japan
Houses of Parliament	London
Jefferson Memorial	Washington, D.C.
John Hancock Center	Chicago
J. Paul Getty Museum	Malibu, California
King's College Chapel	Cambridge, England
Leaning Tower of Pisa	Italy
Louvre	Paris
Millennium Dome	Greenwich, London
Notre-Dame Cathedral	Paris
Pantheon	Rome
Parliament House	Vienna
Parthenon	Athens
Pennsylvania Station	New York
Pentagon	Arlington, Virginia
Petronas Towers	Kuala Lumpur
Pompidou Centre	Paris
President's Palace	Brasília
Pyramids	Egypt
Reichstag	Berlin
Reims Cathedral	France
Sacre Coeur	Paris
Sagrada Familia	Barcelona
St Basil's Cathedral	Moscow
Ste-Chapelle	Paris
St Mark's Cathedral	Venice
St Patrick's Cathedral	New York
St Paul's Cathedral	London
St Peter's	Rome
St Sophia	Istanbul
Sears Tower	Chicago
Sun Temple	Konarak, India
Sydney Opera House	Australia
Taj Mahal	Agra, India
Tower of London	England
Transamerica Pyramid	San Francisco
Trans World Airways Terminal	New York

FAMOUS BUILDINGS (cont.)

(with location)

US Capitol	Washington, D.C.	White House	Washington
		Windsor Castle	England
Versailles	Paris	World Trade	
Westminster Abbey	London	Center	New York

THE MUSICAL SCALE IN TONIC SOL-FA

doh
ray
mi
fah
soh
lah
te

TYPES OF SINGING VOICE

baritone
bass
castrato
contralto *or* alto
counter-tenor
falsetto
mezzo-soprano
soprano
tenor
treble

MUSICAL DIRECTIONS

(with translations)

a battuta	return to strict time	amoroso	tenderly
a cappella	unaccompanied	andante	moderately slow
accelerando	accelerating	andantino	slightly faster than andante
adagietto	fairly slowly		
adagio	slowly	animato	spirited
ad lib(itum)	at will	assai	very
affettuoso	tenderly	a tempo	in the original tempo
agitato	agitated		
al fine	to the end	attacca	continue without stopping
allargando	broadening		
allegretto	fairly lively	bis	repeat
allegro	lively	calando	becoming quieter and slower
al segno	as far as the sign		

MUSICAL DIRECTIONS (cont.)

(with translations)

cantabile	in a singing manner	non troppo	not too much
capriccioso	freely	obbligato	not to be omitted
coda	final part of a movement	ped	pedal
		pesante	heavily
col legno	with stick of the bow	pianissimo, pp	very soft
		p(iano)	soft
con amore	tenderly	più	more
con brio	with vigour	pizz(icato)	plucked
con fuoco	fiery	poco	a little
con sordino	with a mute	portamento	carrying one note into the next
cresc(endo)	becoming louder		
da capo	from the beginning	prestissimo	as fast as possible
dal segno	from the sign	presto	very fast
decrescendo	becoming quieter	rall(entando)	slowing down
dim(inuendo)	becoming quieter	ravvivando	quickening
dolente	sorrowfully	rinforzando, rfz	accentuated
doppio	double	rit(ardando)	slowing down
f(orte)	loudly	ritenuto	more slowly
fortissimo, ff	very loudly	scherzando	playfully
giocoso	playfully	segno	sign
glissando	sliding	semplice	simply
in modo di	in the manner of	sempre	always, throughout
larghetto	fairly slowly		
largo	very slowly	senza	without
legato	tied, smoothly	sf(orzando), sfz	strongly accented
leggiero	lightly	sordino	mute
lento	slowly	sostenuto	sustained
maestoso	majestically	sotto voce	in an undertone
marcato	accented	staccato	detached
marcia	march	stretto	in quicker time
meno mosso	slower pace	stringendo	intensifying
mezza voce	at half strength	subito	immediately
mezzo	half	tacet	instrument remains silent
mezzoforte, mf	fairly loudly		
moderato	moderately	tempo	speed *or* beat
molto	very	ten(uto)	held
morendo	dying away	tutti	whole orchestra
mosso	fast	vivace	lively
moto	motion	vif	lively
nobilmente	nobly	vivement	lively
		zoppa	syncopated

MUSICAL INSTRUMENTS

accordion
acoustic guitar
aeolian harp
alphorn
altohorn
angel chimes
arpeggione
atumpan
auloi
autoharp
bagpipe
balalaika
bandoura
banjo
banjolele
barrel drum
barrel organ
baryton
bassanello
bass drum
bass guitar
bass horn
bassoon
bells
bodhran
bombarde
bombardon
bongo drums
bonnang
bouzouki
bow harp
buccina
bugle
bullroarer
bumbass
bumpa
buzz disk
calliope
carillon
castanets
celeste
cello
chakay
chang
changko

chime
Chinese wood
  block
cimbalom
cipactli
cittern
clappers
clarinet
clarinet
  d'amore
clave
clavichord
clavicor
clavicytherium
claviorgan
cog rattle
componium
contrabass
contrabassoon
cor anglais
cornemuse
cornet
cornett
cornopean
cornu
courtaut
cowbell
crook horn
crotals
crumhorn
crwth
cymbals
cythara anglica
da-daiko
daibyoshi
damaru
darabukka
darbuk
dauli
Deutsche
  schalmei
dhola
didgeridoo
dilruba
diplice

diplo-kithara
djunadjan
dobro
dombak
double bass
double bassoon
doumdouba
drum
dudelsack
dugdugi
dulcimer
electric guitar
entenga
enzenze
erhu
esraj
euphonium
fandur
fiddle
fife
fipple flute
flageolet
flexatone
flugelhorn
flute
French horn
gambang kaya
gansa gambang
gansa jongkok
geigenwerk
glockenspiel
gong
grand piano
guqin
guitar
gusle
handbell
harmonica
harmonium
harp
harpsichord
hawkbell
heckelphone
heikebiwa
helicon

hi-hat cymbals
horn
hu qin
hula ipu
hummel
hurdy-gurdy
jew's harp
jing hu
jingling Johnny
kalimba
kalungu
kamanje
kantele
kanteleharpe
kayageum
kazoo
kena
kenong
kendang
kettledrum
kithara
koboro
ko-kiu
komungo
könighorn
kora
koto
lamellaphone
likembe
lira
lirica
lirone
lithophone
lontar
lute
lyre
mandobass
mandocello
mandola
mandolin
mandolinetto
mandolone
maracas
marimba
masenqo

MUSICAL INSTRUMENTS (cont.)

mayuri
mbira
melodeon
melodica
metallophone
Moog™
  synthesizer
mouth organ
mrdamga
murumbu
musette
mu yü
oboe
ocarina
octavin
o-daiko
okedo
ophicleide
organ
orpharion
orphica
o-tsuzumi
ottavino
p'ai pan
pandora
panhuéhuetl
panpipe
pianino
piano
pianoforte
pianola
piccolo
picco pipe
pien ch'ing
piffaro
pi nai
pipa
pipe
pochette
pommer
psaltery
pu-ilu
putorino
qin
ramkie

ranasringa
raspa
rattle
rauschpfeife
rebab
rebec
recorder
reshoto
rinchik
rommelpot
rote
ruan
sackbut
salpinx
sansa
santur
sanxian
sarangi
sarinda
sarod
saron
sarrusophone
saung-gauk
savernake horn
saw-thai
saxhorn
saxophone
saxotromba
saxtuba
saz
schrillpfeife
shaing
shaker
shakuhachi
shamisen
shanai
shawm
sheng
shiwaya
shô
shofar
side drum
sistrum
sitar
sleigh bells

slide trombone
sona
sonajero
sopile
sordine
sousaphone
spike fiddle
spinet
spitzharfe
sralay
sringara
stamping tube
stock-and-horn
strumento di
  porco
stylophone
surbahar
surnaj
symphonium
synthesizer
syrinx
tabla
tabor
tallharpa
tambourine
tambura
tam-tam
tanpura
teponaztli
terbang
theorbo
thumb piano
tibia
tiktiri
timbales
timpani
tin whistle
tlapanhuéhuetl
tlapiztali
tom-tom
totombito
triangle
triccaballacca
trombone
trumpet

tsuzumi
tuba
tubular bells
tudum
tumyr
tupan
turkish crescent
tympani
ukulele
valiha
vibraphone
vibra slap™
vielle
vihuela
vina
viol
viola
viola bastarda
viola da gamba
viola d'amore
violetta
violin
violoncello
violone
virginal
whistle
whistle flute
wood block
Wurlitzer™
xylophone
xylorimba
yangqin
yangum
yü
yueqin
yun lo
yun ngao
zampogna
zarb
zheng
zither
zobo
zummara
zurla
zurna

TYPES OF JAZZ

acid jazz
Afro-Cuban
avant-garde
bebop
boogie-woogie
bop
cool

Dixieland
free-form
fusion
Harlem
honky-tonk
hot jazz
jive

mainstream
modern
progressive
ragtime
razzmatazz
rooty-toot
skiffle

swing
third stream
trad jazz
west coast

DANCES AND TYPES OF DANCING

allemande
Apache
ballet
ballroom
barn dance
basse danse
beguine
belly dance
black bottom
bolero
boogie
bop
bossa nova
Boston two-step
break-dance
bunny hug
cachucha
cakewalk
cancan
carioca
cha-cha-cha
charleston
clog dance
conga

corroboree
Cossack dance
cotillion
country dance
courante
csardas
devil dance
disco
eightsome reel
fan dance
fandango
farandole
flamenco
fling
folk dance
formation dancing
foxtrot
frug
galliard
gallopade
gavotte
gigue
habanera
haka

[Helston] floral dance
[Helston] furry
Highland fling
hoedown
hokey-cokey
hootchy-kootchy
hornpipe
hula-hula
hully gully
hustle
Irish jig
Irish reel
jazz dance
jig
jitterbug
jive
juba
Lambeth Walk
lancers
limbo
Lindy Hop
Madison
mambo
mashed potato

DANCES AND TYPES OF DANCING (cont.)

maypole dance
mazurka
merengue
Mexican hat
military two-step
minuet
morris dance
old-time
one-step
palais glide
paso doble
Paul Jones
pavane
polka
polonaise
quadrille
quickstep
rain dance

reel
rigadoon
ring-shout
robotic dancing
rock and roll
ronde
round
rumba
Russian dance
samba
saraband
sequence dance
shag
shake
shimmy
shuffle
slam dance
snake

soft-shoe shuffle
square dance
stomp
strathspey
strut
sword dance
tango
tap dance
tarantella
torch
twist
twosome reel
veleta
vogueing
volta
waltz
war dance
zapateado

BALLET STEPS AND POSITIONS

arabesque
attitude
balancé
balloné
batterie
bourrée
brisé volé
cabriole
chaîné
changement
chassé
contretemps
développé

elevation
entrechat
fouetté
glissade
glissé
grands battements
jeté
pas de basque
pas de chat
pas de cheval
pas de deux
petits battements
piqué

pirouette
plié
ronds de jambes à terre
ronds de jambes en l'air
saut
sissonne
soubresaut
temps
tours en l'air

LITERATURE AND LANGUAGE

LITERARY TERMS

absurdism
acmeism
aestheticism
allegory
alliteration
alliterative verse
ambiguity
anachronism
anapaest
anthropomorphism
assonance
Augustan
ballad
bathos
beat generation
blank verse
Bloomsbury group
burlesque
caesura
caricature
catharsis
classicism
cliché
conceit
couplet
courtly love
dactyl
Dadaism
deconstruction
denouement
diction
didacticism
doppelgänger
eclogue
elegy

elision
end stopping
enjambement
epic
epic simile
epigram
episodic
epistle
epistolary novel
epitaph
epithalamium *or*
 epithalamion
euphemism
euphony
euphuism
exemplum
existentialism
expressionism
eye rhyme
fable
fabliau
feminine ending
first person narrative
foot
free indirect style
free verse
futurism
genre
Georgian poets
Gongorism
Gothicism
Gothic novel
half rhyme
Harlem Renaissance
heptameter

hermeticism
heroic couplet
hexameter
Horatian ode
hubris
hyperbole
hypotaxis
iamb
ictus
imagery
imagism
interior monologue
internal rhyme
irony
kenning
Lake poets
lament
leitmotiv *or* leitmotif
limerick
Liverpool poets
lyric
magic realism
malapropism
mannerism
masculine ending
medievalism
metaphor
metaphysical poets
metonymy
metre
Miltonic sonnet
minimalism
mock heroic
modernism
monody

LITERARY TERMS (cont.)

monometer
motif
Movement, the
myth
naturalism
negative capability
nemesis
neoclassicism
neorealism
objective correlative
objectivity
octameter
omniscient narrator
onomatopoeia
oxymoron
paradox
pararhyme
parataxis
parody
pastoralism
pathetic fallacy
pathos
pentameter
personification
Petrarchan sonnet
picaresque
Pléiade, la

postmodernism
post-structuralism
pre-Raphaelitism
pre-Romanticism
primitivism
prosody
prosopopoeia *or*
  prosopopeia
quatrain
realism
Renaissance
  humanism
reported speech
rhetoric
rhyme
Romanticism
Russian formalism
satire
scansion
sentimentality
sibilance
simile
socialist realism
social realism
sonnet
spondee
Spoonerism

stanza
stream of
  consciousness
stress
structuralism
Sturm und Drang
style
subjectivity
subplot
surrealism
syllable
symbolism
synechdoche
tetrameter
theme
third person
  narrative
tragedy
tragicomedy
transcendentalism
trimeter
trochee
ubi sunt
verismo
vorticism

METRES AND METRICAL FEET

alexandrine
amphibrach
amphimacer
anapaest
choree
choriamb
cretic
dactyl

dimeter
dipody
distich
duple metre
elegiac couplet
elegiac distich
heptameter
heroic couplet

hexameter
iamb
iambic
  pentameter
ionic
octameter
paeon
pentameter

pyrrhic
spondee
tetrameter
tribrach
trimeter
trochee

TITLES OF WELL-KNOWN NOVELS

(with authors)

A Christmas Carol (Charles Dickens)
A Clockwork Orange (Anthony Burgess)
A Connecticut Yankee in King Arthur's Court (Mark Twain)
Adam Bede (George Eliot)
A Dance to the Music of Time (Anthony Powell)
A Day in the Life of Ivan Denisovitch (Alexander Solzhenitsyn)
A Dry White Season (André Brink)
A Farewell to Arms (Ernest Hemingway)
Age of Iron (J. M. Coetzee)
Agnes Grey (Anne Brontë)
A High Wind in Jamaica (Richard Hughes)
A Kind of Loving (Stan Barstow)
Alice's Adventures in Wonderland (Lewis Carroll)
A Man of Property (John Galsworthy)
Amelia (Henry Fielding)
A Modern Comedy (John Galsworthy)
And Then There Were None (Agatha Christie)
Animal Farm (George Orwell)
Anna Karenina (Leo Tolstoy)
Anna of the Five Towns (Arnold Bennett)
A Passage to India (E. M. Forster)
A Pocket Full of Rye (Agatha Christie)
A Portrait of the Artist as a Young Man (James Joyce)
A Room with a View (E. M. Forster)
Around the World in Eighty Days (Jules Verne)
A Sentimental Journey (Laurence Sterne)
A Severed Head (Iris Murdoch)
As I Walked Out One Midsummer Morning (Laurie Lee)
A Spell in Winter (Helen Dunmore)
A Suitable Boy (Vikram Seth)
A Tale of Two Cities (Charles Dickens)
A Town like Alice (Nevil Shute)
At Swim-Two-Birds (Flann O'Brien)

Barchester Towers (Anthony Trollope)
Barnaby Rudge (Charles Dickens)
Beau Geste (P. C. Wren)
Behind the Scenes at the Museum (Kate Atkinson)
Ben Hur (Lew Wallace)
Between the Acts (Virginia Woolf)
Billy Liar (Keith Waterhouse)
Black Beauty (Anna Sewell)
Bleak House (Charles Dickens)
Brave New World (Aldous Huxley)
Brideshead Revisited (Evelyn Waugh)
Brighton Rock (Graham Greene)
Burmese Days (George Orwell)
Cakes and Ale (W. Somerset Maugham)
Cal (Bernard MacLaverty)
Camilla (Fanny Burney)
Cancer Ward (Alexander Solzhenitsyn)
Candide (Voltaire)
Cannery Row (John Steinbeck)
Casino Royale (Ian Fleming)
Castle Rackrent (Maria Edgeworth)
Catch-22 (Joseph Heller)
Cat's Eye (Margaret Atwood)
Cecilia (Fanny Burney)
Changing Places (David Lodge)
Chéri (Colette)
Children of the New Forest (Captain Marryat)
Chocky (John Wyndham)
Cider with Rosie (Laurie Lee)
Clarissa (Samuel Richardson)
Clayhanger (Arnold Bennett)
Cold Comfort Farm (Stella Gibbons)
Coningsby (Benjamin Disraeli)
Coral Island (R. M. Ballantyne)
Cousin Bette (Honoré de Balzac)
Cranford (Mrs Gaskell)
Crime and Punishment (Fyodor Dostoevsky)
Crotchet Castle (Thomas Love Peacock)
Cry, the Beloved Country (Alan Paton)
Daisy Miller (Henry James)
Daniel Deronda (George Eliot)

TITLES OF WELL-KNOWN NOVELS (cont.)
(with authors)

David Copperfield (Charles Dickens)
Death on the Nile (Agatha Christie)
Decline and Fall (Evelyn Waugh)
Doctor Zhivago (Boris Pasternak)
Dombey and Son (Charles Dickens)
Don Quixote (Miguel de Cervantes)
Dracula (Bram Stoker)
Dr Jekyll and Mr Hyde (Robert Louis
   Stevenson)
Dr No (Ian Fleming)
Emma (Jane Austen)
Erewhon (Samuel Butler)
Eustace and Hilda (L. P. Hartley)
Evelina (Fanny Burney)
Far from the Madding Crowd
   (Thomas Hardy)
Felicia's Journey (William Trevor)
Finnegans Wake (James Joyce)
For Whom the Bell Tolls (Ernest
   Hemingway)
Frankenstein (Mary Shelley)
Franny and Zooey (J. D. Salinger)
G (John Berger)
Gigi (Colette)
Glenarvon (Lady Caroline Lamb)
Goldfinger (Ian Fleming)
Gone with the Wind (Margaret
   Mitchell)
Goodbye, Mr Chips (James Hilton)
Goodbye to Berlin (Christopher
   Isherwood)
Gormenghast (Mervyn Peake)
Great Expectations (Charles
   Dickens)
Gulliver's Travels (Jonathan Swift)
Guy Mannering (Walter Scott)
Hapworth 16, 1924 (J. D. Salinger)
Hard Times (Charles Dickens)
Headlong Hall (Thomas Love
   Peacock)
Heat and Dust (Ruth Prawer
   Jhabvala)
Holiday (Stanley Middleton)
Hotel du Lac (Anita Brookner)
How Green was My Valley (Richard
   Llewellyn)
How Late It Was, How Late (James
   Kelman)
How Many Miles to Babylon?
   (Jennifer Johnston)

I Claudius (Robert Graves)
In a Free State (V. S. Naipaul)
In Chancery (John Galsworthy)
Ivanhoe (Walter Scott)
Jacob Faithful (Captain Marryat)
Jacob's Room (Virginia Woolf)
Jane Eyre (Charlotte Brontë)
John Halifax, Gentleman (Mrs Craik)
Joseph Andrews (Henry Fielding)
Jude the Obscure (Thomas
   Hardy)
Just-So Stories (Rudyard Kipling)
Keep the Aspidistra Flying (George
   Orwell)
Kenilworth (Walter Scott)
Kidnapped (Robert Louis
   Stevenson)
King Solomon's Mines (Henry Rider
   Haggard)
Kipps (H. G. Wells)
Lady Chatterley's Lover (D. H.
   Lawrence)
Lark Rise to Candleford (Flora
   Thompson)
Last Orders (Graham Swift)
Les Misérables (Victor Hugo)
Life and Times of Michael K (J. M.
   Coetzee)
Little Dorrit (Charles Dickens)
Little Lord Fauntleroy (Frances
   Hodgson Burnett)
Little Women (Louisa M. Alcott)
Live and Let Die (Ian Fleming)
Liza of Lambeth (W. Somerset
   Maugham)
Lolita (Vladimir Nabokov)
Lord of the Flies (William Golding)
Lorna Doone (R. D. Blackmore)
Lost Horizon (James Hilton)
Love, Again (Doris Lessing)
Love in a Time of Cholera (Gabriel
   García Márquez)
Love Story (Erich Segal)
Lucky Jim (Kingsley Amis)
Madame Bovary (Gustave Flaubert)
Mansfield Park (Jane Austen)
Martin Chuzzlewit (Charles Dickens)
Middlemarch (george Eliot)
Midnight's Children (Salman
   Rushdie)

TITLES OF WELL-KNOWN NOVELS (cont.)

(with authors)

Moby Dick (Herman Melville)
Moll Flanders (Daniel Defoe)
Monsieur Beaucaire (Booth Tarkington)
Moon Tiger (Penelope Lively)
Mr Midshipman Easy (Captain Marryat)
Mrs Dalloway (Virginia Woolf)
Murder on the Orient Express (Agatha Christie)
My Brother Jonathan (Francis Brett Young)
Nana (Émile Zola)
Nicholas Nickleby (Charles Dickens)
Nice Work (David Lodge)
Nightmare Abbey (Thomas Love Peacock)
Nineteen Eighty-Four (George Orwell)
North and South (Mrs Gaskell)
Northanger Abbey (Jane Austen)
Offshore (Penelope Fitzgerald)
Of Mice and Men (John Steinbeck)
Oliver Twist (Charles Dickens)
One Hundred Years of Solitude (Gabriel García Márquez)
On the Road (Jack Kerouac)
Oranges Are Not the Only Fruit (Jeanette Winterson)
Orlando (Virginia Woolf)
Oscar and Lucinda (Peter Carey)
Our Man in Havana (Graham Greene)
Our Mutual Friend (Charles Dickens)
Out of the Silent Planet (C. S. Lewis)
Paddy Clarke Ha Ha Ha (Roddy Doyle)
Pamela (Samuel Richardson)
Paradise (Toni Morrison)
Paradise News (David Lodge)
Peregrine Pickle (Tobias Smollett)
Persuasion (Jane Austen)
Phineas Finn (Anthony Trollope)
Pincher Martin (William Golding)
Plague (Albert Camus)
Point Counter Point (Aldous Huxley)
Porgy (Du Bose Heyward)
Portrait of Clare (Francis Brett Young)

Possession (A. S. Byatt)
Prester John (John Buchan)
Pride and Prejudice (Jane Austen)
Rabbit at Rest (John Updike)
Rabbit is Rich (John Updike)
Rabbit Redux (John Updike)
Rabbit, Run (John Updike)
Raffles (E. W. Hornung)
Rasselas (Samuel Johnson)
Reading in the Dark (Seamus Deane)
Rebecca (Daphne Du Maurier)
Rebel (Albert Camus)
Rites of Passage (William Golding)
Robinson Crusoe (Daniel Defoe)
Rob Roy (Walter Scott)
Rogue Justice (Geoffrey Household)
Rogue Male (Geoffrey Household)
Room at the Top (John Braine)
Roxana (Daniel Defoe)
Sacred Hunger (Barry Unsworth)
Saville (David Storey)
Schindler's Ark (Thomas Keneally)
Scoop (Evelyn Waugh)
Sense and Sensibility (Jane Austen)
She (H. Rider Haggard)
Shirley (Charlotte Brontë)
Silas Marner (George Eliot)
Sketches by Boz (Charles Dickens)
Smiley's People (John Le Carré)
Something to Answer For (P. H. Newby)
Sons and Lovers (D. H. Lawrence)
Sorrell and Son (Warwick Deeping)
Staying On (Paul Scott)
Stephen Hero (James Joyce)
Strait is the Gate (André Gide)
Swallows and Amazons (Arthur Ransome)
Swan Song (John Galsworthy)
Sybil (Benjamin Disraeli)
Tarka the Otter (Henry Williamson)
Tender is the Night (F. Scott Fitzgerald)
Tess of the D'Urbervilles (Thomas Hardy)
The Adventures of Huckleberry Finn (Mark Twain)
The Adventures of Sherlock Holmes (Arthur Conan Doyle)

TITLES OF WELL-KNOWN NOVELS (cont.)
(with authors)

The Adventures of Tom Sawyer (Mark Twain)
The Ambassadors (Henry James)
The Beautiful and Damned (F. Scott Fitzgerald)
The Big Sleep (Raymond Chandler)
The Blue Lagoon (H. de Vere Stacpoole)
The Bone People (Keri Hulme)
The Bride of Lammermoor (Walter Scott)
The Brothers Karamazov (Fyodor Dostoevsky)
The Castle of Otranto (Horace Walpole)
The Catcher in the Rye (J. D. Salinger)
The Chimes (Charles Dickens)
The Chrysalids (John Wyndham)
The Conservationist (Nadine Gordimer)
The Country Girls (Edna O'Brien)
The Cricket on the Hearth (Charles Dickens)
The Day of the Triffids (John Wyndham)
The Devils (Fyodor Dostoevsky)
The Devils of Loudun (Aldous Huxley)
The Diary of a Nobody (G. and W. Grossmith)
The Elected Member (Bernice Rubens)
The Emperor of Ice Cream (Brian Moore)
The English Patient (Michael Ondaatje)
The Fall (Albert Camus)
The Famished Road (Ben Okri)
The First Circle (Alexander Solzhenitsyn)
The Forsyte Saga (John Galsworthy)
The French Lieutenant's Woman (John Fowles)
The Ghost Road (Pat Barker)
The Go-Between (L. P. Hartley)
The God of Small Things (Arundhati Roy)
The Golden Bowl (Henry James)

The Grapes of Wrath (John Steinbeck)
The Great Gatsby (F. Scott Fitzgerald)
The Gulag Archipelago (Alexander Solzhenitsyn)
The Heart of Midlothian (Walter Scott)
The Heroes (Charles Kingsley)
The History Man (Malcolm Bradbury)
The History of Henry Esmond (William Makepeace Thackeray)
The History of Mr Polly (H. G. Wells)
The History of Pendennis (William Makepeace Thackeray)
The Hobbit (J. R. R. Tolkien)
The Honourable Schoolboy (John Le Carré)
The Hound of the Baskervilles (Arthur Conan Doyle)
The Idiot (Fyodor Dostoevsky)
The Innocence of Father Brown (G. K. Chesterton)
The Invisible Man (H. G. Wells)
The Island of Doctor Moreau (H. G. Wells)
The Jungle Book (Rudyard Kipling)
The Kraken Wakes (John Wyndham)
The Last of the Mohicans (James Fenimore Cooper)
The Last Tycoon (F. Scott Fitzgerald)
The Lion, The Witch, and The Wardrobe (C. S. Lewis)
The Lonely Passion of Judith Hearne (Brian Moore)
The Long Goodbye (Raymond Chandler)
The Lord of the Rings (J. R. R. Tolkien)
The Lost World (Arthur Conan Doyle)
The Magus (John Fowles)
The Man in the Iron Mask (Alexandre Dumas)
The Memoirs of Sherlock Holmes (Arthur Conan Doyle)
The Midwich Cuckoos (John Wyndham)

TITLES OF WELL-KNOWN NOVELS (cont.)

(with authors)

The Mill on the Floss (George Eliot)
The Moon and Sixpence (W. Somerset Maugham)
The Moonstone (Wilkie Collins)
The Mysteries of Udolpho (Mrs Radcliffe)
The Mysterious Affair at Styles (Agatha Christie)
The Mystery of Edwin Drood (Charles Dickens)
The Name of the Rose (Umberto Eco)
The Old Curiosity Shop (Charles Dickens)
The Old Devils (Kingsley Amis)
The Old Man and the Sea (Ernest Hemingway)
The Outsider (Albert Camus)
The Picture of Dorian Gray (Oscar Wilde)
The Pickwick Papers (Charles Dickens)
The Pilgrim's Progress (John Bunyan)
The Plumed Serpent (D. H. Lawrence)
The Portrait of a Lady (Henry James)
The Prime of Miss Jean Brodie (Muriel Spark)
The Prisoner of Zenda (Anthony Hope)
The Private Memoirs and Confessions of a Justified Sinner (James Hogg)
The Professor (Charlotte Brontë)
The Rainbow (D. H. Lawrence)
The Red Badge of Courage (Stephen Crane)
The Remains of the Day (Kazuo Ishiguro)
Thérèse Raquin (Émile Zola)
The Return of the Native (Thomas Hardy)
The Riddle of the Sands (Erskine Childers)
The Rose and the Ring (William Makepeace Thackeray)
The Satanic Verses (Salman Rushdie)

The Scarlet Letter (Nathaniel Hawthorne)
The Scarlet Pimpernel (Baroness Orczy)
The Screwtape Letters (C. S. Lewis)
The Sea, The Sea (Iris Murdoch)
The Secret Agent (Joseph Conrad)
The Secret Garden (Frances Hodgson Burnett)
The Siege of Krishnapur (J. G. Farrell)
The Silmarillion (J. R. R. Tolkien)
The Silver Spoon (John Galsworthy)
The Tenant of Wildfell Hall (Anne Brontë)
The Thirty-Nine Steps (John Buchan)
The Three Musketeers (Alexandre Dumas)
The Time Machine (H. G. Wells)
The Trumpet Major (Thomas Hardy)
The Unbearable Lightness of Being (Milan Kundera)
The Vicar of Wakefield (Oliver Goldsmith)
The Warden (Anthony Trollope)
The War of the Worlds (H. G. Wells)
The Water-Babies (Charles Kingsley)
The Waves (Virginia Woolf)
The White Company (Arthur Conan Doyle)
The White Monkey (John Galsworthy)
The Wind in the Willows (Kenneth Grahame)
The Wings of the Dove (Henry James)
The Woman in White (Wilkie Collins)
The Woodlanders (Thomas Hardy)
Things Fall Apart (Chinua Achebe)
Three Men in a Boat (Jerome K. Jerome)
Through the Looking-Glass (Lewis Carroll)
Tinker, Tailor, Soldier, Spy (John Le Carré)
Titus Alone (Mervyn Peake)
Titus Groan (Mervyn Peake)

TITLES OF WELL-KNOWN NOVELS (cont.)

(with authors)

Tom Brown's Schooldays (Thomas Hughes)
Tom Jones (Henry Fielding)
To the Lighthouse (Virginia Woolf)
Treasure Island (Robert Louis Stevenson)
Trilby (George du Maurier)
Tristram Shandy (Laurence Sterne)
Twenty Thousand Leagues Under The Sea (Jules Verne)
Two Years Before the Mast (Richard Henry Dana)
Ulysses (James Joyce)
Uncle Tom's Cabin (Harriet Beecher Stowe)
Under the Greenwood Tree (Thomas Hardy)
Vanity Fair (William Makepeace Thackeray)
Vice Versa (F. Anstey)
Villette (Charlotte Brontë)
War and Peace (Leo Tolstoy)
Waverley (Walter Scott)
Westward Ho! (Charles Kingsley)
What Maisie Knew (Henry James)
Wives and Daughters (Mrs Gaskell)
Women in Love (D. H. Lawrence)
Wuthering Heights (Emily Brontë)
Zadig (Voltaire)
Zuleika Dobson (Max Beerbohm)

CHARACTERS FROM WELL-KNOWN WORKS OF FICTION

(with titles and authors)

Abbeville, Horace (*Cannery Row*, John Steinbeck)
Abel (*Middlemarch*, George Eliot)
Ablewhite, Godfrey (*The Moonstone*, Wilkie Collins)
Addenbrooke, Bennett (*Raffles*, E. W. Hornung)
Adler, Irene (*The Adventures of Sherlock Holmes*, Arthur Conan Doyle)
Aisgill, Alice (*Room at the Top*, John Braine)
Aitken (*Prester John*, John Buchan)
Akela (*The Jungle Book*, Rudyard Kipling)
Alibi, Tom (*Waverley*, Walter Scott)
Allan-a-Dale (*Ivanhoe*, Walter Scott)
Allworthy, Squire (*Tom Jones*, Henry Fielding)
Andrews, Joseph (*Joseph Andrews*, Henry Fielding)
Angelica (*The Rose and the Ring*, William Makepeace Thackeray)
Angstrom, Harry (*Rabbit, Run*, John Updike)
Apollyon (*The Pilgrim's Progress*, John Bunyan)
Aramis (*The Three Musketeers*, Alexandre Dumas)
Armitage, Jacob (*The Children of the New Forest*, Captain Marryat)
Arrowpoint (*Daniel Deronda*, George Eliot)
Aslan (*The Lion, the Witch, and the Wardrobe*, C. S. Lewis)
Athos (*The Three Musketeers*, Alexandre Dumas)
Ayesha (*She*, Henry Rider Haggard)
Bagheera (*The Jungle Book*, Rudyard Kipling)
Bagster (*Middlemarch*, George Eliot)
Baloo (*The Jungle Book*, Rudyard Kipling)
Barrymore (*The Hound of the Baskervilles*, Arthur Conan Doyle)
Bede, Adam (*Adam Bede*, George Eliot)
Beesley (*Lucky Jim*, Kingsley Amis)

CHARACTERS FROM WELL-KNOWN WORKS OF FICTION (cont.)

(with titles and authors)

Belladonna (*Vanity Fair*, William Makepeace Thackeray)
Bennet, Catherine (*Pride and Prejudice*, Jane Austen)
Bennet, Elizabeth (*Pride and Prejudice*, Jane Austen)
Bennet, Jane (*Pride and Prejudice*, Jane Austen)
Bennet, Lydia (*Pride and Prejudice*, Jane Austen)
Bennet, Mary (*Pride and Prejudice*, Jane Austen)
Bessie (*Jane Eyre*, Charlotte Brontë)
Bingley, Charles (*Pride and Prejudice*, Jane Austen)
Binkie, Lady Grizzel (*Vanity Fair*, William Makepeace Thackeray)
Black Dog (*Treasure Island*, R. L. Stevenson)
Blake, Franklin (*The Moonstone*, Wilkie Collins)
Bloom, Leopold (*Ulysses*, James Joyce)
Bloom, Molly (*Ulysses*, James Joyce)
Bones, Captain Billy (*Treasure Island*, Robert Louis Stevenson)
Booby, Sir Thomas (*Joseph Andrews*, Henry Fielding)
Bovary, Emma (*Madame Bovary*, Gustave Flaubert)
Brandon, Colonel (*Sense and Sensibility*, Jane Austen)
Brangwen, Gudrun (*The Rainbow, Women in Love*, D. H. Lawrence)
Brangwen, Ursula (*The Rainbow, Women in Love*, D. H. Lawrence)
Brocklehurst (*Jane Eyre*, Charlotte Brontë)
Brooke, Dorothea (*Middlemarch*, George Eliot)
Bruff (*The Moonstone*, Wilkie Collins)
Bulbo, Prince (*The Rose and the Ring*, William Makepeace Thackeray)
Bulstrode, Nicholas (*Middlemarch*, George Eliot)
Butler, Rhett (*Gone with the Wind*, Margaret Mitchell)

Cackle (*Vanity Fair*, William Makepeace Thackeray)
Captain Flint (*Swallows and Amazons*, Arthur Ransome)
Carraway, Nick (*The Great Gatsby*, F. Scott Fitzgerald)
Casaubon, Rev. Edward (*Middlemarch*, George Eliot)
Cass, Eppie (*Silas Marner*, George Eliot)
Casy, Rev. Jim (*The Grapes of Wrath*, John Steinbeck)
Caulfield, Holden (*The Catcher in the Rye*, J. D. Salinger)
Chainmail (*Crotchet Castle*, Thomas Love Peacock)
Challenger, Professor (*The Lost World*, Arthur Conan Doyle)
Chant, Mercy (*Tess of the D'Urbervilles*, Thomas Hardy)
Christian (*The Pilgrim's Progress*, John Bunyan)
Churchill, Frank (*Emma*, Jane Austen)
Clack, Drusilla (*The Moonstone*, Wilkie Collins)
Clare, Angel (*Tess of the D'Urbervilles*, Thomas Hardy)
Collins, Rev. William (*Pride and Prejudice*, Jane Austen)
Conroy, Gabriel ('The Dead', *Dubliners*, James Joyce)
Crawfurd, David (*Prester John*, John Buchan)
Crimsworth, William (*The Professor*, Charlotte Brontë)
Crusoe, Robinson (*Robinson Crusoe*, Daniel Defoe)
Cuff, Sergeant (*The Moonstone*, Wilkie Collins)
Cypress, Mr (*Nightmare Abbey*, Thomas Love Peacock)
Dalloway, Clarissa (*Mrs Dalloway*, Virginia Woolf)
Danvers, Mrs (*Rebecca*, Daphne du Maurier)
Darcy, Fitzwilliam (*Pride and Prejudice*, Jane Austen)
D'Artagnan (*The Three Musketeers*, Alexandre Dumas)

CHARACTERS FROM WELL-KNOWN WORKS OF FICTION
(cont.)
(with titles and authors)

Dashwood, Henry (*Sense and Sensibility*, Jane Austen)

Dean, Ellen (*Wuthering Heights*, Emily Brontë)

Deans, Effie (*The Heart of Midlothian*, Walter Scott)

Deans, Jeanie (*The Heart of Midlothian*, Walter Scott)

De Bourgh, Lady Catherine (*Pride and Prejudice*, Jane Austen)

Dedalus, Simon (*A Portrait of the Artist as a Young Man, Ulysses*, James Joyce)

Dedalus, Stephen (*A Portrait of the Artist as a Young Man, Ulysses*, James Joyce)

Despair, Giant (*The Pilgrim's Progress*, John Bunyan)

De Winter, Maximilian (*Rebecca*, Daphne du Maurier)

Dixon, James (*Lucky Jim*, Kingsley Amis)

Doone, Lorna (*Lorna Doone*, R. D. Blackmore)

Dracula, Count (*Dracula*, Bram Stoker)

Durbeyfield, Tess (*Tess of the D'Urbervilles*, Thomas Hardy)

Eager, Rev. Cuthbert (*A Room with a View*, E. M. Forster)

Earnshaw, Catherine (*Wuthering Heights*, Emily Brontë)

East (*Tom Brown's Schooldays*, Thomas Hughes)

Easy, John (*Mr Midshipman Easy*, Captain Marryat)

Eeyore (*Winnie the Pooh*, A. A. Milne)

Everdene, Bathsheba (*Far from the Madding Crowd*, Thomas Hardy)

Eyre, Jane (*Jane Eyre*, Charlotte Brontë)

Fairfax, Jane (*Emma*, Jane Austen)

Fairfax, Mrs (*Jane Eyre*, Charlotte Brontë)

Fairlie, Frederick (*The Woman in White*, Wilkie Collins)

Fauntleroy, Lord Cedric Errol (*Little Lord Fauntleroy*, Frances Hodgson Burnett)

Fawn, Lord Frederic (*Phineas Finn*, Anthony Trollope)

Ffoulkes, Sir Andrew (*The Scarlet Pimpernel*, Baroness Orczy)

Finn, Huckleberry (*The Adventures of Huckleberry Finn, The Adventures of Tom Sawyer*, Mark Twain)

Finn, Phineas (*Phineas Finn*, Anthony Trollope)

Flanders, Moll (*Moll Flanders*, Daniel Defoe)

Flashman (*Tom Brown's Schooldays*, Thomas Hughes)

Forsyte, Fleur (*The Forsyte Saga*, John Galsworthy)

Forsyte, Irene (*The Forsyte Saga*, John Galsworthy)

Forsyte, Jolyon (*The Forsyte Saga*, John Galsworthy)

Forsyte, Jon (*The Forsyte Saga*, John Galsworthy)

Forsyte, Soames (*The Forsyte Saga*, John Galsworthy)

Fox, Brer (*Uncle Remus*, Joel Chandler Harris)

Frankenstein, Victor (*Frankenstein*, Mary Wollstonecraft Shelley)

Friday (*Robinson Crusoe*, Daniel Defoe)

Gatsby, Major Jay (*The Great Gatsby*, F. Scott Fitzgerald)

George (*Three Men in a Boat*, Jerome K. Jerome)

Geste, Beau (*Beau Geste*, P. C. Wren)

Glover, Catherine (*The Fair Maid of Perth*, Walter Scott)

Goodfellow, Robin (*St Ronan's Well*, Walter Scott)

Gordon, Squire (*Black Beauty*, Anna Sewell)

Grantly, Bishop of Barchester (*The Warden, Barchester Towers*, Anthony Trollope)

Gray, Dorian (*The Picture of Dorian Gray*, Oscar Wilde)

Grimes (*The Water-Babies*, Charles Kingsley)

CHARACTERS FROM WELL-KNOWN WORKS OF FICTION
(cont.)

(with titles and authors)

Gulliver, Lemuel (*Gulliver's Travels*, Jonathan Swift)

Gunn, Ben (*Treasure Island*, Robert Louis Stevenson)

Hands, Israel (*Treasure Island*, Robert Louis Stevenson)

Hannay, Richard (*The Thirty-Nine Steps*, John Buchan)

Harker, Jonathan (*Dracula*, Bram Stoker)

Harker, Minna (*Dracula*, Bram Stoker)

Harman, Joe (*A Town like Alice*, Nevil Shute)

Hatch, Bennet (*The Black Arrow*, Robert Louis Stevenson)

Hawkins, Jim (*Treasure Island*, Robert Louis Stevenson)

HCE (Humphrey Chimpden Earwicker) (*Finnegans Wake*, James Joyce)

Hearne, Judith (*The Lonely Passion of Judith Hearne*, Brian Moore)

Heathcliff (*Wuthering Heights*, Emily Brontë)

Hentzau, Rupert of (*The Prisoner of Zenda*, Anthony Hope)

Holmes, Mycroft (*The Return of Sherlock Holmes*, Arthur Conan Doyle)

Holmes, Sherlock (*The Adventures of Sherlock Holmes, The Hound of the Baskervilles*, etc., Arthur Conan Doyle)

Hornblower, Horatio (The *Hornblower* series, C. S. Forester)

Humpty-Dumpty (*Through the Looking-Glass*, Lewis Carroll)

Hunca Munca (*The Tale of Two Bad Mice*, Beatrix Potter)

Hur, Judah (*Ben Hur*, Lew Wallace)

Hyde, Edward (*Dr Jekyll and Mr Hyde*, Robert Louis Stevenson)

Indian Joe (*The Adventures of Tom Sawyer*, Mark Twain)

Ivanhoe, Wilfred, Knight of (*Ivanhoe*, Walter Scott)

Jabberwocky (*Alice Through the Looking-Glass*, Lewis Carroll)

Jackanapes (*Jackanapes*, Juliana H. Ewing)

Jeeves (*Thank you, Jeeves*, P. G. Wodehouse)

Jekyll, Henry (*Dr Jekyll and Mr Hyde*, Robert Louis Stevenson)

Jim, Lord (*Lord Jim*, Joseph Conrad)

Jones, Tom (*Tom Jones*, Henry Fielding)

Judy (*Wee Willie Winkie*, Rudyard Kipling)

K, Michael (*Life and Times of Michael K*, J. M. Coetzee)

Kanga (*Winnie the Pooh*, A. A. Milne)

Keeldar, Shirley (*Shirley*, Charlotte Brontë)

Kim (*Kim*, Rudyard Kipling)

Kipps, Arthur (*Kipps*, H. G. Wells)

Knightly, George (*Emma*, Jane Austen)

Ladislaw, Will (*Middlemarch*. George Eliot)

Lamb, Leonard (*Middlemarch*, George Eliot)

Lampton, Joe (*Room at the Top*, John Braine)

Latimer, Darsie (*Redgauntlet*, Walter Scott)

Laurence, Theodore (*Little Women*, Louisa M. Alcott)

Laurie (*Little Women*, Louisa M. Alcott)

Lawless (*The Black Arrow*, Robert Louis Stevenson)

Lee, Lorelei (*Gentlemen Prefer Blondes*, Anita Loos)

Legree, Simon (*Uncle Tom's Cabin*, Harriet B. Stowe)

Leicester, Earl of (*Kenilworth*, Walter Scott)

Leigh, Captain Sir Amyas (*Westward Ho!*, Charles Kingsley)

Lessways, Hilda (*The Clayhanger Trilogy*, Arnold Bennett)

Lestrade of Scotland Yard (*A Study in Scarlet*, Arthur Conan Doyle)

Linton, Edgar (*Wuthering Heights*, Emily Brontë)

CHARACTERS FROM WELL-KNOWN WORKS OF FICTION (cont.)

(with titles and authors)

Lockwood (*Wuthering Heights*, Emily Brontë)

Lydgate, Tertius (*Middlemarch*, George Eliot)

Maccrotchet (*Crotchet Castle*, Thomas Love Peacock)

Macgregor, Robin (*Rob Roy*, Walter Scott)

Major, Major (*Catch-22*, Joseph Heller)

Manson, Dr Andrew (*The Citadel*, A. J. Cronin)

March, Amy (*Little Women*, etc., Louisa M. Alcott)

March, Beth (*Little Women*, etc., Louisa M. Alcott)

March, Jo (*Little Women*, etc., Louisa M. Alcott)

March, Meg (*Little Women*, etc., Louisa M. Alcott)

March Hare, The (*Alice in Wonderland*, Lewis Carroll)

Marchmain, Teresa (*Brideshead Revisited*, Evelyn Waugh)

Marchmain, Earl of Brideshead (*Brideshead Revisited*, Evelyn Waugh)

Marchmain, Lady Cordelia (*Brideshead Revisited*, Evelyn Waugh)

Marchmain, Lady Julia (*Brideshead Revisited*, Evelyn Waugh)

Marchmain, Lord Sebastian (*Brideshead Revisited*, Evelyn Waugh)

Markham, Gilbert (*The Tenant of Wildfell Hall*, Anne Brontë)

Marner, Silas (*Silas Marner*, George Eliot)

Marple, Jane (*A Pocket Full of Rye*, Agatha Christie)

Mauleverer, Lord (*Cranford*, Mrs Gaskell)

Mercy (*The Pilgrim's Progress*, John Bunyan)

Merrilies, Meg (*Guy Mannering*, Walter Scott)

Messala (*Ben Hur*, Lew Wallace)

Michael, Duke of Strelsau (*The Prisoner of Zenda*, Anthony Hope)

Mitty, Walter (*The Secret Life of Walter Mitty*, James Thurber)

Mock Turtle, The (*Alice's Adventures in Wonderland*, Lewis Carroll)

Mole, Mr (*The Wind in the Willows*, Kenneth Grahame)

Montmorency, the dog (*Three Men in a Boat*, Jerome K. Jerome)

Moore, Mrs (*A Passage to India*, E. M. Forster)

Moreau, Dr (*The Island of Dr Moreau*, H. G. Wells)

Morel, Paul (*Sons and Lovers*, D. H. Lawrence)

Morgan, Angharad (*How Green Was My Valley*, Richard Llewellyn)

Morgan, Huw (*How Green Was My Valley*, Richard Llewellyn)

Moriarty, Dean (*On the Road*, Jack Kerouac)

Moriarty, Professor James (*Memoirs of Sherlock Holmes*, Arthur Conan Doyle)

Morland, Catherine (*Northanger Abbey*, Jane Austen)

Mowgli (*The Jungle Book*, Rudyard Kipling)

Napoleon (*Animal Farm*, George Orwell)

Nash, Richard (Beau) (*Monsieur Beaucaire*, Booth Tarkington)

Nutkin, Squirrel (*The Tale of Squirrel Nutkin*, Beatrix Potter)

O'Ferrall, Trilby (*Trilby*, George du Maurier)

O'Hara, Kimball (*Kim*, Rudyard Kipling)

O'Hara, Scarlett (*Gone with the Wind*, Margaret Mitchell)

Olifaunt, Nigel (*The Fortunes of Nigel*, Walter Scott)

Omnium, Duke of (Family name Palliser) (The 'Palliser' series, Anthony Trollope, the 'Barsetshire' series Angela Thirkell)

Otter, Mr (*The Wind in the Willows*, Kenneth Grahame)

Owl (*Winnie the Pooh*, A. A. Milne)

CHARACTERS FROM WELL-KNOWN WORKS OF FICTION (cont.)

(with titles and authors)

Palliser, Lady Glencora (*Phineas Finn*, Anthony Trollope)

Palliser, Plantagenet (*Phineas Finn*, Anthony Trollope)

Paradise, Sal (*On the Road*, Jack Kerouac)

Pendennis, Arthur (Pen) (*Pendennis*, William Makepeace Thackeray)

Pennyfeather, Paul (*Decline and Fall*, Evelyn Waugh)

Pickle, Peregrine (*Peregrine Pickle*, Tobias Smollett)

Piggy (*Lord of the Flies*, William Golding)

Piglet, Henry Pootel (*Winnie the Pooh*, A. A. Milne)

Pinkie (*Brighton Rock*, Graham Greene)

Poirot, Hercule (*The Mysterious Affair at Styles*, etc., Agatha Christie)

Polly, Alfred (*The History of Mr Polly*, H. G. Wells)

Poole, Grace (*Jane Eyre*, Charlotte Brontë)

Porgy (*Porgy*, Du Bose Heywood)

Porthos (*The Three Musketeers*, Alexandre Dumas)

Proudie, Dr (*Framley Parsonage* and other 'Barsetshire' novels, Anthony Trollope)

Proudie, Mrs (*Framley Parsonage* and other 'Barsetshire' novels, Anthony Trollope)

Puck (Robin Goodfellow) (*Puck of Pook's Hill*, Rudyard Kipling)

Punch (*Wee Willie Winkie*, Rudyard Kipling)

Quantock, Mrs Daisy (*Queen Lucia*, E. F. Benson)

Quatermain, Allan (*King Solomon's Mines*, Henry Rider Haggard)

Quirk, Thady (*Castle Rackrent*, Maria Edgeworth)

Rabbit (*Winnie the Pooh*, A. A. Milne)

Rabbit, 'Brer' (*Uncle Remus*, Joel Chandler Harris)

Rabbit, The White (*Alice's Adventures in Wonderland*, Lewis Carroll)

Raffles, A. J. (*Raffles* series, E. W. Hornung)

Ralph (*Lord of the Flies*, William Golding)

Rama (Tiger Tiger) (*The Jungle Book*, Rudyard Kipling)

Ramsay, Mr (*To the Lighthouse*, Virginia Woolf)

Ramsay, Mrs (*To the Lighthouse*, Virginia Woolf)

Randall, Rebecca (*Rebecca of Sunnybrook Farm*, Kate D. Wiggin)

Rassendyll, Rudolf (*The Prisoner of Zenda*, Anthony Hope)

Rattler, Martin (*Martin Rattler*, R. M. Ballantyne)

Ready, Masterman (*Masterman Ready*, Captain Marryat)

Rebecca (*Rebecca*, Daphne du Maurier)

Rebecca (*Rebecca of Sunnybrook Farm*, Kate D. Wiggin)

Redgauntlet, Sir Arthur Darsie (*Redgauntlet*, Walter Scott)

Red King (*Through the Looking-Glass*, Lewis Carroll)

Red Knight (*Through the Looking-Glass*, Lewis Carroll)

Red Queen (*Through the Looking-Glass*, Lewis Carroll)

Reed, Mrs (*Jane Eyre*, Charlotte Brontë)

Remus, Uncle (*Uncle Remus* series, Joel Chandler Harris)

Ridd, John (*Lorna Doone*, R. D. Blackmore)

Rikki-Tikki-Tavi (*The Jungle Book*, Rudyard Kipling)

Rivers, St John (*Jane Eyre*, Charlotte Brontë)

Robsart, Amy (*Kenilworth*, Walter Scott)

Rochester, Bertha (*Jane Eyre*, Charlotte Brontë)

Rochester, Edward Fairfax (*Jane Eyre*, Charlotte Brontë)

Roo (*Winnie the Pooh*, A. A. Milne)

Roxana (*Roxana*, Daniel Defoe)

CHARACTERS FROM WELL-KNOWN WORKS OF FICTION
(cont.)

(with titles and authors)

Ryder, Charles (*Brideshead Revisited*, Evelyn Waugh)

St Bungay, Duke of (*Phineas Finn*, Anthony Trollope)

St Clare, Evangeline (Little Eva) (*Uncle Tom's Cabin*, Harriet Beecher Stowe)

Sambo (*Just-So Stories*, Rudyard Kipling)

Sanders (Sandi) (*Sanders of the River*, Edgar Wallace)

Sawyer, Tom (*The Adventures of Tom Sawyer*, Mark Twain)

Seal, Basil (*Put Out More Flags*, Evelyn Waugh)

Shandy, Tristram (*Tristram Shandy*, Laurence Sterne)

Sharp, Rebecca (Becky) (*Vanity Fair*, William Makepeace Thackeray)

Shelton, Richard (*The Black Arrow*, Robert Louis Stevenson)

Shere Khan (Lungri) (*The Jungle Book*, Rudyard Kipling)

Shipton, Mother (*The Luck of Roaring Camp*, Bret Harte)

Silver, Long John (*Treasure Island*, Robert Louis Stevenson)

Slope, Rev. Obadiah (*Barchester Towers*, Anthony Trollope)

Sloth (*The Pilgrim's Progress*, John Bunyan)

Smith, Winston (*Nineteen Eight-Four*, George Orwell)

Smollet, Captain (*Treasure Island*, Robert Louis Stevenson)

Snowe, Lucy (*Villette*, Charlotte Brontë)

Sorrel, Hetty (*Adam Bede*, George Eliot)

Sorrell, Kit (*Sorrell and Son*, Warwick Deeping)

Southdown, Earl of (*Vanity Fair*, William Makepeace Thackeray)

Square (*Tom Jones*, Henry Fielding)

Starkadder, Judith (*Cold Comfort Farm*, Stella Gibbons)

Starkadder, Old Mrs (*Cold Comfort Farm*, Stella Gibbons)

Svengali (*Trilby*, George du Maurier)

Tarka (*Tarka the Otter*, Henry Williamson)

Temple, Miss (*Jane Eyre*, Charlotte Brontë)

Thatcher, Becky (*The Adventures of Tom Sawyer*, Mark Twain)

Thorne, Dr Thomas (*Doctor Thorne*, Anthony Trollope)

Thorpe, Isabella (*Northanger Abbey*, Jane Austen)

Thwackum (*Tom Jones*, Henry Fielding)

Thumb, Tom (*The Tale of Two Bad Mice*, Beatrix Potter)

Tiddler, Tom (*Adam's Opera*, Clemence Dane)

Tiger Lily (*Peter Pan*, J. M. Barrie)

Tiggy-Winkle, Mrs (*The Tale of Mrs Tiggy-Winkle*, Beatrix Potter)

Tilney, Henry (*Northanger Abbey*, Jane Austen)

Tinker Bell (*Peter Pan*, J. M. Barrie)

Tittlemouse, Mrs Thomasina (*The Tale of Mrs Tittlemouse*, Beatrix Potter)

Toad, Mr (*The Wind in the Willows*, Kenneth Grahame)

Tom (*The Water-Babies*, Charles Kingsley)

Tom, 'Uncle' (*Uncle Tom's Cabin*, Harriet Beecher Stowe)

Topsy (*Uncle Tom's Cabin*, Harriet Beecher Stowe)

Trelawney, Squire (*Treasure Island*, Robert Louis Stevenson)

Troy, Sergeant Francis (*Far from the Madding Crowd*, Thomas Hardy)

Trumpington, Lady (*The Virginians*, William Makepeace Thackeray)

Tulliver, Maggie (*The Mill on the Floss*, George Eliot)

Tulliver, Tom (*The Mill on the Floss*, George Eliot)

Turner, Jim (Captain Flint) (*Swallows and Amazons*, Arthur Ransome)

Tweedledee (*Through the Looking-Glass*, Lewis Carroll)

CHARACTERS FROM WELL-KNOWN WORKS OF FICTION
(cont.)

(with titles and authors)

Tweedledum (*Through the Looking-Glass*, Lewis Carroll)

Twitchett, Mrs Tabitha (*The Tale of Tom Kitten*, Beatrix Potter)

Umpopa (*King Solomon's Mines*, Henry Rider Haggard)

Uncas (*The Last of the Mohicans*, James Fennimore Cooper)

Valiant-for-Truth (*The Pilgrim's Progress*, John Bunyan)

Vane, Harriet (*Strong Poison*, Dorothy L. Sayers)

Vane, Lady Isabel (*East Lynne*, Mrs Henry Wood)

Verinder, Lady Julia (*The Moonstone*, Wilkie Collins)

Violet Elizabeth (*Just William*, Richmal Crompton)

Virginian, The (*The Virginian*, Owen Wister)

Walker, John (*Swallows and Amazons*, Arthur Ransome)

Walker, Roger (*Swallows and Amazons*, Arthur Ransome)

Walker, Susan (*Swallows and Amazons*, Arthur Ransome)

Walker, Titty (*Swallows and Amazons*, Arthur Ransome)

Walker, Vicky (*Swallows and Amazons*, Arthur Ransome)

Water Rat (Ratty) (*The Wind in the Willows*, Kenneth Grahame)

Waverley, Edward (*Waverley*, Walter Scott)

Western, Mrs (*Tom Jones*, Henry Fielding)

Western, Sophia (*Tom Jones*, Henry Fielding)

Western, Squire (*Tom Jones*, Henry Fielding)

Weston, Mrs (*Emma*, Jane Austen)

Whiteoak (family) (*The Whiteoak Chronicles*, Mazo de la Roche)

White-Tip (*Tarka the Otter*, Henry Williamson)

Whittier, Pollyanna (*Pollyanna*, Eleanor H. Porter)

Wilkes, Ashley (*Gone with the Wind*, Margaret Mitchell)

Wilkes, India (*Gone with the Wind*, Margaret Mitchell)

William (*Just William*, Richmal Crompton)

Williams, Percival William (*Wee Willie Winkie*, Rudyard Kipling)

Willoughby, John (*Sense and Sensibility*, Jane Austen)

Wimsey, Lord Peter Death Bredon (*Whose Body?*, Dorothy L. Sayers)

Winnie-the-Pooh (Edward Bear) (*Winnie-the-Pooh*, A. A. Milne)

Wolf, 'Brer' (*Uncle Remus*, Joel Chandler Harris)

Woodhouse, Emma (*Emma*, Jane Austen)

Woodhouse, Isabella (*Emma*, Jane Austen)

Wooster, Bertie (*Thank You, Jeeves*, etc., P. G. Wodehouse)

Worldly-Wiseman (*The Pilgrim's Progress*, John Bunyan)

Yossarian, Captain John (*Catch-22*, Joseph Heller)

CHARACTERS FROM THE NOVELS OF CHARLES DICKENS
(with novels)

Adams, Jack (Dombey and Son)
Akershem, Sophronia (Our Mutual Friend)
Allen, Arabella (The Pickwick Papers)
Allen, Benjamin (The Pickwick Papers)
Anne (Dombey and Son)
Ayresleigh, Mr (The Pickwick Papers)
Badger, Dr Bayham (Bleak House)
Badger, Laura (Bleak House)
Badger, Malta (Bleak House)
Badger, Matthew (Bleak House)
Badger, Quebec (Bleak House)
Badger, Woolwich (Bleak House)
Bagstock, Major (Dombey and Son)
Bailey, Benjamin (Martin Chuzzlewit)
Bailey, Captain (David Copperfield)
Baillie, Gabriel (The Pickwick Papers)
Balderstone, T. (Sketches by Boz)
Bamber, Jack (The Pickwick Papers)
Bangham, Mrs (Little Dorrit)
Bantam, Angelo Cyrus (The Pickwick Papers)
Baps (Dombey and Son)
Barbara (The Old Curiosity Shop)
Barbary, Miss (Bleak House)
Bardell, Mrs Martha (The Pickwick Papers)
Bardell, Tommy (The Pickwick Papers)
Barker, Phil (Oliver Twist)
Barkis (David Copperfield)
Barley, Clara (Great Expectations)
Barney (Oliver Twist)
Barnwell, B. B. (Martin Chuzzlewit)
Barton, Jacob (Sketches by Boz)
Barton, Mrs (Sketches by Boz)
Bates, Charley (Oliver Twist)
Bedwin, Mrs (Oliver Twist)
Begs, Mrs Ridger (David Copperfield)
Belling, Master (Nicholas Nickleby)
Belvawney, Miss (Nicholas Nickleby)
Berinthia (Dombey and Son)
Bet, Betsy (Oliver Twist)

Betsey, Jane (Dombey and Son)
Betsy (The Pickwick Papers)
Bitzer (Hard Times)
Blackpool, Stephen (Hard Times)
Blimber, Dr (Dombey and Son)
Blotton (The Pickwick Papers)
Bobster, Cecilia (Nicholas Nickleby)
Bobster, Mr (Nicholas Nickleby)
Boffin, Henrietta (Our Mutual Friend)
Boffin, Nicodemus (Our Mutual Friend)
Boldwig, Captain (The Pickwick Papers)
Bonney (Nicholas Nickleby)
Bounderby, Josiah (Hard Times)
Boythorn, Lawrence (Bleak House)
Brass, Sally (The Old Curiosity Shop)
Brass, Sampson (The Old Curiosity Shop)
Bravassa, Miss (Nicholas Nickleby)
Bray, Madeline (Nicholas Nickleby)
Bray, Walter (Nicholas Nickleby)
Brick, Jefferson (Martin Chuzzlewit)
Briggs (Dombey and Son)
Brogley (Dombey and Son)
Brooker (Nicholas Nickleby)
Browdie, John (Nicholas Nickleby)
Brown, Alice (Dombey and Son)
Brown, Mrs (Dombey and Son)
Brownlow, Mr (Oliver Twist)
Budden, Alexander August (Sketches by Boz)
Budden, Amelia (Sketches by Boz)
Budden, Octavius (Sketches by Boz)
Bullamy (Martin Chuzzlewit)
Bullseye (Oliver Twist)
Bumble (Oliver Twist)
Bunsby, Captain (Dombey and Son)
Buzuz, Sergeant (The Pickwick Papers)
Calton (Sketches by Boz)
Carker, Harriet (Dombey and Son)
Carker, James (Dombey and Son)
Carker, John (Dombey and Son)
Carton, Sydney (A Tale of Two Cities)
Casby, Christopher (Little Dorrit)
Charley (David Copperfield)

CHARACTERS FROM THE NOVELS OF CHARLES DICKENS (cont.)

(with novels)

Cheeryble, Charles (Nicholas Nickleby)
Cheeryble, Frank (Nicholas Nickleby)
Cheeryble, Ned (Nicholas Nickleby)
Cheggs, Alick (The Old Curiosity Shop)
Chester, Edward (Barnaby Rudge)
Chester, Sir John (Barnaby Rudge)
Chick, John (Dombey and Son)
Chick, Louisa (Dombey and Son)
Chickweed, Conkey (Oliver Twist)
Chillip, Dr (David Copperfield)
Chivery, John (Little Dorrit)
Chollop, Hannibal (Martin Chuzzlewit)
Chuckster (The Old Curiosity Shop)
Chuffey (Martin Chuzzlewit)
Chuzzlewit, Anthony (Martin Chuzzlewit)
Chuzzlewit, Diggory (Martin Chuzzlewit)
Chuzzlewit, George (Martin Chuzzlewit)
Chuzzlewit, Jonas (Martin Chuzzlewit)
Chuzzlewit, Martin (Martin Chuzzlewit)
Chuzzlewit, Mrs Ned (Martin Chuzzlewit)
Chuzzlewit, Toby (Martin Chuzzlewit)
Clare, Ada (Bleak House)
Clark (Dombey and Son)
Clarke (The Pickwick Papers)
Claypole, Noah (Oliver Twist)
Cleaver, Fanny (Our Mutual Friend)
Clennam, Arthur (Little Dorrit)
Clive (Little Dorrit)
Clubber, Sir Thomas (The Pickwick Papers)
Cluppins (The Pickwick Papers)
Cly (A Tale of Two Cities)
Codger, Mrs (Martin Chuzzlewit)
Codlin, Thomas (The Old Curiosity Shop)
Compeyson (Great Expectations)
Conway, General (Barnaby Rudge)
Cooper, Augustus (Sketches by Boz)
Cooper, Mrs (Sketches by Boz)

Copperfield, Clara (David Copperfield)
Copperfield, David (David Copperfield)
Corney, Mrs (Oliver Twist)
Crackit, Toby (Oliver Twist)
Craddock, Mrs (The Pickwick Papers)
Cratchit, Belinda (A Christmas Carol)
Cratchit, Bob (A Christmas Carol)
Cratchit, Tiny Tim (A Christmas Carol)
Crawley, Young Mr (The Pickwick Papers)
Creakle (David Copperfield)
Crewler, Mrs (David Copperfield)
Crewler, Rev Horace (David Copperfield)
Crewler, Sophy (David Copperfield)
Crimple, David (Martin Chuzzlewit)
Cripples, Mr (Little Dorrit)
Crookey (The Pickwick Papers)
Crowl (Nicholas Nickleby)
Crummles, Ninetta (Nicholas Nickleby)
Crummles, Vincent (Nicholas Nickleby)
Crumpton, Miss Amelia (Sketches by Boz)
Crumpton, Miss Maria (Sketches by Boz)
Cruncher, Jeremiah (A Tale of Two Cities)
Cruncher, Jerry (A Tale of Two Cities)
Crupp, Mrs (David Copperfield)
Crushton, Hon Mr (The Pickwick Papers)
Curdle (Nicholas Nickleby)
Cutler, Mr (Nicholas Nickleby)
Cutler, Mrs (Nicholas Nickleby)
Cuttle, Captain Ned (Dombey and Son)
Dadson (Sketches by Boz)
Daisy, Solomon (Barnaby Rudge)
Darnay, Charles (A Tale of Two Cities)
Dartle, Rosa (David Copperfield)
D'Aulnais (A Tale of Two Cities)

CHARACTERS FROM THE NOVELS OF CHARLES DICKENS
(cont.)
(with novels)

David (Nicholas Nickleby)
Dawes, Mary (Dombey and Son)
Dawkins, Jack (Oliver Twist)
Dedlock, Sir Leicester (Bleak House)
Dedlock, Volumnia (Bleak House)
Defarge, Madame (A Tale of Two Cities)
Dennis, Ned (Barnaby Rudge)
Dibabs, Mrs (Nicholas Nickleby)
Dingo, Professor (Bleak House)
Dingwall, M. P. (Sketches by Boz)
'Dismal Jimmy' (The Pickwick Papers)
Diver, Colonel (Martin Chuzzlewit)
Dodson (The Pickwick Papers)
Dolloby (David Copperfield)
Dombey, Fanny (Dombey and Son)
Dombey, Florence (Dombey and Son)
Dombey, Louisa (Dombey and Son)
Dombey, Paul (Dombey and Son)
Donny, Mrs (Bleak House)
Dorker (Nicholas Nickleby)
Dorrit, Amy (Little Dorrit)
Dorrit, Edward (Little Dorrit)
Dorrit, Fanny (Little Dorrit)
Dorrit, Frederick (Little Dorrit)
Dorrit, William (Little Dorrit)
Dowler, Captain (The Pickwick Papers)
Doyce, Daniel (Little Dorrit)
Drood, Edwin (Edwin Drood)
Drummle, Bentley (Great Expectations)
Dubbley (The Pickwick Papers)
Dumps, Nicodemus (Sketches by Boz, Pickwick Papers)
Edmunds, John (The Pickwick Papers)
Estella (Great Expectations)
Evans, Jemima (Sketches by Boz)
Evenson, John (Sketches by Boz)
Fagin (Oliver Twist)
Feeder (Dombey and Son)
Feenix (Dombey and Son)
Fibbitson, Mrs (David Copperfield)
Finching, Mrs Flora (Little Dorrit)
Fips, Mr (Martin Chuzzlewit)
Fizkin, Horatio (The Pickwick Papers)

Flamwell, Mr (Sketches by Boz)
Fledgeby, Old (Our Mutual Friend)
Fledgeby, Young (Our Mutual Friend)
Fleming, Agnes (Oliver Twist)
Flintwinch, Affery (Little Dorrit)
Flintwinch, Ephraim (Little Dorrit)
Flintwinch, Jeremiah (Little Dorrit)
Flite, Miss (Bleak House)
Fogg (The Pickwick Papers)
Foliar (Nicholas Nickleby)
Gabelle, Theophile (A Tale of Two Cities)
'Game Chicken', The (Dombey and Son)
Gamp, Mrs Sarah (Martin Chuzzlewit)
Gargery, Biddy (Great Expectations)
Gargery, Joe (Great Expectations)
Gargery, Pip (Great Expectations)
Garland, Abel (The Old Curiosity Shop)
Garland, Mr (The Old Curiosity Shop)
Garland, Mrs (The Old Curiosity Shop)
Gashford (Barnaby Rudge)
Gaspard (A Tale of Two Cities)
Gay, Walter (Dombey and Son)
Gazingi, Miss (Nicholas Nickleby)
General, Mrs (Little Dorrit)
George, Mr (Bleak House)
George (The Pickwick Papers)
George (The Old Curiosity Shop)
Gilbert, Mark (Barnaby Rudge)
Gills, Solomon (Dombey and Son)
Gordon, Lord George (Barnaby Rudge)
Gowan, Harry (Little Dorrit)
Gradgrind, Louisa (Hard Times)
Gradgrind, Thomas (Hard Times)
Graham, Mary (Martin Chuzzlewit)
Granger, Edith (Dombey and Son)
Green, Tom (Barnaby Rudge)
Gregsbury (Nicholas Nickleby)
Gride, Arthur (Nicholas Nickleby)
Gridley (Bleak House)
Grimwig (Oliver Twist)
Grip (Barnaby Rudge)

CHARACTERS FROM THE NOVELS OF CHARLES DICKENS (cont.)

(with novels)

Groves, 'Honest' James (The Old Curiosity Shop)
Grudden, Mrs (Nicholas Nickleby)
Gunter (The Pickwick Papers)
Guppy, William (Bleak House)
Haggage, Dr (Little Dorrit)
Hardy, Mr (Sketches by Boz)
Haredale, Emma (Barnaby Rudge)
Haredale, Geoffrey (Barnaby Rudge)
Haredale, Reuben (Barnaby Rudge)
Harmon, John (Our Mutual Friend)
Harris, Mrs (Martin Chuzzlewit)
Harthouse, James (Hard Times)
Havisham, Miss (Great Expectations)
Hawdon, Captain (Bleak House)
Hawk, Sir Mulberry (Nicholas Nickleby)
Headstone, Bradley (Our Mutual Friend)
Heep, Uriah (David Copperfield)
Hexam, Charlie (Our Mutual Friend)
Hexam, Jesse (Our Mutual Friend)
Hexam, Lizzie (Our Mutual Friend)
Heyling, George (The Pickwick Papers)
Higden, Betty (Our Mutual Friend)
Hominy, Major (Martin Chuzzlewit)
Hortense (Bleak House)
Howler, Rev M. (Dombey and Son)
Hugh (Barnaby Rudge)
Jaggers (Great Expectations)
Janet (David Copperfield)
Jarley, Mrs (The Old Curiosity Shop)
Jarndyce, John (Bleak House)
Jellyby, Caddy (Bleak House)
Jellyby, Mrs (Bleak House)
Jellyby, Peepy (Bleak House)
Jingle, Alfred (The Pickwick Papers)
Jinkins (Martin Chuzzlewit)
Jo (Bleak House)
Jobling, Dr John (Martin Chuzzlewit)
Jobling, Tony (Bleak House)
Joe (The Pickwick Papers)
Johnson, Mr (Nicholas Nickleby)
Jones, Mary (Barnaby Rudge)
Jorkins (David Copperfield)
Jowl, Mat (The Old Curiosity Shop)
Jupe, Cecilia (Hard Times)

Kags (Oliver Twist)
Kedgick, Captain (Martin Chuzzlewit)
Kenwigs, Morleena (Nicholas Nickleby)
Kettle, La Fayette (Martin Chuzzlewit)
Kitterbell, Charles (Sketches by Boz)
Knag, Miss (Nicholas Nickleby)
Krook (Bleak House)
La Creevy, Miss (Nicholas Nickleby)
Lammle, Alfred (Our Mutual Friend)
Langdale (Barnaby Rudge)
Larkins, Mr (David Copperfield)
Leeford, Edward (Oliver Twist)
Lenville (Nicholas Nickleby)
Lewsome (Martin Chuzzlewit)
Lightwood, Mortimer (Our Mutual Friend)
Lillyvick (Nicholas Nickleby)
List, Isaac (The Old Curiosity Shop)
Littimer (David Copperfield)
Lobbs, Maria (The Pickwick Papers)
Lobbs, 'Old' (The Pickwick Papers)
Lorry, Jarvis (A Tale of Two Cities)
Losberne (Oliver Twist)
Lucas, Solomon (The Pickwick Papers)
Lumley, Dr (Nicholas Nickleby)
Lupin, Mrs (Martin Chuzzlewit)
Macstinger, Mrs (Dombey and Son)
Magnus, Peter (The Pickwick Papers)
Magwitch, Abel (Great Expectations)
Malden, Jack (David Copperfield)
Malderton, Mr (Sketches by Boz)
Mallard (The Pickwick Papers)
Manette, Dr (A Tale of Two Cities)
Manette, Lucie (A Tale of Two Cities)
Mann, Mrs (Oliver Twist)
Mantalini, Mr (Nicholas Nickleby)
Marchioness, The (The Old Curiosity Shop)
Marley, Jacob (A Christmas Carol)
Marton (The Old Curiosity Shop)
Mary Anne (David Copperfield)
Mary (The Pickwick Papers)
Matthews (Nicholas Nickleby)

CHARACTERS FROM THE NOVELS OF CHARLES DICKENS
(cont.)

(with novels)

Maylie, Harrie (Oliver Twist)
Maylie, Mrs (Oliver Twist)
Maylie, Rose (Oliver Twist)
Meagles (Little Dorrit)
Mealy (David Copperfield)
Mell, Charles (David Copperfield)
Merdle, Mr (Little Dorrit)
Micawber, Wilkins (David
  Copperfield)
Miff, Mrs (Dombey and Son)
Miggs, Miss (Barnaby Rudge)
Mills, Julia (David Copperfield)
Milvey, Rev Frank (Our Mutual
  Friend)
Minerva (The Pickwick Papers)
Minus (Sketches by Boz)
Mivins (The Pickwick Papers)
Moddle, Augustus (Martin
  Chuzzlewit)
Molly (Great Expectations)
Morfin (Dombey and Son)
Mould (Martin Chuzzlewit)
Mowcher, Miss (David Copperfield)
Mullet, Professor (Martin
  Chuzzlewit)
Murdstone, Edward (David
  Copperfield)
Murdstone, Jane (David
  Copperfield)
Mutanhed, Lord (The Pickwick
  Papers)
Nadgett (Martin Chuzzlewit)
Nancy (Oliver Twist)
Nandy, John Edward (Little Dorrit)
Neckett, Charlotte (Bleak House)
Neckett, Emma (Bleak House)
Neckett, Tom (Bleak House)
Nickleby, Godfrey (Nicholas
  Nickleby)
Nickleby, Kate (Nicholas Nickleby)
Nickleby, Nicholas (Nicholas
  Nickleby)
Nickleby, Ralph (Nicholas Nickleby)
Nipper, Susan (Dombey and Son)
Noakes, Percy (Sketches by Boz)
Noggs, Newman (Nicholas
  Nickleby)
Nubbles, Christopher (The Old
  Curiosity Shop)

Nupkins, George (The Pickwick
  Papers)
O'Bleary (Sketches by Boz)
Old Barley (Great Expectations)
Omer (David Copperfield)
Pancks (Little Dorrit)
Pardiggle, Francis (Bleak House)
Pardiggle, O. A. (Bleak House)
Parsons, Gabriel (Sketches by Boz)
Pawkins, Major (Martin Chuzzlewit)
Peak (Barnaby Rudge)
Pecksniff, Charity (Martin
  Chuzzlewit)
Pecksniff, Mercy (Martin Chuzzlewit)
Pecksniff, Seth (Martin Chuzzlewit)
Peggotty, Clara (David Copperfield)
Peggotty, Daniel (David
  Copperfield)
Peggotty, Ham (David Copperfield)
Peggotty, Little Em'ly (David
  Copperfield)
Pell, Solomon (The Pickwick Papers)
Peps, Dr Parker (Dombey and Son)
Perch (Dombey and Son)
Perker (The Pickwick Papers)
Phunky (The Pickwick Papers)
Pickwick, Samuel (The Pickwick
  Papers)
Pilkins, Dr (Dombey and Son)
Pinch, Ruth (Martin Chuzzlewit)
Pinch, Tom (Martin Chuzzlewit)
Pipchin, Mrs (Dombey and Son)
Pipkin, Nathaniel (The Pickwick
  Papers)
Pirrip, Philip (Pip) (Great
  Expectations)
Plornish, Thomas (Little Dorrit)
Pocket, Herbert (Great
  Expectations)
Pocket, Matthew (Great
  Expectations)
Pocket, Sarah (Great Expectations)
Podsnap, Georgiana (Our Mutual
  Friend)
Podsnap, Mr (Our Mutual Friend)
Pogram, Elijah (Martin Chuzzlewit)
Potatoes (David Copperfield)
Pott, Minverva (The Pickwick
  Papers)
Price, 'Tilda (Nicholas Nickleby)

CHARACTERS FROM THE NOVELS OF CHARLES DICKENS
(cont.)
(with novels)

Priscilla (Bleak House)
Pross, Miss (A Tale of Two Cities)
Pross, Solomon (A Tale of Two Cities)
Pumblechook (Great Expectations)
Quale (Bleak House)
Quilp, Daniel (The Old Curiosity Shop)
Quinion (David Copperfield)
Raddle, Mr (The Pickwick Papers)
Raddle, Mrs (The Pickwick Papers)
Riah (Our Mutual Friend)
Riderhood, Pleasant (Our Mutual Friend)
Riderhood, Roger (Our Mutual Friend)
Rigaud, Monsieur (Little Dorrit)
Rouncewell, Mrs (Bleak House)
Rudge, Barnaby (Barnaby Rudge)
Rudge, Mary (Barnaby Rudge)
Rugg, Anastasia (Little Dorrit)
St Evremonde, Marquis de (A Tale of Two Cities)
St Evremonde, Marquise de (A Tale of Two Cities)
Sampson, George (Our Mutual Friend)
Sawyer, Bob (The Pickwick Papers)
Scadder, Zephaniah (Martin Chuzzlewit)
Scadgers, Lady (Hard Times)
Scaley (Nicholas Nickleby)
Scott, Tom (The Old Curiosity Shop)
Scrooge, Ebenezer (A Christmas Carol)
Sharp (David Copperfield)
'Shiny William' (The Pickwick Papers)
Sikes, Bill (Oliver Twist)
Simmons, Beadle (Sketches by Boz)
Simmons, William (Martin Chuzzlewit)
Skewton, Hon Mrs (Dombey and Son)
Skiffins, Miss (Great Expectations)
Skimpole, Arethusa (Bleak House)
Skimpole, Harold (Bleak House)
Skimpole, Kitty (Bleak House)
Skimpole, Laura (Bleak House)
Skittles, Sir Barnet (Dombey and Son)

Skylark, Mr (David Copperfield)
Slammer, Dr (The Pickwick Papers)
Sleary, Josephine (Hard Times)
Sloppy (Our Mutual Friend)
Slumkey, Hon Samuel (The Pickwick Papers)
Slurk (The Pickwick Papers)
Slyme, Chevy (Martin Chuzzlewit)
Smallweed, Bartholomew (Bleak House)
Smallweed, Joshua (Bleak House)
Smallweed, Judy (Bleak House)
Smiggers, Joseph (The Pickwick Papers)
Smike (Nicholas Nickleby)
Smorltork, Count (The Pickwick Papers)
Snagsby (Bleak House)
Snawley (Nicholas Nickleby)
Snevellici, Miss (Nicholas Nickleby)
Snobb, The Hon (Nicholas Nickleby)
Snodgrass, Augustus (The Pickwick Papers)
Snubbin, Sergeant (The Pickwick Papers)
Sowerberry (Oliver Twist)
Sownds (Dombey and Son)
Sparkler, Edmund (Little Dorrit)
Sparsit, Mrs (Hard Times)
Spenlow, Dora (David Copperfield)
Spottletoes, Mrs (Martin Chuzzlewit)
Squeers, Fanny (Nicholas Nickleby)
Squeers, Wackford (Nicholas Nickleby)
Squod, Phil (Bleak House)
Stagg (Barnaby Rudge)
Stareleigh, Justice (The Pickwick Papers)
Startop (Great Expectations)
Steerforth, James (David Copperfield)
Stiggins (The Pickwick Papers)
Strong, Dr (David Copperfield)
Stryver, C. J. (A Tale of Two Cities)
Summerson, Esther (Bleak House)
Sweedlepipe, Paul (Martin Chuzzlewit)
Sweet William (The Old Curiosity Shop)

CHARACTERS FROM THE NOVELS OF CHARLES DICKENS (cont.)

(with novels)

Swiveller, Richard (The Old Curiosity Shop)
Tacker (Martin Chuzzlewit)
Tamaroo, Miss (Martin Chuzzlewit)
Tapley, Mark (Martin Chuzzlewit)
Tappertit, Simon (Barnaby Rudge)
Tattycoram (Little Dorrit)
Taunton, Mrs (Sketches by Boz)
Tibbs, Mrs (Sketches by Boz)
Tigg, Montague (Martin Chuzzlewit)
Tippin, Lady (Our Mutual Friend)
Tisher, Mrs (Edwin Drood)
Tite-Barnacle, Clarence (Little Dorrit)
Tite-Barnacle, Ferdinand (Little Dorrit)
Tite-Barnacle, Junior (Little Dorrit)
Tite-Barnacle, Lord Decimus (Little Dorrit)
Tite-Barnacle, Mr (Little Dorrit)
Todgers, Mrs (Martin Chuzzlewit)
Toodle (Dombey and Son)
Toots, Mr P. (Dombey and Son)
Tottle, Watkins (Sketches by Boz)
Tox, Miss (Dombey and Son)
Trabb (Great Expectations)
Traddles, Tom (David Copperfield)
Trent, Frederick (The Old Curiosity Shop)
Trent, Nellie (The Old Curiosity Shop)
Trimmer, Mr (Sketches by Boz)
Trott, Alexander (Sketches by Boz)
Trotter, Job (The Pickwick Papers)
Trotwood, Betsey (David Copperfield)
Trundle (The Pickwick Papers)
Tuggs, Charlotte (Sketches by Boz)
Tuggs, Joseph (Sketches by Boz)
Tuggs, Simon (Sketches by Boz)
Tulkinghorn (Bleak House)
Tupman, Tracy (The Pickwick Papers)
Tupple (Sketches by Boz)
Turveydrop, Prince (Bleak House)
Twist, Oliver (Oliver Twist)
Varden, Dolly (Barnaby Rudge)
Varden, Gabriel (Barnaby Rudge)
Veneering, Anastasia (Our Mutual Friend)

Veneering, Hamilton (Our Mutual Friend)
Venus, Mr (Our Mutual Friend)
Verisopht, Lord Frederick (Nicholas Nickleby)
Vholes (Bleak House)
Von Koeldwethout (Nicholas Nickleby)
Vuffin (The Old Curiosity Shop)
Wackles, Jane (The Old Curiosity Shop)
Wackles, Melissa (The Old Curiosity Shop)
Wackles, Sophie (The Old Curiosity Shop)
Wade, Miss (Little Dorrit)
Walker, Mick (David Copperfield)
Wardle, Emily (The Pickwick Papers)
Wardle, Isabella (The Pickwick Papers)
Wardle, Mr (The Pickwick Papers)
Wardle, Rachel (The Pickwick Papers)
Waterbrook (David Copperfield)
Watkins (Nicholas Nickleby)
Watty (The Pickwick Papers)
Wegg, Silas (Our Mutual Friend)
Weller, Sam (The Pickwick Papers)
Weller, Tony (The Pickwick Papers)
Wemmick (Great Expectations)
Westlock, John (Martin Chuzzlewit)
Wickfield, Agnes (David Copperfield)
Wickfield, Mr (David Copperfield)
Wickham, Mrs (Dombey and Son)
Wilfer, Bella (Our Mutual Friend)
Wilfer, Lavinia (Our Mutual Friend)
Wilfer, Reginald (Our Mutual Friend)
Willet, Joe (Barnaby Rudge)
Willet, John (Barnaby Rudge)
Winkle, Nathaniel (The Pickwick Papers)
Witherden, Mr (The Old Curiosity Shop)
Withers (Dombey and Son)
Wititterly, Julia (Nicholas Nickleby)
Woodcourt, Allan (Bleak House)
Wopsle (Great Expectations)
Wrayburn, Eugene (Our Mutual Friend)

TITLES OF WELL-KNOWN PLAYS
(with playwrights)

Abigail's Party (Mike Leigh)
Accidental Death of an Anarchist (Dario Fo)
A Cuckoo in the Nest (Ben Travers)
A Day in the Death of Joe Egg (Peter Nichols)
A Doll's House (Henrik Ibsen)
After the Fall (Arthur Miller)
All for Love (John Dryden)
All God's Chillun got Wings (Eugene O'Neill)
All My Sons (Arthur Miller)
All's Well that Ends Well (William Shakespeare)
Amadeus (Peter Shaffer)
A Man for All Seasons (Robert Bolt)
A Midsummer Night's Dream (William Shakespeare)
Androcles and the Lion (G. B. Shaw)
Andromaque (Jean Racine)
An Ideal Husband (Oscar Wilde)
An Inspector Calls (J. B. Priestley)
An Italian Straw Hat (Eugène Labiche)
Anna Christie (Eugene O'Neill)
Antigone (Sophocles)
Antony and Cleopatra (William Shakespeare)
Arms and the Man (G. B. Shaw)
Arsenic and Old Lace (Joseph Kesselring)
A Streetcar Named Desire (Tennessee Williams)
As You Like It (William Shakespeare)
A Taste of Honey (Shelagh Delaney)
Athalie (Jean Racine)
Aureng-Zebe (John Dryden)
A Woman of No Importance (Oscar Wilde)
Barefoot in the Park (Neil Simon)
Bartholomew Fair (Ben Jonson)
Billy Liar (Willis Hall and Keith Waterhouse)
Blithe Spirit (Noël Coward)
Blood Wedding (Federico García Lorca)
Broken Glass (Arthur Miller)
Caesar and Cleopatra (G. B. Shaw)
Candida (G. B. Shaw)

Can't Pay? Won't Pay! (Dario Fo)
Captain Brassbound's Conversion (G. B. Shaw)
Caste (T. W. Robertson)
Cat on a Hot Tin Roof (Tennessee Williams)
Cavalcade (Noël Coward)
Charley's Aunt (Brandon Thomas)
Chips with Everything (Arnold Wesker)
Coriolanus (William Shakespeare)
Cymbeline (William Shakespeare)
Dancing at Lughnasa (Brian Friel)
Dangerous Corner (J. B. Priestley)
Death of a Salesman (Arthur Miller)
Design For Living (Noël Coward)
Dr Faustus (Christopher Marlowe)
Duel of Angels (Jean Giraudoux)
Edward II (Christopher Marlowe)
Electra (Sophocles)
Endgame (Samuel Beckett)
Entertaining Mr Sloane (Joe Orton)
Faust (Goethe)
Five Finger Exercise (Peter Shaffer)
Flare Path (Terence Rattigan)
French without Tears (Terence Rattigan)
Galileo (Bertolt Brecht)
Ghosts (Henrik Ibsen)
Golden Boy (Clifford Odets)
Hamlet, Prince of Denmark (William Shakespeare)
Haunting Julia (Alan Ayckbourn)
Happy Days (Samuel Beckett)
Hay Fever (Noël Coward)
Heartbreak House (G. B. Shaw)
Henry IV [Parts 1 and 2] (William Shakespeare)
Henry V (William Shakespeare)
Henry VI [Parts 1, 2, and 3] (William Shakespeare)
Henry VIII (William Shakespeare)
Hobson's Choice (Harold Brighouse)
I Am a Camera (John van Druten)
Inadmissible Evidence (John Osborne)
Indian Ink (Tom Stoppard)
Journey's End (R. C. Sherriff)
Julius Caesar (William Shakespeare)
Jumpers (Tom Stoppard)

TITLES OF WELL-KNOWN PLAYS (cont.)
(with playwrights)

Juno and the Paycock (Sean O'Casey)
King John (William Shakespeare)
King Lear (William Shakespeare)
Krapp's Last Tape (Samuel Beckett)
Lady Windermere's Fan (Oscar Wilde)
Le Misanthrope (Molière)
Look Back in Anger (John Osborne)
Loot (Joe Orton)
Love for Love (William Congreve)
Love's Labour's Lost (William Shakespeare)
Macbeth (William Shakespeare)
Major Barbara (G. B. Shaw)
Man and Superman (G. B. Shaw)
Marriage à la Mode (John Dryden)
Measure for Measure (William Shakespeare)
Medea (Euripides)
Moonlight (Harold Pinter)
Mourning becomes Electra (Eugene O'Neill)
Much Ado about Nothing (William Shakespeare)
Murder in the Cathedral (T. S. Eliot)
Oedipus Rex (Sophocles)
Othello (William Shakespeare)
Pandora's Box (Frank Wedekind)
Pericles (William Shakespeare)
Perkin Warbeck (John Ford)
Peter Pan (J. M. Barrie)
Phèdre (Jean Racine)
Pillars of Society (Henrik Ibsen)
Plenty (David Hare)
Present Laughter (Noël Coward)
Private Lives (Noël Coward)
Pygmalion (G. B. Shaw)
Quality Street (J. M. Barrie)
Racing Demon (David Hare)
Richard II (William Shakespeare)
Richard III (William Shakespeare)
Ring Round the Moon (Jean Anouilh)
Romanoff and Juliet (Peter Ustinov)
Romeo and Juliet (William Shakespeare)
Rookery Nook (Ben Travers)
Roots (Arnold Wesker)

Rosencrantz and Guildenstern are Dead (Tom Stoppard)
Ross (Terence Rattigan)
Saint Joan (G. B. Shaw)
Separate Tables (Terence Rattigan)
She Stoops to Conquer (Oliver Goldsmith)
Sizwe Bansi is Dead (Athol Fugard)
Strife (John Galsworthy)
Suddenly Last Summer (Tennessee Williams)
Tamburlaine the Great (Christopher Marlowe)
Tartuffe (Molière)
The Acharnians (Aristophanes)
The Adding Machine (Elmer Rice)
The Admirable Crichton (J. M. Barrie)
The Alchemist (Ben Jonson)
The American Dream (Edward Albee)
The Anatomist (James Bridie)
The Apple Cart (G. B. Shaw)
The Bacchae (Euripides)
The Balcony (Jean Genet)
The Bankrupt (Alexander Ostrovsky)
The Barretts of Wimpole Street (Rudolf Besier)
The Beaux' Stratagem (George Farquhar)
The Birds (Aristophanes)
The Birthday Party (Harold Pinter)
The Broken Heart (John Ford)
The Broken Jug (Heinrich von Kleist)
The Browning Version (Terence Rattigan)
The Caretaker (Harold Pinter)
The Caucasian Chalk Circle (Bertolt Brecht)
The Cherry Orchard (Anton Chekhov)
The Circle (W. Somerset Maugham)
The Cocktail Party (T. S. Eliot)
The Comedy of Errors (William Shakespeare)
The Constant Wife (W. Somerset Maugham)
The Contrast (Royall Tyler)
The Corn is Green (Emlyn Williams)

TITLES OF WELL-KNOWN PLAYS (cont.)
(with playwrights)

The Country Girl (Clifford Odets)
The Critic (Richard Brinsley Sheridan)
The Crucible (Arthur Miller)
The Deep Blue Sea (Terence Rattigan)
The Devil's Disciple (G. B. Shaw)
The Devils (John Whiting)
The Doctor's Dilemma (G. B. Shaw)
The Duchess of Malfi (John Webster)
The Dumb Waiter (Harold Pinter)
The Family Reunion (T. S. Eliot)
The Fire-Raisers (Max Frisch)
The Frogs (Aristophanes)
The Ghost Sonata (August Strindberg)
The Glass Menagerie (Tennessee Williams)
The Good-Natured Man (Oliver Goldsmith)
The Government Inspector (Nikolai Gogol)
The Hostage (Brendan Behan)
The Iceman Cometh (Eugene O'Neill)
The Importance of Being Earnest (Oscar Wilde)
The Jew of Malta (Christopher Marlowe)
The Lady's not for Burning (Christopher Fry)
The Lark (Jean Anouilh)
The Linden Tree (J. B. Priestley)
The Madness of George III (Alan Bennet)
The Magistrate (Pinero)
The Maid's Tragedy (Francis Beaumont and John Fletcher)
The Master Builder (Henrik Ibsen)
The Matchmaker (Thornton Wilder)
The Merchant of Venice (William Shakespeare)
The Merry Wives of Windsor (William Shakespeare)
The Miser (Molière)
The Mousetrap (Agatha Christie)
The Old Bachelor (William Congreve)
The Philanderer (G. B. Shaw)

The Plough and the Stars (Sean O'Casey)
The Revenger's Tragedy (Cyril Tourneur)
The Rivals (Richard Brinsley Sheridan)
The Romans in Britain (Howard Brenton)
The Room (Harold Pinter)
The School for Scandal (Richard Brinsley Sheridan)
The School for Wives (Molière)
The Seagull (Anton Chekhov)
The Second Mrs Tanqueray (Pinero)
The Shadow of a Gunman (Sean O'Casey)
The Spanish Tragedy (Thomas Kyd)
The Suppliant Women (Aeschylus)
The Taming of the Shrew (William Shakespeare)
The Tempest (William Shakespeare)
The Tricks of the Trade (Dario Fo)
The Trojan Women (Euripides)
The Two Gentlemen of Verona (William Shakespeare)
The White Devil (John Webster)
The Wild Duck (Henrik Ibsen)
The Winslow Boy (Terence Rattigan)
The Winter's Tale (William Shakespeare)
This Happy Breed (Noël Coward)
Three Sisters (Anton Chekhov)
Three Tall Women (Edward Albee)
Timon of Athens (William Shakespeare)
'tis Pity She's a Whore (John Ford)
Titus Andronicus (William Shakespeare)
Translations (Brian Friel)
Travesties (Tom Stoppard)
Troilus and Cressida (William Shakespeare)
Twelfth Night (William Shakespeare)
Two Noble Kinsmen (William Shakespeare and John Fletcher)
Uncle Vanya (Anton Chekhov)
Under Milk Wood (Dylan Thomas)
Venice Preserved (Thomas Otway)

TITLES OF WELL-KNOWN PLAYS (cont.)
(with playwrights)

Volpone (Ben Jonson)
Waiting for Godot (Samuel Beckett)
What Every Woman Knows (J. M. Barrie)

What the Butler Saw (Joe Orton)
Who's Afraid of Virginia Woolf? (Edward Albee)
Women Beware Women (Thomas Middleton)

CHARACTERS FROM THE PLAYS OF WILLIAM SHAKESPEARE
(with plays)

Aaron (Titus Andronicus)
Achilles (Troilus and Cressida)
Adam (As You Like It)
Adriana (The Comedy of Errors)
Aegeon (The Comedy of Errors)
Aemilia (The Comedy of Errors)
Agamemnon (Troilus and Cressida)
Agrippa (Julius Caesar, Antony and Cleopatra)
Aguecheek, Sir Andrew (Twelfth Night)
Ajax (Troilus and Cressida)
Alarbus (Titus Andronicus)
Albany, Duke of (King Lear)
Alonso (The Tempest)
Angelo (Measure for Measure)
Anne (Richard III)
Antiochus (Pericles)
Antipholus (The Comedy of Errors)
Antonio (The Merchant of Venice, The Tempest)
Antony (Julius Caesar, Antony and Cleopatra)
Ariel (The Tempest)
Armado (Love's Labour's Lost)
Arviragus (Cymbeline)
Audrey (As You Like It)
Aufidius (Coriolanus)
Banquo (Macbeth)
Baptista (The Taming of the Shrew)
Bardolph (1 Henry IV, 2 Henry IV, Henry V, The Merry Wives of Windsor)
Bassanio (The Merchant of Venice)
Bassianus (Titus Andronicus)

Beatrice (Much Ado About Nothing)
Belarius (Cymbeline)
Belch, Sir Toby (Twelfth Night)
Benedick (Much Ado About Nothing)
Benvolio (Romeo and Juliet)
Bernardo (Hamlet)
Berowne (Love's Labour's Lost)
Bertram (All's Well That Ends Well)
Bianca (The Taming of the Shrew, Othello)
Blunt (2 Henry IV)
Bolingbroke, Henry [Henry IV] (Richard II)
Bottom (A Midsummer Night's Dream)
Brabantio (Othello)
Brutus (Julius Caesar, Coriolanu)
Calchas (Troilus and Cressida)
Caliban (The Tempest)
Cambridge (Henry V)
Capulet (Romeo and Juliet)
Cassio (Othello)
Celia (As You Like It)
Cesario (Twelfth Night)
Charmian (Antony and Cleopatra)
Chiron (Titus Andronicus)
Clarence, George, Duke of (3 Henry VI, Richard III)
Claudio (Much Ado About Nothing, Measure for Measure)
Claudius (Hamlet)
Cleon (Pericles)
Cleopatra (Antony and Cleopatra)
Cloten (Cymbeline)

CHARACTERS FROM THE PLAYS OF WILLIAM SHAKESPEARE (cont.)

(with plays)

Cominius (Coriolanus)
Cordelia (King Lear)
Cornelius (Hamlet)
Cornwall, Duke of (King Lear)
Corin (As You Like It)
Coriolanus (Coriolanus)
Costard (Love's Labour's Lost)
Cressida (Troilus and Cressida)
Cymbeline (Cymbeline)
Demetrius (Titus Andronicus, A Midsummer Night's Dream, Antony and Cleopatra)
Dennis (As You Like It)
Desdemona (Othello)
Diana (All's Well that Ends Well)
Diomedes (Antony and Cleopatra, Troilus and Cressida)
Dionyza (Pericles)
Dogberry (Much Ado About Nothing)
Don Pedro (Much Ado About Nothing)
Donalbain (Macbeth)
Douglas (1 Henry IV)
Dromio (The Comedy of Errors)
Dumain (Love's Labour's Lost)
Duncan (Macbeth)
Edgar (King Lear)
Edmund (King Lear)
Edward IV (2 Henry VI, 3 Henry VI)
Elbow (Measure for Measure)
Elizabeth (Henry VI, Richard III)
Emilia (Othello)
Enobarbus (Antony and Cleopatra)
Eros (Antony and Cleopatra)
Escalus (Measure for Measure)
Fabian (Twelfth Night)
Falstaff (1 Henry IV, 2 Henry IV, The Merry Wives of Windsor)
Ferdinand (Love's Labour's Lost, The Tempest)
Feste (Twelfth Night)
Fleance (Macbeth)
Florizel (The Winter's Tale)
Flute (A Midsummer Night's Dream)
Fortinbras (Hamlet)
Frederick (As You Like It)
Froth (Measure for Measure)
Fulvia (Antony and Cleopatra)

George, Duke of Clarence (Henry VI, Richard III)
Gertrude (Hamlet)
Glendower, Owen (1 Henry IV)
Gloucester, Earl of (King Lear)
Gloucester, Richard, Duke of (2 Henry 3 Henry VI, Richard III)
Goneril (King Lear)
Gonzalo (The Tempest)
Gratiano (The Merchant of Venice, Othello)
Grey (Henry V)
Guiderius (Cymbeline)
Guildenstern (Hamlet)
Hal [Henry V] (1 Henry IV)
Hamlet (Hamlet)
Hecate (Macbeth)
Hector (Troilus and Cressida)
Helenus (Troilus and Cressida)
Helena (A Midsummer Night's Dream, All's Well That Ends Well)
Helicanus (Pericles)
Henry IV (Richard II, 1 Henry IV, 2 Henry IV)
Henry V (1 Henry IV, 2 Henry IV, Henry V)
Henry VI (1 Henry VI, 2 Henry VI, 3 Henry VI)
Henry VIII (Henry VIII)
Henry, Earl of Richmond [Henry VII] (Richard III)
Hermia (A Midsummer Night's Dream)
Hermione (The Winter's Tale)
Hero (Much Ado About Nothing)
Hippolyta (A Midsummer Night's Dream)
Horatio (Hamlet)
Hortensio (The Taming of the Shrew)
Hotspur (1 Henry IV)
Iachimo (Cymbeline)
Iago (Othello)
Imogen (Cymbeline)
Iras (Antony and Cleopatra)
Isabella (Measure for Measure)
Jacques (As You Like It)
Jaquenetta (Love's Labour's Lost)
Jessica (The Merchant of Venice)

CHARACTERS FROM THE PLAYS OF WILLIAM SHAKESPEARE (cont.)

(with plays)

Juliet (Romeo and Juliet, Measure for Measure)
Julius Caesar (Julius Caesar)
Katherina (The Taming of the Shrew)
Katherine (Henry V, Love's Labour's Lost)
Laertes (Hamlet)
Lafew (All's Well That Ends Well)
Laurence, Friar (Romeo and Juliet)
Lavinia (Titus Andronicus)
Lear (King Lear)
Leontes (The Winter's Tale)
Lepidus (Julius Caesar, Antony and Cleopatra)
Longaville (Love's Labour's Lost)
Lorenzo (The Merchant of Venice)
Lucentio (The Taming of the Shrew)
Luciana (The Comedy of Errors)
Lucius (Titus Andronicus)
Lysander (A Midsummer Night's Dream)
Lysimachus (Pericles)
Macbeth (Macbeth)
Macbeth, Lady (Macbeth)
Macduff (Macbeth)
Macduff, Lady (Macbeth)
Malcolm (Macbeth)
Malvolio (Twelfth Night)
Mamillius (The Winter's Tale)
Marcellus (Hamlet)
Margaret (2 Henry VI, 3 Henry VI, Richard III)
Maria (Love's Labour's Lost, Twelfth Night)
Mariana (Measure for Measure, All's Well That Ends Well)
Marina (Pericles)
Mark Antony (Julius Caesar, Antony and Cleopatra)
Martius (Titus Andronicus)
Menenius (Coriolanus)
Mercutio (Romeo and Juliet)
Miranda (The Tempest)
Montague (Romeo and Juliet)
Mortimer (1 Henry IV)
Mutius (Titus Andronicus)
Nerissa (The Merchant of Venice)
Nym (Henry V, The Merry Wives of Windsor)

Oberon (A Midsummer Night's Dream)
Octavia (Antony and Cleopatra)
Octavius, Caesar (Julius Caesar, Antony and Cleopatra)
Oliver (As You Like It)
Olivia (Twelfth Night)
Ophelia (Hamlet)
Orlando (As You Like It)
Orsino (Twelfth Night)
Osric (Hamlet)
Oswald (King Lear)
Othello (Othello)
Pandarus (Troilus and Cressida)
Paris (Troilus and Cressida)
Parolles (All's Well That Ends Well)
Patroclus (Troilus and Cressida)
Paulina (The Winter's Tale)
Percy (1 Henry IV)
Perdita (The Winter's Tale)
Pericles (Pericles)
Peto (2 Henry IV)
Petruchio (The Taming of the Shrew)
Phebe (As You Like It)
Philoten (Pericles)
Pinch (The Comedy of Errors)
Pisanio (Cymbeline)
Pistol (2 Henry IV, Henry V, The Merry Wives of Windsor)
Poins (1 Henry IV, 2 Henry IV)
Polixenes (The Winter's Tale)
Polonius (Hamlet)
Pompey (Measure for Measure, Antony and Cleopatra)
Portia (The Merchant of Venice)
Posthumus (Cymbeline)
Priam (Troilus and Cressida)
Prospero (The Tempest)
Proteus (The Two Gentlemen of Verona)
Puck (A Midsummer Night's Dream)
Quickly, Mistress (1 Henry IV, 2 Henry IV, The Merry Wives of Windsor)
Quince (A Midsummer Night's Dream)
Quintus (Titus Andronicus)
Regan (King Lear)

CHARACTERS FROM THE PLAYS OF WILLIAM SHAKESPEARE (cont.)

(with plays)

Richard II (Richard II)
Richard III (2 Henry VI, 3 Henry VI, Richard III)
Richard, Duke of Gloucester [Richard III] (2 Henry VI, 3 Henry VI, Richard III)
Richmond, Henry, Earl of [Henry VII] (Richard III)
Roderigo (Othello)
Romeo (Romeo and Juliet)
Rosalind (As You Like It)
Rosaline (Love's Labour's Lost)
Rosencrantz (Hamlet)
Rumour (2 Henry IV)
Saturninus (Titus Andronicus)
Scroop (Henry IV)
Sebastian (The Tempest, Twelfth Night)
Shallow, Justice (2 Henry IV, The Merry Wives of Windsor)
Shylock (The Merchant of Venice)
Sicinius (Coriolanus)
Silence (2 Henry IV)
Silvius (As You Like It)
Slender (The Merry Wives of Windsor)
Christopher Sly (The Taming of the Shrew)

Snout (A Midsummer Night's Dream)
Snug (A Midsummer Night's Dream)
Solinus (The Comedy of Errors)
Stephano (The Tempest)
Tamora (Titus Andronicus)
Tearsheet, Doll (2 Henry IV)
Thasia (Pericles)
Theseus (A Midsummer Night's Dream)
Titania (A Midsummer Night's Dream)
Titus (Titus Andronicus)
Touchstone (As You Like It)
Trinculo (The Tempest)
Troilus (Troilus and Cressida)
Tybalt (Romeo and Juliet)
Ulysses (Troilus and Cressida)
Verges (Much Ado About Nothing)
Vincentio (Measure for Measure, The Taming of the Shrew)
Viola (Twelfth Night)
Violenta (All's Well That Ends Well)
Voltimand (Hamlet)
Volumnia (Coriolanus)
William (As You Like It)

RHETORICAL DEVICES

alliteration
anacoluthon
anadiplosis
anaphora
anastrophe
antiphrasis
antistrophe
aporia
antithesis

assonance
catechresis
chiasmus
diacope
enallage
epanalepsis
epanorthosis
epiphora
epistrophe

epizeuxis
hendiadys
hypallage
hyperbaton
hyperbole
hysteron proteron
isocolon
litotes

metaphor
palindrome
paralipsis
periphrasis
polyptoton
prosopopoeia
simile
symploce
trope

THEATRICAL TERMS

above
act
act drop
actor
actor-manager
actress
ad lib
advertisement
  curtain
agent
alienation effect
amphitheatre
anti-masque
apron
arc light
arena
aside
asphaleian
  system
assistant stage
  manager
  (ASM)
audition
auditorium
author's night
backcloth
backing flat
backstage
balcony
barn door
  shutter
barrel
batten
below
benefit
bespeak
  performance
blackout
blocking
blue
boards
boat truck
book
book ceiling
book flat

book wing
boom
border
border light
box office
box set
bridge
bristle trap
built stuff
business
busk
buskin
call
call board
call boy
call door
carpenter's
  scene
carpet cut
carriage-and-
  frame system
catastrophe
catwalk
cauldron trap
ceiling-cloth
cellar
centre stage
chariot-and-
  pole system
chorus
circle
circuit
cloth
clouding
collective
  creation
colour wheel
command
  performance
composite
  setting
corner trap
corsican trap
coryphaeus
cothurnus

counterweight
  system
critic
crush bar
cue
curtain
curtain call
curtain-raiser
curtain set
cut-cloth
cyclorama
designer
detail scenery
deus ex
  machina
deuteragonist
dimmer
diorama
director
diseuse
double take
downstage
drag artist
dramatis
  personae
drapery setting
dress circle
dress rehearsal
dressing room
drop
drum-and-shaft
  system
dumb show
elevator
encore
enter
epilogue
exit
falling flap
fan effect
female
  impersonator
flat
flexible staging
flies

flipper
float
floodlight
flying effect
flyman
follow spot
footlight
footlights trap
formal stage
fox wedge
foyer
fresnel spot
frontcloth
front of house
gaff
gallery
gauze
gel
general utility
ghost glide
glory
GOBO
gods
grave trap
green room
grid
grooves system
ground row
gypsy
halls
ham
hand-props
hand worked
  house
heavy
hoist
house
house light
impresario
improvisation
incidental
  music
inner stage
inset
in the round

THEATRICAL TERMS (cont.)

iris
jackknife stage
jornada
juvenile
knockabout
kuppelhorizont
lanterna magica
lashline
leg
leko
libretto
light batten
light console
lighting
light pipe
limelight
linsenschein-
   werfer
lobsterscope
low comedian
LX
lycopodium
make-up
manager
manet
marionette
mask
masking piece
masque
matinée
mezzanine floor
mime
mise en scéne
multiple setting
mummer
noises off
odeum
off-broadway
off-off-
   broadway
off stage
old man
old woman
olio
on stage

open stage
orchestra
orchestra pit
pageant lantern
panorama
paradiso
parallel
pass door
pepper's ghost
perch
periaktoi
pinspot
pipe
pipe batten
pit
platform
platform stage
playbill
plot sheet
portal opening
producer
profile board
profile spot
projector
prologue
promenade
promenade
   production
prompt book
prompter
prompt side
prop
property
proscenium
   arch
proscenium
   border
proscenium
   doors
protagonist
puppet
quick-change
   room
rain box
rake

reflector
rehearsal
rep
repertory
resting
return
revolving stage
revue
rise-and-sink
rod-puppet
roll ceiling
rope house
rose
rostrum
run
rundhorizont
runway
saddle-iron
safety curtain
sand-cloth
scene
scene dock
scenery
sciopticon
scissor cross
scrim
scruto
sea row
set
set piece
set waters
show portal
sightline
silicon
   controlled
   rectifier
sill iron
simultaneous
   setting
skene
sky border
sky cloth
sky dome
slapstick
slips

slip stage
slote
sock
soubrette
sound effects
spieltreppe
spot bar
spotlight
stage
stage brace
stage cloth
stage crew
stage direction
stage door
stage-door
   keeper
stage lighting
stage manager
   (SM)
stage rake
stage setting
stalls
star trap
stereopticon
stichomythia
stock company
strip light
strobe light
supernumerary
switchboard
synchronous
   winch system
tableau
tabs
tail
teaser
technical
   rehearsal
throwline
thunder run
thundersheet
thyristor
toggle
top drop
tormentor

THEATRICAL TERMS (cont.)

touring
  company
transformation
  scene
transparency
trap
traveller

traverse curtain
tree border
trickwork
tritagonist
truck
tumbler
understudy

unities
upper circle
upstage
utility
valance
vamp trap
visor

wagon stage
walk-on
wardrobe
water rows
wind machine
wings
word rehearsal

LANGUAGES

Abkhazian
Achinese
Afrikaans
Ainu
Akkadian
Akan
Albanian
Aleut
Amharic
Andaman
Anglo-Saxon
Annamese
Arabic
Aramaic
Aranda
Armenian
Assamese
Assyrian
Avar
Aymara
Azerbaijani
Aztec
Babylonian
Bahasa
  Indonesia
Bajau
Balinese

Baluchi
Barotse
Bashkir
Basque
Batak
Beach-la-mar
Beja
Belorussian
Bemba
Bengali
Bihari
Bokmål
Brahui
Breton
Bugis
Bulgarian
Burmese
Buryat or Buriat
Cantonese
Catalan
Chagatai
Chagga
Chaldee or
  Chaldean
Chechen
Cheremiss
Chichewa

Chin
Chinese
Chinook Jargon
Chukchi
Chuvash
Circassian
Congolese
Coptic
Cornish
Creole
Croatian
Czech
Danakil
Dani
Danish
Dinka
Divehi
Duala
Dusun
Dutch
Dyak
Dyula
Dzongkha
Edo
Efik
Egyptian
Elamite

English
Estonian
Etruscan
Ewe
Faeroese
Fan
Fante
Farsi
Fijian
Finnish
Flemish
Fon
Formosan
French
Frisian
Fulah
Fulani
Fulfulde
Ga
Gaelic
Galibi
Galician
Galla
Garo
Gaulish
Ge'ez
Georgian

LANGUAGES (cont.)

German
Gilbertese
Gond
Gothic
Greek
Guarani
Guaycuru
Gujarati
Gurkhali
Gurung
Hausa
Hawaiian
Hebrew
Herero
Himyaritic
Hindi
Hindustani
Hittite
Hmong
Ho
Hottentot
Hungarian
Ibanag
Ibibio
Ibo
Icelandic
Ido
Igbo
Ijo
Ila
Ingush
Inuktitut
Irish
Italian
Japanese
Javanese
Jivaro
Kabardian
Kachin
Kalmuck *or*
  Kalmyk
Kamba
Kanarese
Kannada
Kara-Kalpak

Karamojong
Karelian
Karen
Kashmiri
Kashubian
Kawi
Kazakh
Khalkha
Khasi
Khmer
Kikongo
Kikuyu
Kingwana
Kirundi
Kissi
Kiswahili
Kolami
Komi
Kond
Kongo
Konkani
Kono
Koranko
Korean
Korwa
Koryak
Krio
Kru
Kuki
Kumyk
Kurdish
Kurukh
Kyrgyz *or*
  Kirghiz
Ladino
Lai
Lahnda
Lamba
Lamut
Langobardic
langue d'oc
langue d'oïl
Laotian *or* Lao
Lapp *or* Lappish
Latin

Latvian
Laz
Lepcha
Lesghian
Limbu
Lingala
Lithuanian
Livonian
Loma
Lozi
Luba
Luganda
Lugbara
Lunda
Luo
Lusatian
Lushai
Lycaonian
Lycian
Macedonian
Madurese
Magyar
Malagasy
Malay
Malayalam
Malinke
Maltese
Manchu
Mandarin
Manganja
Manipuri
Manx
Maori
Marathi
Marquesan
Marshallese
Masai
Mende
Messapic
Miao
Mingrelian
Mixtec
Modoc
Mon

Mongol *or*
  Mongolian
Mordvin
Mossi
Motu
Mysian
Naga
Nama
Ndebele
Nenets
Nepali
Newari
Ngbandi
Nguni
Nicobarese
Niuean
Nogay
Norn
Norse
Norwegian
Nuba
Nuer
Nupe
Nyanja
Nyamwezi
Nyasa
Nyoro
Occitan
Oraon
Oriya
Osmanli
Ossetian
Ostyak
Otomi
Ovambo
Pahari
Pahlavi
Palauan
Palaung
Pali
Pampangan
Pangasinan
Panjabi *or*
  Punjabi
Pano

LANGUAGES (cont.)

Pashto	Samburu	Sulu	Tupi
Peguan	Samoan	Sumerian	Turkish
Persian	San	Sundanese	Turkmen
Phoenician	Sandawe	Susu	Tuva
Phrygian	Sango	Swahili	Twi
Pictish	Sanskrit	Swazi	Udmurt
Pintupi	Santali	Swedish	Uduk
Police Motu	Sardinian	Syriac	Ugaritic
Polish	Sasak	Tagalog	Uigur
Portuguese	Sauk	Tahitian	Ukrainian
Prakrit	Scythian	Taino	Urdu
Provençal	Sebei	Taita	Uzbek
Prussian	Senoi	Tajik	Vai
Punic	Sepik	Tamang	Venda
Quechua	Serbian	Tamashek	Venetic
Quiché	Serbo-Croat	Tamil	Veps
Rai	Sesotho	Tatar	Vietnamese
Rajasthani	Setswana	Tehuelche	Vogul
Rajmahali	Shan	Telugu	Volapük
Rarotongan	Shelta	Temne	Wa
Rawang	Sherbro	Teso	Wapishana
Rejang	Shilha	Thai	Warao
Rhaetian	Shilluk	Thracian	Warlpiri
Riff	Shina	Tibetan	Welsh
Riksmål	Siamese	Ticuna	Wendish
Romaic	Sidamo	Tigré	Wolof
Romanes	Sindebele	Tigrinya	Xhosa
Romanian	Sindhi	Tiv	Yaghnobi
Romansch	Sinhalese	Tocharian	Yakut
Romany	Slovak	Toda	Yao
Ronga	Slovene	Tolai	Yenisei
Russian	Sogdian	Tonga	Yiddish
Ruthenian	Somali	Tongan	Yoruba
Rwanda	Songhai	Tshiluba	Yupik
Sabaean	Sorbian	Tsonga	Zande
Sahaptin	Sotho	Tswana	Zulu
Saharan	Spanish	Tulu	Zyrian
Sakai	Suk	Tumbuka	
Samal	Sukuma	Tungus	

ACCENTS AND DIACRITICAL MARKS

acute	háček
breve	hamza
cedilla	macron
circumflex	tilde
diaeresis	umlaut
grave	

PHONETIC ALPHABET

Alpha	November
Bravo	Oscar
Charlie	Papa
Delta	Quebec
Echo	Romeo
Foxtrot	Sierra
Golf	Tango
Hotel	Uniform
India	Victor
Juliet	Whisky
Kilo	X-ray
Lima	Yankee
Mike	Zulu

PUNCTUATION MARKS

accent	inverted
apostrophe	comma
asterisk	obelus
asterism	omission mark
brace	parenthesis
bracket	period
caret	point
colon	printer's mark
comma	question mark
dagger	quotation mark
dash	semicolon
diacritical mark	solidus
ellipsis	square bracket
em dash *or* rule	stop
en dash *or* rule	stroke
exclamation	swung dash
mark	virgule
full stop	
hyphen	

GRAMMATICAL TERMS

ablative	auxiliary verb	copula	disjunct
ablative	binding	countable	distributive
absolute	case	dative	dual
accusative	causative	declension	enclitic
active voice	clause	defective verb	ergative
adjective	cognate	definite article	feminine
adjunct	collective noun	deictic	final clause
adverb	comparative	deixis	finite verb
affix	complement	demonstrative	frequentative
anaphora	conditional	deponent	future perfect
antecedent	conjugation	determiner	future tense
aorist	conjunct	diminutive	gender
aspect	conjunction	direct object	genitive

GRAMMATICAL TERMS (cont.)

gerund
gerundive
govern
government
imperative
imperfect
imperfective
impersonal
  verb
indeclinable
indefinite article
indicative
indicative
indirect object
infinitive
infix
inflect
inflection
instrumental
intensifier
interjection
interrogative
intransitive
  verb
irregular verb

iterative
jussive
locative
main clause
masculine
mass noun
middle voice
modal verb
modifier
mood
negative
neuter
nominative
noun
number
object
objective case
oblique case
optative
paratactic
parataxis
participle
particle
partitive
passive voice

passive voice
past tense
perfective
perfect tense
periphrastic
person
personal
  pronoun
phrasal verb
phrase
pluperfect
plural
possessive
postpositive
predeterminer
predicate
predicate
prefix
preposition
present tense
preterite
proclitic
pronoun
proper noun
reciprocal

reflexive
relative clause
relative
  pronoun
sandhi
sentence
singular
strong verb
subject
subjective case
subjunct
subjunctive
substantive
suffix
superlative
tense
tmesis
transitive verb
uncountable
  noun
verb
vocative
voice
weak verb

BRANCHES OF PHILOSOPHY

aesthetics
analytical philosophy
axiology
bioethics
cosmology
deontology
epistemology
ethics
formal logic
gnosiology
ideology
legal ethics

linguistic philosophy
logic
mathematical
  philosophy
metaethics
metaphysics
metempirics
modal logic
moral philosophy
ontology
phenomenology

philosophy of
  language
philosophy of law
philosophy of
  mathematics
philosophy of mind
philosophy of
  psychology
philosophy of religion
philosophy of science
political philosophy
teleology

SPORTS

SPORTS AND SPORTING ACTIVITIES

aeroball
aerobatics
aikido
airgun shooting
air racing
Alpine climbing
Alpine combined
  event
Alpine skiing
American football or
  gridiron
angling
archery
association football or
  soccer
asymmetric bars
athletics
Australian rules
  football
autocross
badminton
ballooning
bandy
baseball
basketball
beagling
beam
bear baiting
biathlon
big-game fishing
blood sports
bobsleigh racing
bouldering
boules or boccie
bowling

boxing
bullfighting
bunji jumping
caber tossing
Canadian 5-pin
  bowling
Canadian canoe
  racing
Canadian football
canoeing
canoe polo
canoe sailing
canoe slalom racing
canoe sprint racing
carom billiards
caving
clay pigeon shooting
climbing
coarse fishing
cock fighting
coursing
court handball
cricket
croquet
cross bow archery
cross-country skiing
  or Nordic skiing
crown-green bowls
curling
cycle racing
darts
darts cricket
darts football
decathlon
deerstalking

discus
diving
downhill racing
down-the-line
  shooting
drag racing
dressage
English billiards
equestrianism
Eton wall game
falconry
fell running
fencing
ferreting
field archery
field events
field hockey
figure skating
flat-green bowls
flat racing
floor exercises
fly-fishing
football
fox hunting
freefall
free pistol shooting
freestyle skiing
French cricket
Gaelic football
game fishing
giant slalom
gliding
golf
greyhound racing
grouse shooting

SPORTS AND SPORTING ACTIVITIES (cont.)

gymkhana
gymnastics
hammer
handball
hang-gliding
haphido
harness horseracing
heptathlon
high bar *or* horizontal
  bar
high jump
hiking
hillwalking
horizontal bar *or* high
  bar
horseracing
horseshoe pitching
hurdles
hurling
ice climbing
ice-dancing
ice hockey
jai alai *or* pelota
javelin
jet skiing
judo
jujitsu
kabaddi
karate
karting
kayaking
kendo
kenipo
kick boxing
kiting
korfball
kung fu
lacrosse
langlauf
laser sailing
lawn tennis
long-distance running
long jump
luge
marathon

martial arts
match fishing
middle-distance
  running
mink hunting
modern pentathlon
moto-cross
motorcycle racing
motor racing
mountain biking
mountaineering
mountain running
netball
Nordic combined
  event
Nordic skiing *or* cross-
  country skiing
off-piste skiing
offshore yacht racing
Olympic French
  shooting
orienteering
otter hunting
parachuting
paragliding
parallel bars
parascending
pato
pelota *or* jai alai
petanque
pheasant shooting
pigeon racing
pigeon shooting
ping-pong *or* table
  tennis
pistol shooting
point-to-point
pole vault
polo
pommel horse
pool
potholing
powerboat racing
puissance
racquetball

rally cross
rambling
rapid-fire pistol
  shooting
relay racing
rhythmic gymnastics
rifle shooting
rings
rock climbing
rodeo
roller blading
roller derby
roller hockey
roller hockey
roller skating
roller skiing
rough shooting
rounders
rowing
rugby fives
rugby league
rugby union
running game target
  shooting
sailplaning
scrambling
scuba diving
sculling
sea fishing
sepak takrow
sharpshooting
shinty
shooting
short board sailing
short tennis
short-track speed
  skating
shot put
showjumping
sidecar racing
skateboarding
skeet shooting
skibob racing
ski-jumping
ski-mountaineering

SPORTS AND SPORTING ACTIVITIES (cont.)

skittles
skydiving
slalom
sled-dog racing
snooker
snorkelling
snowboarding
soccer *or* association
  football
softball
speedball
speed-skating
speedway
spelunking
sports aerobics
sprint
squash *or* squash
  rackets
steeplechase
stock-car racing

stoolball
super-G
surfing
swimming
synchronized
  swimming
table tennis *or* ping-
  pong
tae kwon do
tang soo do
target archery
team handball
tennis
tenpin bowling
Thai boxing
three-day event
tobogganing
track events
trampolining
trapshooting

triathlon
triple jump
trotting
tug of war
tumbling
underwater diving
vault
volleyball
volleyball
walking
water polo
water sports
weightlifting
white water rafting
wildfowling
wild water racing
windsurfing
winter sports
wrestling
yacht racing

SPORTING TERMS

abseil
ace
advantage
albatross
alley
arabesque
arena
away
back crawl
backhand
back heel
back pass
backstroke
batsman
batter
belay
bell
birdie

blade
blitz
block
bogey
bowler
breaststroke
bully off
bunker
butterfly
by-ball
bye
by-line
cannon
cartwheel
catcher
centre back
centre fielder
centre forward

centre half
chequered flag
chicane
coach
conversion
corner
count
course
court
cover point
cox
crawl
cross bar
cue
curl
dead ball
dead heat
defence

deuce
dive
division
doubles
draw
dribble
drive
drop ball
drop goal
drop kick
drop shot
dummy
dunk
eagle
end
end zone
en rappel
épée

SPORTING TERMS (cont.)

extra cover
extra time
fairway
false start
fault
feint
fielder
field goal
final
flanker back
flick
foil
follow-through
forehand
forward pass
Fosbury flop
foul
frame
free ball
free hit
free kick
freestyle
front crawl
fullback
full time
fumble
give and go
goal
goal attack
goal defence
goal difference
goalkeeper
goal kick
goal line
goal post(s)
goal shooter
halfback
half-time
half volley
handball
handicap
hat trick
heat
high feet
high tackle

home goal
home leg
home run
home straight
infielder
injury time
inside left
inside right
karabiner
kickoff
kiss shot
knockout or k.o.
lap
left back
left centre-back
left defenseman
left fielder
left forward
left half
left hook
left wing
left wing-back
let
linebacker
line-out
linesman
links
lob
man-to-man
  marking
midfield
miscue
nominated ball
nose guard
obstruction
offence
offside
offside trap
onside
on the ropes
out
outfielder
outside left
outside right
overhead kick

own goal or
  o.g.
pacemaker or
  pacer
par
parry
pass
peel off
penalty
penalty corner
penalty flick
penalty kick
penalty shoot-
  out
penalty spot
photo finish
piste
pitcher
pit lane
piton
pit stop
pivot
place kick
playoff
pocket
pole position
possession
post
pot
promotion
prusiking
puck
push
put-in
putt
qualify
quarter
quarterback
quarterfinal
race
racket
rally
rank(ing)
rappel
raquet

referee
regatta
relegation
replay
reserves
return game
right back
right centre-
  back
right
  defenseman
right fielder
right forward
right half
right hook
right wing
right wing-back
ruck
running back
sabre
save
scissors kick
scoop
scrum
scrum half
scrummage
scull
seed
serve
short corner
shortstop
shuttlecock or
  shuttle
sidestroke
silver
slalom
slam dunk
slip-streaming
somersault
spar
speech play
split end
springboard
sprint
stanchion

SPORTING TERMS (cont.)

stand-off half
starting blocks
starting pistol
stoppage time
striker
stroke
substitute
sudden death
sweeper

tackle
tailback
tee off
three quarter
through-ball
throw-in
tight end
time-out
toe-poke

touchdown
touching ball
touchline
try
tuck
uppercut
volley
wide receiver
wildcard

wing
wing attack
wing back
wing defence
wing forward
zonal defence

ATHLETIC EVENTS

biathlon
cross-country run
decathlon
discus
800m race
fell run
1,500m race
50km walk
50m race
5,000m race
400m hurdles
400m race
400m relay
half-marathon
hammer throw
heptathlon

high jump
hurdling
javelin
long-distance race
long jump
marathon
middle-distance race
modern pentathlon
one-mile race
110m hurdles
100m race
pole vault
relay race
shotput
1,600m relay
sprint

steeplechase
10,000m race
tetrathlon
3,000m steeplechase
tossing the caber
triathlon
triple jump
tug-of-war
20km walk
200m race
women's 100m
 hurdles
women's 3,000m race
women's 200m
 hurdles
women's 80m hurdles

GYMNASTIC EVENTS

asymmetric bars
beam
floor exercises
high bar
horse vault
parallel bars
pommel horse

rhythmic gymnastics
rings
side horse vault
sports aerobics
trampolining
tumbling

TROPHIES, AWARDS, AND EVENTS
(with sport)

Admiral's Cup	sailing
African Nations Cup	football
Air Canada Silver Broom	curling
All-England (Wimbledon) Championships	tennis
All-Ireland Championship	Gaelic football, hurling
Alpine Championships	skiing
America's Cup	sailing
Ashes	cricket
Australian Open	tennis
Badminton Horse Trials	equestrian
Boat Race	rowing
British Open Championship	golf, snooker
Camanachd Association Challenge Cup	shinty
Cambridge Blue	
Cheltenham Gold Cup	horse racing
Classics	horse racing
Coca Cola (League) Cup	football
Commonwealth Games	athletics
Cornhill Test	cricket
Davis Cup	tennis
Daytona 500	motor racing
Derby	horse racing
English Greyhound Derby	greyhound racing
European Champions' Cup	football, basketball
European Championships	football
European Cup-Winners' Cup	football
European Super Cup	football
Federation Cup	tennis
FA (Football Association) Challenge Cup	football
FA Charity Shield	football
FIFA (International Federation of Association Football) World Cup	football
Five Nations' Championship	rugby
Football League Championship	football
Football League Cup	football
Formula One Drivers' World Championship	motor racing
French Open	tennis
Full Cap	football, rugby
Gillette Cup	cricket
Golden Boot Award	football
Gorden International Medal	curling
Grand National	greyhound racing
Grand National Steeplechase	horse racing
Grand Prix	motor racing
Grand Slam	tennis

TROPHIES, AWARDS, AND EVENTS (cont.)

(with sport)

Guinness Trophy	tiddlywinks
Harmsworth Trophy	powerboat racing
Henley Royal Regatta	rowing
Highland Games	
IBF (International Boxing Federation) Championships	boxing
Icy Smith Cup	ice hockey
Indianapolis 500 *or* Indy 500	motor racing
International Championship	bowls
International Cross-country Championship	athletics
International Inter-city Industrial Fairs Cup	football
Iroquois Cup	lacrosse
Isle of Man TT	motorcycle racing
Jules Rimet Trophy	football
King George V Gold Cup	equestrian
Kinnaird Cup	fives
Le Mans 24-Hour Race	motor racing
Lombard Rally	motor racing
Lonsdale Belt	boxing
Macrobertson International Shield	croquet
Man of the Match	cricket, football
Marathon	athletics
Middlesex Sevens	rugby union
Milk Race	cycling
Monte Carlo Rally	motor racing
Most Valuable Player	American football, basketball
National Coarse Championship	angling
National Hunt Jockey Championship	horse racing
National Westminster Bank Trophy	cricket
Nordic Championships	skiing
Oaks	horse racing
Olympic Games	
One Thousand Guineas	horse racing
Open Croquet Championship	croquet
Oxford Blue	
Palio	horse racing
PFA (Professional Footballers' Association) Footballer of the year	football
PFA Manager of the Year	football
Premier League Championship	football
Prudential World Cup	cricket
Queen Elizabeth II Cup	equestrian
RAC Tourist Trophy	motor racing

TROPHIES, AWARDS, AND EVENTS (cont.)

(with sport)

Rose Bowl	American football
Royal Hunt Cup	horse racing
Rugby League Challenge Cup	rugby league
St Leger	horse racing
SFA (Scottish Football Association) Cup	football
South American Championship	football
Stanley Cup	ice hockey
Strathcona Cup	curling
Sudirman Cup	badminton
Superbowl	American football
Super Cup	handball
Swaythling Cup	table tennis
Test Series	cricket, rugby union
Tour de France	cycling
Triple Crown	rugby union
Two Thousand Guineas	horse racing
Uber Cup	badminton
UEFA (Union of European Football Associations) Cup	football
Uniroyal World Junior Championships	curling
US Masters	golf
US Open	tennis, golf
US PGA (Professional Golf Association) Championships	golf
Walker Cup	golf
Wightman Cup	sailing
Wimbledon	tennis
Wingfield Skulls	rowing
World Bowl	American football
World Championship	snooker
WBA (World Boxing Association) Championships	boxing
WBC (World Boxing Council) Championships	boxing
World Club Championship	football
World Cup	football
World Masters Championships	darts
World Series	baseball
Yellow Jersey	cycling

STADIUMS AND VENUES

(with main sport)

Aintree	horse racing
Anaheim Stadium, California	baseball
Anfield, Liverpool	football
Ascot	horse racing
Azteca Stadium, Mexico City	Olympics, football
Belfry, The	golf
Belmont Park, Long Island	horse racing
Bernabau Stadium, Madrid	football
Big Four Curling Rink	curling
Brands Hatch	motor racing
Brooklands	motor racing
Caesar's Palace, Las Vegas	boxing
Cardiff Arms Park	rugby union
Celtic Park, Glasgow	football
Central Stadium, Kiev	football
Cleveland Municipal Stadium	baseball
Corporation Stadium, Calicur	cricket
Croke Park, Dublin	Gaelic football, hurling
Crucibal, Sheffield	snooker
Crystal Palace	athletics
Daytona International Speedway	motor racing, motor cycling
Eden Gardens, Calcutta	cricket
Edgbaston	cricket
Epsom Downs	horse racing
Forum, The	gymnastics
Francorchamps, Belgium	motor racing
Goodison Park, Liverpool	football
Hampden Park, Glasgow	football
Headingley	cricket
Heysel Stadium, Brussels	football
Highbury, London	football
Hillsborough, Sheffield	football
Ibrox, Glasgow	football
Lahore	cricket
Landsdowne Road, Dublin	rugby union
Lenin Stadium, Moscow	football
Lords Cricket Ground	cricket
Louisiana Superdome	most sports
Maracana Stadium, Brazil	football
Meadowbank	athletics
Memorial Coliseum, Los Angeles	most sports
Moor Park, Rickmansworth	golf
Munich Olympic Stadium	athletics, football
Murrayfield	rugby union
Newlands, Cape Town	cricket, rugby union

STADIUMS AND VENUES (cont.)

(with main sport)

Newmarket	horse racing
Nou Camp, Barcelona	football
Odsal Stadium, Bradford	rugby league
Old Trafford, Manchester	cricket, football
Olympic Stadium, Berlin	athletics, football
Oval, The	cricket
Royal and Ancient Golf Club of St Andrews	golf
San Siro, Milan	football
Senayan Main Stadium, Jakarta	cricket
Shanghai Stadium	gymnastics
Silverstone	motor racing
Stahov Stadium, Prague	gymnastics
Texas Stadium	most sports
Twickenham	rugby union
Villa Park, Birmingham	football
Wembley Conference Centre	darts
Wembley Stadium	football, rugby
White City	greyhound racing
White Hart Lane, London	football
Wimbledon	tennis
Windsor Park, Belfast	football

UK FOOTBALL CLUBS

Aberdeen	Blackpool	Carlisle United
Airdrieonians	Bolton Wanderers	Celtic
Albion Rovers	Bournemouth	Charlton Athletic
Aldershot	Bradford City	Chelsea
Alloa	Brechin City	Chester City
Arbroath	Brentford	Chesterfield
Ards	Brighton & Hove	Clyde
Arsenal	Albion	Clydebank
Aston Villa	Bristol City	Colchester United
Ayr United	Bristol Rovers	Coventry City
Barnsley	Burnley	Cowdenbeath
Berwick Rangers	Bury	Crewe Alexandra
Birmingham City	Cambridge United	Crusaders
Blackburn Rovers	Cardiff City	Crystal Palace

UK FOOTBALL CLUBS (cont.)

Darlington
Derby County
Doncaster Rovers
Dumbarton
Dundee
Dundee United
Dunfermline Athletic
East Fife
East Stirlingshire
Everton
Exeter City
Falkirk
Forfar Athletic
Fulham
Gillingham
Glenavon
Glentoran
Grimsby Town
Halifax Town
Hamilton Academical
Hartlepool United
Heart of Midlothian
Hereford United
Hibernian
Huddersfield Town
Hull City
Ipswich Town
Kilmarnock
Larne
Leeds United
Leicester City
Leyton Orient
Lincoln City

Linfield
Liverpool
Luton Town
Manchester City
Manchester United
Mansfield Town
Meadowbank Thistle
Middlesbrough
Millwall
Montrose
Morton
Motherwell
Newcastle United
Northampton Town
Norwich City
Nottingham Forest
Notts County
Oldham Athletic
Oxford United
Partick Thistle
Peterborough United
Plymouth Argyle
Portsmouth
Port Vale
Preston North End
Queen of the South
Queen's Park
Queen's Park Rangers
Raith Rovers
Rangers
Reading
Rochdale
Rotherham United

Scarborough
Scunthorpe United
Sheffield United
Sheffield Wednesday
Shrewsbury Town
Southampton
Southend United
Stenhousemuir
Stirling Albion
St Johnstone
St Mirren
Stockport County
Stoke City
Stranraer
Sunderland
Swansea City
Swindon Town
Torquay United
Tottenham Hotspur *or*
  Spurs
Tranmere Rovers
Walsall
Watford
West Bromwich
  Albion
West Ham United
Wigan Athletic
Wimbledon
Wolverhampton
  Wanderers *or*
  Wolves
Wrexham
York City

EUROPEAN FOOTBALL CLUBS

(with country)

AC Milan	Italy	Hansa Rostock	Germany
AEK Athens	Greece	IFK Gothenburg	Sweden
AIK Stockholm	Sweden	Inter Milan	Italy
Ajax	The Netherlands	Internazionale	Italy
Amadora	Portugal	JC Kerkrade	The Netherlands
Anderlecht	Belgium	Juventus	Italy
AS Roma	Italy	Karlsruhe	Germany
Atalanta	Italy	Lazio	Italy
Atlético de		Legia Warsaw	Poland
Bilbao	Spain	Le Havre	France
Atlético de		Lille	France
Madrid	Spain	Lyons	France
Auxerre	France	Marseilles	France
Barcelona	Spain	Metz	France
Bastia	France	Monaco	France
Bayer		Montpellier	France
Leverkusen	Germany	Munich	Germany
Bayern Munich	Germany	Nantes	France
Benfica	Portugal	Napoli	Italy
Boavista	Portugal	Nice	France
Bologna	Italy	Olympiakos	Germany
Bordeaux	France	Panathinaikos	Germany
Borussia		Paris Saint	
Dortmund	Germany	Germain	France
Borussia Mönchen-		Parma	Italy
gladbach	Germany	Perugia	Italy
Braga	Portugal	Piacenza	Italy
Brann Bergen	Germany	Porto	Portugal
Brondby	Denmark	PSV Eindhoven	The Netherlands
Cagliari	Italy	Racing	
Cologne	Germany	Santander	Spain
CSKA Moscow	Russia	Rapid Vienna	Austria
Duisburg	Germany	Real Madrid	Spain
Dynamo Kiev	Ukraine	Real Sociedad	Spain
Ekeren	Belgium	Real Zaragoza	Spain
Español	Spain	RKC Waalwijk	The Netherlands
Farense	Portugal	Royal Antwerp	Belgium
FC Bruges	Belgium	Salzburg	Austria
FC Volendam	The Netherlands	Sampdoria	Italy
Feyenoord	The Netherlands	Setubal	Portugal
Fiorentina	Italy	Sevilla	Spain
Fortuna Sittard	The Netherlands	Slavia Prague	Czech Republic
Galatasaray	Germany	Spartak Moscow	Russia
Hajouk Split	Croatia	Sparta Prague	Czech Republic
Hamburg	Germany	Sporting Gijón	Spain

EUROPEAN FOOTBALL CLUBS (cont.)

(with country)

Sporting Lisbon	Portugal	Valencia	Spain
Standard Liège	Belgium	Verona	Italy
Steaua		VFB Stuttgart	Germany
Bucharest	Romania	Vicenza	Italy
Strasbourg	France	Vitesse	
Tilburg	The Netherlands	Arnhem	The Netherlands
Utrecht	The Netherlands	Werder Bremen	Germany

AMERICAN FOOTBALL TEAMS

Atlanta Falcons
Buffalo Bills
Chicago Bears
Cleveland Browns
Dallas Cowboys
Denver Broncos
Detroit Lions
Green Bay Packers
Houston Oilers
Indianapolis Colts
Kansas City Chiefs
Los Angeles Raiders
Los Angeles Rams
Miami Dolphins
Minnesota Vikings
New England Patriots
New Orleans Saints
New York Giants
New York Jets
Philadelphia Eagles
Phoenix Cardinals
Pittsburgh Steelers
San Diego Chargers
San Francisco 49ers
Seattle Seahawks
Tampa Bay Buccaneers
Washington Redskins

BASEBALL TEAMS

Atlanta Braves
Baltimore Orioles
Boston Red Sox
Brooklyn Dodgers
California Angels
Chicago Cubs
Chicago White Sox
Cincinnati Reds
Cleveland Indians
Detroit Tigers
Kansas City Royals
Los Angeles Dodgers
Milwaukee Braves
Minnesota Twins
New York Giants
New York Mets
New York Yankees
Oakland Athletics
Philadelphia Phillies
Pittsburgh Pirates
St Louis Browns
St Louis Cardinals
San Francisco Giants
Texas Rangers
Toronto Blue Jays
Washington Senators

CRICKETING TERMS AND EXPRESSIONS

all-rounder
bail
batsman *or* batswoman
beamer
body-line
bosie
bouncer
boundary
bowler
bye
century
chinaman
cover
cow-shot
crease
cut
daisy-cutter
deep square leg
duck
fielder
fine leg

flipper
googly
golden duck
gully
hat-trick
hit wicket
hook
how's that! *or* howzat!
innings
in-swinger
late cut
leg before wicket (l.b.w.)
leg bye
leg glance
leg-side fielder
leg slip
leg spin
leg-theory bowling
long hop

long leg
long off
long on
longstop
maiden
mid-off
mid-on
mid-wicket
no-ball
non-striker
offside fielder
off spin
out-swinger
over
overthrow
run
scorer
seamer
shooter
short leg
sight-screen
silly mid-off

silly mid-on
silly point
slips
square cut
square leg
sticky dog
sticky wicket
stonewalling
striker
stumped
sweep
test match
third man
ton
top-spinner
twelfth man
umpire
wicket
wicketkeeper
yorker

GOLFING TERMS

ace
addressing the ball
albatross
backswing
baff
birdie
bisque
blaster
bogey
brassie
bunker
bye
caddie

dead ball
divot
dog-leg hole
dormy
downswing
driver
driving iron
dubbed shot
eagle
fairway
flagstick
follow-through
fore!
forecaddie

green
handicap
hanging ball
hole-high ball
hole in one
iron
lofted shot
mashie iron
midiron
niblick
nineteenth hole
par
pin
pitch and putt

putter
recovery shot
rough
rub of the green
sand shot
sclaff
spot putting
tee
tee off
trap
upswing
water hazard
wedge
wood shot

RUGBY POSITIONS AND ROLES

attacker
back row
back-row forward
ball carrier
blocker
centre
defender
flanker
fly-half
forward
front row
front-row forward
full-back

half-back
hooker
jumper
left centre three-
    quarter
left wing three-quarter
lock (forward)
loose head (prop)
loose forward
number eight
prop (forward)
right centre three-
    quarter

right wing three-
    quarter
scrum half
second row
second-row forward
stand-off half
three-quarter
tight end
tight head (prop)
try scorer
winger
wing forward
wing (three-quarter)

BOXING WEIGHT DIVISIONS

bantamweight
cruiserweight
featherweight
flyweight
heavyweight
junior lightweight
light flyweight

light heavyweight
light middleweight
lightweight
light welterweight
middleweight
welterweight

FENCING TERMS

blade
corps à corps
counterattack
counter-riposte
coupé
cutover
electrical foil

en garde *or* on
    guard
épée
feint
flèche
foil
foil button

foil grip
foil guard
guard
lunge
mask
parry
piste

remise
riposte
running attack
sabre
supination
touch
touché

MISCELLANEOUS

COOKERY TERMS

baking
barbecuing
boiling
braising
broiling
casseroling
charbroiling
coddling
curing
currying
deep-frying
fricasseeing
frying
grilling
marinating
oven-roasting
parboiling
pickling
poaching
pot-roasting
roasting
sautéeing
scrambling
simmering
smoking
spit-roasting
steaming
stewing
stir-frying
toasting

HERBS

angelica
anise
basil
bay leaf
bergamot
borage
camomile
chervil
chicory
chives
comfrey
dill
fennel
fenugreek
lavender
lemon mint
lovage
marjoram
mint
oregano
parsley
peppermint
pot-herb
rosemary
rue
saffron
sage
savory
sesame
sorrel
spearmint
sweet cicely
tarragon
thyme

SPICES

allspice
black pepper
capers
caraway seeds
cardamom
cassia
cayenne pepper
chilli
cinnamon
cloves
coriander
cumin
curcuma
five spices
garam masala
garlic
ginger
ginseng
green pepper
juniper berries
mace
mustard
nutmeg
paprika
pimento
turmeric
vanilla
white pepper

CHEESES

Ami du Chambertin
Beaufort
Bel Paese
blue brie
blue cheese
blue vinney
Boursin
Brie
Caerphilly
Cambozola
Camembert
Cantal
Chaumes
Cheddar
Cheshire
chèvre
Churnton™
Colby
cottage cheese
cream cheese
curd cheese

Danish blue
Derby
Dolcelatte
double Gloucester
Dunlop
Edam
Emmental
feta
fromage frais
Gervais
gjetost
Gloucester
Gorgonzola
Gouda
grana
Gruyère
halloumi
Ilchester
Jarlesburg
Lancashire
Leicester

Liederkranz
Limburger
Liptauer
Livarot
mascarpone
Monterey
Monterey Jack
mozzarella
Neufchâtel
Oka
Parmesan
pecorino
Port Salut
provolone
quark
Reblochon
Red Leicester
Reggiano
ricotta
Romano
Roquefort
Sage Derby

Saint Agur
Sainte Honoré
Saint Nectaire
Samsoe
Stilton
stracchino
Swiss cheese
taleggio
Tillamook
Tilsit
Tomme de Savoie
tvorog
vacherin
Vignotte
Wensleydale
Wiltshire
Windsor
Windsor Red

TYPES OF PASTA

agnolotti
annellini
bigoli
bucatini
cannelloni
capelli
cappelletti
conchiglie
cravattine
ditali
ditalini
ditaloni
farfalle
farfalline
fettucce
fettuccine

fidelini
fusilli
gramigna
lasagne
linguine
lumache
macaroni
manicotti
noodles
orecchiette
paglia e fieno
pappardelle
penne
pipe
ravioli
rigatoni

risoni
rotelle
rotini
spaghetti
spaghettini
spaghettone
stelline
tagliatelle
tagliolini
taglioni
tortellini
tortelloni
tortiglioni
trenette
tuffoloni
vermicelli

BEANS AND PEAS

adzuki bean
bean sprout
black-eyed bean
broad bean
butter-bean
chickpea
flageolet
French bean
garden pea
haricot bean

horse bean
kidney bean
lentil
lima bean
mangetout
mung bean
pea-bean
petit pois
pinto bean
red bean

runner bean
scarlet runner
soya bean
split pea
string bean
sugar pea
sugar snap pea
wax-pod bean

DESSERTS

Apfelstrudel
apple charlotte
apple pie
baked Alaska
baklava
banana split
banoffi pie
bavaroise
Black Forest gateau
blancmange
bread-and-butter
  pudding
Brown Betty
cabinet pudding
cajeta
charlotte russe
Christmas pudding
cobbler
compote
crème caramel
crêpes Suzette
crumble
custard
dairy ice cream
death by chocolate

egg custard
entremets
Eve's pudding
floating island
fool
fresh fruit
fruit cup
fruit flan
fruit salad
granita
ice cream
jam tart
jelly
junket
kissel
Knickerbocker Glory
Mississippi mud pie
mousse
pandowdy
pavlova
peach Melba
plum pudding
rice pudding
roly-poly
semolina

shoofly pie *Am.*
sorbet
soufflé
sponge pudding
spotted dick
spumoni
steamed pudding
stewed fruit
suet pudding
summer pudding
sundae
tapioca
tipsy-cake
tiramisu
treacle tart
trifle
upside-down
  pudding
Viennoise
  [pudding]
water ice
whip (gooseberry
  whip)
yogurt
zabaglione

CAKES

almond cake
angel cake
baba
Bakewell tart
baklava
bannock
Battenburg
brownie
cheesecake
cruller
cupcake
Danish pastry
devil's food
  cake
doughnut

drop scone
Dundee cake
Eccles cake
éclair
fairy cake
flapjack
frangipane
fruit cake
gateau
Genoa cake
gingerbread
hoecake
koeksister
kuchen
ladyfinger

lardy-cake
Madeira cake
madeleine
marble cake
meringue
millefeuille
muffin
pancake
pandowdy
parkin
pavlova
plum cake
pound cake
queen cake
rock cake

scone
seedcake
shortcake
simnel cake
sponge cake
strudel
Swiss roll
teacake
tipsy-cake
torte
upside-down
  cake
Victoria sponge
wedding cake
yule log

WINES AND VARIETIES OF GRAPES

Aleatico
Aligoté
Aloxe-Corton
Alsace
Amontillado
Bandol
Barbaresco
Barbera
Barolo
Barsac
Beaujolais
Beaune
Blanc Fumé
Blanquette de
  Limoux
Bordeaux
Bourgueil
Brouilly
Bual
Bull's Blood
Burgundy
Byrrh

Cabernet Franc
Cabernet
  Sauvignon
Cahors
Campari
Carignan
Cassis
Chablis
Chambolle-
  Musigny
Champagne
Chardonnay
Chassagne-
  Montrachet
Château
  d'Yquem
Château Haut-
  Brion
Château Lafite
Château Latour
Château
  Margaux

Château
  Mouton-
  Rothschild
Chenin Blanc
Chianti
Chinon
Cinsaut
Claret
Colombard
Corton-
  Charlemagne
Côte-Rôtie
Côtes-de-
  Provence
Côtes-du-Rhône
Côtes-du-
  Roussillon
Côtes-du-
  Ventoux
Côtes-du-
  Vivarais
Crémant

Crépy
Crozes-
  Hermitage
Dolcetto
Dubonnet
Entre-Deux-
  Mers
Falerno
Fino
Fitou
Frangy
Fumé Blanc
Furmint
Gaillac
Gamay
Gevrey-
  Chambertin
Gewürztra-
  miner
Gigondas
Graves
Grenache

WINES AND VARIETIES OF GRAPES (cont.)

Grignolino
Grüner Veltliner
Haut Poitou
  Wines
Hermitage
Hock
Kerner
Lacrima Christi
Lambrusco
Madeira
Málaga
Malbec
Malvasia
  Bianca
Mammolo
Mandelaria
Manseng
Manzanilla
Margaux
Marsala
Marsanne
Martini
Médoc
Mercurey
Merlot
Meunier

Meursault
Monbazillac
Montagny
Montepulciano
Montilla
Montlouis
Montrachet
Morey-Saint-
  Denis
Mosel
Moselle
Mourvedre
Müller-Thurgau
Muscadelle
Muscadet
Muscat
Nebbiolo
Nuits-Saint-
  Georges
Orvieto
Pauillac
Pinotage
Pinot Blanc
Pinot Gris
Pinot Noir
Pommard

Port
Pouilly-Fuissé
Pouilly-Fumé
Retsina
Richebourg
Riesling
Rioja
Rivesaltes
Romanée-Conti
Rosé
Saint-Emilion
Saint Estephe
Saint Julien
Sancerre
Sangiovese
Santenay
Saumur
Sauternes
Sauvignon
  Blanc
Savigny-lès-
  Beaune
Sémillon
Sherry
Shiraz or Syrah
Sylvaner

Tavel
Tempranillo
Tocai Friulano
Tokay
Trebbiano
Valençay
Valpolicella
Verdejo
Verdelho
Verdello
Verdicchio
Verduzzo
Vermentino
Vermouth
Vernaccia
Vin de Paille
Vinho Verde
Vin Jaune
Viognier
Volnay
Vosne-
  Romanée
Vouvray
Zinfandel

CHAMPAGNE MEASURES

magnum = 2 bottles
jeroboam = 2 magnums
rehoboam = 3 magnums
methuselah = 4 magnums
salmanazar = 6 magnums
balthazar = 8 magnums
nebuchadnezzar = 10 magnums

BEERS

ale
bitter
bottled beer
brown ale
canned beer
draught beer
ice beer
keg beer
lager
low-alcohol
  beer

lite
mild
pale ale
porter
real ale
steam-brewed
  beer
stout
strong ale

GAMES

Aunt Sally
bagatelle
beetle
bingo
blind man's
  buff
bumble-puppy
catch
cat's cradle
charades
Chinese
  whispers
conkers
consequences
cowboys and
  Indians
crambo
craps
curling
darts
diabolo
dominoes
ducks and
  drakes

dumb crambo
fan-tan
fivestones
follow-my-
  leader
forfeits
fox and geese
grandmother's
  footsteps
hangman
hazard
hide-and-seek
hoopla
hopscotch
hunt the slipper
hunt the
  thimble
I spy
it
jacks
jackstraws
jukskei
keno
kickean

leapfrog
liar dice
lotto
mah-jong
marbles
murder in the
  dark
musical chairs
nim
noughts and
  crosses
pachinko
paintball
pall-mall
pass the parcel
piggy
pig in the
  middle
pinball
pin the tail on
  the donkey
pitch-and-toss
poker dice

postman's
  knock
prison base
quoits
roulette
sardines
shove-
  halfpenny
shovelboard
Simon Says
spillikins
spin the bottle
swy
tag
taw
tick-tack-toe
tiddlywinks
tig
tipcat
trap-ball
twenty
  questions
two-up

BOARD GAMES

backgammon
checkers *Am.*
chess
Chinese chequers
Chinese chess
Cluedo™
draughts
fox and geese
go
gobang
goose

halma
kono
ludo
mancala
merrill
Monopoly™
pachisi
peggotty
Pictionary™
race game
Risk™

salta
Scrabble™
shogi
snakes and ladders
solitaire
steeplechase
Trivial Pursuit™
uckers
wari
wei ch'i

CARD GAMES

all fours
auction
  bridge
baccarat
banker
basset
beggar-my-
  neighbour
belote
bezique
blackjack
Black Maria
blind poker
Boston
brag
bridge
California
  jack
canasta
Canfield
cassino
cheat

chemin de
  fer
cinch
coon-can
comet
cribbage
Dom Pedro
duplicate
  bridge
écarté
euchre
fan-tan
faro
five
  hundred
forty-five
gleek
happy
  families
hearts
high-low
imperial
klaberjass

Klondike
lansquenet
loo
lottery
matrimony
Michigan
monte
muggins
nap
Newmarket
noddy
old maid
ombre
Pam
panguingue
patience
pedro
Pelmanism
penny ante
pinochle
piquet
pitch
poker

pontoon
Pope Joan
primero
quadrille
quinze
red dog
reverse
rouge et
  noir
rubber
  bridge
ruff
rummy
Russian
  Bank
Sancho
  Pedro
scopa
seven-up
sixty-six
skat
skin
slapjack

snap
snip-snap-
  snorum
solitaire
  Am.
speculation
spite and
  malice
strip Jack
  naked
thirty-one
three-card
  monte
tredrille
twenty-five
vingt-et-un
vint
whipper-
  ginny
whist

FABRICS AND FIBRES

acetate
acrylic
alpaca
angora
astrakhan
baize
brocade
brocatelle
buckram
bunting
burlap
calico
cambric
camel hair
Canton crepe

canvas
cashmere
challis
chambray
cheesecloth
chenille
cheviot
chiffon
chinchilla
chino
chintz
coconut
  matting
coir
cord

corduroy
cotton
crepe
crepe-back
  satin
crepe de Chine
crimplene™
crinoline
Dacron™
damask
denim
doeskin
Donegal tweed
drill
duffel

dungaree
faille
felt
flannel
flannelette
gabardine
gauze
Georgette crepe
gingham
gossamer
grenadine
gunny
haircloth
Harris tweed
hemp

FABRICS AND FIBRES (cont.)

herringbone
hessian
hopsack
horsehair
huckaback
jacquard
jean
jersey
jute
lamé
leatherette™
linen
linsey-woolsey
long cloth
Lycra™
Mackinaw *Am.*
mackintosh
madras
Malines
marocain
Marseilles

matting
melton
microfibre
mohair
moire
moleskin
mousseline
muslin
nankeen
netting
nylon
oiled silk
organdie
organza
Orlon™
Paisley
panne velvet
piqué
plaid
plush
polyester

poplin
polyvinyl
   chloride (PVC)
rayon
sackcloth
sailcloth
sarsenet
sateen
satin
say
serge
sharkskin
sheer
shoddy
silk
stammel
stockinet
suede
swansdown
tabaret
tabby

tapestry
tarpaulin
Terylene™
ticking
toile
towelling
tricot
Tricotine
tulle
tweed
twill
velour
velvet
velveteen
vicuña
viscose
webbing
wool
worsted

SEWING TECHNIQUES

appliqué
basting
binding
couching
crocheting
cutwork
darning
drawn-work
embroidery
facing
faggoting

fine-drawing
gathering
laid work
mitring
needlepoint
overcasting
overlocking
oversewing
patchwork
pleating
quilting

ruching
ruffling
scalloping
shirring
smocking
topstitching
tucking
whitework

SEWING STITCHES

backstitch
blanket stitch
blind stitch
buttonhole
  stitch
chain stitch
cross stitch
crow's foot

feather stitch
Florentine stitch
French knot
gros point
hemstitch
herringbone
  stitch
kettle stitch

lazy daisy stitch
lock stitch
needlepoint
overstitch
petit point
running stitch
satin stitch
stay stitch

stem stitch
tack
tailor's tack
tent stitch
topstitch
whip-stitch

KNITTING TERMS

argyle
bawneen (wool)
Berlin (wool)
cable stitch
chain
crochet
double knitting

Fair Isle
fingering (wool)
fisherman
foundation
garter stitch
graft
increase

intarsia
moss stitch
plain stitch
purl stitch
raschel
ribbing
shell-stitch

slip-stitch
stocking stitch
trellis stitch
warp
worsted
yarn

KNOTS

bend
Blackwall hitch
bow
bowknot
bowline
bowline on the
  bight
carrick bend
cat's-paw
clove hitch
diamond knot
Englishman's
  tie
figure-of-eight
  knot

fisherman's
  bend
fisherman's
  knot
granny knot
half hitch
hangman's knot
harness hitch
hawser-bend
Hercules knot
hitch
loop-knot
love-knot
Matthew
  Walker

mesh knot
overhand knot
prusik
reef knot
rolling hitch
round turn and
  two half
  hitches
running
  bowline
running knot
sailor's knot
sheepshank
sheet bend
shroud-knot

slip-knot
square knot
surgeon's knot
thumb knot
timber hitch
true-love knot
Turk's head
wall-knot
wale-knot
water-knot
weaver's knot
Windsor knot

CERAMICS

agate-ware
Arita ware
Berlin ware
bisque
bone china
Castleford ware
Castor ware
champlevé
Chantilly ware
Chelsea
  porcelain
Ch'ing
  porcelain
cloisonné
Coalport
creamware
Crown Derby
Delft
Dresden china

earthenware
eggshell china
faience
fine china
fired porcelain
flatware
hard-paste
hollowware
Imari ware
ironstone
jasper ware
Kakiemon ware
Kutani ware
Limoges
maiolica or
  majolica
Meissen ware
mezza-maiolica
Ming ware

Nabeshima
  ware
Nanking ware
Parian
  porcelain
porcelain
porcelain
  enamel
queen's ware
raku
Rockingham
  ware
Royal Doulton
Royal
  Worcester
salt-glaze
Satsuma
  porcelain
semi-porcelain

Seto ware
Sèvres
soft-paste
  porcelain
Spode ware
stone china
stoneware
Staffordshire
  ware
Sung ware
Talavera ware
Tang ware
Ting ware
Toft ware
Vincennes ware
Wedgwood
Worcester

TYPES AND STYLES OF FURNITURE

Bauhaus
bentwood
bombé
boulle
cabriole
Chippendale

Duncan Phyfe
Empire
Gothic Revival
Hepplewhite
inlaid
Jacobean

Louis Quatorze
Louis Quinze
Louis Seize
Louis Treize
Queen Anne
Regency

reproduction
rustic
Scandinavian
Shaker
Sheraton

GEMSTONES AND SEMI-PRECIOUS STONES

agate
almandine
amber
amethyst
aquamarine
bloodstone
cairngorm

carbuncle
carnelian
cat's-eye
chalcedony
corundum
diamond
emerald

fire-opal
garnet
hawk's-eye
hyacinth
jade
jasper
lapis lazuli

moss agate
greenstone
onyx
opal
plasma
ruby
sapphire

sardonyx
topaz
tourmaline
turquoise
zircon

COLOURS

amber	cerulean	green	olive	saffron
apricot	cherry	grey	opal	salmon
aquamarine	chestnut	hazel	orange	sapphire
auburn	chocolate	indigo	peach	scarlet
azure	cinnamon	iris	pea green	sea green
beige	claret	ivory	pearl	sepia
black	cobalt	jade	pink	silver
blue	copper	jet	powder	sky blue
bottle green	coral	khaki	blue	tan
bronze	cream	lavender	primrose	tawny
brown	crimson	lemon	puce	Titian red
buff	cyan	lime green	purple	topaz
burgundy	dun	magenta	raven	turquoise
burnt ochre	ebony	mahogany	red	ultramarine
burnt	ecru	maroon	rose	umber
sienna	emerald	mauve	royal blue	vermilion
burnt	fawn	mushroom	ruby	violet
umber	fuchsia	mustard	russet	viridian
camel	ginger	navy	rust	white
caramel	gold	ochre	sable	yellow

BIRTHSTONES
(with dates)

garnet	Jan.
amethyst	Feb.
bloodstone	Mar.
diamond	Apr.
emerald	May
pearl	June
ruby	July
sardonyx	Aug.
sapphire	Sept.
opal	Oct.
topaz	Nov.
turquoise	Dec.

SIGNS OF THE ZODIAC
(with dates)

Aries	Mar. 21 – Apr. 19
Taurus	Apr. 20 – May 20
Gemini	May 21 – June 21
Cancer	June 22 – July 22
Leo	July 23 – Aug. 22
Virgo	Aug. 23 – Sept. 22
Libra	Sept. 23 – Oct. 23
Scorpio	Oct. 24 – Nov. 21
Sagittarius	Nov. 22 – Dec. 21
Capricorn	Dec. 22 – Jan. 19
Aquarius	Jan. 20 – Feb. 18
Pisces	Feb. 19 – Mar. 20

WEDDING ANNIVERSARIES

paper	1st	pottery or		china	20th
cotton	2nd	willow	9th	silver	25th
leather	3rd	tin or		pearl	30th
fruit or flowers	4th	aluminium	10th	coral	35th
wood	5th	steel	11th	ruby	40th
iron	6th	silk or linen	12th	sapphire	45th
wool or copper	7th	lace	13th	gold	50th
bronze or		ivory	14th	emerald	55th
pottery	8th	crystal	15th	diamond	60th

GIRLS' NAMES

Abanya	Alana	Alison	Aneira	Anstey
Abbie	Alanna	Alix	Angel	Anstice
Abby	Alannah	Allegra	Angela	Anthea
Abigail	Alberta	Allie	Angelica	Antoine
Ada	Albertina	Allison	Angelina	Antoinette
Adela	Albertine	Ally	Angeline	Antonia
Adelaide	Albina	Alma	Angelique	Antonina
Adele	Albinia	Aloysia	Angharad	Anwen
Adeline	Albreda	Alphonsina	Angie	Anya
Adina	Alda	Althea	Anis	Anyetta
Adriana	Aldith	Alva	Anita	Aphra
Adrianne	Aldreda	Alvie	Ann	Apollonia
Adrienne	Aledwen	Alvina	Anna	Appolina
Agatha	Alethea	Amalia	Annabel	April
Aggie	Aletta	Amalie	Annabella	Arabella
Agnes	Alex	Amanda	Annabelle	Araminta
Agneta	Alexa	Amaryllis	Annalisa	Aramintha
Agnetha	Alexandra	Amata	Annaple	Ariadne
Aileen	Alexandria	Amber	Anne	Ariane
Ailsa	Alexandrina	Amelia	Anneliese	Arianna
Aimee	Alexia	Amicia	Annette	Arlene
Aine	Alexis	Amina	Annice	Arletta
Ainsley	Alfreda	Aminta	Annie	Arline
Ainslie	Ali	Amy	Annika	Armina
Aisha	Alia	Anaïs	Annis	Artemisia
Aisling	Alice	Anastasia	Annora	Ashley
Aislinn	Alicia	Andie	Anona	Asma
Aithne	Alina	Andrea	Anouska	Aspasia
Alabama	Aline	Andrée	Anselma	Astra

GIRLS' NAMES (cont.)

Astrid	Bernadette	Brenda	Carole	Charmian
Athena	Bernadina	Bride	Carolina	Chattie
Athene	Bernardina	Bridget	Caroline	Cher
Audra	Bernardotte	Bridie	Carolyn	Cherelle
Audrey	Bernice	Brighid	Carrie	Cherie
Augusta	Bernie	Brigid	Cary	Cherry
Augustina	Berny	Brigit	Caryl	Cheryl
Aurea	Berry	Brigitta	Carys	Chloe
Aurelia	Berta	Brigitte	Casey	Chris
Aureole	Bertha	Briony	Cass	Chrissie
Auriel	Beryl	Brita	Cassandra	Chrissy
Aurora	Bess	Britannia	Cassie	Christa
Ava	Bessie	Britt	Cat	Christabel
Aveline	Bessy	Brona	Cath	Christian
Averil	Beta	Bronwen	Catharine	Christiana
Avice	Beth	Bronwyn	Catherine	Christiania
Avis	Bethan	Brunetta	Cathleen	Christie
Avril	Bethany	Bryony	Cathy	Christina
Ayesha	Bethia	Caitlin	Catrin	Christine
Aziza	Betsy	Cal	Catrina	Christmas
Bab	Bette	Cameron	Catriona	Christy
Babette	Bettina	Camilla	Caz	Ciara
Babs	Bettrys	Camille	Cecile	Cicely
Barbara	Betty	Candace	Cecilia	Cilla
Barbie	Beulah	Candice	Cecilie	Cinderella
Barbra	Beverley	Candida	Cecily	Cindy
Basma	Beverly	Candy	Ceinwen	Cis
Bathsheba	Bianca	Canice	Celeste	Ciss
Bea	Biddy	Caprice	Celestina	Cissie
Beata	Billie	Cara	Celestine	Cissy
Beatrice	Bina	Carey	Celia	Claire
Beatrix	Birdie	Carina	Celina	Clara
Beattie	Birgit	Carita	Celine	Clarabel
Beatty	Birgitta	Carla	Ceri	Clare
Bebe	Blanch	Carleen	Ceridwen	Claribel
Becky	Blanche	Carlene	Cerys	Clarice
Bedelia	Blodwen	Carlotta	Charis	Clarinda
Bee	Blodyn	Carly	Charissa	Clarissa
Bel	Blossom	Carlyn	Charity	Claudette
Belinda	Blythe	Carmel	Charlene	Claudia
Bell	Bobbie	Carmela	Charley	Claudine
Bella	Bonita	Carmelita	Charlie	Clem
Belle	Bonnie	Carmen	Charlotte	Clemence
Benita	Bonny	Carol	Charmaine	Clemency
Berenice	Branwen	Carola	Charmanay	Clementia

GIRLS' NAMES (cont.)

Clementina	Davida	Donna	Elined	Esmeralda
Clementine	Davina	Dora	Elinor	Estella
Cleo	Davinia	Dorcas	Elisabeth	Estelle
Cleopatra	Dawn	Doreen	Elise	Esther
Clodagh	Deanna	Dorette	Elisha	Ethel
Clotilda	Deanne	Doria	Elissa	Etheldreda
Colette	Deb	Dorice	Eliza	Ethelinda
Colina	Debbie	Dorinda	Elizabeth	Ethne
Colleen	Deborah	Doris	Ella	Etta
Columbina	Debra	Dorita	Elle	Ettie
Columbine	Dede	Dorothea	Ellen	Etty
Concepta	Dee	Dorothy	Ellie	Eudora
Concetta	Deirdre	Dorrie	Elma	Eugenia
Connie	Delia	Dot	Eloisa	Eugenie
Constance	Delilah	Dottie	Eloise	Eulalia
Constancy	Della	Dreda	Elroy	Eulalie
Constantia	Delma	Dulcie	Elsa	Eunice
Cora	Delphine	Dymphna	Elsie	Euphemia
Coral	Delwen	Dympna	Elspeth	Eustacia
Coralie	Delwyn	Eartha	Elspie	Eva
Cordelia	Delyth	Easter	Eluned	Evadne
Corinna	Demelza	Eda	Elvie	Evangelina
Corinne	Denise	Eden	Elvina	Evangeline
Cornelia	Dennie	Edie	Elvira	Eve
Courtenay	Dervla	Edina	Em	Evelina
Courteney	Deryn	Edith	Emanuela	Eveline
Courtney	Desdemona	Edna	Emeline	Evelyn
Cressida	Desiree	Edwina	Emelyn	Evie
Crystal	Di	Effie	Emerald	Evita
Cynthia	Diamond	Eileen	Emilia	Evonne
Cytherea	Diana	Eiluned	Emily	Fabiana
Daff	Diane	Eilwen	Emma	Faith
Dagmar	Dianne	Eily	Emmanuela	Fan
Daisy	Dilys	Eira	Emmeline	Fanny
Dale	Dina	Eirian	Emmie	Farah
Damaris	Dinah	Eithne	Ena	Faron
Dana	Dione	Elain	Enid	Farran
Dani	Dionne	Elaine	Erica	Farren
Danette	Dionysia	Eldreda	Erika	Fatima
Daniella	Dodie	Eleanor	Erin	Faustina
Danielle	Doll	Eleanora	Ermintrude	Fay
Daph	Dolly	Elena	Ermyntrude	Faye
Daphne	Dolores	Eleonora	Ernestine	Felicia
Darcy	Dominica	Elfreda	Eryl	Felicity
Darlene	Dominique	Elfrida	Esme	Fenella

GIRLS' NAMES (cont.)

Fern	Garnet	Gracie	Héloïse	Inez
Ffyona	Gay	Grainne	Hennie	Ingeborg
Fidelia	Gaye	Grania	Henny	Ingrid
Fifi	Gayle	Greta	Henrietta	Iola
Finola	Gaynor	Gretchen	Henriette	Iolanthe
Fiona	Gemma	Gretel	Hepsie	Iona
Fionnghuala	Genevieve	Griselda	Hepzibah	Irene
Fionnuala	Genevra	Grizel	Hermia	Iris
Flavia	Georgette	Grizzel	Hermione	Irma
Fleur	Georgia	Guendolen	Hester	Isa
Flo	Georgiana	Guinevere	Hetty	Isabel
Flora	Georgie	Gusta	Heulwen	Isabella
Florence	Georgina	Gwen	Hilary	Isabelle
Floretta	Geraldine	Gwenda	Hilda	Isadora
Flossie	Gerda	Gwendolen	Hildegard	Iseult
Flower	Germaine	Gwendoline	Hildegarde	Ishbel
Floy	Gerry	Gwendolyn	Hillary	Isla
Fortune	Gertie	Gwenllian	Hippolyta	Ismay
Foster	Gertrude	Gwyn	Holly	Isobel
Fran	Ghislaine	Gwynedd	Honora	Isolde
Franca	Gilberta	Gwyneth	Honoria	Ita
Frances	Gilbertine	Gwynneth	Hope	Ivah
Francesca	Gilda	Hadassah	Horatia	Ivy
Francie	Gill	Hagar	Horry	Jacinta
Francine	Gillian	Haidee	Hortense	Jacintha
Francisca	Gina	Halcyon	Hortensia	Jackie
Frankie	Ginette	Hannah	Howard	Jacky
Frannie	Ginevra	Harriet	Hulda	Jacoba
Franny	Ginger	Harriette	Huldah	Jacobina
Freda	Ginny	Hasna	Hyacinth	Jacqueline
Frederica	Gisela	Hattie	Hyacintha	Jacquelyn
Frederika	Giselle	Hatty	Hylda	Jacquetta
Fredrica	Giulielma	Haya	Hypatia	Jacqui
Fredrika	Gladys	Hayley	Ianthe	Jade
Freya	Glenda	Hazel	Ida	Jael
Frieda	Glenis	Heather	Idonea	Jan
Gabbie	Glenna	Hebe	Ilma	Jancis
Gabby	Glenys	Hedda	Ilona	Jane
Gabi	Glinys	Hedwig	Ilse	Janet
Gabriella	Gloria	Hedy	Iman	Janetta
Gabrielle	Glory	Heidi	Imani	Janette
Gaby	Glynis	Helen	Immy	Janey
Gaenor	Golda	Helena	Imogen	Janice
Gail	Goldie	Helene	Ina	Janie
Gale	Grace	Helga	Indira	Janine

GIRLS' NAMES (cont.)

Janis	Josepha	Keren	Laverne	Lily
Jansis	Josephine	Keri	Lavina	Lina
Jasmine	Josette	Kerri	Lavinia	Linda
Jay	Josie	Kerrie	Lea	Lindsay
Jayleen	Joss	Kerris	Leah	Lindsey
Jayne	Joy	Kerry	Leanne	Lindy
Jean	Joyce	Keturah	Lee	Linette
Jeanette	Juanita	Kezia	Leigh	Linnet
Jeanie	Judi	Keziah	Leila	Lisa
Jeanne	Judith	Khaleda	Leilah	Lisbeth
Jeannette	Judoc	Kim	Lela	Lise
Jeannie	Judy	Kimberley	Lena	Lisette
Jeannine	Julia	Kimberly	Lennie	Lita
Jemima	Juliana	Kirby	Lenny	Liz
Jemma	Julianne	Kirsten	Lenore	Liza
Jen	Julie	Kirsty	Leona	Lizanne
Jenifer	Julienne	Kit	Leonie	Lizbeth
Jenna	Juliet	Kitty	Leonora	Lizzie
Jennie	Juliette	Kristen	Les	Lizzy
Jennifer	Julitta	Kristin	Lesley	Llinos
Jenny	June	Kristina	Lesli	Lois
Jessamine	Justina	Kristine	Leslie	Lola
Jessamyn	Justine	Kula	Leta	Lolita
Jessica	Kara	Kylie	Letitia	Lolly
Jessie	Karen	Laetitia	Lettice	Lora
Jewel	Karin	Lalage	Lettie	Loraine
Jill	Karina	Lalla	Letty	Loreen
Jillian	Kate	Lana	Liana	Loren
Jinny	Kath	Laraine	Lianne	Loretta
Jo	Katharine	Larissa	Libby	Lorette
Joan	Katherine	Larraine	Liddy	Lori
Joanna	Kathleen	Laura	Liesel	Lorinda
Joanne	Kathryn	Lauraine	Liesl	Lorn
Jocasta	Kathy	Laureen	Lil	Lorna
Jocelyn	Katie	Laurel	Lila	Lorraine
Jodi	Katrina	Lauren	Lilac	Lottie
Jodie	Katrine	Laurencia	Lili	Lotty
Jody	Katy	Laurentia	Lilian	Lou
Johanna	Kay	Lauretta	Lilias	Louella
Joleen	Kaz	Laurette	Lilith	Louisa
Jolene	Keeley	Lauri	Lilla	Louise
Joni	Kelda	Laurie	Lillah	Lu
Jonquil	Kellie	Laurina	Lillian	Lucasta
Jonti	Kelly	Laurinda	Lillias	Luce
Joscelin	Kendra	Lavena	Lillie	Lucetta

GIRLS' NAMES (cont.)

Lucette	Mair	Marla	Mélisande	Modesty
Lucia	Maire	Marlene	Melissa	Moira
Luciana	Mairin	Marlin	Melloney	Moll
Lucie	Maisie	Marlyn	Melodie	Molly
Lucille	Malvina	Marni	Melody	Mona
Lucina	Mamie	Marnie	Melva	Monica
Lucinda	Mandy	Marsha	Melvina	Monique
Lucky	Manuela	Marta	Mercedes	Morag
Lucrece	Mara	Martha	Mercia	Morna
Lucretia	Marah	Marti	Mercy	Morwenna
Lucrezia	Marcella	Martie	Meredith	Moyna
Lucy	Marcelle	Martina	Meriel	Moyra
Luella	Marcia	Martine	Merilyn	Muna
Lulu	Marcie	Marty	Merle	Muriel
Lydia	Marcy	Mary	Merrilyn	Myfanwy
Lyn	Margaret	Maryam	Merrion	Myra
Lynda	Margareta	Matilda	Merry	Myrna
Lynette	Margaretta	Mattie	Meryl	Myrtilla
Lynn	Margarita	Matty	Meta	Myrtle
Lynne	Margarita	Maud	Mia	Mysie
Lynnette	Marge	Maude	Michaela	Nadia
Lynzi	Margie	Maudie	Michele	Nadine
Lyra	Margo	Maura	Michelle	Nahum
Mabel	Margot	Maureen	Milborough	Nan
Mabelle	Marguerita	Mavis	Mildred	Nance
Mable	Marguerite	Maxine	Millicent	Nancy
Maddie	Maria	May	Millie	Nanette
Maddy	Mariabella	Meave	Milly	Nanny
Madeleine	Mariam	Meg	Mima	Naomi
Madelina	Mariamne	Megan	Mimi	Natalia
Madeline	Marian	Meggie	Mina	Natalie
Madge	Marianne	Meggy	Minerva	Natasha
Madonna	Marie	Meghan	Minna	Nawal
Mae	Mariel	Mehala	Minnie	Nell
Maeve	Marietta	Mehalah	Minty	Nellie
Magda	Mariette	Mehalia	Mira	Nelly
Magdalen	Marigold	Mehetabel	Mirabel	Nerina
Magdalena	Marika	Mehitabel	Mirabella	Nerissa
Magdalene	Marilyn	Meirion	Mirabelle	Nerys
Maggie	Marina	Mel	Miranda	Nessa
Magnolia	Marion	Melania	Miriam	Nessie
Mahala	Marisa	Melanie	Mirvat	Nesta
Mahalah	Marissa	Melba	Miryam	Netta
Mahalia	Marita	Melicent	Mitzi	Nettie
Maidie	Marjorie	Melinda	Mo	Neva

GIRLS' NAMES (cont.)

Nichola	Ozzy	Phyllis	Rhonwen	Rosina
Nicky	Pam	Pia	Ria	Rosita
Nicola	Pamela	Pippa	Rica	Roslyn
Nicole	Pamelia	Poll	Ricarda	Rowan
Nicolette	Pandita	Polly	Richmal	Rowena
Nikki	Pandora	Pollyanna	Rika	Roxana
Nina	Pansy	Poppy	Rina	Roxane
Ninette	Pascale	Portia	Rita	Roxanna
Nita	Pat	Primrose	Roberta	Roxanne
Noele	Patience	Prisca	Robina	Roxy
Noeleen	Patricia	Priscilla	Robyn	Ruby
Noeline	Patsy	Prudence	Rochelle	Ruth
Noelle	Patti	Prue	Roisin	Ruthie
Nola	Pattie	Prunella	Roma	Sabina
Nona	Patty	Queena	Romaine	Sabrina
Nora	Paula	Queenie	Rona	Sadie
Norah	Paulette	Queeny	Ronalda	Saffron
Noreen	Pauline	Rachael	Ronna	Sal
Norma	Peace	Rachel	Ronnette	Salena
Nova	Pearl	Rae	Ros	Salina
Nuala	Peg	Raelene	Rosa	Sally
Nyree	Peggy	Rafaela	Rosabel	Salome
Octavia	Pen	Raina	Rosabella	Sam
Odette	Penelope	Raine	Rosabelle	Samantha
Odile	Penny	Raiyah	Rosaleen	Sammy
Odilia	Pepita	Ramani	Rosalia	Sanchia
Oenone	Perdita	Ramona	Rosalie	Sandie
Olga	Peronel	Raphaela	Rosalind	Sandra
Olive	Perpetua	Raquel	Rosalinda	Sandy
Olivet	Peta	Raymonde	Rosaline	Sara
Olivia	Petra	Rebecca	Rosalyn	Sarah
Ollie	Petrina	Rebekah	Rosamond	Saranna
Olwen	Petronella	Regina	Rosamund	Sarina
Olwyn	Petronilla	Reine	Rosanna	Sarita
Olympia	Petula	Rena	Rosanne	Sarra
Ona	Phebe	Renata	Rose	Scarlet
Oona	Phemie	Rene	Roseann	Scarlett
Oonagh	Phil	Renée	Roseanna	Seana
Opal	Philippa	Renie	Roseanne	Selena
Ophelia	Phillida	Rhea	Roseline	Selina
Oriana	Phillipa	Rhian	Roselyn	Selma
Oriel	Phillippa	Rhiannon	Rosemarie	Senga
Ottilia	Philomena	Rhoda	Rosemary	Septima
Ottilie	Phoebe	Rhona	Rosetta	Seraphina
Owena	Phyllida	Rhonda	Rosie	Serena

GIRLS' NAMES (cont.)

Shani	Sophia	Terry	Trudy	Vivienne
Shannon	Sophie	Tess	Ulrica	Walburga
Shari	Sophronia	Tessa	Ulrika	Wallis
Sharon	Sorcha	Tessie	Una	Wanda
Sharron	Stacey	Thea	Unity	Wendy
Shauna	Stacy	Thelma	Ursula	Wilfreda
Shaz	Stefanie	Theodora	Val	Wilfrida
Sheba	Stella	Theodosia	Valda	Wilhelmina
Sheelagh	Stephanie	Theophania	Valentina	Willa
Sheena	Stevie	Theophila	Valentine	Williamina
Sheila	Sue	Theresa	Valerie	Wilma
Sheilah	Sukey	Thérèse	Vanessa	Win
Shelagh	Susan	Theresia	Vashti	Winefred
Shelley	Susanna	Thirsa	Velda	Winifred
Shelly	Susannah	Thirza	Velma	Winnie
Shena	Susanne	Thomasina	Venetia	Winnifred
Sherri	Susie	Thomasine	Venus	Wynn
Sherry	Suzanna	Thora	Vera	Wynne
Sheryl	Suzanne	Thyone	Verena	Xanthe
Shirl	Suzette	Thyra	Verity	Xenia
Shirley	Suzy	Tibby	Verna	Yasmin
Shona	Sybella	Tiffany	Verona	Yolanda
Sian	Sybil	Tilda	Veronica	Yvette
Sibbie	Sybilla	Tilly	Véronique	Yvonne
Sibby	Sylvia	Timothea	Vi	Zana
Sibella	Sylvie	Tina	Vicki	Zandra
Sibilla	Tabitha	Tirzah	Vicky	Zara
Sibyl	Talitha	Tisha	Victoria	Zarina
Sibylla	Tallulah	Toni	Victorine	Zein
Sidonia	Tamar	Tonia	Vikki	Zelda
Sidony	Tamara	Tonya	Vilma	Zelma
Síle	Tamasine	Topsy	Vina	Zena
Silvana	Tammy	Toru	Vinny	Zenobia
Silvia	Tamsin	Totty	Viola	Zillah
Simona	Tania	Tracey	Violet	Zinnia
Simone	Tanith	Tracy	Violetta	Zita
Síne	Tansy	Tricia	Violette	Zoë
Sinead	Tanya	Trina	Virginia	Zohra
Siobhan	Tara	Tris	Vita	Zola
Siri	Tatiana	Trisha	Viv	Zora
Sisley	Tegan	Trissie	Viva	Zorah
Sissy	Tegwen	Trix	Vivia	Zoulika
Sonia	Temperance	Trixie	Vivian	Zuleika
Sonja	Teresa	Trudi	Viviana	
Sonya	Terri	Trudie	Vivien	

BOYS' NAMES

Aaron	Aled	Angel	Austen	Bernard
Abdul	Alex	Angelo	Austin	Bernardo
Abdullah	Alexander	Angus	Avery	Bernhard
Abe	Alexis	Ansel	Axel	Bernie
Abel	Alf	Ansell	Aylmer	Berny
Abner	Alfie	Anselm	Aylwin	Bert
Abraham	Alfonso	Anthony	Azariah	Berthold
Abram	Alfred	Anton	Baldwin	Bertie
Adair	Alger	Antonio	Balthasar	Bertram
Adal	Algernon	Antony	Balthazar	Bertrand
Adam	Algie	Anwar	Barclay	Bethel
Adamnan	Algy	Aquila	Barnabas	Beverley
Adamu	Ali	Archelaus	Barnaby	Bevis
Adolf	Alick	Archer	Barnard	Bez
Adolph	Alistair	Archibald	Barnet	Bill
Adolphe	Allan	Archie	Barney	Billie
Adolphus	Allen	Archy	Baron	Billy
Adrian	Allistair	Armand	Barrett	Bing
Aeneas	Allister	Armando	Barrie	Bjorn
Ahmad	Alonzo	Armin	Barrington	Blaine
Ahmed	Aloysius	Arnaud	Barron	Blair
Aidan	Alphonse	Arnie	Barry	Blaise
Ainsley	Alphonso	Arnold	Bart	Blake
Ainslie	Alphonsus	Art	Barthol-	Blane
Ajay	Alun	Artemas	omew	Blase
Al	Alured	Artemus	Bas	Boaz
Alain	Alvah	Arthur	Basie	Bob
Alan	Alvar	Artie	Basil	Bobbie
Alaric	Alvie	Arturo	Bastian	Bobby
Alasdair	Alvin	Arty	Bat	Bonar
Alastair	Alvis	Asa	Baz	Boniface
Alban	Alwyn	Asher	Beau	Boris
Albany	Amadou	Ashley	Ben	Botolf
Alberic	Ambrose	Assim	Benedick	Botolph
Albert	Amos	Athelstan	Benedict	Botulf
Alden	Amyas	Athol	Benet	Boyce
Aldhelm	Ananda	Atom	Benito	Boyd
Aldis	Anatoly	Auberon	Benjamin	Brad
Aldo	Ancel	Aubert	Benji	Bradley
Aldous	André	Aubrey	Bennet	Bram
Aldred	Andreas	August	Bennett	Bramwell
Aldus	Andrew	Augustin	Benny	Brandan
Aldwin	Andy	Augustine	Bentley	Brandon
Aldwyn	Aneirin	Augustus	Berenger	Brendan
Alec	Aneurin	Aulay	Berkeley	Brent

BOYS' NAMES (cont.)

Bret, Brett, Brian, Brice, Brock, Broderick, Bruce, Bruno, Bryan, Bryce, Bryn, Bud, Burt, Buster, Byron, Cadel, Cadell, Cadwallader, Caesar, Cai, Caius, Cal, Caleb, Callum, Calum, Calvin, Cameron, Camillus, Campbell, Caractacus, Caradoc, Caradog, Carey, Carl, Carleton, Carlo, Carlos, Carlton, Carol, Carolus, Carter, Cary, Casey, Caspar

Cassim, Cecil, Cedric, Cedrych, Cerdic, Ceri, Chad, Chandler, Charles, Charley, Charlie, Charlton, Chas, Chauncey, Chauncy, Chay, Chester, Chris, Christian, Christie, Christmas, Christopher, Christy, Chrystal, Chuck, Ciaran, Clarence, Clark, Claud, Claude, Claudius, Clayton, Cledwyn, Clem, Clement, Cliff, Clifford, Clifton, Clint, Clinton, Clive, Clyde, Clym, Cole, Colin

Colley, Colm, Colum, Columba, Conan, Conn, Connor, Conor, Conrad, Constant, Constantine, Cormac, Cornelius, Corney, Cosimo, Cosmo, Courtenay, Courtney, Craig, Crispian, Crispin, Crystal, Cuddie, Cuddy, Curt, Curtis, Cuthbert, Cy, Cyprian, Cyril, Cyrus, Dafydd, Dai, Dale, Damian, Damien, Damon, Dan, Daniel, Danny, Dante, Darby, Darcy, Darrel, Darrell

Darren, Darryl, Daryl, Dave, David, Davy, Dean, Declan, Dee, Del, Delbert, Delroy, Den, Denholm, Denis, Dennis, Denny, Denys, Denzil, Derby, Derek, Dermot, Derrick, Derry, Deryck, Deryk, Des, Desmond, Dewi, Dexter, Diarmait, Diarmid, Diarmuid, Dick, Dickie, Dickon, Dicky, Digby, Diggory, Dillon, Dion, Dionysius, Dirk, Dominic, Dominick

Don, Donal, Donald, Donny, Donovan, Doran, Dorian, Doug, Dougal, Dougie, Douglas, Drew, Drogo, Duane, Dud, Dudley, Dugald, Duggie, Duke, Duncan, Dunstan, Durand, Dustin, Dwayne, Dwight, Dylan, Eamon, Eamonn, Earl, Earnest, Eben, Ebenezer, Ed, Eddie, Eddy, Eden, Edgar, Edmond, Edmund, Edom, Edward, Edwin, Edwyn, Egbert, Eldon

BOYS' NAMES (cont.)

Eldred	Evelyn	Gaius	Goldwyn	Harley
Eleazar	Everard	Gamaliel	Gordon	Harold
Eli	Ewan	Gareth	Graeme	Haroun
Elias	Ewen	Garfield	Graham	Harrison
Elihu	Ezekiel	Garnet	Grahame	Harry
Elijah	Ezra	Garret	Grant	Hartley
Eliot	Fabian	Garrick	Granville	Harun
Ellery	Faron	Garry	Grayburn	Harvey
Elliot	Farquhar	Garth	Greg	Hashim
Ellis	Farran	Gary	Gregor	Hassan
Elmer	Farren	Gaspar	Gregory	Hayden
Elton	Feargus	Gavin	Grenville	Haydon
Elvin	Felix	Gawain	Griffith	Heath
Elvis	Ferdinand	Gaylord	Grover	Heber
Elwyn	Fergie	Gaz	Guido	Hector
Emanuel	Fergus	Gene	Gunter	Hedley
Emery	Fernando	Geoff	Gunther	Henri
Emil	Fidel	Geoffrey	Gus	Henry
Emile	Finlay	Geordie	Gussie	Herb
Emlyn	Fitzroy	George	Gustaf	Herbert
Emmanuel	Fletcher	Georgie	Gustav	Herbie
Emrys	Florian	Geraint	Gustave	Hercules
Enoch	Floyd	Gerald	Gustavus	Hereward
Enos	Fluellen	Gerard	Guy	Herman
Eoghan	Flurry	Gerrard	Gwilym	Hermann
Ephraim	Fortunatus	Gerry	Gwylim	Hervé
Eppie	Francesco	Gershom	Gwyn	Hervey
Erasmus	Francis	Gervais	Gwynfor	Hew
Eric	Francisco	Gervase	Gyles	Hezekiah
Erik	Franco	Gerwyn	Hadrian	Hieronymus
Erle	Frank	Gethin	Hal	Hilary
Ern	Frankie	Gib	Ham	Hillary
Ernest	Franklin	Gideon	Hamil	Hippolytus
Ernie	Fraser	Gidon	Hamilton	Hiram
Errol	Frasier	Gil	Hamish	Hob
Esau	Frazer	Gilbert	Hamlet	Hobart
Esme	Fred	Giles	Hamlyn	Holden
Esmond	Freddie	Gillean	Hammond	Homer
Ethan	Freddy	Gillian	Hamnet	Honor
Ethelbert	Frederic	Gilroy	Hamo	Honour
Ethelred	Frederick	Glen	Hamon	Hopi
Eugene	Fredric	Glyn	Hank	Horace
Eustace	Fredrick	Godfrey	Hannibal	Horatio
Evan	Fulbert	Godwin	Hans	Horry
Evander	Gabriel	Goldwin	Hardy	Howard

BOYS' NAMES (cont.)

Howel	Ivor	Jillian	Kay	Launce
Howell	Izaak	Jim	Keir	Launcelot
Hubert	Jabez	Jimmy	Keith	Lauren
Huey	Jack	Joachim	Kelvin	Laurence
Hugh	Jackie	Job	Ken	Lauri
Hughie	Jacky	Jocelyn	Kendal	Laurie
Hugo	Jacob	Jock	Kendall	Lawrence
Humbert	Jacques	Joe	Kenelm	Lawrie
Humph	Jacqui	Joel	Kenneth	Layton
Humphrey	Jago	Joey	Kenny	Lazarus
Husain	Jahangir	Johannes	Kenred	Leander
Hussein	Jake	John	Kenrick	Lee
Huw	James	Johnnie	Kent	Leigh
Hyman	Jamie	Johnny	Kentigern	Leighton
Hymie	Jamshed	Johnston	Kenton	Lemuel
Hywel	Jan	Jolyon	Kester	Len
Iain	Japhet	Jon	Kevin	Lennox
Ian	Japheth	Jonah	Khaled	Leo
Ibrahim	Jared	Jonas	Khalid	Leofric
Ichabod	Jarred	Jonathan	Khurshid	Leoline
Idris	Jarrod	Jools	Kieran	Leon
Ifor	Jarvis	Jordan	Kilroy	Leonard
Ignatius	Jason	Joscelin	Kim	Leopold
Igor	Jasper	José	Kimball	Leroi
Ike	Javed	Joseph	Kimberley	Leroy
Imran	Jawaharlal	Josh	Kimberly	Les
Ingram	Jay	Joshua	King	Leslie
Inigo	Jed	Josiah	Kingsley	Lester
Iolo	Jedidiah	Josias	Kirby	Levi
Iorwerth	Jeff	Jotham	Kirk	Lew
Ira	Jefferson	Juan	Kit	Lewis
Irvin	Jeffery	Judah	Kofi	Lex
Irvine	Jeffrey	Judas	Kris	Liam
Irving	Jem	Judd	Krishnan	Lincoln
Irwin	Jemmy	Jude	Kurt	Lindsay
Isa	Jeremiah	Jules	Kyle	Lionel
Isaac	Jeremias	Julian	Kyren	Llewellyn
Isaiah	Jeremy	Julius	Laban	Llewelyn
Isidore	Jermaine	Junior	Lachlan	Lloyd
Israel	Jerome	Justin	Lambert	Lonnie
Ithel	Jerry	Jyoti	Lance	Loren
Itzhak	Jess	Kamal	Lancelot	Lorenzo
Ivan	Jesse	Kane	Lanty	Lori
Ives	Jesus	Karl	Larry	Lorin
Ivo	Jethro	Karol	Lars	Lorn

BOYS' NAMES (cont.)

Lorne	Marshall	Montgom-	Nicol	Oswald
Lou	Martin	ery	Nicolas	Oswin
Louie	Marty	Monty	Nigel	Otho
Louis	Martyn	Morarji	Nik	Otis
Lovell	Marvin	Moray	Niles	Otto
Lowell	Marvyn	Mordecai	Ninian	Owain
Lucas	Mat	Morgan	Noah	Owen
Lucian	Matt	Morris	Noam	Ozzie
Lucien	Matthew	Mort	Noel	Pablo
Lucius	Matthias	Mortimer	Nolan	Paddy
Ludo	Maurice	Morty	Norbert	Padraig
Ludovic	Max	Moses	Norm	Palmer
Luke	Maximilian	Moshe	Norman	Paolo
Luther	Maxwell	Moss	Norris	Parker
Lyle	Maynard	Mostafa	Norton	Parry
Lyn	Meirion	Motilal	Nowell	Pascal
Lyndon	Mel	Muhammad	Nye	Pascoe
Lynn	Melford	Muir	Obadiah	Pat
Madoc	Melville	Mungo	Oberon	Patrick
Magnus	Melvin	Murdoch	Octavian	Paul
Malachi	Melvyn	Murray	Octavius	Pedro
Malachy	Meredith	Murtagh	Odo	Pelham
Malcolm	Merlin	Myles	Ogden	Perce
Malise	Merrion	Myron	Olaf	Perceval
Mallory	Merton	Napoleon	Olav	Percival
Malory	Merv	Nat	Olave	Percy
Malvin	Mervin	Nathan	Oliver	Peregrine
Manasses	Mervyn	Nathanael	Olivier	Perry
Manfred	Micah	Nathaniel	Ollie	Pete
Manley	Michael	Neal	Omar	Peter
Manny	Mick	Ned	Onuphrius	Phil
Manohar	Mickey	Neddie	Orlando	Philemon
Mansel	Micky	Neddy	Orrell	Philibert
Mansur	Mike	Nehemiah	Orson	Philip
Manuel	Milburn	Neil	Orval	Phillip
Manus	Miles	Neill	Orville	Phineas
Marc	Milo	Nelson	Osbert	Phinehas
Marcel	Milton	Nevil	Osborn	Pierre
Marcellus	Mitch	Neville	Osborne	Piers
Marco	Mitchell	Newton	Oscar	Piet
Marcus	Mohammed	Niall	Osho	Pip
Mario	Mohandas	Nicholas	Osmond	Piran
Marius	Montagu	Nick	Osmund	Poldie
Mark	Montague	Nicky	Ossie	Prescott
Marmaduke	Monte	Nicodemus	Ossy	Preston

BOYS' NAMES (cont.)

Prince	Ricky	St John	Sigismund	Taylor
Quentin	Rik	Salamon	Sigmund	Ted
Quincy	Rikki	Salman	Silas	Teddie
Quinn	Roald	Salvador	Silvanus	Teddy
Quintin	Rob	Salvatore	Silvester	Tel
Rab	Robbie	Sam	Sim	Terence
Rabbie	Robert	Sammy	Simeon	Terrence
Radcliff	Robin	Sampson	Simon	Terri
Rafael	Rod	Samson	Sinclair	Terry
Rafe	Roddy	Samuel	Sitaram	Tertius
Rainer	Roderick	Satyendra	Sol	Tex
Rajiv	Rodger	Saul	Solly	Thaddeus
Ralph	Rodney	Saxon	Solomon	Theo
Ramlal	Rodolph	Scott	Spencer	Theobald
Ramon	Rodrigo	Seamus	Stafford	Theodore
Ramsay	Roger	Sean	Stan	Theodoric
Ramsey	Roland	Seb	Stanford	Theophilus
Ranald	Rolf	Sebastian	Stanislaus	Thom
Randal	Rollo	Sefton	Stanley	Thomas
Randall	Rolly	Selby	Stephen	Thorley
Randolph	Rolph	Selwyn	Steve	Thornton
Randy	Roly	Septimus	Steven	Thurstan
Raoul	Ron	Serge	Stevie	Thurston
Raphael	Ronald	Sergei	Stew	Tim
Rashid	Ronnie	Sergio	Stewart	Timmy
Ray	Rory	Sergius	Stirling	Timothy
Raymond	Ross	Seth	Stu	Titus
Raymund	Rowan	Seumas	Stuart	Tobias
Rayner	Rowland	Seward	Subhas	Toby
Raynor	Roy	Sextus	Sunil	Todd
Reg	Royal	Seymour	Swithin	Tolly
Reggie	Royston	Shamus	Syd	Tom
Reginald	Rudi	Shane	Sydney	Tommy
René	Rudolf	Shannon	Syed	Tony
Reuben	Rudolph	Shaun	Sylvanus	Torquil
Rex	Rudy	Shaw	Sylvester	Travers
Reynard	Rufus	Shawn	Taffy	Travis
Reynold	Rupert	Sheldon	Talal	Trefor
Rhys	Russ	Shelley	Talbot	Trev
Riccardo	Russel	Shem	Taliesin	Trevor
Rich	Russell	Sheridan	Tam	Tristan
Richard	Ruud	Sholto	Tancred	Tristram
Richie	Ryan	Sid	Tariq	Troy
Rick	Sacha	Sidney	Tarquil	Tudor
Ricki	Sacheverell	Siegfried	Tarquin	Turlough

BOYS' NAMES (cont.)

Ty	Vin	Warwick	Willy	Wystan
Tyrone	Vince	Washington	Wilmer	Xavier
Ulric	Vincent	Wat	Wilmot	Yehudi
Ulysses	Vinnie	Wayne	Win	Yossef
Upton	Virgil	Wendell	Windsor	Yusuf
Urban	Vitus	Wesley	Winfred	Yves
Uriah	Wade	Wilbert	Winfrid	Zachariah
Valentine	Wal	Wilbur	Winnie	Zacharias
Valery	Waldo	Wilf	Winston	Zachary
Vaughan	Wallace	Wilfred	Winthrop	Zack
Vaughn	Wallis	Wilfrid	Woodrow	Zak
Vere	Wally	Will	Wyatt	Zane
Vernon	Walt	Willard	Wybert	Zechariah
Vic	Walter	William	Wyndham	Zedekiah
Vick	Ward	Willie	Wynford	Zeke
Victor	Warner	Willis	Wynn	Zephaniah
Vijay	Warren	Willoughby	Wynne	Zoran

TOOLS

adze	edging shears	mallet	scraper
auger	file	mattock	screwdriver
awl	fork	mitre	scribe
axe	fretsaw	nippers	scythe
beetle	gavel	perforator	secateurs
bevel	glass cutter	pickaxe	shears
billhook	grinder	pincers	shovel
blowlamp	hacksaw	pitchfork	sickle
blowtorch	hammer	plane	sledgehammer
brace bit	hammer drill	pliers	soldering iron
bradawl	hand-axe	pruning hook	spade
burnisher	handsaw	punch	spanner
chainsaw	handspike	rake	spokeshave
chisel	hedge clipper	ram	swage
clamp	hoe	rasp	trowel
claw hammer	jack	riddle	tweezers
clough	jemmy	ripsaw	vice
crowbar	jigsaw	roller	wedge
cultivator	knife	sander	wire cutter
dibber	lawn mower	sandpaper	wire stripper
drill	lever	saw	wrench

CURRENCIES OF THE WORLD

(with countries)

afghani	Afghanistan		Tuvalu, Uganda,
agora *pl.* -rot	Israel		USA, Zimbabwe
at	Laos	cént	Peru
baht	Thailand	centas *pl.* -ai	Lithuania
baiza	Oman	centavo	Argentina, Bolivia,
balboa	Panama		Brazil, Cape Verde,
ban *pl.* bani	Moldova,		Chile, Colombia,
	Romania		Cuba, Dominican
birr	Ethiopia		Republic, Ecuador,
bolívar	Venezuela		El Salvador,
boliviano	Bolivia		Guatemala,
butut	The Gambia		Guinea-Bissau,
cauris	Guinea		Honduras, Mexico,
cedi	Ghana		Mozambique,
cent	Antigua and		Nicaragua,
	Barbuda, Australia,		Philippines,
	The Bahamas,		Portugal
	Barbados, Belau,	centesimo *pl.*	
	Belize, Brunei,	-mi	Italy, San Marino,
	Canada, Cyprus,		Vatican City
	Dominica, Estonia,	centésimo	Panama, Uruguay
	Ethiopia, Fiji,	centime	Algeria, Andorra,
	Grenada, Guyana,		Belgium, Benin,
	Jamaica, Kenya,		Burkina Faso,
	Kiribati, Liberia,		Burundi,
	Malaysia, Malta,		Cameroon, Central
	Marshall Islands,		African Republic,
	Mauritius,		Chad, Comoros,
	Micronesia,		Congo, Democratic
	Namibia, Nauru,		Republic of Congo,
	The Netherlands,		Côte d'Ivoire,
	New Zealand,		Djibouti, Equatorial
	Panama, St Kitts		Guinea, France,
	and Nevis, St		Gabon, Guinea,
	Lucia, St Vincent		Haiti,
	and the Grena-		Liechtenstein,
	dines, The		Luxembourg,
	Seychelles, Sierra		Madagascar, Mali,
	Leone, Singapore,		Monaco, Morocco,
	Solomon Islands,		Niger, Rwanda,
	Somalia, South		Senegal,
	Africa, Sri Lanka,		Switzerland, Togo,
	Suriname, Taiwan,		Vanuatu
	Tanzania, Trinidad	cêntimo	São Tomé and
	and Tobago,		Principe

CURRENCIES OF THE WORLD (cont.)

(with countries)

céntimo	Andorra, Costa Rica, Paraguay, Spain, Venezuela
CFA franc	Benin, Burkina Faso, Central African Republic, Chad, Congo, Equatorial Guinea, Senegal, Togo
chetrum	Bhutan
chon	North Korea, South Korea
colón *pl.* colónes *or* colóns	Costa Rica, El Salvador
córdoba oro	Nicaragua
dalasi	The Gambia
denar	Macedonia
Deutsche Mark *or* Deutschmark	Germany
dinar	Algeria, Bahrain, Bosnia-Herzegovina, Iraq, Jordan, Kuwait, Libya, Sudan, Tunisia, Yemen, Yugoslavia
dirham *or* dirhem	Libya, Morocco, Qatar, United Arab Emirates
dobra	São Tomé and Principe
dollar	Australia, The Bahamas, Barbados, Belau, Belize, Brunei, Canada, Fiji, Guyana, Jamaica, Kiribati, Liberia, Malaysia, Marshall Islands, Micronesia, Namibia, Nauru, New Zealand, Singapore, Solomon Islands, Taiwan, Trinidad and Tobago, Tuvalu, USA, Zimbabwe
dong	Vietnam
drachma *pl.* -ae, -as	Greece
dram	Armenia
East Caribbean dollar	Antigua and Barbuda, Dominica, Grenada, St Kitts and Nevis, St Lucia, St Vincent and the Grenadines
escudo	Cape Verde, Portugal
eyrir *pl.* aurar	Iceland
fen	China
filler	Hungary
fils	Bahrain, Iraq, Jordan, Kuwait, United Arab Emirates, Yemen
forint	Hungary
franc	Andorra, Belgium, Burundi, Cameroon, Comoros, Democratic Republic of Congo, Djibouti, France, Gabon, Guinea, Ivory Coast, Luxembourg, Madagascar, Mali, Monaco, Niger, Rwanda, Switzerland
gopik	Azerbaijan
gourde	Haiti

CURRENCIES OF THE WORLD (cont.)
(with countries)

groschen	Austria
grosz *pl.*	
groszy	Poland
guaraní	Paraguay
guilder	The Netherlands,
	Suriname
halala	Saudi Arabia
haler *or* halier *pl.* haleru	
or halierov	Czech Republic,
	Slovakia
hryvna *or*	
hryvnya	Ukraine
jeon	South Korea
jun	North Korea
khoum	Mauritania
kina	Papua New Guinea
kip	Laos
kobo	Nigeria
kopeck, kopek, copeck *or*	
copek	Belarus, Russia,
	Tajikistan
kopiyka	Ukraine
koruna	Czech Republic,
	Slovakia
krona	Sweden
króna *pl.* -nur	Iceland
krone *pl.*	
kroner	Denmark, Norway
kroon *pl.* -ni	Estonia
kuna *pl.* kune	Croatia
kuruş *or*	
kurush	Turkey
kwacha	Malawi, Zambia
kwanza	Angola
kyat	Myanmar
laari	Maldives
lari	Georgia
lats *pl.* lati	Latvia
lek	Albania
lempira	Honduras
leone	Sierra Leone
lepton pl. -ta	Greece
leu *pl.* lei	Moldova, Romania
lev *pl.* leva	Bulgaria
lilangeni *pl.*	
emalangeni	Swaziland
lipa	Croatia
lira *pl.* lire	Italy, Malta, San
	Marino, Turkey,
	Vatican City
lisente	Lesotho
litas *pl.* litai	Lithuania
loti *pl.*	
maloti	Lesotho
luma	Armenia
lwei	Angola
manat	Azerbaijan,
	Turkenistan
markka	Finland
metical	Mozambique
millime	Tunisia
möngö	Mongola
naira	Nigeria
nakfa	Eritrea
ngultrum	Bhutan
ngwee	Zambia
øre	Denmark, Norway
öre	Sweden
ouguiya	Mauritania
pa'anga	Tonga
paisa *pl.*	
paise	Bangladesh, India,
	Nepal, Pakistan
para	Bosnia-Herzegovina,
	Macedonia,
	Yugoslavia
penni *pl.* -nia	
or -nis	Finland
penny *pl.*	
pence	Republic of Ireland,
	UK
peseta	Spain
pesewa	Ghana
peso	Argentina, Chile,
	Colombia, Cuba,
	Dominican
	Republic, Guinea-
	Bissau, Mexico,
	Philippines,
	Uruguay
pfennig *pl.*	
-nige	Germany

CURRENCIES OF THE WORLD (cont.)

(with countries)

piastre	Egypt, Lebanon, Syria
pound	Cyprus, Egypt, Lebanon, Syria, UK
pul *pl.* puli *or* puls	Afghanistan
pula	Botswana
punt	Republic of Ireland
pya	Myanmar
qindar *or* qintar *pl.* -arka	Albania
quetzal *pl.* -zales	Guatemala
rand	South Africa
real	Brazil
rial	Iran, Oman, Yemen
riel	Cambodia
ringgit	Malaysia
riyal	Qatar, Saudi Arabia
rouble	Belarus, Russia, Tajikstan
rufiyaa	Maldives
rupee	India, Mauritius, Nepal, Pakistan, Seychelles, Sri Lanka
rupiah	Indonesia
santimi	Latvia
satang	Thailand
schilling	Austria
sen	Cambodia, Indonesia, Japan, Malaysia
sene	Samoa
seniti	Tonga
sent *pl.* senti	Estonia
shekel *or* sheqel	Israel
shilling	Kenya, Somalia,Tanzania, Uganda
sol *pl.* soles	Peru
som	Kyrgyzstan
stotin	Slovenia
stotinka *pl.* -inki	Bulgaria
sucre	Ecuador
sum *pl.* sumy	Uzbekistan
taka	Bangladesh
tala	Samoa
tambala	Malawi
tanga	Tajikistan
tenge	Kazakhstan, Turkmenistan
tetri	Georgia
thebe	Botswana
toea	Papua New Guinea
tolar *pl.* -arji	Slovenia
tugrik	Mongolia
tyiyn	Kyrgyzstan
vatu	Vanuatu
won	North Korea, South Korea
xu	Vietnam
yen	Japan
yuan	China
zloty	Poland

ECONOMIC TERMS AND THEORIES

added value
aggregate demand
balanced budget
bear market
boom or bust cycle
broad money
bull market
capitalism
centrally planned
  economy
colonialism
command economy
competition
consumerism
corporate state
cost of production
deficit financing
demand curve
demand economy
depression
dialectical materialism
diminishing returns
division of labour
duopoly
econometrics
economic classicism
economic equilibrium
economic growth
economic policy
economic rent
economies of scale
elasticity of demand
exchange value
FIFO
fiscal drag
fiscal policy
five-year plan
free market
free trade
fungible

futures market
gold standard
gross domestic
  product (GDP)
gross national
  product (GNP)
imperialism
inelastic
inflationary gap
institutionalism
investment
Keynesianism
labour theory of value
laissez-faire
  economics
Leninism
liquidity
M1 or M2 or M3 or
  M4
macroeconomics
marginal efficiency of
  capital
marginalism
market forces
Marxism
materialism
means of production
mercantilism
microeconomics
mixed economy
monetarism
monetary policy
monopoly
multiplier [effect]
narrow money
national income
neo-classicism
New Deal
New Economics
oligopoly

options market
perfect competition
physiocracy
positional goods
prices and incomes
  policy
principle of
  acceleration
private sector
productivity
property
protection
public sector
put option
quantity theory of
  money
recession
retail price index
revisionism
slavery
slump
stagflation
statics
supply and demand
supply-side
  economics
surplus
surplus value
syndicalism
totalitarianism
trade barrier
trade cycle
Trotskyism
value added
velocity of money
wage-price spiral
welfare economics
windfall profit

FINANCIAL TERMS

agio
agiotage
arbitrage
bank rate
bill of exchange
bimetallism
capital-expenditure
  budget
deflation
depreciation
devaluation
disinflation
effective rate
equalization fund
exchange premium
exchange rate

financial year
floating currency
foreign exchange
  market
gilt-edged securities
gold standard
Income Bonds
inflation
inflationary spiral
interest rate
ISA
managed currency
minimum lending rate
MIRAS
money market
par

parity
PEP
personal pension
rallying
reflation
revolving fund
shares
sinking fund
snake
stagflation
strong currency
TESSA
unit trust
valuta
venture capital

ROMAN NUMERALS

I	1	XVI	16
II	2	XVII	17
III	3	XVIII	18
IV	4	XIX	19
V	5	XX	20
VI	6	L	50
VII	7	C	100
VIII	8	D	500
IX	9	$\underline{M}$	1000
X	10	$\underline{V}$	5000
XI	11	$\underline{X}$	10 000
XII	12	$\underline{L}$	50 000
XIII	13	$\underline{C}$	100 000
XIV	14	$\underline{D}$	500 000
XV	15	$\underline{M}$	1 000 000